NO-FAULT APPROACHES IN THE NHS

This book explores how concerns can be raised about the NHS, why raising concerns hasn't always improved standards, and how a no-fault open culture approach could drive improvements.

The book describes a wide range of mechanisms for raising concerns about the NHS, including complaints, the ombudsman, litigation, HSIB, and the major inquiries since 2000, across the various UK jurisdictions. The NHS approach is contextualised within the broader societal developments in dispute resolution, accountability and regulation.

The authors take a holistic view, and outline practical solutions for reforming how the NHS responds to problems. These should improve the situation for those raising concerns and for those working within the NHS, as well as providing cost savings. The no-fault approaches proposed in the book provide long-term sustainable solutions to systemic problems, which are particularly timely given the impact of the COVID-19 pandemic on the NHS.

The book will be of interest to academics, researchers, ADR practitioners, practising lawyers and policy makers.

Volume 14 in the series Civil Justice Systems

Civil Justice Systems

Series General Editor: Christopher Hodges,
Centre for Socio-Legal Studies, University of Oxford

This series covers new theoretical and empirical research on the mechanisms for resolution of civil disputes, including courts, tribunals, arbitration, compensation schemes, ombudsmen, codes of practice, complaint mechanisms, mediation and various forms of Alternative Dispute Resolution. It examines frameworks for dispute resolution that comprise combinations of the above mechanisms, and the parameters and conditions for selecting certain types of techniques and procedures rather than others. It also evaluates individual techniques, against parameters such as cost, duration, accessibility, and delivery of desired outcomes, and illuminates how legal rights and obligations are operated in practice.

Volume 1: *The Costs and Funding of Civil Litigation: A Comparative Perspective*
edited by Christopher Hodges, Stefan Vogenauer and Magdalena Tulibacka

Volume 2: *Consumer ADR in Europe*
Christopher Hodges, Iris Benöhr and Naomi Creutzfeldt-Banda

Volume 3: *Law and Corporate Behaviour: Integrating Theories of Regulation, Enforcement, Compliance and Ethics*
Christopher Hodges

Volume 4: *A Comparative Examination of Multi-Party Actions*
Joanne Blennerhassett

Volume 5: *Redress Schemes for Personal Injuries*
Sonia Macleod and Christopher Hodges

Volume 6: *Ethical Business Practice and Regulation: A Behavioural and Values-Based Approach to Compliance and Enforcement*
Christopher Hodges and Ruth Steinholtz

Volume 7: *Delivering Collective Redress: New Technologies*
Christopher Hodges and Stefaan Voet

Volume 8: *Pharmaceutical and Medical Device Safety: A Study in Public and Private Regulation*
Sonia Macleod and Sweta Chakraborty

Volume 9: *Delivering Dispute Resolution: A Holistic Review of Models in England and Wales*
Christopher Hodges

Volume 10: *Regulatory Delivery*
Graham Russell and Christopher Hodges

Volume 11: *Access to Justice for the Chinese Consumer: Handling Consumer Disputes in Contemporary China*
Ling Zhou

Volume 12: *Public and Private Enforcement of Securities Laws: The Regulator and the Class Action in Australia's Continuous Disclosure Regime*
Michael Legg

Volume 13: *Outcome-Based Cooperation: In Communities, Business, Regulation, and Dispute Resolution*
Christopher Hodges

Volume 14: *No-Fault Approaches in the NHS: Raising Concerns and Raising Standards*
Sonia Macleod and Christopher Hodges

No-Fault Approaches in the NHS

Raising Concerns and Raising Standards

Sonia Macleod
and
Christopher Hodges

•HART•
OXFORD • LONDON • NEW YORK • NEW DELHI • SYDNEY

HART PUBLISHING

Bloomsbury Publishing Plc

Kemp House, Chawley Park, Cumnor Hill, Oxford, OX2 9PH, UK

1385 Broadway, New York, NY 10018, USA

29 Earlsfort Terrace, Dublin 2, Ireland

HART PUBLISHING, the Hart/Stag logo, BLOOMSBURY and the Diana logo are
trademarks of Bloomsbury Publishing Plc

First published in Great Britain 2022

A catalogue record for this book is available from the British Library.

Library of Congress Cataloging-in-Publication data

Names: Macleod, Sonia, author. | Hodges, Christopher J. S., author.

Title: No-fault approaches in the NHS : raising concerns and raising standards / Sonia Macleod and Christopher Hodges.

Description: Oxford ; New York : Hart, 2022. | Series: Civil justice systems ; volume 14 | Includes bibliographical references
and index. | Summary: "This book explores how concerns can be raised about the NHS, why raising concerns hasn't always
improved standards, and how a no-fault open culture approach could drive improvements. The book describes a wide range of
mechanisms for raising concerns about the NHS, including complaints, the ombudsman, litigation, HSIB, and the major inquiries
since 2000, across the various UK jurisdictions. The NHS approach is contextualised within the broader societal developments in
dispute resolution, accountability, and regulation. The authors take a holistic view, and outline practical solutions for reforming how
the NHS responds to problems. These should improve the situation for those raising concerns and for those working within the
NHS, as well as providing cost savings. The no-fault approaches proposed in the book provide long-term sustainable solutions
to systemic problems, which are particularly timely given the impact of the COVID-19 pandemic on the NHS. The book will be
of interest to academics, researchers, ADR practitioners, practicing lawyers, and policy makers"—Provided by publisher.

Identifiers: LCCN 2022036548 | ISBN 9781509916658 (hardback) | ISBN 9781509960880 (paperback) |
ISBN 9781509916665 (pdf) | ISBN 9781509916672 (Epub)

Subjects: LCSH: Great Britain. National Health Service. | National health services—England. | Medical care—Law and
legislation—England. | Medical personnel—Malpractice—England.

Classification: LCC KD3210 .M33 2022 | DDC 344.42/02—dc23/eng/20220924

LC record available at https://lccn.loc.gov/2022036548

ISBN: HB: 978-1-50991-665-8
       ePDF: 978-1-50991-666-5
       ePub: 978-1-50991-667-2

Typeset by Compuscript Ltd, Shannon

To find out more about our authors and books visit www.hartpublishing.co.uk. Here you will find extracts, author information,
details of forthcoming events and the option to sign up for our newsletters.

PREFACE

This book was planned and started prior to the pandemic. The effects of the pandemic and of subsequent energy and austerity crises seem to us to make it even more important to create an NHS that delivers desired outcomes of health and social care through a cooperative and learning culture. The system for raising concerns has to be directed at identifying and solving problems, and then learning and improving. It has to be a system that delivers *care* and *performance* in achieving *outcomes*.

It was our intention to highlight a number of the mechanisms by which patients can raise concerns about healthcare. We do not intend this to be a comprehensive list of all the possible routes by which concerns can be communicated. One of the most notable omissions is that we have not focused on the role of the third sector. This is because there is a such a diversity of organisations – from the large national charities, such as HealthWatch, to bijou single-issue groups. While some of these groups are small, and focus on specific issues, they can have significant impact; the Cure, the NHS campaign group, secured the Mid-Staffordshire Public Inquiry and resulting reforms such as the Duty of Candour, which have been felt across the NHS. The move towards integrated care systems will further enhance the role of the third sector in health and social care and the future relationships, complaints pathways and attributions of liability need careful thought.

The pandemic has put the NHS under unimaginable pressure. During the initial wave there were no vaccines, no licenced treatments, and no guarantee that the NHS would be able to cope. The 'Stay Home; Protect the NHS; Save Lives' mantra encapsulated the seriousness of the situation to those outside the NHS. Those who were working within health and social care did not need reminding of the gravity of the situation, and working through this has inevitably taken its toll on staff. There has been no meaningful respite for healthcare staff following this initial ordeal; subsequent waves of infection have been followed by the pressures of trying to relieve the backlog. One consequence of the pandemic has been an excess of 1,500 cancer deaths and delays to treatment that have left many, many people suffering with their condition. At the time of writing (November 2022) there are nearly seven million patients waiting for elective care, and hospitals are carrying out fewer operations than they were pre-pandemic. It has been widely reported that efforts to reduce the backlog have been undermined by a lack of workforce planning, and it is noteworthy that in his Autumn Statement the Chancellor (and former Health Secretary) Jeremy Hunt committed to the government to publishing independently verified forecasts of how many staff the NHS needs in the next five, ten and fifteen years as part of a longer-term planning strategy. Having enough staff is fundamental. In many other safety-critical sectors staffing levels are non-negotiable; a plane will not fly without a *full* complement of staff, this requirement protects both service users and the service providers. The reforms we suggest depend on a properly staffed NHS, which is not the current position. As we write this, the NHS is currently short of just over 2,500 midwives, increasing the pressure on those who remain.

Given this, it isn't entirely surprising that in a 2021 RCM survey almost 60% of midwives who responded said that they were considering leaving the NHS in the next year. This is clearly not sustainable.

In August the proposed pay scales for nurses were announced which included an increase of 4%. There have been widespread media reports of nurses being unable to make ends meet due to the cost of living crisis and resorting to using food banks. The Royal College of Nurses had sought a pay increase of 5% over inflation, around 15%, and have balloted their members, who have voted for strike action. The strikes are due to take place in December 2022 and would be the first ever national strike action by nurses. It is very clear that there is considerable dissatisfaction with the current offer for nursing staff and that staff are considering leaving. It is difficult to see how the existing 47,000 nursing, midwifery and health visitor vacancies in England will be filled despite a recruitment drive by NHS England. Funding of the service has to include adequately funding the wages of those who provide the service.

The cost of living crisis has led to both a substantial squeeze on individuals and a tightening of government spending. The planned Health and Social Care levy has been scrapped and therefore this additional source of revenue is not available. Health and social care spending has been prioritised, with health revenue spending increased by £3.3 billion over the next two years. There will be a slight increase in capital spending and the New Hospital Programme will be unaffected. In return for this spending there is an expectation of further efficiency savings and improved performance, particularly around ambulance response times, A&E waiting times and access to primary care.

Social care funding remains a key issue. Reforms to limit the amount individuals will be asked to contribute to their social care have been proposed. Under these proposals an £86,000 cap would limit the amount that anyone in England would be asked to contribute towards their social care. Anyone with assets of less than £20,000 would have their care funded by the local authority. Those individuals with assets of over £100,000 will self-fund their social care until either they reach the £86,000 cap from which point the care will be funded by the local authority or until the value of their assets drops below £100,000. Those with assets between £20,000 and £100,000 would be expected to make a contribution towards their care (never more than 20% of the asset value) until either they reach the £86,000 cap or the value of their assets drops below £20,000, at which point the local authority will fund their care. These reforms were due to commence in October 2023, but as part of the spending controls in the Autumn statement implementation has been delayed for a year. The savings from delaying this policy, combined with increased council tax payments and increased central government spend has enabled social care spending to increase by £2.8 billion next year and £4.7 billion the year after. This increase in social care funding includes £1 billion which is earmarked for supporting discharges from hospitals into the community in 2024/25 to help support the NHS.

In this book we have set out the mechanisms for raising concerns and also some of the worst examples of NHS failings. Given the current state of the NHS, we are sure there will be some who question whether this is an appropriate time for this book. We would argue that this is the most appropriate time, change is clearly needed and will support improvements. We have set out how the system can be developed so it provides better care for patients and for the staff who care for them.

This work would not have been possible without the funding provided by Swiss-Re and the European Justice Forum who have generously provided unfettered support for our research for many years. The views expressed here are ours and do not represent the views of these or any other organisations. We warmly thank many people who have contributed to our knowledge and research over many years. There are simply too many to name. We certainly thank Roberta Bassi, Helen Kitto, Tom Adams, Elizabeth Morris and Emma Platt at Hart Publishing for yet another seamless collaboration. Finally, we would like to thank our colleagues and associates at CSLS.

BRIEF CONTENTS

Preface.. *v*

Contents.. *xi*

1. Introduction.. 1

PART I
THE NHS

2. Our Wonderful NHS... 7

3. The Long Term Plan... 14

4. The NHS Patient Safety Strategy.. 32

5. NHS Policy on Responding to Mistakes.. 50

PART II
RAISING CONCERNS

6. Mechanisms for Dealing with Staff Concerns... 57

7. NHS Complaints.. 58

8. UK Health Service Ombudsman.. 97

9. Clinical Claims Against the NHS.. 116

10. Public Inquiries and Reviews.. 169

11. The Health Services Safety Investigation Branch.. 207

12. Complaints to Regulators... 219

PART III
RAISING STANDARDS

13. Raising Concerns and Raising Standards.. 257

14. Conclusion... 287

Index *291*

CONTENTS

Preface.. *v*

Brief Contents... *ix*

1. Introduction... 1
   The Structure of This Book 2

PART I
THE NHS

2. Our Wonderful NHS 7
   I. The Health and Social Care Levy.. 9
   II. Public Perceptions of the NHS.. 9
   III. Satisfaction and Dissatisfaction with the NHS 10
   IV. Evolution of the NHS 10
   V. NHS Patient Experience and Metrics.. 11
   VI. COVID-19 and the NHS 12

3. The Long Term Plan 14
   I. New Service Model for the NHS.. 14
      A. 'Out of Hospital' Care, Primary and Community Health Services 15
   II. Action on Prevention and Health Inequalities 17
      A. Health Inequalities... 17
      B. Smoking.. 18
      C. Obesity.. 18
      D. Alcohol 18
      E. Air Pollution 19
      F. Antimicrobial Resistance 19
   III. Further Progress on Care Quality and Outcomes 19
      A. Children and Young People 19
      B. Major Health Conditions 19
   IV. NHS Staff Getting the Backing They Need...................................... 20
      A. The Workforce Implementation Plan 20
      B. Increasing the Number of Nurses, Midwives, Allied Health
         Professionals and Other Staff.. 20
      C. Growing the Medical Workforce.. 21
      D. International Recruitment 21

E. Supporting NHS Staff...21
F. Enabling Productive Working..22
G. Leadership and Talent Management 23
H. Volunteers 23
V. Digitally-enabled Care Going Mainstream Across the NHS.............23
A. Empowering People...24
B. Supporting Health and Care Professionals...................................25
C. Supporting Clinical Care 25
D. Improving Population Health 25
E. Improving Clinical Efficiency and Safety.....................................26
VI. Taxpayers' Investments Being Used to Maximum Effect 27
A. Test 1: The NHS Will Return to Financial Balance 27
B. Test 2: The NHS Will Achieve Productivity Growth of at Least
1.1 Per Cent...28
C. Test 3: The NHS Will Use Better Integration and Prevention to
Drive Down the Growth in Demand for Care 29
D. Test 4: The NHS Will Reduce Unjustified Performance Variation............30
E. Test 5: The NHS Will Make Better Use of Capital Investment
and Assets 30
VII. Next Steps 30
VIII. Long Term Plan Conclusions...31

4. The NHS Patient Safety Strategy 32
I. Insight 33
A. Learn from Patient Safety Events (LFPSE) 33
B. Patient Safety Incident Response Framework................................34
C. The Medical Examiner System..35
D. National Clinical Review and Response 36
E. The National Patient Safety Alerts System...................................36
F. The National Patient Safety Committee.......................................37
G. The Healthcare Safety Investigation Branch/Health Services Safety
Investigations Body...37
H. Clinical Negligence and Litigation 37
i. Getting it Right First Time (GIRFT) 37
II. Involvement..39
A. Patient and Public Voice Partners...39
B. Patient Safety Education and Training...40
C. Patient Safety Specialists 40
D. Safety I and Safety II...41
E. The Independent Sector 41
III. Improvement...42
A. The National Patient Safety Improvement Programme...................42
B. Patient Safety Workstreams 42
C. Continuous Improvement 43
D. The Maternity and Neonatal Safety Improvement Programme 43
E. The Medicines Safety Improvement Programme 44

F.   The Mental Health Safety Improvement Programme 44
G.   Safety Issues That Particularly Affect Older People......................................45
H.   Safety and Learning Disabilities...45
I.   Antimicrobial Resistance and Healthcare Associated Infections 47
J.   Research and Innovation..47
K.   Managing Deterioration Safety Improvement Programme.........................48
L.   The Adoption and Spread Safety Improvement Programme 48
IV. National Patient Safety Strategy Conclusions 49

5. NHS Policy on Responding to Mistakes...50
I.   Being Open...50
II. Candour and Apologies 51
A.   Statutory Duty of Candour 52
III. NHS Policy on Responding to Mistakes Conclusions 53

PART II
RAISING CONCERNS

6. Mechanisms for Dealing with Staff Concerns..57
I.   Mechanisms for NHS Staff to Raise Concerns..57
II. Resolving Concerns Raised by Staff and Employers 57

7. NHS Complaints 58
I.   Public Service Complaints in England..58
II. NHS Complaints in England...59
A.   Support and Advocacy Services for Complainants 61
B.   Complaints and Healthcare Staff..62
C.   Complaints Processes 63
    i.   English NHS Complaints Processes and Parameters........................63
    ii.   1960s to 1980s...64
    iii. 1990s to 2000..64
    iv.   2000 to 2020 65
    v.   Overview of English Complaints Data 69
D.   Reviews and Reports Considering NHS Complaint Handling....................69
    i.   Dr Harold Shipman..69
    ii.   The Three Inquiries 70
    iii. Robert Francis QC: Mid-Staffs Independent Inquiry 2010 71
    iv.   Health Select Committee 2011 71
    v.   Robert Francis QC: Mid-Staffs Public Inquiry 2013.......................71
    vi.   Berwick 2013..72
    vii. Clwyd and Hart 2013 73
    viii. PHSO's 2015 Review of Complaints 75
    ix.   Southern Health Review (Stage I) 2021...78
    x.   Baroness Julia Cumberlege: IMMDS 2020..78
    xi.   Ockenden Reports 2020 and 2022 79

III.   NHS Complaints in Wales 80
    A.   Welsh Public Service Complaints 80
    B.   Welsh NHS Complaints Overview 83
    C.   Welsh NHS Complaints Processes and Parameters 84
       i.   Keith Evans 2014 86
       ii.   The Once for Wales Concerns Management System 88
IV.   NHS Complaints in Scotland 88
    A.   Scottish Public Service Complaints 88
    B.   Scottish NHS Complaints Overview 90
    C.   Scottish NHS Complaints Processes and Parameters 90
       i.   Overview of Scottish Complaints Data 92
V.   Conclusions: Complaints 93

8. UK Health Service Ombudsman 97
I.   The UK Ombudsman Landscape 97
II.   The Parliamentary Ombudsman Background 97
III.   Health Service Ombudsman Background 98
    A.   Overview of PHSO's Activity 98
    B.   PHSO's Process for Healthcare Complaints 99
    C.   A Unified Public Services Ombudsman for England 102
IV.   Scottish Public Services Ombudsman (SPSO) Background 104
    A.   Overview of SPSO's Activity 104
V.   The Public Services Ombudsman for Wales (PSOW) Background 107
    A.   Overview of PSOW's Activity 107
    B.   PSOW's Healthcare Complaints 109
VI.   The Northern Ireland Public Ombudsman Services (NIPSO) Background 110
    A.   Overview of NIPSO's Activity 111
    B.   NIPSO's Healthcare Complaints 113
VII.   Conclusions: Ombudsmen 114
    A.   Scotland and Wales 114

9. Clinical Claims Against the NHS 116
I.   Clinical Negligence Litigation as a Compensation Mechanism 116
    A.   Liability and the Thresholds Used to Assess Individuals 116
       i.   Diagnosis Cases: Reasonable Care and Skill Cases 117
       ii.   Consent Cases 118
       iii.   Liability Thresholds 119
    B.   Institutional Non-delegable Duties of Care 119
II.   Threshold Conclusions 121
III.   Clinical Claims Against the NHS in England 122
    A.   NHS Clinical Negligence Claims in England Overview 122
       i.   National Audit Office Report 2001 123
       ii.   Marsh Report 2011 123
       iii.   National Audit Office Report 2017 123

iv. Civil Justice Council Report into Fixed Recoverable Cost
in Lower Value Clinical Negligence Claims..124
v. Health and Social Care Select Committee Inquiry into NHS..........124
vi. Overview of NHS Resolution's Clinical Claim Handling
Activity..125
a. The Filtering and Funding of Potential Clinical Negligence
Claims in England...125
b. The Handling of Clinical Negligence Claims in England..........126
B. Claims Against the NHS in England Conclusions....................................131
IV. Clinical Claims Against the NHS in Scotland..131
A. NHS Clinical Negligence Litigation in Scotland Overview.....................131
B. CNORIS and the Central Legal Office...132
i. Overview of CNORIS..133
a. The Filtering and Funding of Potential Clinical Negligence
Claims in Scotland..133
b. The Handling of Potential Clinical Negligence Claims
in Scotland...135
C. Claims Against the NHS in Scotland Conclusions...................................137
V. Clinical Claims Against the NHS in Wales...138
A. NHS Clinical Negligence Claims in Wales Overview...............................138
i. Claims under £25,000: The NHS Redress Scheme...........................138
ii. Claims Over £25,000...139
B. NHS Redress Arrangements...140
C. Welsh Risk Pool Claims Handling...142
D. Learning from Events..145
i. Learning from Litigated Cases...145
ii. Learning from Redress Cases...147
E. Conclusions on the Welsh Scheme..147
VI. Clinical Claims Against the NHS in Northern Ireland....................................148
A. NHS Clinical Negligence Claims in Northern Ireland Overview...........148
i. The Filtering and Funding of Potential Clinical Negligence
Claims in Northern Ireland...148
ii. The Handling of Potential Clinical Negligence Claims
in Northern Ireland..149
B. Northern Ireland Clinical Negligence Conclusions.................................153
VII. Conclusions: Clinical Negligence..153
A. Clinical Negligence Litigation in the Home Nations...............................153
B. Litigation for Clinical Negligence..155
i. Clinical Negligence: Financial Aspects..157
ii. Woolf: Mediation and Pre-Action Protocols.....................................157
iii. Litigation Funding, Costs and Successive Reforms..........................159
iv. Jackson: Costs Controls and Management...161
v. Further Funding Cuts..164
vi. Clinical Negligence: Financial Efficiency..165
a. Fixed Recoverable Costs for Clinical Negligence......................166
VIII. Conclusions on Litigation 167

10. Public Inquiries and Reviews 169
    I.   Rodney Ledward...170
    II.   Bristol Royal Infirmary..171
    III.   Dr Harold Shipman..173
    IV.   The Three Inquiries: Clifford Ayling Independent Inquiry; Richard Neale
        Independent Inquiry; William Kerr and Michael Haslam Independent
        Inquiry 174
        A.   Clifford Ayling..174
        B.   Richard Neale 176
        C.   William Kerr and Michael Haslam..178
            i.   William Kerr..178
            ii.   Michael Haslam 179
            iii.   Conclusions on Kerr/Haslam..180
        D.   Response to the Three Inquiries...180
    V.   Mid Staffordshire Hospital Trust Independent Inquiry 181
    VI.   Winterbourne View Hospital...183
    VII.   The Keogh Hospitals Review 184
    VIII.   Mid Staffordshire Hospital Trust Public Inquiry 185
    IX.   Morecambe Bay 186
    X.   Abertawe Bro Morgannwg University Health Board...189
    XI.   Gosport War Memorial Hospital...191
    XII.   Ian Paterson..193
    XIII.   The Independent Medicines and Medical Devices Safety Review...................195
    XIV.   The Ockenden Review of Maternity Services at Shrewsbury and
        Telford Hospital NHS Trust 196
    XV.   Conclusions on Inquiries and Reviews...199

11. The Health Services Safety Investigation Branch...207
    I.   HSSIB Background...207
        A.   The Expert Advisory Group Report 207
    II.   Establishing the HSIB/HSSIB and its Statutory Framework 209
    III.   HSIB Internal Culture..210
    IV.   HSIB Investigations..210
    V.   HSIB Maternity Investigations 211
        A.   Maternity Investigation Statistics..212
        B.   HSIB Maternity Investigation Conclusions.................................213
    VI.   HSIB National Investigations...214
        A.   National Investigation Statistics...215
        B.   HSIB National Investigation Conclusions 216
    VII.   HSIB Conclusions 216

12. Complaints to Regulators 219
    I.   Complaints to Activity and Entity Regulators..221
    II.   Complaints to Professional Regulators...222
        A.   Separating the Investigation and Adjudication in Fitness to
            Practise Hearings 223

B. Standard of Proof Required in Fitness to Practise Hearings 223
C. Fitness to Practise Procedures...223
D. Oversight of Professional Regulators' Responses to Public Concerns........228
    i. Annual Reviews...228
    ii. Special Reviews 229
E. The General Medical Council (GMC)...229
    i. Jack Adcock's Death, the GMC and Dr Hadiza Bawa-Garda's
       Sanctions 230
    ii. Current GMC Fitness to Practise Procedures.......................................233
       a. The MPTS 233
       b. GMC Statistics..235
F. The Nursing and Midwifery Council (NMC) 237
    i. 2008 and 2012 CHRE Reviews of NMC Fitness to Practise
       Procedures 238
    ii. Morecambe Bay and the NMC..239
    iii. Current NMC Fitness to Practise Procedures......................................243
    iv. NMC Statistics...244
G. The Healthcare Professionals Council (HCPC) 246
    i. Current HCPC Fitness to Practise Procedures 246
       a. The HCPTS...247
    ii. HCPC Statistics 250
III. Conclusions on Complaints to Regulators 252

PART III
RAISING STANDARDS

13. Raising Concerns and Raising Standards 257
I. The Rationale: Delivering Care and Improving Performance 257
II. What Do People Want When They Raise Concerns?..259
    A. NHS Complaints 260
    B. NHS Clinical Negligence Claims 261
    C. Healthcare Investigations...265
    D. International Research..266
    E. Conclusions on What People Want 266
    F. Some Challenges in Delivering What People Want.....................................267
III. The Core Objectives...268
    A. Caring for Those Who Have Been Harmed (the Caring Objective) 268
    B. Reporting Concerns (the Reporting Objective)..269
    C. Establishing What Happened and Any Deviation from Good
       Practice (the Investigation Objective) 269
    D. Demonstrating Systemic and Actual Learning (the Learning
       Objective)..270
    E. Financial Efficiency (the Financial Objective) 270
IV. The Just Culture Model 271

V.   Open and Just Culture in the NHS 273
VI.   Outcome Based Cooperation...276
VII.   Barriers to an Open and Just Culture 276
    A.   Improving Operational Culture 277
    B.   Reducing Barriers to Reporting Concerns 278
    C.   Removing Blame Culture..279
        i.   Improving Dispute Resolution...280
        ii.   Fundamental Reforms in Dispute Resolution Systems:
             Techniques, Processes, Pathways, Functions, Institutions,
             Landscapes...281
        iii.   Early Facilitated Dispute Resolution...285
VIII.   Conclusions on the Social Policy Objectives 286

14. Conclusion...287

Index *291*

1

Introduction

This book cannot possibly do justice to the experiences of those who have been harmed by substandard NHS care, and whose initial harms have been compounded by poor responses when concerns are raised. Improvements to these systems are long overdue.

In this book we will examine how complaints and claims are dealt with in the NHS – and how they should be dealt with. This inquiry encompasses not just an inquiry into complaint mechanisms and various dispute resolution techniques and architectures but also understanding the purposes that underlie the NHS and the outcomes that matter to patients, and how these may be achieved, especially through outcome- and performance-related cultures in operational, management and regulatory systems.

The book follows a series of inquiries by the authors and other colleagues into dispute resolution systems in England and Wales generally,[1] redress schemes for personal injuries across the globe,[2] mechanisms in Europe for delivering collective redress to groups of people,[3] consumer alternative dispute resolution mechanisms across Europe, especially relating to Ombudsmen,[4] mechanisms for funding litigation and its costs[5] and means of affecting behaviour, especially though management of organisations and through regulation.[6] It will be seen that this body of work charts the considerable evolution that has been occurring in both dispute resolution and regulatory systems. A critical change is to consider what affects firstly the behaviour of healthcare professionals and patients by applying the findings of behavioural psychology and secondly considering what actually impacts on the culture of organisations, rather than by resting on the traditional assumptions on how to affect behaviour that are grounded in theorising about legal and economic systems.

The principal finding of the book is that there is a major need to modernise how complaints and injuries are dealt with by the NHS. This is not only so as to align with

---

[1] C Hodges, *Delivering Dispute Resolution: A Holistic Review of Models in England & Wales* (Hart, 2019).

[2] S Macleod and C Hodges, *Redress Schemes for Personal Injuries* (Hart, 2017).

[3] C Hodges and S Voet, *Delivering Collective Redress: New Technologies* (Hart, 2018); DR Hensler, C Hodges and I Tzankova (eds), *Class Actions in Context: How Culture, Economics and Politics Shape Collective Litigation* (Edward Elgar, 2016); C Hodges and A Stadler (eds), *Resolving Mass Disputes: ADR and Settlement of Mass Claims* (Edward Elgar, 2013).

[4] C Hodges, I Benöhr and N Creutzfeldt-Banda, *Consumer ADR in Europe* (Hart Publishing, 2012).

[5] C Hodges, S Vogenauer and M Tulibacka (eds), *The Costs and Funding of Civil Litigation: A Comparative Approach* (Hart Publishing, 2010); C Hodges, J Peysner and A Nurse, Report: *Litigation Funding. Status and Issues* (Centre for Socio-Legal Studies, Oxford and Lincoln University, 2012) at www.csls.ox.ac.uk/documents/ReportLitigationFunding.pdf.

[6] C Hodges, *Outcome-Based Cooperation in Communities, Organisations, Regulation and Dispute Resolution* (Hart, 2022); G Russell and C Hodges (eds), *Regulatory Delivery* (Hart, 2019); C Hodges and R Steinholtz, *Ethical Business Practice and Regulation: A Behavioural and Values-Based Approach to Compliance and Enforcement* (Hart, 2017); C Hodges, *Law and Corporate Behaviour: Integrating Theories of Regulation, Enforcement, Culture and Ethics* (Hart Publishing, 2015).

widespread developments in how disputes are dealt with by courts, ombudsmen and others in a digital modern world. It is also so as to remove a major impediment to enabling the NHS to learn from mistakes and risk, and improve performance and reduce risk. The key learning here is that a system that is built on adversarialism and finding blame (negligence) will never be one in which those involved share the essential information on which such learning and improvement depends.

The first, dispute resolution, aspect has been very well recognised for many years. The fact that courts and traditional dispute resolution systems involve processes that are too slow, costly, difficult to access and use, has been widely discussed for decades. Where simple alternatives have been created, people have voted with their feet in preferring them. That has happened in most consumer markets, where complaints are now handled online or on the phone, backed by ombudsman systems in most regulated market sectors, and lawyers and courts are almost never used.

The second, behavioural learning, aspect is much less widely recognised, even though it forms the basis of other high risk activities, such as aviation safety. A revolution is currently underway in regulatory systems generally, as a result of challenges to traditional ideas about deterrence and enforcement, and the adoption of approaches that identify underlying causes of problems and support learning, improved performance and reduced risk. This book does not cover such broad changes in detail, or in relation to regulatory policy and practice in the healthcare sector, but does outline the broad and highly significant developments.

The book calls for change not just to the procedures but also to the criteria that are applied, both for triggering care and support, and for accountability and institutional learn-ing. There should be a move away from blame and adversarialism to an open, just and learning culture in which care and financial support are triggered by criteria of need, and professional, managerial and regulatory intervention are aimed at supporting improvement. Without these changes, the organisational culture of the NHS will not improve. With these changes, the culture, relations between staff and patients and feelings of trust, confidence and pride will all improve, as will outcomes.

The Structure of This Book

This book contains the following Parts: 'The NHS'; 'Raising Concerns'; and 'Raising Standards'. Each Part can be read independently, but they are best considered as parts of a whole.

Part I will give an overview of the NHS, with a focus on the current approaches to patient safety, responding to mistakes and a very brief overview of some of the mechanisms for staff to raise concerns.

Part II, 'Raising Concerns', examines the formal mechanisms[7] by which patient concerns about NHS care can be raised, including examining complaints, claims and independent reports and inquiries into a series of major scandals in the delivery of NHS care. Each chap-ter will provide a very brief overview of the types of concerns and the process used for raising them, followed by an analysis of reviews or reports into how to improve the system

---

[7] Informal mechanisms, such as the use of social media or websites rating care, will not be considered.

and prevent reoccurrence of these problems. This analysis will focus on findings related to how NHS culture shapes how problems are dealt with. Each chapter will conclude with key findings. There will be an overall conclusion on raising concerns.

Part III, 'Raising Standards', will look at the mechanisms which can be used to hold the NHS to account. This includes an assessment of what people want from an accountability mechanism and how effective the mechanisms for raising concerns are at holding the NHS to account. This Part will consider why, despite the seemingly endless recommendations to correct underlying issues in the delivery of healthcare, and to improve the systems for complaints and redress, issues have not always been resolved and further scandals have not always been prevented. This Part will then look to how adapting approaches to behaviour, regulation and redress could provide workable policy solutions to these problems for the NHS.

The NHS

2

Our Wonderful NHS

The NHS was established in 1948 to provide free health, dental, optical and nursing care to all, funded essentially from general taxation.[1] Some modest co-payment was introduced in 1951 for dentistry[2] and a year later for prescription medicines for some people. These co-payments are only charged for patients in the community, there are no co-payments for inpatients. There are exceptions from all NHS co-payment charges for certain groups.[3] The co-payments that have been added to the NHS are relatively modest: the concept of a taxation-funded free-at-the-point-of-delivery NHS for all those who are 'ordinarily resident' in the UK has endured. While this century has seen a substantial but quiet increase in private health insurance take-up by many employers and less commonly by individuals, this remains a minority option. Only around 10 per cent of the UK population hold private healthcare policies.[4] Private healthcare in the UK tends to focus on elective secondary treatments; primary care remains almost exclusively public. The size and coverage of the NHS means it dwarfs the UK private healthcare sector.

This book will focus on the more recent history of the NHS in the twenty-first century. The NHS is a large and complex organisation, which has contact with more than 1.5 million patients, families and carers daily.[5] It is the fifth largest employer in the world.[6] Although

---

[1] See J Laing and McHale J, *Principles of Medical Law* 4th edn (Oxford University Press, 2017); C Webster, *The National Health Service. A Political History* 2nd edn (Oxford University Press, 2002).

[2] In 1951 a charge was introduced for NHS dentures, and charges for other treatments soon followed.

[3] Dental treatment exists in a hybrid model: NHS dental treatment is available free of charge to certain groups (including children, pregnant women/women who have given birth in the previous 12 months and those on low incomes) the remainder of the population pay for NHS dentistry. Charges for NHS dental treatments are currently organised into three charging bands, www.nhs.uk/common-health-questions/dental-health/what-is-included-in-each-nhs-dental-band-charge/. A similar model exists for opticians with free NHS eyesight tests for certain groups and NHS optical vouchers to contribute towards the cost of glasses/contact lenses, www.nhs.uk/using-the-nhs/help-with-health-costs/free-nhs-eye-tests-and-optical-vouchers/. Prescription charges are paid per prescription and are not related to the cost of the item that has been prescribed. There is no charge for individuals who are over 60, children, pregnant women/women who have given birth in the previous 12 months, those with specified medical conditions who have a valid medical exemption certificate, those with a war pension if the prescription is for their accepted disability and those on low incomes, www.nhs.uk/nhs-services/prescriptions-and-pharmacies/who-can-get-free-prescriptions/. There are also options to purchase a prescription pre-payment certificate which covers all prescriptions required for a specified time period and will work out less costly for those who average more than one prescribed item per month.

[4] Country profile for England from Roosa Tikkanen, Robin Osborn, Elias Mossialos, Ana Djordjevic and George Wharton, *International Profiles of Health Care Systems 2020* (Commonweath Fund, 5 June 2020) available at www.commonwealthfund.org/international-health-policy-center/countries/england.

[5] *Understanding the New NHS: A Guide for Everyone Working and Training within the NHS* (NHS England, 2014) 4.

[6] L Rolewicz and B Palmer, *The NHS Workforce in Numbers: Facts on Staffing and Staff Shortages in England* (Nuffield Trust, published 8 May 2019, updated 19 February 2020) available at www.nuffieldtrust.org.uk/resource/the-nhs-workforce-in-numbers.

they are the face of the NHS, doctors and nurses (150,000 and 330,000 respectively at February 2020) make up only around one-third of the total workforce. NHS employees include almost 350,000 people providing support to clinical staff; just over 320,000 nurses and midwives; 182,000 NHS infrastructure support staff; 146,000 scientific, therapeutic and technical staff; just under 118,000 hospital and community health service doctors; 83,000 GP support and administrative staff; 34,000 GPs; nearly 17,000 GP practice nurses; just under 17,000 ambulance staff; and around 2,000 other staff. Some NHS clinical services are delivered by non-NHS organisations: at least 55,000 individuals are employed by independent healthcare providers, but it is not known how many of them provide NHS commissioned clinical services.[7] In actuality many more people work in the NHS indirectly, for example employees of companies the NHS contracts to provide services such as cleaning, laundry, etc.

In fact, the NHS is not a single organisation. To date it was best visualised as a series of interlocking systems, see Figure 1, modified from Charles 2019.[8] The major components are hospitals and community health services, general practitioners (GPs) and mental health services, each of which has had separate funding and incentives. Since April 2013 Public Health is no longer an NHS responsibility and is run by Local Authorities and Public Health England in 2013.[9] However, the Long Term Plan sets out further integration which will significantly alter the inter-relationships between these systems, see the New Service Model section of the Long Term Plan below.

Figure 1 Diagram of NHS Health Services

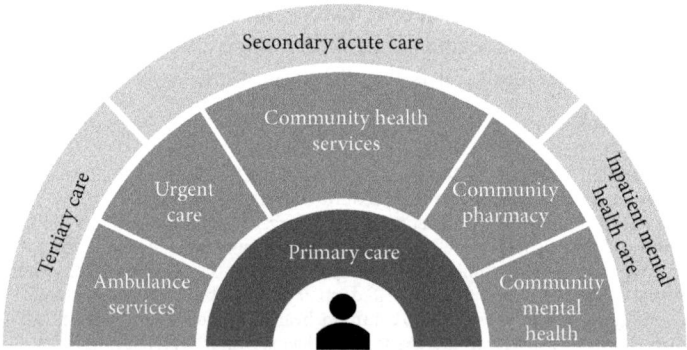

Social care is run by local councils and is not part of the NHS but the advent of integrated care has meant it is closely linked in practice and likely to become more so under the Long

[7] See https://digital.nhs.uk/data-and-information/publications/statistical/independent-healthcare-provider-workforce-statistics.

[8] Anna Charles, *Community Health Services Explained* (The Kings Fund, 14 January 2019) available at www.kingsfund.org.uk/publications/community-health-services-explained.

[9] Public health was the responsibility of the NHS but this was changed by the Health and Social Care Act 2012 (2012 c 7). Since 1 April 2013 local authorities have been responsible for improving the health of their local population and for public health services including most sexual health services and services aimed at reducing drug and alcohol misuse. The Secretary of State continues to have overall responsibility for improving health, with national public health functions delegated to Public Health England.

Term Plan. The structure of the social care market, which is predominantly private providers, is very different to the structure of the NHS.

I.   The Health and Social Care Levy

Government plans for social care have been long-awaited and an announcement was made by the Prime Minister Boris Johnson on 7 September 2021. From April 2022 a 1.25 per cent increase in employee, employer and self-employed national insurance contributions and dividend tax, termed the health and social care levy, was introduced. This is predicted to generate an additional £12 billion per year. Over the first three years £5.4 billion is allocated to social care in England (£500 million is earmarked for training); £16 billion will go towards NHS England funding; £8.9 billion will be spent on the 'health-based Covid response' including dealing with the backlogs caused by the pandemic; and £5.7 billion will go to the devolved nations to cover health and social care there. Although touted as a social care spending reform it is unclear how the levy would be split after the initial three years. This may be a moot point; at present the future of the levy is uncertain.

II.   Public Perceptions of the NHS

The British public are proud of the NHS. In his memoire the former Chancellor of the Exchequer Nigel Lawson described the NHS as the closest thing the English people have to a religion.[10] An insight into how important the NHS is to the national psyche was clear from the 2012 London Olympic opening ceremony, designed by the Oscar-winning film director Danny Boyle, which featured over 800 NHS volunteers. According to the Olympic media guide,[11] the opening ceremony honoured 'two of Britain's greatest achievements: its amazing body of children's literature and its National Health Service'.

The COVID-19 pandemic sharply focussed public perception of the NHS and social care, and particularly on the individuals who make up the service. The £38.9 million raised for NHS charities by Captain Sir Tom Moore[12] and the 'clap for carers'[13] that occurred from March to May 2020 provided very tangible expressions of the appreciation that members of the public have for health and social care staff and other key workers. This tallies with consistent findings from the Friends and Families Test data,[14] where the vast majority of service users report a positive experience of the NHS and would recommend the service to friends or family.

---

[10] Nigel Lawson, *The View from No. 11: Memoirs of a Tory Radical* (Bantam Press, 1992).

[11] Media guide: London 2012 Olympic Games opening ceremony/The London Organising Committee of the Olympic Games and Paralympic Games Ltd (Summer Olympic Games. Organizing Committee. 30, 2012, London) available at https://library.olympic.org/Default/doc/SYRACUSE/60858/media-guide-london-2012-olympic-games-opening-ceremony.

[12] https://captaintom.org/.

[13] Clap for Carers involved members of the UK public standing on their doorsteps to applaud key workers during the first wave of the COVID-19 pandemic. It was held weekly on Thursday evenings at 8pm for 10 weeks from 25 March 2020 to 28 May 2020, and will subsequently be an annual event on 25 March, see https://clapforourcarers.co.uk/.

[14] See www.nhs.uk/using-the-nhs/about-the-nhs/friends-and-family-test-fft/.

However, more recent findings indicate that there is growing dissatisfaction with the NHS, attributed to longer delays and difficulties obtaining services in an NHS that is still struggling with the aftershocks of the pandemic. Dr Katherine Hederson, a senior A&E consultant and president of the Royal College of Emergency Medicine describes the experiences of A&E staff:

> During the pandemic people were being very positive about healthcare workers. But now the public are frustrated that services aren't getting back to normal. Maybe people who weren't the source of abuse before are now being the source of abuse. Abuse may be physical or verbal, it may be through social media, or it may be racial or misogynistic.[15]

This places an additional pressure on an already stretched service.

III. Satisfaction and Dissatisfaction with the NHS

From its inception onwards the vast majority of British people have felt positively about the NHS and at present COVID-19 appears to have generated an overwhelming feeling of goodwill towards the NHS. An insight into user satisfaction can be gained from the Friends and Family test data.[16] Overall, across the services the NHS offers the percentage of users who would recommend that service to their family and friends usually ranges from the mid-80s to almost 100 per cent recommendation levels. Although most members of the British public would recommend the NHS this does not mean they are entirely satisfied, their views may be nuanced. There often seems to be a dichotomy between the way people think about the NHS as an institution and service, and the way they think about their personal experiences of NHS care. For example, on the one hand people may call to mind the good work of individual NHS staff members, while also reflecting less favourably on issues such as waiting times, the unavailability of expensive drugs for people in need and constant reforms to NHS structures. Another factor that can influence perceptions of the NHS is the series of major failings that have been given extensive publicity in the popular media.

There are clearly a number of units that have consistently delivered high quality care year after year. Despite the huge amount of good work delivered by the NHS, there have been some blemishes on its reputation. Successive serious scandals have occurred, and resultant official investigations have consistently noted the failings in supporting the necessary culture across the NHS.

IV. Evolution of the NHS

Since its inception the NHS has been constantly evolving and the service it delivers has changed dramatically. The number of medical acts and the complexity of techniques continues to increase significantly, not least because of the increasing number of elderly people

---

[15] Denis Campbell, '"People Are Very Angry With Us": A&E Doctor on Abuse of Staff' *The Guardian* (10 October 2021) available at www.theguardian.com/society/2021/oct/10/people-are-being-very-angry-with-us-ae-doctor-on-abuse-of-nhs-staff.

[16] www.england.nhs.uk/fft/friends-and-family-test-data/.

and the availability of innovative, and often costly, treatments.[17] As the eminent British paediatrician Sir Cyril Chantler reflected in 1998 'Medicine used to be simple, ineffective, and relatively safe. It is now complex, effective, and potentially dangerous.'[18]

There has been a clear pattern of continued improvements in the effectiveness of treatments which has continued into this century. In a 2015 policy statement, the NHS leadership asserted that the NHS had dramatically improved since 2000, with better cancer and cardiac outcomes, shorter waits and much higher patient satisfaction, whilst accepting that quality of care can be variable, preventable illness is widespread and health inequalities deep-rooted.[19]

V. NHS Patient Experience and Metrics

While there are clear improvements in outcomes there are also several notable examples from the NHS where both the quality of the clinical care delivered and the patient experience have been utterly unacceptable. Mid-Staffs, for example, has become short-hand for dreadful NHS care. One of the particularly troubling aspects of Mid-Staffs was that although patients and their families knew the care was substandard the official 'risk governance' reports and assessments did not recognise this. Mid-Staffs was rated as 'good' under the self-assessment rating awarded by the Healthcare Commission (the precursor of the Care Quality Commission). However, just six months later the Independent Inquiry[20] slammed the culture of the hospital trust reporting that it was not conducive to providing good quality and safe patient care.

Similarly, a disconnect between patient satisfaction and outcomes and official critiques of the service has occurred with NHS Resolution's Maternity Incentives Scheme. This consists of 10 'safety actions'; a Trust that completes these 10 actions will get a rebate from the money they have paid to NHS Resolution to cover their clinical negligence costs. It was widely reported that several NHS Trusts have had to pay back millions to the scheme after their assessments of their maternity safety were found to be incorrect.[21] For example, almost £1 million was paid to Shrewsbury & Telford Trust for completing these 'safety actions', shortly afterwards the maternity care they provided was judged 'inadequate' by the Care Quality Commission (CQC) and Donna Ockenden was asked to carry out a major

---

[17] C Newdick, *Who Should We Treat? Rights, Rationing and Resources in the NHS* 2nd edn (Oxford University Press, 2005).

[18] C Chantler, *BMJ* 1998;317:1666 doi: https://doi.org/10.1136/bmj.317.7173.1666b (published 12 December 1998).

[19] *NHS Five Year Forward View* (NHS England, October 2014) available at www.england.nhs.uk/publication/nhs-five-year-forward-view/.

[20] *Independent Inquiry into Care Provided by Mid Staffordshire NHS Foundation Trust January 2005–March 2009 Volumes I and II. Chaired by Robert Francis QC*, HC375-I and HC375-II (24 February 2010) available at www.gov.uk/government/publications/independent-inquiry-into-care-provided-by-mid-staffordshire-nhs-foundation-trust-january-2001-to-march-2009.

[21] Shaun Litern, 'Hospitals Forced to Repay Millions After Falsely Claiming Their Maternity Units Were Safe' *The Independent* (8 March 2021) available at www.independent.co.uk/news/health/maternity-safety-nhs-hospitals-shrewsbury-b1804683.html?fbclid=IwAR2vSrgUCbbzOnX3lkIgtxrA_575RpBzDIjrqGWB2TZEGBoV_WcRq6EtPZ4.

review of their maternity services (see Part II, chapter 10, 'Public Inquiries and Reviews'). Similarly, East Kent are paying back money and are the subject of an inquiry into maternity safety as well as a criminal prosecution by the CQC over the death of baby Harry Richford in 2017.

While clear safety and outcomes achievements have been delivered by the majority of NHS services, there are questions over whether systems based on targets, control measures and bureaucratic controls are the best fit for a complex entity like the NHS as they do not always reflect patient experience. For example, Brown and Calnan[22] described how this 'audit culture' erodes the less tangible, but vital, communication and caring aspects of healthcare interactions, causing a negative impact on both staff and patients. Patient input is vital, and there are moves to include more patient inputs and reports, for example the involvement strand of the patient safety strategy is explicit about including patient perspectives.

VI. COVID-19 and the NHS

The NHS Long Term Plan and the NHS Patient Safety Strategy are described in more detail in chapters three and four. They were drawn up before COVID-19 and they outline the template for taking the NHS forwards for the next few years. However, the NHS has undoubtedly been significantly impacted by the pandemic. Managing and treating COVID-19 has caused enormous knock-ons for other NHS services. Over the financial years 2022/23–2025/26 £8.9 billion from the Health and Social Care levy will go towards providing catch-up services. There have been some vocal critics stating that this will not be enough to clear the backlog caused by the pandemic.

However, even before COVID-19 the NHS had for many years been subject to a series of pressures, including increasing demand with seasonal fluctuations, budgetary constraints, resource problems and – not least – a series of structural reorganisations imposed by different governments. There have been concerns over the availability of care, long waiting lists, people left on hospital trolleys, unresponsiveness to complaints and major scandals and breakdowns in communication and trust. Governments focused on delivery of care at controllable cost, and the resultant policymaking prioritised operational measures and targets and has arguably diverted attention from aspects of the quality of care delivered to patients.

COVID-19 has shown that when it needs to the NHS can move at speed and adapt the care provided. Reorganisations that might have seemed nigh on impossible have been successfully managed in exceptionally short timeframes. As well as the promised additional financial resources a similar flexible and innovative approach that was taken to treating the pandemic will be needed to clear the vast backlog of non-urgent care that COVID-19 has caused. The pandemic has also shown the importance of caring. The compassion and kindness shown by NHS hospital staff caring for patients whose families were not allowed to

---

[22] P Brown and M Calnan, 'The Risks of Managing Uncertainty: The Limitations of Governance and Choice, and the Potential for Trust' (2009) 9(1) *Social Policy & Society* 13–24.

physically visit provided some of the defining images of the pandemic. The potential toll this takes on staff should not be underestimated; it is clear that the NHS must care not just for its patients but for its staff as well. There is an opportunity to analyse what changes to aspects of service delivery worked well during the acute phases of the pandemic. This analysis should inform both how care should be organised and what aspects of providing healthcare need to be prioritised going forward.

3

The Long Term Plan

The NHS Long Term Plan,[1] published in January 2019, sets out the plan for the next decade for the NHS. It outlines three 'truths':

> There's been pride in our Health Service's enduring success, and in the shared social commitment it represents. There's been concern – about funding, staffing, increasing inequalities and pressures from a growing and ageing population. But there's also been optimism – about the possibilities for continuing medical advance and better outcomes of care.

Taking these three truths as its starting point the Long Term Plan outlines how the NHS will be future-proofed. The five-year funding agreement at an average of a 3.4 per cent increase per year, the consensus on the changes that are needed and the practical experience gained from implementing the NHS Five Year Forward View[2] are held up as enabling factors for the Long Term Plan.

The Long Term Plan set out in seven chapters the actions needed to future proof the NHS. These are a new service model; actions on prevention and health inequalities; progress on care quality and outcomes; support for NHS staff; the roll out of digital care; delivering financial sustainability from NHS; and implementation of the Long Term Plan.

I. New Service Model for the NHS

Three key objectives are set out under this heading: for the NHS to be more joined up and co-ordinated in its care; for it to be more proactive in the services it provides; and more differentiated in the support offered to individuals. In order to achieve these ambitions the Long Term Plan sets out five major changes to the NHS Service model. These are:

1. We will *boost 'out-of-hospital' care*, and finally dissolve the historic divide between primary and community health services.
2. The NHS will *redesign and reduce pressure on emergency hospital services*.
3. People will get more control over their own health, and *more personalised care* when they need it.
4. *Digitally-enabled primary and outpatient care* will go mainstream across the NHS.

---

[1] *NHS Long Term Plan* (NHS England, January 2019) available at www.longtermplan.nhs.uk/.
[2] *NHS Five Year Forward View* (NHS England, October 2014) available at www.england.nhs.uk/publication/nhs-five-year-forward-view/.

5.   Local NHS organisations will increasingly *focus on population health* and local part-
     nerships with local authority-funded services, through new Integrated Care Systems
     (ICSs) everywhere.

It is very clear that the proposals laid out involve major changes to the way services are delivered by the NHS. Changes to the NHS service model are particularly important in terms of
accountability, new organisational structures and arrangements may not fit into the existing
structures. It has long been recognised that the systems for raising concerns about NHS care
are multifarious and difficult to navigate, changes to the service model risk exacerbating this
existing fault.

A. 'Out of Hospital' Care, Primary and Community Health Services

As part of the *Five Year Forward View* NHS organisations and partnership were invited to form
'vanguards' to develop and implement new models of care. Initially in March 2015 three types
of vanguards were created. 'Integrated primary and acute care systems' joined up GP, hospital,
community and mental health services. 'Multispecialty community providers' (MCPs) moved
specialist care out of hospitals into the community. 'Enhanced health in care homes' offered
older people better, joined-up health, care and rehabilitation services. In July 2015 'Urgent
and emergency care' vanguards were created, they developed new approaches to improve the
coordination of services and to reduce pressure on A&E departments. Vanguards in the fifth
care model, 'Acute care collaborations', started in September 2015. Their aim was to link hospitals together to improve clinical and financial viability and to reduce variations in care and in
efficiency.[3] The vanguards programme ended in March 2018 and responsibility for new care
models was transferred to the System Transformation Group.

   Integrated Care Systems (ICSs)[4] have been tested as new models for health and care
services. They represent a significant shift from the previous emphasis on organisational
autonomy and competition. ICSs and pave the way for stronger public sector partnerships
and the erosion of 'Payment by Results' and market-based reform.[5] ICSs do not have a
mandated structure, instead they are developed and led locally to meet the needs of the
community in that area. In their guidance on designing integrated care systems[6] NHS
England describe ICSs as

> a pragmatic way to join up planning and service delivery across historical divides: primary and
> specialist care, physical and mental health, health and social care. They are also helping to priori-
> tise self-care and prevention so that people can live healthier and more independent daily lives.

---

[3] For more detail on vanguards see the NAO, 'Developing new care models through NHS vanguards' HC 1129,
Session 2017–2019 (29 June 2018) available at www.nao.org.uk/wp-content/uploads/2018/06/Developing-new-
care-models-through-NHS-Vanguards.pdf.

[4] www.england.nhs.uk/integratedcare/.

[5] In particular concerns were raised that the integrated care provider contract no longer paid a specified amount
for each treatment given to each patient, but instead provides a fixed annual amount for a whole range of services
for all the patients in a given area. This was judicially reviewed and the Court of Appeal found in favour of the
respondent in *Jennifer Shepherd (On Behalf of 999 Call for the NHS), R (On the Application Of) v (1) NHS Calderd-
ale Clinical Commissioning Group (2) Monitor* [2018] EWCA Civ 2849 (20 December 2018) available at www.bailii.
org/ew/cases/EWCA/Civ/2018/2849.html.

[6] *Designing Integrated Care Systems (ICSs) in England* (NHS England, June 2019) available at www.england.nhs.
uk/wp-content/uploads/2019/06/designing-integrated-care-systems-in-england.pdf.

ICSs evolved from Sustainability and Transformation Partnerships[7] (STPs) – partnerships between NHS and local government which were formed to develop long-term plans to improve local health and care services.

From April 2021 there have been 42 ICSs covering the whole of England. Each ICS can cover a large geographic area with a substantial population, typically between one and three million. In their guidance three levels are described.

Systems (populations circa one million to three million people) – in which the whole area's health and care partners in different sectors come together to set strategic direction and to develop economies of scale

Places (populations circa 250,000 to 500,000 people) – served by a set of health and care providers in a town or district, connecting primary care networks to broader services including those provided by local councils, community hospitals or voluntary organisations.

Neighbourhoods (populations circa 30,000 to 50,000 people) – served by groups of GP practices working with NHS community services, social care and other providers to deliver more coordinated and proactive services, including through primary care networks.

There is clear variation. In early ICSs Gloucestershire had a total population of 528,000 with only one recognised 'place', in contrast West Yorkshire & Harrogate had a population of 2.7 million and six 'places'.

Despite their prominence in the Long Term Plan, Integrated Care Systems do not currently have any basis in legislation and, as of May 2022, no formal powers or accountabilities. ICSs blur the traditional boundaries between commissioners and providers and also between the NHS and local authorities. This has implications for accountability and transparency. There are examples of ICSs incorporating local democratic oversight, developing novel governance structures, and meeting in public and/or publishing papers and information. However, such actions are discretionary and variable and implementation has been patchy. Recommendations were made to the Government and Parliament for putting Integrated Care Systems onto a statutory footing by NHS England.[8] These have been incorporated by the Government into the Health and Care Act 2022, which broadly mirrors NHS England's recommendations. Concerningly, quite fundamental questions have been raised as to how effectively ICSs deliver care. The Centre for Policy Studies report 'Is Manchester Greater? A New Analysis of NHS Integration'[9] reported some worrying trends, including delays in transfers of care and decreased productivity, despite increased funding. This analysis was of pre-pandemic data, and was such that the Centre for Policy Studies called for a pause on putting ICSs on a statutory footing to allow time for more analysis of their impact. This has clearly not happened and the Government has signalled a clear intention to progress ICSs.

---

[7] See www.england.nhs.uk/integratedcare/how-did-we-get-here/.

[8] www.england.nhs.uk/publication/legislating-for-integrated-care-systems-five-recommendations-to-government-and-parliament/ and www.england.nhs.uk/publication/integrating-care-next-steps-to-building-strong-and-effective-integrated-care-systems-across-england/.

[9] Centre for Policy Studies *Is Manchester Greater? An Analysis of NHS Integration* (2021) available at www.cps.org.uk/research/is-manchester-greater-a-new-analysis-of-nhs-integration/.

Placing ICSs on a statutory footing should lead to greater transparency and accountability. However, the proposed statutory footing for ICSs has scope for substantial flexibility and this approach has inherent risks. Any ICS should include clear instructions on how learning and liability following adverse events should be approached. If an adverse event occurs as part of the care provided by an integrated care system this could involve multiple agencies, both public and private entities (pharmacists, opticians, etc) who are covered by different liability arrangements. There is a risk that there may be a tendency to try to apportion blame and/or liability to pay compensation to other organisations/professions that make up the ICS. This will inhibit the flow of clear information which could be used to learn from such events.

II. Action on Prevention and Health Inequalities

The pandemic has brought health inequalities into sharp focus, however the Long Term Plan had already highlighted the need for work on health inequalities and also on prevention. The introduction to chapter two, 'The NHS', mentions the overlap between NHS services and local government responsibilities for funding and commissioning public health services, including smoking cessation, drug and alcohol services, sexual health and early years support for children such as school nursing and health visitors. However, Chapter Two of the Long Term Plan set out at paragraph 2.4:

> As many of these services are closely linked to NHS care, and in many case provided by NHS trusts, the Government and the NHS will consider whether there is a stronger role for the NHS in commissioning sexual health services, health visitors, and school nurses, and what best future commissioning arrangements might therefore be.

Prior to 2013 these services were the responsibility of the NHS, and it appears that some retrenchment on the 2013 reforms may be forthcoming.

The chapter focusses on six specific areas; health inequalities; smoking; obesity; alcohol; air pollution; and antimicrobial resistance.

A. Health Inequalities

While the Long Term Plan is clear that the NHS cannot treat its way out of health inequalities, it can ensure that actions to drive down health inequalities are taken. Specific interventions mentioned are enhanced and targeted continuity of care for mothers from Black, Asian and minority ethnic (BAME)[10] and socioeconomically deprived groups; providing smoking cessation services to pregnant women; increasing the number of severely mentally ill patients who are offered physical health checks; a number of interventions aimed at increasing the

---

[10] BAME mothers are at higher risk of pregnancy- and birth-related complications and poor outcomes. For example, Black mothers have an almost five-times greater risk of maternal mortality than white mothers, for Asian mothers the risk was twice that of white mothers, see the 2020 MBRRACE report: www.npeu.ox.ac.uk/mbrrace-uk/reports.

health and lifespan of people with autism and learning disabilities; enhancing the healthcare provision available for rough sleepers; identifying and supporting carers, including young carers; increasing NHS provision for those with serious gambling problems; and engaging with and commissioning third sector organisations to provide services and support to vulnerable and at-risk groups.

B. Smoking

Smoking accounts for more years of lost life than any other modifiable risk factor and is a significant cost to the NHS both in GP appointments and hospital admissions. From 2023/24 treatment based on the Ottowa smoking cessation model will be offered to anyone admitted to hospital; to expectant mothers and their partners, and as part of specialist services provided to those with long-term mental health needs and those with learning disabilities.

C. Obesity

Obesity and poor diet are linked with type 2 diabetes, high blood pressure, high cholesterol and increased risk of respiratory, musculoskeletal and liver disease. Obese people have an increased risk of certain cancers, for example a three-fold increased risk of developing colon cancer. UK obesity rates are among the worst in Europe, with almost two-thirds of adults in England being either overweight or obese. Childhood obesity is also a significant concern, with a third of children leaving primary school either overweight or obese. Levels of obesity are not evenly distributed among different socioeconomic groups, with much higher rates among the most deprived populations. The risk of developing diabetes is up to six times higher in some BAME groups, necessitating targeted approaches in these groups. The Long Term Plan details how the NHS will double the NHS Diabetes Prevention Programme; will offer access to primary care weight management services for type 2 diabetics and those with a BMI of 30+ and hypertension; will pilot the use of very low calorie diets for obese people with type 2 diabetes; will take action to ensure the food offered in NHS premises is healthier; and will improve the consistency of the nutrition training provided for doctors at medical school.

D. Alcohol

Alcohol puts substantial pressure on the NHS. It contributes to various conditions including cardiovascular disease, cancer and liver disease and to harm from accidents, violence and self-harm. Hospitals with the highest rate of alcohol dependence-related admissions will develop Alcohol Care Teams (ACTs). ACTs have been demonstrated to significantly reduce A&E attendances, bed days, readmission and ambulance call outs. ACTs will be funded from their clinical commissioning groups health inequalities funding supplement, working in partnership with local authority commissioners of drug and alcohol services.

E. Air Pollution

The Long Term Plan acknowledges the impact of air pollution and that almost 30 per cent of preventable deaths in England are due to non-communicable diseases specifically attributed to air pollution. By 2028 at least 90 per cent of the NHS fleet will be low emission vehicles; heating NHS sites using coal and oil will be phased out; and the greater use of virtual appointments will reduce travel to and from NHS appointments.

F. Antimicrobial Resistance

The NHS has reduced primary care antibiotic prescriptions and will continue to support and implement the five-year action plan on antimicrobial resistance.[11]

III. Further Progress on Care Quality and Outcomes

Chapter three of the Long Term Plan states at 3.1:

> For all major conditions, the quality of care and the outcomes for patients are now measurably better than a decade ago. Childbirth is the safest it has ever been, cancer survival is at an all-time high, deaths from cardiovascular disease have halved since 1990, and male suicide is at a 31-year low.

However, the Long Term Plan is clear that there is scope for further improvement and makes explicit commitments including improving cancer survival by increasing early diagnosis and reiterating the Government's aim of halving maternity deaths by 2025. The plan also sets out a specific improvement focus on two areas: providing a strong start for children and young people and delivering better care for major health conditions.

A. Children and Young People

Improvement priorities for children and young people include: maternity and neonatal services; child and young people's mental health services; learning disability and autism provisions; cancer services; as well as the redesign of other health services.

B. Major Health Conditions

Priorities in the care of major health conditions include a focus on diabetes; strokes; cardiovascular disease; respiratory disease; cancer and adult mental health services. Ambitions for achieving short waits for planned care are set out in sections 3.107–3.111. It is clear that all

---

[11] 'UK 5-year Action Plan for Antimicrobial resistance 2019 to 2024' available at www.gov.uk/government/publications/uk-5-year-action-plan-for-antimicrobial-resistance-2019-to-2024.

of these aims, particularly the commitment to improve early diagnosis of cancers,[12] have been significantly impacted by the COVID-19 pandemic, and this impact will continue for some time to come.

IV. NHS Staff Getting the Backing They Need

The Long Term Plan acknowledges the NHS has a shortfall in staffing that is unsustainable, and there is a need both to train more staff and also to improve staff retainment rates. Staff retention has been made more difficult by the incredibly challenging working conditions presented by the first wave of the pandemic and the knock-on that has had on treatment provision. Although hospitals were the public focus of the first wave the impact extends into primary care as well.

A. The Workforce Implementation Plan

NHS Improvement, NHS England and Health Education England established a working group, and in partnership with a range of organisations across the NHS, including NHS managers, NHS staff unions, the Academy of Medical Royal Colleges, the Royal College of Nursing and the British Medical Association, they have developed an interim NHS people plan.[13] The interim plan focuses on three key areas – recruiting more staff; making the NHS a great place to work; and equipping the NHS to meet the challenges of twenty-first century healthcare.

B. Increasing the Number of Nurses, Midwives, Allied Health Professionals and Other Staff

There are different routes into nursing and the Interim Plan seeks to develop a clear model that provides information on these different routes to inform entrants and employers. The Long Term Plan sets out inconsistencies between the entry standards required by Higher Education Institutions (HEIs) for nursing degrees and the fact that not all HEIs can guarantee clinical placements required. In response the Long Term Plan pledges to provide funding for additional clinical placements up to a 50 per cent increase and to offer all nursing or midwifery graduates a five-year NHS job guarantee in the area where they qualified. The Long Term Plan states that increasing the number of nursing apprenticeships and a new blended practical/online nursing degree with reduced fees both aim to widen participation. The Interim Plan states that the blended degree is being developed, and outlines funding available to trainees during their courses.

---

[12] For example see M Limb, 'Covid-19: Early Stage Cancer Diagnoses Fell by Third in First Lockdown' (2021) 373(1179) *BMJ*, doi: https://doi.org/10.1136/bmj.n1179.
[13] www.england.nhs.uk/2019/06/more-staff-not-enough-nhs-must-also-be-best-place-to-work-says-new-nhs-people-plan/.

Allied health professionals (AHPs) will be used to support patient flow, with specific recommendations for AHPs that are currently undersupplied. Apprenticeships in such specialties, both clinical and non-clinical, will be used.

C. Growing the Medical Workforce

While the recruitment gap is starkest for nurses there are also gaps for doctors. There is a clear need to examine how to increase the numbers going into primary care. The Long Term Plan sets out intentions that primary care networks expand to include health care professionals to create multi-disciplinary teams. Two-year primary care fellowships will be created for newly qualified doctors and nurses to provide a secure employment contract and to help nurses in particular to consider primary care as a first destination role. A new indemnity scheme for GPs[14] was launched by NHS Resolution in April 2019, which will cover the multi-disciplinary teams (MDTs) as well as GPs themselves. Various reforms will be undertaken in collaboration with the British Medical Association (BMA), the General Medical Council (GMC), the Royal Colleges and providers around: enabling trainees to switch between specialities more fluidly; developing credentialling to allow doctors to broaden their practice; reforming the Associate Specialist grade; increasing generalist training to meet the needs of an aging population; and developing incentives to ensure trainee specialities match local needs.

D. International Recruitment

In the short- to medium-term it is clear that the NHS workforce will need to recruit internationally to meet the existing skills gap. Removing visa requirements for doctors and nurses and ensuring there are no immigration caps on Healthcare Professionals (HCPs) where there is a shortage have already been undertaken. The Interim People Plan lays out intentions to develop a new procurement framework of approved international recruitment agencies for 'lead recruiters' to draw on. This aims to support increased international recruitment by ensuring consistent operational and ethical standards. In addition, the Department of Health and Social Care (DHSC) and professional regulators will look to drive improvements to regulatory processes, in particular to streamline registration processes and reduce of recruitment timelines.

E. Supporting NHS Staff

Retaining staff, particularly nurses, is key, and NHS Improvement's Retention Collaboration will be rolled out to all NHS employers. This was drawn up before the pandemic and so does not include measures to address the additional stress that COVID-19 has put on the NHS

---

[14] https://resolution.nhs.uk/services/claims-management/clinical-schemes/general-practice-indemnity/clinical-negligence-scheme-for-general-practice.

workforce and the resulting psychological trauma and post-traumatic stress affecting many NHS staff. Projects such as Hopeline19[15] aim to support NHS staff and raise awareness of these issues, but given the scale of the issue[16] it seems likely that delivering staff retention will require far more to be done to than was originally envisaged in the Long Term Plan.

The Long Term Plan recognises that inflexible and unpredictable working patterns disincentivise NHS workers. The plan sets out how the NHS will more consistently adopt a more modern workplace ethos promoting flexibility, wellbeing and career development. Lack of career development and progress is a reason for many staff leaving, increased multi-professional credentialing and greater investment in CPD will provided to address this.

NHS staff face harassment, bullying and abuse – a quarter of staff report they have experienced such behaviour from other staff. Working in collaboration with employers and trade unions, efforts to address discrimination, bullying and harassment of staff will be stepped up. These efforts include £1 million of additional funding for the Workforce Race Equality Standard,[17] further work on closing the gender pay gap, strengthening support for LGBT+ staff, expanding the Practitioner Health Programme[18] (which provides confidential support for doctors with mental health needs) as well as looking at staff-led solutions, for example using the Talk Health and Care online forum.

Violence against NHS staff is a key concern, at the start of 2021 the NHS launched the violence prevention and reduction standard to provide a safe working environment for NHS staff.[19] Further efforts to reduce violence against staff include working with the police and Crown Prosecution Service to secure swift prosecutions, improved staff training in how to deal with violence and prompt mental health support for staff who have been victims of violence. A roll-out of body worn cameras for paramedics is underway, three years ahead of the Long Term Plan target date, following successful pilot studies.[20]

F. Enabling Productive Working

The Long Term Plan was clear that technology could, and should, be used to enable staff to focus on patient care. This included elements such as increasing the use of telephone triage and telephone/online consultations. The uptake of such measures has been brought forward by the COVID-19 pandemic. Other technological improvements, such as online access to test results, the use of more functional technology in the workplace and the increased use of technology to improve administration efficiency will free up staff time.

E-job plans will be developed for all staff except those who work exclusively in one clinical area. These provide a digital resource detailing the professional activities involved in each role. When combined with e-rostering this will enable Trusts to match capacity to

---

[15] Hopeline was set up to provide a morale boost for NHS staff, who can ring to listen to messages from members of the public telling them how valued they are www.frontline19.com/hopeline19/.

[16] Rebecca Café, 'Nurses' Mental Health: "Most People in the NHS, They Are Sad' *BBC News* (23 November 2021) available at www.bbc.co.uk/news/uk-england-london-59104738.

[17] www.england.nhs.uk/about/equality/equality-hub/equality-standard/.

[18] www.england.nhs.uk/2018/10/nhs-to-prioritise-doctors-mental-health/.

[19] www.england.nhs.uk/publication/violence-prevention-and-reduction-standard/.

[20] www.england.nhs.uk/2021/06/nhs-roll-out-of-body-cams-in-boost-to-ambulance-crews-safety/.

expected demand. NHS England have developed levels of attainment and meaningful use standards to assist Trusts with their e-job planning.[21]

G. Leadership and Talent Management

The Long Term Plan recognises that NHS leadership directly impacts on the quality of care and organisational performance, but that the NHS does not have a sufficient pipeline of skilled senior leaders. The 'NHS Leadership Code' will be developed and will enshrine the cultural values and leadership behaviours expected within the NHS. A more systematic approach will be adopted to identifying the next generation of leaders and to supporting leaders. A more inclusive culture will be developed building on the 2016 Developing People: Improving Care framework, including: programmes to develop a more inclusive culture and to ensure a more diverse leadership cadre that is representative of all staff and the population they serve; leadership development offers for staff at all levels; a faculty of coaches/mentors to support senior leaders; ensuring widespread knowledge of improvement skills and how to apply them for all levels of leadership in the NHS.

H. Volunteers

Volunteers contribute to the NHS in a range of roles, but the levels of volunteers varies substantially between Trusts. The Long Term Plan pledges that NHS England will provide £2.3 million to scale up volunteering across England, with the aim to double the number of volunteers within three years.

V. Digitally-enabled Care Going Mainstream Across the NHS

The Long Term Plan lays the priorities for digital transformation across the NHS. There are clear success stories of embedding digital transformation within the NHS, for electronic prescribing is used by 93 per cent of GP practices and the e-Referral Service now covers all hospitals and GP practices. In order to facilitate the spread of good practice digitally advanced Trusts are supported to become Exemplars. Exemplars are then partnered with international healthcare organisations who successfully utilise digital technology, to learn from them, in the process becoming 'Global Digital Exemplars'.[22] Global Digital Exemplars (GDEs) are then partnered with 'fast followers' UK Trusts who will support the spread of best practice. Funding from NHS England (NHSE)/DHSC is matched locally allowing GDEs and fast followers to develop and test digital models to improve care that, if successful, can then be rolled out more widely across the NHS.

While improvements have been made there is scope for more progress. For patients this involves creating straightforward access to patient records, giving them control over

---

[21] www.england.nhs.uk/wp-content/uploads/2020/09/E-job_planning_meaningful_use_standards.pdf.
[22] www.england.nhs.uk/digitaltechnology/connecteddigitalsystems/exemplars/.

their medical record while protecting their privacy and using software to support patients to manage their health condition. For individual clinical staff the desired improvements are to ensure that clinicians can interact with patient records wherever they are; to reduce data collection burdens by using software and tools to capture data; to use AI and decision support algorithms to help clinicians apply best practice and to reduce variation. At a system level predictive software will be used to support planning care to meet local needs; linkage between clinical, genomic and other data will support the development of new treatments; data captured during healthcare will be made available, as open data, for clinical research; aggregate metrics will be used to ascertain NHS performance and service. Underpinning these is a commitment to ensuring that NHS systems and NHS data are secure; that technology standards are enforced to ensure interoperable accessible data; and efforts are made to support software developers and innovators within the English health IT industry.

In order to implement these aims in June 2021 the Government produced their draft data strategy, 'Data saves lives: reshaping health and social care with data'.[23] Some proposals in the draft strategy, such as the extraction of GP records onto a centralised database without asking patients for consent, have proved controversial, and a two-month delay was put in place to give time to raise awareness.

A. Empowering People

The Long Term Plan commits to providing people with the ability to access, manage and contribute to their healthcare using digital tools and resources both for preventative care and during treatment. The NHS App, the NHS login and the NHS Apps library all deliver personalised content and provide trustworthy healthcare information. The Plan commits to working with the NHS, the third sector, developers and individuals to create apps tailored to specific conditions, such as diabetes, anxiety and depression. There is a commitment to incorporate additional modes of delivery, such as virtual and augmented reality.

The Long Term Plan lays out plans for the NHS App to provide seamless access to local and national NHS services. The COVID-19 pandemic has dramatically impacted on NHS App use. Following the announcement on 12 May 2021 that the NHS App would be used for vaccine passports the number of people who have downloaded it increased substantially from 3.5 million to almost five million.

Better Births, the National Maternity Review, recommended that women should have electronic, interoperable maternity records. The Long Term Plan commits to extending the coverage to the whole country by 2023/24 and to ensure that a digital 'red book', which records information about the child including growth and immunisation records, will also be available.

---

[23] www.gov.uk/government/publications/data-saves-lives-reshaping-health-and-social-care-with-data-draft/data-saves-lives-reshaping-health-and-social-care-with-data-draft.

B. Supporting Health and Care Professionals

There is a recognition that NHS staff need more efficient technology than is currently in place. The Long Term Plan sets out that staff will be provided with the tools they need to effectively deliver care, including facilitating digital data collection at the point of care.

There are known issues with mobile working, for example community nurses face challenges such as poor connectivity in patient homes, inability to access GP records, limited training on digital devices and software compatibility issues. The plan outlines an expansion of the use of mobile digital services in community settings for both prevention and emergency care including community-based staff and ambulance staff having access to digital patient care records and plans.

Digital leadership in each organisation will be driven by board level leadership on informatics, with increased digital training for all staff and the expansion of the NHS Digital Academy programme.[24]

C. Supporting Clinical Care

At the start of the Long Term Plan some elements of the NHS remained paper-based, all providers in acute, community and mental health settings are expected to achieve core levels of digitisation by 2024. To enable this electronic Patient Record systems and associated apps, including cloud-based variants, will be rolled out. All digitisation must meet nationally agreed standards to enable integration with the local health and care record.

The Long Term Plan sets out how there will be increased digital options for people seeking NHS care. The NHS App will provide a 24/7 triage function to enable individuals to manage their health needs or to connect them to local services when appropriate. The COVID-19 pandemic has accelerated the transition to virtual appointments and the redesign of clinical pathways. There is now much greater use of virtual clinics rather than physical ones and there is greater use of digital resources, such as photographs and questionnaires for patients seeking a referral to a specialist.

An integrated child protection system will be developed that replaces multiple legacy systems and will provide a screening and vaccination system for children.

D. Improving Population Health

Population health management systems will be deployed to Integrated Care Systems. The Long Term Plan's aim is that these systems will learn and become more adept at identifying at-risk groups and those who are most likely to benefit from particular interventions. These systems will also be able to identify and monitor whether patients have missed care.

---

[24] www.hee.nhs.uk/our-work/nhs-digital-academy.

Depersonalised data will be extracted from local records to support greater population health management approaches and enable more research. Working with developers and industry the NHS will work towards the frictionless integration of healthcare information and smart home and wearable devices. This development will be facilitated by NHS developed application programming interfaces (APIs) to manage the flow of information between these different systems.

E. Improving Clinical Efficiency and Safety

Digital technology will be used to help the NHS to deliver care more efficiently and safely, for example diagnostic imaging networks will enable rapid sharing of clinical images with specialist clinicians improving diagnostic efficiency. This must be done securely, both at a system level with appropriate cybersecurity protection and at the individual level by educating individual staff. To provide the most effective service any digital solutions created or commissioned by the NHS should be open source so the developer community can enhance and improve on them. All local health care record data platforms should provide free APIs to facilitate the creation of new digital solutions. The centralised NHS digital capabilities must be adaptable and capable of being deployed both locally and nationally.

The Long Term Plan sets out several digital technology milestones.

- 2019: introducing controls to ensure new systems purchased by the NHS comply with agreed standards, including those set out in 'The Future of Healthcare'.
- 2020: five geographies will deliver a longitudinal health and care record platform linking NHS and local authority organisations, three further areas will follow in 2021.
- 2020/21: people will have access to their care plan and communications from their care professionals via the NHS App; the care plan will move to the individual's Local Health and Care Record (LHCR) over the next five years.
- Summer 2021: 100 per cent compliance with mandated cyber security standards across all NHS organisations in the health and care system.
- 2021/22: systems that support population health management will be operating in all Integrated Care System across England, with a Chief Clinical Information Officer (CCIO) or Chief Information Officer (CIO) on every local NHS organisation board.
- 2022/23: the Child Protection Information system will be extended to cover all health care settings, including general practices.
- 2023/24: all patients in England will have access to a digital first primary care offer.
- 2024: secondary care providers in England, including acute, community and mental health care settings, will be fully digitised, including clinical and operational processes across all settings, locations and departments. Data will be captured, stored and transmitted electronically, supported by robust IT infrastructure and cyber security, and LHCRs will cover the whole country.

VI. Taxpayers' Investments Being Used to Maximum Effect

In June 2018 the Prime Minister set out that NHS England's revenue would average 3.4 per cent growth per year in real terms in the next five years, delivering a real term increase of £20.5 billion by 2023/24. This additional spending was to deal with existing pressures, demographic changes and new priorities. These original plans have been overridden by the COVID-19 pandemic. The funding given for COVID-19 dwarves the original provision: as at March 2021 the addition support package for the health services was at £92 billion.[25] A health and social care levy to supplement the funding for health and social care has been implemented from April 2022. This indicates a clear Government commitment as the levy was launched despite considerable pressure to delay its implementation due to the UK experiencing substantial cost of living increases.

The Long Term Plan sets out that the NHS will be put back onto a sustainable financial path and five tests are set out to demonstrate this. These will be briefly outlined below, but in practice this is rather a moot point. The impact of COVID-19 means that the funding arrangements for the NHS will differ significantly from the proposals set out in the Long Term Plan.

A. Test 1: The NHS Will Return to Financial Balance

The Long Term Plan commits to returning the overall NHS provider sector to balance by 2020/21, and to eliminating any GGC/Trust deficits by 2023/24. The evidence for the first part of 2020/21 before COVID hit was that the NHS would have achieved an overall provider balance and that the number of providers in deficit had approximately halved from the previous year. While clear progress was being made the impacts of COVID will be felt for many years, not least in the number of delayed 'routine' procedures and the 'missed' diagnoses for cancer, heart disease, etc which may lead to more serious illness that require more intensive treatment. These have led to the additional funding set out in the section above.

Other key changes outlined in returning the NHS to balance were:

– changes to payments and allocations so they better match the cost of service delivery;

– reforming the payment system from activity-based payments to population-based funding including:

    o   moving to a blended payment model for providers, starting with urgent and emergency care. The new blended model will be composed of fixed and variable elements. The fixed element covers the cost of delivering the activity required. The variable element is a marginal rate payable for elective activities and other locally agreed services.

---

[25] www.gov.uk/government/news/7billion-for-nhs-and-social-care-for-covid-19-response-and-recovery.

- o reforming the Commissioning for Quality and Innovation System (CQUIN). CQUINs, introduced in 2009, made a proportion of healthcare providers' income conditional on demonstrating quality improvement and innovation goals agreed between the Trust and its commissioners.
- o Two elements will not form part of the new payment model, the marginal rate for emergency tariff[26] and the emergency readmission rule.[27]

- The Accelerated Turnaround programme will be put in place by NHS Improvement for the worst performing 30 Trusts.
- ICSs will be supported by further financial reforms, with a focus on earned financial autonomy to give local health systems greater control over their resources where they have demonstrated strong financial and performance delivery.
- 2019/20 was to be a transitional year, with rebased control totals.[28] The rebased control totals were nationally financially neutral in aggregate and took into account changes in various factors. The overall aim was for control totals and the provider sustainability fund[29] to end in 2020/21.
- A Financial Recovery Fund (FRF) was to be created. This one-off fund was aimed at Trusts that agree and deliver upon a control total, but still record a deficit. The aim set out in the Long Term Plan was to eliminate all Trust deficits by 2023/24.

B. Test 2: The NHS Will Achieve Productivity Growth of at Least 1.1 Per Cent

While the NHS has been improving efficiency and making productivity gains there is scope for further improvement. The government set a target of efficiency and productivity gains

---

[26] Introduced in 2010/11 the marginal rate emergency rule (MRET) was a response to an increase in short duration (less than 48 hours) emergency admissions in England that could not be explained by population growth and Accident & Emergency (A&E) attendance growth alone. The intention was to limit emergency admissions. A baseline emergency admissions level was set and for emergency admissions above this baseline, the provider received just 30 per cent of the normal price under the Default Tariff Rollover (DTR) tariff. The remaining 70 per cent was retained by the commissioner and had to be spent on managing the demand for admitted emergency care.

[27] Similar to MRETs (see above) the emergency readmission rule has meant that hospitals were not reimbursed for certain types of emergency readmissions which were above locally agreed thresholds.

[28] NHS Trusts, Foundation Trusts STPs and ICSs are offered a 'control total', a financial target for that year, which they can chose to accept or reject. Access to some forms of national funding, such as national sustainability and transformation funding (see note 29 below), is conditional on providers agreeing and delivering their control total.

[29] Originally set up with £1.8 billion in 2016/17 as the Sustainability and Transformation Fund, then rebranded and uprated in 2018/19 as the Provider Sustainability Fund with £2.45 billion, this fund was used to incentivise deficit reduction. The control totals for some Trusts were set so that in order to meet them these Trusts had to spent more than they earned in a financial year. In effect this was a real-term spending cut over and above what the Trust needed to break even. The incentive for meeting these stringent control totals was that if a Trust got to the end of the year having managed to deliver this underspend they then got funding from the STRF/PSF that matched the underspend. For a more detailed description see S Gainsbury, 'Having Your Fudge and Eating It' (Nuffield Trust Comment, 2019) available at www.nuffieldtrust.org.uk/news-item/having-your-fudge-and-eating-it#costsbenefits.

of 1.1 per cent per year, which would be retained by the NHS and re-invested in services. Ten priority areas were selected:

- Improving clinical workforce management to optimise service provision and reduce bank and agency costs.[30]
- Using centralised bulk procurement for hospital consumables.[31]
- Addressing the lack of capacity in pathology and diagnostic services.[32]
- Improving efficiency in community health services, mental health and primary care.[33]
- Delivering value for money on medicines.[34]
- Improving NHS administration efficiency both nationally and locally.[35]
- Improving the way the NHS uses its estates and equipment.[36]
- Reducing the use of interventions that are not clinically effective or are effective in limited circumstances in the NHS.[37]
- Reducing the costs associated with patient-harms by improving patient safety.[38]
- Tackling patient, contractor, payroll or procurement fraud.[39]

C. Test 3: The NHS Will Use Better Integration and Prevention to Drive Down the Growth in Demand for Care

The Long Term Plan states that the mechanisms for reducing the demand for healthcare by providing better integration and prevention are set out in chapters one (see Section I above), two (see Section II above) and three (see Section III above).

---

[30] This will be achieved using electronic rosters/e-job plans. By 2023 all providers should deploy evidence-based approaches to determine required staffing levels.

[31] A new centralised NHS procurement agency, Supply Chain Coordination Limited, will deliver bulk purchase savings for commonly used hospital consumables.

[32] The focus will be on expanding the workforce, and setting up hubs and networks underpinned by digital imaging capacity that enables the image to be taken in a setting local to the patient and examined by an expert clinician irrespective of the clinician's location.

[33] The Long Term Plan sets out investments to improve these services. Specifically: making use of digital resources as described above in Section V; working with primary care networks to ensure effective use of allied health professionals, such as physiotherapists, pharmacists, etc in the new service model; and expanding the GIRFT programme (see the description of GIRFT in Chapter 4, section I 'Insight'; subsection 'H. Clinical Negligence and Litigation') into mental health and community health services.

[34] This includes a raft of measures to improve value for money including: e-prescribing to reduce errors and medicine related hospital admissions; greater use of pharmacists to ensure patients take their medicines as intended; reducing prescribing of low clinical value items and readily available over-the-counter (OTC) medicines; new statutory and voluntary pricing agreements; and the use of augmented intelligence to analyse prescribing data and reduce fraud.

[35] This was expected to save £700 million by 2023/24 and consisted of simplifying costly bureaucratic processes; reforming the payment system; and automating call core transactional services.

[36] This involves disposing of unnecessary land and buildings; reducing the amount of non-clinical space; and reducing the NHS's carbon footprint, for example by using LED lighting, smart energy management and less polluting ambulances.

[37] This joint project between NICE, the Academy of Medical Royal Colleges, NHS E/I, and clinical commissioners.

[38] The patient safety strategy, set out in chapter four, outlines the measures that will be used to improve patient safety and reduces the costs associated with patient harms.

[39] NHS business services manage a large-scale patient eligibility checking service.

D. Test 4: The NHS Will Reduce Unjustified Performance Variation

Variation includes NHS providers' operational and financial performance as well as clinical practices. Targeted programmes designed to reduce health inequalities and variation in outcomes will be utilised. This includes improving participation in marginalised groups, for example by modernising the bowel cancer screening programme. Increasing best practice, for example 'Getting it Right First Time' (GIRFT), identifies and compares best clinical practice, and this information can be used to drive improvements, particularly when underpinned by initiatives such as the Model Hospital.

The Long Term Plan states that the mechanisms for reducing unjustified variation in performance are set out in further detail in chapters two (see Section II above), three (see Section IV above) and six (see this section).

As well as targeted programmes a system-wide quality improvement approach will be used. Staff will be trained in the skills and methodologies required to improve care and reduce costs. This includes solutions like the NHS RightCare programme,[40] which uses an evidence-based approach to design optimum care pathways.

A key function of ICSs will be to reduce unwarranted variation, with support from national programmes. ICSs will be expected to co-ordinate clinicians and managers to implement standardised evidence based pathways.

E. Test 5: The NHS Will Make Better Use of Capital Investment and Assets

This involves managing both NHS's physical and digital estates to meet patient needs. Estates plans will sit alongside clinical and services strategies and will include pipeline proposals for potential capital investments. Going forward the NHS's capital regime must ensure capital funding: is prioritised and allocated effectively; supports service transformation and increased productivity; and allows for efficient planning and expenditure control.

Further details of this test are set out in the capital settlement in the Spending Review.

VII. Next Steps

There are clearly many steps and stages to implementing a comprehensive Long Term Plan, which build on pre-existing strategies (including the cancer, maternity, mental health, GP and learning disabilities strategies) and plans set out in the Five Year Forward View. Local health systems are expected to produce local implementation plans based on indicative budgets. The intention was to ensure that local health systems can shape how the Long Term Plan is implemented and develop the capacity to use systematic quality improvement approaches.

---

[40] www.england.nhs.uk/rightcare/.

Central to the Long Term Plan are ICSs, which were envisaged as a means of driving forward improvement. How successful this approach will be has been questioned.[41] Despite the concerns that have been raised there are no signs that ICSs will be delayed or further evaluated before large-scale implementation.

VIII. Long Term Plan Conclusions

The 2019 Long Term Plan was intended to drive substantial change in the NHS. However, the COVID-19 pandemic is likely to have a far more seismic impact on the NHS at least in the short- to medium-term. It is currently far too early to judge the effectiveness of the Long Term Plan, and it may never be possible to fully disentangle the relative contributions of the Plan, COVID-19 and the additional funding in driving changes to the NHS.

One of the concerns is the lack of real time feedback. The Long Term Plan sets a 10-year strategy, which for the NHS is a longer time period than previous plans. This cannot preclude responsive changes when situations change. The COVID pandemic is an obvious example of adaptations of the plan, but these were very much forced by circumstance. What is slightly more concerning is a seeming lack of responsiveness to feedback and evidence that contradicts the direction of travel. Just because a plan is in place does not mean it should be rigorously adhered to if the evidence starts to indicate that it may not be working as was originally intended. For example, the continued roll out of ICSs despite concerns being raised about their effectiveness. By not publicly addressing these issues it is unclear whether they have been considered and discounted, whether the plans have been adapted or whether nothing has changed from the original plan. There is a need to develop both adaptive service delivery, as was seen during the pandemic, and to demonstrate more accessible, evidence-based strategic oversight. Openness and accountability must be seen from the topdown as well as at the service delivery frontline.

The focus on supporting the workforce, including hiring is vital. Inadequate staffing levels can have devastating impacts on patient safety and on staff morale. Concerns over unfilled vacancies have existed for years. However, the covid pandemic has created a perfect storm of backlog, burnout and almost unbearable pressure on some specialties. The Health and Social Care Select Committee's July 2022 report into Workforce: Recruitment, training and retention in health and social care[42] is clear that persistent understaffing of the NHS now poses a serious risk to staff and patient safety:

> The refusal to do proper workforce planning also risks the Government's principal objective for the NHS at the moment, namely to tackle the Covid backlog.

While the Long Term Plan recognises these issues it does not set out the detailed workforce planning which is sorely needed. Worryingly strategic workforce planning in social care is even more limited.

---

[41] See The Centre for Policy Studies, *Is Manchester Greater? An Analysis of NHS Integration* (2021) available at www.cps.org.uk/research/is-manchester-greater-a-new-analysis-of-nhs-integration/.

[42] Health and Social Care Select Committee, *Workforce: Recruitment, training and retention in health and social*, Third Report of Session 2022–23, HC 115, 25 June 2022, available at https://committees.parliament.uk/work/1647/workforce-recruitment-training-and-retention-in-health-and-social-care/publications/.

4

The NHS Patient Safety Strategy

Ensuring patient safety has long been an absolute priority for the NHS. In 2000 in his seminal report, *An Organisation with a Memory*,[1] the then Chief Medical Officer Liam Donaldson recognised that patient safety had been somewhat of a Cinderella specialty and that a greater focus was needed of the importance of system errors. The Department of Health's response, *Building a Safer NHS for Patients*[2] set out a plan for implementing the recommendations of *An Organisation with a Memory*. The key elements were

– setting up a new 'national reporting and learning system' (NRLS) for learning from adverse events;

– building expertise in the NHS in root cause analysis;

– promoting a culture of incident reporting and patient safety in NHS organisations; and

– ensuring a more consistent approach to the commissioning of investigations to respond to failures of whole services or major systems weaknesses.

A new National Patient Safety Agency (NPSA) was set up to oversee the new national learning system, to analyse trends and to issue guidance on safety solutions to address the most serious problems identified by the system.

Patient safety has clearly evolved in the intervening 20 years, and sitting alongside the NHS Long Term Plan is the NHS's Patient Safety Strategy.[3] This was developed by NHS Improvement and NHS England, and was overseen by the first NHS National Director of Patient Safety, Dr Aidan Fowler.[4] The Patient Safety Strategy Summary outlines the NHS's safety vision and built on two foundations; a patient safety culture and a patient safety system. It says that the following three strategic aims will support the development of both the patient safety culture and the patient safety system:

• improving understanding of safety by drawing intelligence from multiple sources of patient safety information **(Insight).**

• equipping patients, staff and partners with the skills and opportunities to improve patient safety throughout the whole system **(Involvement).**

[1] An Organisation with a Memory (Department of Health, June 2000).

[2] Building a Safer NHS for Patients: Implementing 'An Organisation with a Memory' (Department of Health, June 2001).

[3] www.england.nhs.uk/wp-content/uploads/2020/08/190708_Patient_Safety_Strategy_for_website_v4.pdf. The 2021 update is available from www.england.nhs.uk/publication/nhs-patient-safety-strategy-2021-update/.

[4] Dr Fowler was appointed as NHS National Director of Patient Safety and as a Deputy Chief Medical Officer in July 2018.

- designing and supporting programmes that deliver effective and sustainable change in the most important areas **(Improvement)**.

It is very clear that the pandemic has impacted on the development of both the patient safety culture and the patient safety system. This is outlined in the 2021 update to the patient safety strategy,[5] which outlines what has changed and why. These updates are discussed below.

I. Insight

There are various sources of intelligence listed in the strategy. These include the Healthcare Safety Investigation Branch (Branch) and clinical negligence litigation. These provide mechanisms for patients or members of the public to raise concerns, so will be outlined here and also discussed in greater detail in their own chapters.

Other information sources listed are the Patient Safety Incident Management System (PSIMS)/Learn from Patient Safety Events (LFPSE); the new Patient Safety Incident Response Framework (PSIRF) (which is to replace the Serious Incident Framework (SIF)); the medical examiner system; the national clinical review and response; and the National Patient Safety Alerts System. These are briefly summarised below.

A. Learn from Patient Safety Events (LFPSE)

In 2019 the system the NHS uses to record patient safety incidents underwent a major upgrade. Previously patient safety incidents were reported to the National Patient Safety Agency's NRLS. In mid-2019 the NHS started to transition from the NRLS to a new system, the Learning from Patient Safety Events (previously known as Development of the Patient Safety Incident Management System (DPSIMS) during development).[6] Qualifying patient safety incidents that occur during NHS care must be reported.[7] Of the almost 2.25 million patient safety incident reports made from April to March 2020 the vast majority did not result in any harm, see Table 1.[8] This pattern has been consistent throughout previous years.[9]

---

[5] NHS England & Improvement *NHS Patient Safety Strategy: 2021 Update* (February 2021) available at www.england.nhs.uk/wp-content/uploads/2021/02/B0225-NHS-Patient-Safety-Strategy-update-Feb-2021-Final-v2.pdf.

[6] See www.england.nhs.uk/patient-safety/learn-from-patient-safety-events-service/. LFPSE is a major upgrade and creates a single national NHS system for recording patient safety events.

[7] There is an option for the general public to report patient safety incidents, defined as 'any unintended or unexpected incident which could have, or did, lead to harm for one or more patients receiving healthcare'. See www.england.nhs.uk/patient-safety/report-patient-safety-incident/.

[8] Taken from NRLS national patient safety incidents reports: Commentary NHS England and Improvement September 2020 available at www.england.nhs.uk/wp-content/uploads/2020/03/NAPSIR-commentary-Sept-2020-FINAL.pdf.

[9] The transition from NRLS to PSIMS/LFPSE has meant changes to the type of data that is required and the way in which it is shared and reported. These differences mean that the data recorded on NRLS and PSIMS/LFPSE are not comparable and NHS Improvement warned in 2019 that there is the potential for unpredictable fluctuations in report numbers during the shift from NRLS to PSIMS/LFPSE. See https://webarchive.nationalarchives.gov.uk/20200501112017/https://improvement.nhs.uk/documents/5074/Changes_to_patient_safety_data_publications_September_2019_v2.pdf. While the numbers should be treated with caution the pattern that the majority of patient safety incidents cause no harm is consistent.

Changes in the other harm categories are less consistent, but they are also much lower numbers so small changes in the number of reports would have a more pronounced impact on the percentage change.

Table 1 Reported incidents by reported degree of harm in England reported as occurring from April 2018 to March 2019 and from April 2019 to March 2020*

Reported degree of harm	April 2018 to March 2019		April 2019 to March 2020		% change
	N	%	N	%	
No Harm	1,50,124	74.0	1,609,520	71.6	6.7
Low	467,429	23.0	567,323	25.3	21.4
Moderate	51,110	2.5	59,594	2.7	16.6
Severe	5,426	0.3	5,919	0.3	9.1
Death	4,568	0.2	4,241	0.2	−7.2
Total	2,036,657	100	2,246,597	100	10.3

* Excludes reports where the degree of harm was not reported.

B. Patient Safety Incident Response Framework

The Serious Incident Framework[10] set out how serious incidents should be investigated by the NHS. It was last revised in March 2015.[11] The new PSIRF is being used by early adopters. The roll out of the PSIRF was significantly impacted by the pandemic; it commenced in spring 2022 and organisations will gradually transition to using it.

The change from the SIF to the PSIRF follows a realisation that organisations routinely struggle to meet the expectations of the SIF. In March 2018 NHS Improvement launched an engagement programme to seek views from a wide range of stakeholders about how and when patient safety incidents should be investigated. The engagement feedback[12] identified

> those affected by incidents are not appropriately supported or involved in the investigation process; the quality of investigation reports is generally poor; and improvements to prevent the recurrence of harm are not effectively implemented. Early exploration of these issues (as described in the engagement document) identified that problems are driven by: (1) defensive cultures and lack of trust; (2) inappropriate use of the Serious Incident investigation process; (3) misaligned oversight and assurance processes; (4) lack of time and expertise; and (5) lack of uptake of an evidence-based approach.

The new PSIRF is very clear that patient safety incident investigations are conducted with the benefit of hindsight and should carry out a careful analysis to identify the causal factors and steps that could be taken to help prevent future recurrence. It is very explicitly stated

---

[10] www.england.nhs.uk/patient-safety/serious-incident-framework/.

[11] www.england.nhs.uk/wp-content/uploads/2020/08/serious-incidnt-framwrk.pdf.

[12] NHS Improvement, *The Future of NHS Patient Safety Investigation: Rngagement Feedback* (November 2018) available at https://webarchive.nationalarchives.gov.uk/20200501112315/https://improvement.nhs.uk/documents/3519/Future_of_NHS_patient_safety_investigations_engagement_feedback_FINAL.pdf.

that judgements about culpability are not part of the investigation. Several reasons are outlined for this. Firstly, hindsight bias makes an incident appear more predictable, and therefore preventable, than it actually was.

Secondly, there is a concern that determining preventability involves judging the degree of attribution. The fear is that people or organisations that are the subject of such a judgement could feel blamed and become closed and fearful, making them reluctant to help investigators. This could create a culture of concealment which limits the opportunity for learning and improvement.

The third and final reason given is that a Patient Safety Incident Investigation or PSII is a retrospective analysis that focuses on identifying firstly the causal factors and then the steps that could be taken to help prevent future recurrence. If the investigator were also to be tasked with drawing conclusions about whether the outcome was foreseeable, avoidable or preventable at the time of the incident, the two statements can appear contradictory and invite challenge around objectivity. The draft framework is clear that a PSII must only focus on identifying the problems, why they occurred and actions to help prevent them in the future.

C. The Medical Examiner System

Medical examiners are senior doctors who in the immediate period before a death is registered (five days) independently scrutinise the causes of death. This is part of the NHS's Learning from Deaths strategy. Prior to the Medical Examiner System there had been guidance for Trusts on working with bereaved families and carers,[13] but there had not been a mechanism to ensuring that all deaths are subject to independent scrutiny. The Medical Examiner System[14] provides a formalised channel for families and carers to raise any concerns they have over the care the deceased received. Participation by families is voluntary.

Each medical examiner office team will:

- agree the proposed cause of death with the qualified attending practitioner to ensure the death certificate is accurate.

- for non-coroner cases, discuss the cause of death with the next of kin and establish if they have any concerns with the care provided.

- act as a source of medical advice to the local coroner and facilitate notification of deaths to them appropriately.

From 2019/20 acute trusts in England were asked to establish medical examiner offices, with the intention that in 2020/21 this service would be expanded to all deaths, including those occurring in the community and in independent providers. The COVID-19 Pandemic has impacted on this, with the implementation of the Medical Examiner System paused during the first wave. The revised timeline aims to have all deaths covered by Q1 2022/2023.[15]

---

[13] www.england.nhs.uk/publication/learning-from-deaths-guidance-for-nhs-trusts-on-working-with-bereaved-families-and-carers/.
[14] www.england.nhs.uk/establishing-medical-examiner-system-nhs/.
[15] NHS England & Improvement, *NHS Patient Safety Strategy: 2021 Update* (February 2021) available at www.england.nhs.uk/wp-content/uploads/2021/02/B0225-NHS-Patient-Safety-Strategy-update-Feb-2021-Final-v2.pdf.

From July 2020 medical examiners were asked to consider whether there is a reason to suspect that the death of health service and adult social care staff who died after contracting COVID-19 was a result of the person being exposed to COVID-19 at work. They were asked to report their conclusions to the National Medical Examiner's office. The contribution that medical examiners made during the acute phase of the pandemic has been recognised in the 2021 patient safety update and their importance in any future pandemic has been highlighted.

Medical examiner offices impact at local, regional and national levels. The scrutiny they provide is triangulated with other information, such as mortality indices and local intelligence, enabling issues of concern and trends or patterns that merit further exploration to be identified. The first National Medical Examiner Report[16] was published in April 2021. This report covered 2020, so was significantly impacted by COVID-19.

D. National Clinical Review and Response

National incident data is continuously analysed to identify new and under-recognised issues which can be addressed through national action. NHS England and NHS Improvement estimate 160 lives and £13.5 million in treatment costs are currently saved every year. Continuous review and developments in machine learning will be used to drive further improvement and savings. Ongoing work with partner organisations will determine if issues are best addressed at source or by professional organisations, other safety partners or using an NHS Improvement Patient Safety Alert.

E. The National Patient Safety Alerts System

Issuing safety advice and guidance to the NHS does not automatically lead to the required outcome. In 2018 the National Patient Safety Alerting Committee (NaPSAC) was set up to improve the effectiveness of such alerts.

One of the issues is that multiple different stakeholders issue many different types of safety communication through the Central Alerting System (CAS). The Chief Medical Officer, the Department of Health and Social Care (DHSC) Supply Disruption, Medicines and Healthcare products Regulatory Agency (MHRA), NHS Digital, NHS England, NHS Improvement Estates and Facilities, national patient safety team and Public Health England (PHE) all currently issue safety messages, notices, letters or alerts using CAS. The initial task for NaPSAC is to develop common standards and thresholds across these organisations. Alerts will adhere to a single format that clearly outlines to recipients what they need to do, by when and why. The standards and thresholds agreed by NaPSAC will underpin CQC's inspection of National Patient Safety Alerts and any regulatory response to non-compliance. NaPSAC ceased to exist as of November 2020, with functions transferred to the National Patient Safety Committee.

---

[16] www.england.nhs.uk/publication/national-medical-examiner-reports/.

F. The National Patient Safety Committee

The aim of this committee is for it to become a safety committee akin to the safety boards that exist for other safety critical industries like transport. The committee will have oversight of the implementation of Healthcare Safety Investigation Branch (HSIB) recommendations. It will hold to account all its contributing organisations for progress on actions agreed in response to these recommendations. The Committee will also request progress reports from non-healthcare bodies to which HSIB recommendations are directed.

G. The Healthcare Safety Investigation Branch/Health Services Safety Investigations Body

HSIB was established in April 2017 to carry out independent investigations into systemic safety risks. From April 2018 HSIB started undertaking maternity investigations. HSIB's four key contributions to the Patient Safety Strategy are listed as:

- Developing and testing healthcare safety investigation processes to improve effectiveness both nationally and locally.
- Facilitating maternity safety improvements using their maternity investigations.
- Producing reports that demonstrate the benefits of using specialist safety investigators.
- Reinforcing patient involvement in understanding and preventing patient harm.

The Health and Care Act 2022 created a statutory framework for HSIB and renamed it the Health Services Safety Investigations Body and removed the maternity investigations which will be passed to a new Strategic Health Authority.

H. Clinical Negligence and Litigation

The patient safety strategy is clear on the impact and cost of clinical negligence litigation. It outlines plans to facilitate learning from clinical negligence claims, including the early notification scheme for obstetric brain injuries,[17] the Clinical Negligence Scheme for Trusts (CNST) maternity incentives scheme, claims scorecards for members, thematic reviews and research.

i. Getting it Right First Time (GIRFT)[18]

The patient safety strategy also outlines how NHS Resolution will work with the GIRFT programme using intelligence gained from claims to improve care quality by reducing unwarranted variation. GIRFT began in 2012 as an analysis of orthopaedic outcomes to

---

[17] The early notification scheme requires that NHS Resolution is notified within 30 days of a qualifying incident, which allows for much earlier investigation and admissions of liability in birth-related brain injury cases.
[18] www.gettingitrightfirsttime.co.uk/.

address variation in clinical practice and improve care by providing benchmarking data and in-depth analysis of services to drive evidence-based change. GIRFT aims to identify approaches that improve outcomes and patient experience and to spread this good practice. GIRFT started in orthopaedics and in the first 12 months after the pilot programme it achieved an estimated £30–£50 million savings in orthopaedic care mainly through reducing inpatient stay lengths and improved procurement.

GIRFT consists of five key strands

– A data gathering and analysis exercise which creates a detailed picture of national practice, outcomes and other related factors.

– Direct clinical engagement between GIRFT clinical specialists with the Trust (including its senior clinicians) to examine how practices at that Trust fit with the national picture, identifying where the Trust is doing well and where improvements could be made.

– A national report which draws on the data analysis and the engagement with Trusts to identify opportunities for improvement across that service.

– An implementation phase where the GIRFT teams support Trusts, commissioners and ICSs to deliver the recommended improvements.

– Best practice guidance and support for standardised/integrated patient pathways and elective recovery work in 'high volume/low complexity' specialities.

The original GIRFT programme which proved highly successful was in orthopaedics. Orthopaedics has the advantage that there is a comprehensive national joint registry (NJR)[19] which has been collecting data on implanted joints since 2003. It is very clear that the NJR was the single most important data source for the original GIRFT programme. The Indepenent Medicines and Medical Devices Safety Review (IMMDS review) recommended that all implantable medical devices should be included in a national database, while that recommendation is being implemented it will be a number of years before mature registries exist. GIRFT has now been expanded into over 40 clinical specialities, many of which do not have comparable data-resources. It will be interesting to see whether the gains made in the original GIRFT area of orthopaedics can be matched in these other clinical areas.

GIRFT has a litigation work stream which applies a similar approach to learning from litigation. In 2017 GIRFT and NHS Resolution jointly released the Surgical Specialities Litigation Data Pack, which contained speciality-specific litigation metrics, allowing Trusts to benchmark their performance against the national picture. Specific action points for local systems were also put forward, including careful review of each claim, benchmarking each department against the national average, informing NHS Resolution of coding errors and triangulating claims with learning from complaints, inquests and Serious Incident reports. An updated Litigation Pack was released in 2019.

In May 2021 GIRFT issued Learning from Litigation Claims[20] jointly with NHS Resolution. This is intended to provide a structured tool to improve learning from claims, which will be led by Trust legal departments with support from clinicians and managers. All learning should be encouraged, but it should be remembered that the proportion of harmed

---

[19] www.njrcentre.org.uk/njrcentre/default.aspx.

[20] www.gettingitrightfirsttime.co.uk/bpl/litigation/.

individuals who complain and/or claim is very small, for this reason this approach simply cannot capture most of the information around harms.

II. Involvement

Five headings are listed in the strategy under this heading. These include:

- Patients, carers, families and lay people as partners
- Patient safety education and training
- Patient safety specialists
- Safety I and Safety II
- Independent sector

A. Patient and Public Voice Partners

The NHS Patient Safety Strategy highlights how patients, carers and families are not just passive recipients of healthcare but also key participants in delivering patient safety. As such the strategy calls firstly for greater support to enable patients to be involved in their own safety and secondly it envisages the creation of patient safety partner (PSP) roles.

> Patient safety partners (PSPs) are patients, carers, family members or other lay people (including NHS professionals from another organisation working in a lay capacity)5 who are recruited to work in partnership with staff to influence and improve the governance and leadership of safety within an NHS organisation.[21]

The NHS Patient strategy lays out how PSPs will be involved in:

- Service and pathway design.
- Safety governance, for example, by sitting on relevant committees to support compliance monitoring, responding to safety issues, reviewing data and reports and providing appropriate challenge to ensure learning and change.
- Strategy and policy. PSPs could ensure patients' perspectives are considered and provide valuable insights on the risks to patients; for example, where transitions in care and integration of care pathways are being considered.

In June 2021 NHS Improvement published the Framework for Involving Patients in Patient Safety[22] following a consultation[23] on the draft framework and other elements.

---

[21] As defined in the draft framework for involving patients in patient safety, https://engage.improvement.nhs.uk/policy-strategy-and-delivery-management/framework-for-involving-patients-in-patient-safety/user_uploads/200310-draft-framework-for-involving-patients-in-patient-safety.pdf.

[22] www.england.nhs.uk/wp-content/uploads/2021/06/B0435-framework-for-involving-patients-in-patient-safety.pdf.

[23] https://engage.improvement.nhs.uk/policy-strategy-and-delivery-management/framework-for-involving-patients-in-patient-safety/user_uploads/200310-draft-framework-for-involving-patients-in-patient-safety.pdf.

This framework builds on the recommendations made in Don Berwick's 2013 report[24] into patient safety in the NHS which called for greater power and involvement for patients and carers.

B. Patient Safety Education and Training

This is a flagship element of the Patient safety strategy, and it is envisaged that 'if successful, it will have more impact than any other action in this strategy'. It is a complex and lengthy programme of work focussing on teaching everyone working in healthcare that error is normal and what the right approaches are to reduce risk and maximise the chances of things going well. The key objectives set out in the Patient Safety Strategy are:

- To develop a robust, achievable and aspirational plan for patient safety training for the NHS.
- To make safety training within professional educational programmes explicit and mapped to the competencies in a national syllabus.
- To ensure every member of the NHS has access to patient safety training; from ward to board and from commissioner to provider.

A national patient safety syllabus[25] was launched on 13 May 2021. The syllabus fits into existing training programmes both within the NHS and at external organisations such as universities and higher education institutes. All staff will follow the same syllabus at an appropriate level starting with a universal 'Essentials' introduction for all new NHS staff and progressing to more specialist 'Access to Practice' training modules for patient safety specialists.

To inspire confidence training needs to be high quality. Health Education England (HEE) will be heavily involved initially in ensuring the implementation of the patient safety syllabus across the NHS and subsequently in applying its quality framework to evaluate training and assure quality.

C. Patient Safety Specialists

NHS organisations are required to identify at least one person to be their patient safety specialist. No new roles will be created, individuals in existing posts in that organisation will become the patient safety specialist on a full-time basis. They are expected to support the development of a patient safety culture within the organisation and to engage with the executive team. A patient safety specialist network will encourage the sharing of good practice and learning.

---

[24] National Advisory Group on the Safety of Patients in England, *A Promise to Learn – A Commitment to Act Improving the Safety of Patients in England* (August 2013) available at www.gov.uk/government/publications/berwick-review-into-patient-safety.

[25] www.aomrc.org.uk/news-and-views/nhs-patient-safety-syllabus-launched-to-save-lives/.

D. Safety I and Safety II

The origins of Safety I and Safety II are outlined in a 2015 white paper by Hollnagel et al.[26] They write

> Safety-I, safety is defined as a state where as few things as possible go wrong. A Safety-I approach presumes that things go wrong because of identifiable failures or malfunctions of specific components: technology, procedures, the human workers and the organisations in which they are embedded. Humans – acting alone or collectively – are therefore viewed predominantly as a liability or hazard, principally because they are the most variable of these components. The purpose of accident investigation in Safety-I is to identify the causes and contributory factors of adverse outcomes, while risk assessment aims to determine their likelihood. The safety management principle is to respond when something happens or is categorised as an unacceptable risk, usually by trying to eliminate causes or improve barriers, or both.

This is distinguished from Safety II which they say

> relates to the system's ability to succeed under varying conditions. A Safety-II approach assumes that everyday performance variability provides the adaptations that are needed to respond to varying conditions, and hence is the reason why things go right. Humans are consequently seen as a resource necessary for system flexibility and resilience. In Safety-II the purpose of investigations changes to become an understanding of how things usually go right, since that is the basis for explaining how things occasionally go wrong. Risk assessment tries to understand the conditions where performance variability can become difficult or impossible to monitor and control. The safety management principle is to facilitate everyday work, to anticipate developments and events, and to maintain the adaptive capacity to respond effectively to the inevitable surprises (Finkel 2011[27]).

There is a shift away from these original definitions in the Patient Safety Strategy, which focusses on a more simplistic interpretation of 'a focus on the rare examples of things going wrong ("Safety I") to why things routinely go right in healthcare ("Safety II")'. This doesn't encompass the shift in the perceptions of the roles of people as outlined by Hollnagel et al and the description of integrating Safety II provided in the Patient Safety Strategy is quite amorphous, which may make it difficult to implement in a consistent manner across different organisations.

E. The Independent Sector

Private providers and the NHS have different reporting requirements. The development of the Acute Data Alignment Programme ADAPt by the Private Healthcare Information Network (PHIN) and NHS Digital is key to integrating the different information sets and enabling the private sector to submit data to key NHS safety databases and to contribute to clinical audits.

Additionally, the private sector will continue to support improvements in good practice, whistleblowing and speaking up culture, including appointing Freedom to Speak Up Guardians where they are not already in post.

---

[26] E Hollnagel, RL Wears and J Braithwaite, 'From Safety-I to Safety-II: A White Paper' (2015) www.england.nhs.uk/signuptosafety/wp-content/uploads/sites/16/2015/10/safety-1-safety-2- whte-papr.pdf.
[27] M Finkel, *On Flexibility: Recovery from Technological and Doctrinal Surprise on the Battlefield* (Stanford University Press, 2011).

III. Improvement

The aim of this workstream is to develop and support safety improvement programmes. Successful safety improvement programmes should prioritise the most important safety issues and employ consistent measurement and effective improvement methods.

A. The National Patient Safety Improvement Programme[28]

This initiative is managed and led nationally by the National Patient Safety Team, but delivered locally. Improvement programmes are delivered by one of 15 regional Patient Safety Collaboratives (PSCs). PSCs and the Patient Safety Collaborative programme were established in 2014 in the light of the Mid Staff public inquiry[29] and Don Berwick's *A Promise to Learn – A Commitment to Act* report[30] commissioned in response to this scandal. PSCs are made up of the NHS providers and commissioners in a geographical region. They include hospitals, community, primary care, mental health and ambulance services and clinical commissioning groups.

PSCs are commissioned through, and hosted by, 15 regional Academic Health Science Networks (AHSNs). AHSNs are made up of NHS staff, patients, carers, academics, quality improvement and safety experts.

Four national priorities were identified for 2019/20. These are:

- Preventing deterioration and sepsis
- Medicines safety
- Maternal and neonatal safety
- Adoption and spread of tested interventions

Preventing deterioration and sepsis falls into the Managing Deterioration Safety Improvement Programme (ManDetSIP), see below.

B. Patient Safety Workstreams

In addition to 'Continuous Improvement' there are a number of specific improvement subheadings listed in the National Patient Safety Strategy which are explored below:

- Maternal and Neonatal safety;
- Medicines safety;
- Mental Health Safety;

---

[28] www.england.nhs.uk/patient-safety/patient-safety-improvement-programmes/.

[29] *Report of the Mid Staffordshire NHS Foundation Trust Public Inquiry. February 2013 Chaired by Robert Francis QC*, HC947, available at www.gov.uk/government/publications/report-of-the-mid-staffordshire-nhs-foundation-trust-public-inquiry.

[30] National Advisory Group on the Safety of Patients in England, *A Promise to Learn – A Commitment to Act Improving the Safety of Patients in England* (August 2013) available at www.gov.uk/government/publications/berwick-review-into-patient-safety.

- Safety issues that particularly affect older people;
- Safety and learning difficulties;
- Antimicrobial resistance and healthcare associated infection, and
- Research and innovation.

Related to these and listed in the National patient safety programme are

- the Managing Deterioration Safety Improvement Programme, and
- the Adoption and Spread Safety Improvement Programme.

C. Continuous Improvement

It should go without saying that the NHS safety system must support continuous sustainable improvement. Quality improvement, the systematic use of specific methodologies and tools, will be used to continuously improve outcomes for patients. Key to this is understanding causes of variation, building learning and capability, and determining which evidence-based interventions and implementation approaches achieve the desired improvements.

D. The Maternity and Neonatal Safety Improvement Programme

This programme sits within the Maternity Transformation Programme, which was developed to implement the findings of the National Maternity Review, *Better Births*.[31] The implementation of *Better Births* is overseen by the Maternity Transformation Programme Board, whose work also includes delivering the national objective[32] to halve the rates of Stillbirths, Neonatal and Maternal Deaths and Asphyxial brain injuries between 2015 and 2025. Progress is being made towards this target. However, one of the issues is that a Trust must report the same qualifying incident to multiple organisations (Each Baby Counts, the Healthcare Safety Investigation Branch (HSIB), the Mothers and Babies: Reducing Risk through Audits and Confidential Enquiries across the UK (MBRRACE) programme, NHS Resolution) as well as carrying out an internal investigation. The Patient Safety Strategy lays out plans to rationalise this so that any incident is only reported to one single portal.

The Programme identifies five clinical priorities: increasing the proportion of smoke-free pregnancies; improving the optimisation and stabilisation of very preterm infants; improving the diagnosis and management of gestational diabetes; improving the diagnosis and management of neonatal hypoglycaemia; and improving the recognition and management of deterioration during labour and the early post-partum period. The Saving Baby Lives

---

[31] *Better Births: Improving Outcomes of Maternity Services in England: A Five Year Forward View for Maternity Care* (National Maternity Review, 2016).
[32] www.gov.uk/government/news/new-ambition-to-halve-rate-of-stillbirths-and-infant-deaths.

Care Bundle (2019)[33] with its five core aims[34] will also be supported by the Improvement programme.

E. The Medicines Safety Improvement Programme

The Medicines Safety Improvement Programme aims to reduce medication-related harms in the NHS by focussing on high risk drugs and situations, and vulnerable patients. This is a serious issue, with an estimated 237 million medication errors in England each year, of which 66 million are clinically significant. Key to delivering this objective are implementing electronic prescribing, focussing on patient reported outcomes related to safety and a focus on shared decision-making between patients and healthcare professionals.

The 2021 Patient Safety Strategy update provides more clarity. The initial focusses will be on: reducing medicine administration errors in care homes; regular medicine review in care homes including looking at problematic polypharmacy; structured medicine reviews in community settings including looking for problematic polypharmacy; best practice guidance on transitioning patients on anticoagulants from hospital to care homes; reducing harm by reducing the prescribing and supply of methotrexate, and shared decision-making training for pharmacists when working with patients with atrial fibrillation on anticoagulants or patients starting on opioids for non-chronic, non-cancer related pain.

F. The Mental Health Safety Improvement Programme

The Mental Health Safety Improvement Programme clearly has substantial work to do. In their review, *The State of Care in Mental Health Services 2014–17*,[35] the CQC identified safety as the factor that was most often rated as requiring improvement or inadequate. The safety of acute wards and Psychiatric Intensive Care Units was particularly concerning with only 18 per cent of such services rated as good and just 1 per cent as outstanding. The Improvement Programme works with the providers, CQC (local teams and central) and NHS I local teams.

There are two main components.

– Engagement with Trusts to develop, implement and maintain a safety plan.

– The improvement collaborative programmes, which have a focus on improving specific aspects of mental health safety, such as reducing restrictive practices (restraint, seclusion and rapid tranquillisation), improving sexual safety on inpatient mental health wards

---

[33] www.england.nhs.uk/publication/saving-babies-lives-version-two-a-care-bundle-for-reducing-perinatal-mortality/.

[34] These are (1) reducing smoking in pregnancy; (2) risk assessment, prevention and surveillance of pregnancies at risk of fetal growth restriction; (3) raising awareness of reduced fetal movement; (4) effective fetal monitoring during labour; (5) reducing preterm birth.

[35] Care Quality Commission, *The State of Care in Mental Health Services 2014–2017. Findings from the CQC's Programme of Comprehensive Inspections of Specialist Mental Health Services* (2017) available at www.cqc.org.uk/publications/major-report/state-care-mental-health-services-2014-2017.

and learning disability services for both patients and staff and reducing self-harm and suicide in inpatient mental health services.

G. Safety Issues That Particularly Affect Older People

As we have an aging population the importance of safety issues that impact on older adults, such as falls, pressure sores, infections and ensuring appropriate nutrition and hydration, will grow. This initiative is multifactorial with several key focusses. These include the Stop the Pressure programme,[36] falls prevention[37],[38] and the development of an anticipatory care framework which incorporates identifying those living with frailty and/or complex needs, carrying out a holistic needs assessment which is used to create a personalised care and support plan.[39] These approaches span both primary and secondary care, and the development of ICSs is expected to generate new care models to deliver joined up health and care services.

H. Safety and Learning Disabilities

There have long been concerns over the quality of care provided to people with learning disabilities, with some utterly horrendous failings, such as were seen at Winterbourne View (for more details see chapter 10). The Long Term Plan is clear that people with learning disabilities have poorer health outcomes, including premature death, and this needs to be resolved. The Learning Disabilities Mortality Review (LeDeR) Programme[40] investigates the deaths of those with a learning disability (from late 2021 individuals with autism will also be included). Their 2020 annual report contains some stark findings; for instance in 2019 85 per cent of the UK population lived to be over 65, by contrast the proportion of people

---

[36] This is incorporated as part of the National Wound Care Strategy Programme, see www.nationalwoundcare-strategy.net/.

[37] This includes falls collaboratives to develop local models in collaboration with other partner agencies, for example see the Bradford District Care NHS Foundation Trust work with the West Yorkshire Fire and Rescue Service, www.england.nhs.uk/atlas_case_study/falls-prevention-nurses-lead-collaborative-falls-service-improvement-with-west-yorkshire-fire-and-rescue-service/ as well as national online guidance, for example the NICE Clinical Guideline [CG161] Falls in Older People: assessing risk and prevention, (NICE 12 June 2013) available at www.nice.org.uk/guidance/cg161.

[38] In 2019/20 a Commissioning for Quality and Innovation (CQUIN) payment framework was created to incentivise Acute Trusts and Community hospitals to reduce inpatient falls in older patients, see www.england.nhs.uk/wp-content/uploads/2019/03/CQUIN-Guidance-1920-080319.pdf.

[39] Changes to the GP contract in 20178/18 introduced routine frailty identification for all patients aged 65 and over. This requires that the GPs undertake an annual medicines review, a falls assessment risk (if clinically appropriate) and promote the enriched Summary Care record for all patients identified as living with severe frailty. For those identified as living with moderate frailty the GP must consider undertaking these actions. To facilitate this an electronic Frailty Index (eFI) may be used www.england.nhs.uk/ourwork/clinical-policy/older-people/frailty/efi/#should-the-practice-i-work-in-use-the-efi-to-identify-people-who-may-be-living-with-frailty. The eFI analyses key indicators within the electronic health record to create a score that is predictive of the risk of frailty for this patient. See also the NHS Right Care: Frailty Toolkit for further detail available at www.england.nhs.uk/rightcare/wp-content/uploads/sites/40/2019/07/frailty-toolkit-june-2019-v1.pdf.

[40] The Learning Disabilities Mortality Review programme LeDeR, https://leder.nhs.uk/about.

with learning disabilities living to over 65 was just 38 per cent. The LeDeR programme is being supported by and aligned with the medical examiner system.

Particular focus will be given to:

- Preventing the overmedication of people with learning disabilities with psychotropic medications;[41]

- ensuring patients with learning disabilities and/or autism and their families are treated properly and listened to when they raise a concern or give feedback;[42]

- widening the use of Care and Treatment Reviews (CTRs)[43] or, for children and young people, Care, Education and Treatment Reviews (CETRs). CTRs and CETRs are carried out by independent panel, and can be either (a) a pre-admission review to assess whether an alternative to hospitalisation is more appropriate or (b) if the patient is already in hospital, a review of what can be done to improve the quality of in-patient care and/ or to make plans for a smooth transition from hospital to other care. NHS England produce toolkits[44] for CTRs and CETRs which detail expected standards, and outline discharge steps, including a 12-point discharge plan, to ensure consistency of approach and to monitor effectiveness. During COVID CTRs and CETRs have moved online.

- The patient safety strategy sets out the aim that by 2024 all NHS care will meet the four learning disability improvement standards.[45] The first three standards are for all Trusts, the fourth is only for specialist Trusts that provide services commissioned exclusively for people with learning disabilities, autism or both. The standards concern
  - ° Respecting and protecting rights[46]
  - ° Inclusion and engagement[47]
  - ° Workforce[48]
  - ° Learning disability standards aimed solely at specialist mental health trusts providing care to people with learning disabilities, autism or both.[49]

---

[41] 17 per cent of people with a learning disability receive antipsychotic medication, compared with 1 per cent of the general population and there are c 30,000–35,0000 people with a learning disability who receive daily antipsychotic medication despite having no clinical reason for this in their GP notes. To combat this STOMP and STAMP will be expanded. STOMP stands for Stopping Over Medication of People with a Learning Disability, autism or both, see www.england.nhs.uk/learning-disabilities/improving-health/stomp/ for more detail. STOMP looks at adults, STAMP (Supporting Treatment and Appropriate Medication in Paediatrics) is the equivalent for children and young people, see www.england.nhs.uk/learning-disabilities/improving-health/stamp/.

[42] 'Ask Listen Do' provides support and resources to help organisations learn from and improve the care offered to those with a learning disability, autism or both, by improving the experience of these patients and their families when giving feedback, raising concerns or complaining. See www.england.nhs.uk/learning-disabilities/about/ask-listen-do/.

[43] www.england.nhs.uk/learning-disabilities/care/ctr/.

[44] www.england.nhs.uk/publication/care-and-treatment-review-code-and-toolkit/.

[45] www.england.nhs.uk/learning-disabilities/about/resources/the-learning-disability-improvement-standards-for-nhs-trusts/.

[46] All trusts must ensure that they meet their Equality Act Duties to people with learning disabilities, autism or both, and that the wider human rights of these people are respected and protected, as required by the Human Rights Act.

[47] Every trust must ensure all people with learning disabilities, autism or both and their families and carers are empowered to be partners in the care they receive.

[48] All trusts must have the skills and capacity to meet the needs of people with learning disabilities, autism or both by providing safe and sustainable staffing, with effective leadership at all levels.

[49] Trusts that provide specialist learning disabilities services commissioned solely for the use of people with learning disabilities, autism or both must fulfil the objectives of national policy and strategy.

Compliance with these standards requires trusts to assure themselves that they have the necessary structures and processes, workforce and skills to deliver the outcomes that people with learning disabilities, autism or both, their families and carers expect and deserve. For further details see the 2018 *The Learning Disability Improvement Standards for NHS Trusts* published by NHS Improvement.[50]

I. Antimicrobial Resistance and Healthcare Associated Infections

The 2011 Annual CMO report highlighted antimicrobial resistance,[51] since then there have been notable successes in tackling infections such as methicillin-resistance *Staphylococcus aureus* (MRSA) and *Clostridium difficile*, though it should be remembered that these were often nosocomial infections. The rise of antimicrobial resistance, coupled with the dearth of development of new antibiotics, presents a potentially significant issue for all health-care providers. A national Action Plan for Anti-microbial Resistance was launched in January 2019. It is multi-faceted, and includes: aiming to halve nosocomial gram negative blood stream infections by 2023/24 by supporting better management of urinary tract infections (UTIs) in older patients in primary care; using a CQUIN to incentivise improvements in the diagnosis and management of UTIs in older patients in secondary care settings;[52] the GIRFT surgical site infection programme; increasing influenza vaccination uptake to reduce the risk of secondary respiratory tract infections; improved antimicrobial prescribing in secondary care (aligning with the medication safety improvement programme); and a CQUIN incentivising appropriate antibiotic prophylaxis for colorectal surgery.

J. Research and Innovation

There is a clear recognition in the patient safety strategy that a reciprocal flow of information is needed between the frontline care providers and those researching the evidence base behind safety innovations. This 'bridge' is provided by National Institute for Health Research (NIHR)-funded Patient Safety Translational Research Centres (PSTRCs), several of which have received significant funding. They aim to translate basic clinical, applied and health services research relevant to patient safety into early pilot/feasibility studies. The spread of successful innovations will be assisted by AHSNs and partner organisations. The updated tasks in the 2021 update include a focus on developing new technical solutions to never events as well as supporting the safety innovation pipeline more widely.

---

[50] NHS Improvement, *The Learning Disability Improvement Standards for NHS Trusts* (June 2018) available at www.england.nhs.uk/wp-content/uploads/2020/08/v1.17_Improvement_Standards_added_note.pdf.

[51] Dame Sally Davies, *Chief Medical Officer Annual Report 2011: Volume Two Infections and the Rise of Antimicrobial Resistance* (March 2013) available at https://assets.publishing.service.gov.uk/government/uploads/system/uploads/attachment_data/file/138331/CMO_Annual_Report_Volume_2_2011.pdf.

[52] This will include a package of measures to ensure the adoption of PHE and NICE's diagnostic and antimicrobial guidance, such as the 'To Dip or Not To Dip' toolkit and other associated resources.

Unlike some more traditional scientific research models patient safety innovation requires validation from patients and staff throughout. The PSTRCs' research and innovation strategy hinges on the principles explained in 'Involvement', Section II above.

K. Managing Deterioration Safety Improvement Programme

The Managing Deterioration Safety Improvement Programme (ManDetSIP) spans both health and social care. This programme aims to improve the way care systems approach prevention, identification, escalation and responses to physical deterioration. Harm reduction will be achieved by better system co-ordination and the use of safe reliable care pathways. Three key ambitions are:

–   To support the spread and adoption of the COVID-19 oximetry@home[53] and COVID virtual ward[54] (this was updated to become a distinct national patient safety improvement programme).

–   To support the adoption of a single standardised national Paediatric Early Warning Score (PEWS) and system-wide paediatric observation tracker across all appropriate care settings. Multiple slightly different PEWS exist, the 2021 patient safety update indicates that small-scale testing of the PEWS is underway ahead of a national scale-up.

–   To support an increase in the spread and adoption of deterioration management tools (e.g. NEWS2,[55] RESTORE2,[56] RESTORE2 mini, SBARD[57] etc), reliable personalised care and support planning (PCSP), and approaches encompassing end of life care principles, to support learning disabilities, mental health and dementia care management in relation to deterioration in at least 80 per cent of all appropriate non-acute settings across health and social care by March 2024.

L. The Adoption and Spread Safety Improvement Programme

This programme (A&S-SIP) aims to identify and support the adoption and spread of effective and safe evidence-based interventions and practice across England. The objectives

---

[53] This involves primary care services providing pulse oximeters to patients who have been diagnosed with coronavirus and who are most at risk of becoming seriously unwell enabling patients to monitor their own oxygen levels, www.england.nhs.uk/nhs-at-home/covid-oximetry-at-home/.

[54] Virtual wards involve hospitals discharging patients with a pulse oximeter and supporting information which enables the hospital to monitor their oxygen levels at home, www.england.nhs.uk/nhs-at-home/covid-virtual-wards/.

[55] National Early Warning Score 2 (NEWS2). NEWS2 is an aggregated scoring system which assesses patients based on measuring and scoring six physiological parameters: respiration rate; oxygen saturation; systolic blood pressure; pulse rate; level of consciousness or new confusion; temperature.

[56] Recognise Early Soft Signs, Take Observations, Respond, Escalate2 (RESTORE2) is a physical deterioration an escalation tool for care/nursing homes. It was designed by NHS West Hampshire CCG and is free to use. RESTORE2 mini is a condensed version of RESTORE2 see www.hampshiresouthamptonandisleofwightccg.nhs.uk/your-health/restore-official.

[57] Situation, Background, Assessment, Recommendation is an evidence based tool for escalating clinical problems or to facilitate effective handovers, see www.england.nhs.uk/improvement-hub/wp-content/uploads/sites/44/2017/11/SBAR-Implementation-and-Training-Guide.pdf.

specifically set out in the patient safety improvement strategy were to increase the use of the British Thoracic Society (BTS) Chronic Obstructive Pulmonary Disease (COPD) discharge care bundle[58] in acute hospital discharges; to increase the adoption of three evidence-based tracheostomy safety interventions;[59] to increase the proportion of acute hospital patients receiving all the elements of the asthma discharge care bundle[60] which they are eligible for; and to increase the proportion of patients receiving all the elements of the emergency laparotomy discharge care bundle[61] which they are eligible for.

IV. National Patient Safety Strategy Conclusions

The aims set out in the strategy are laudable, and it is a real positive to have what were previously disparate projects and pieces of guidance unified into a single source. Insight, Section I, outlines proposals to gather data, including improvements to and evolutions of the various reporting systems. Setting out the issues provides clarity, but it does not necessarily resolve the problems. For example, a new set of thresholds for National Patient Safety alerts is clearly a good thing, but we know that alert fatigue is a common issue and so actually the key issue is the response to such alerts and the strategy is currently silent on this. No mention is made of any way to assess how effective such alerts are in driving change. Similarly, the medical examiner system is a really valuable resource, but it has the scope to deliver more. Collecting data is essential for patient safety – you cannot drive improvement from a base of ignorance – but it is not enough on its own.

Similarly, the approach laid out in Involvement, Section II, or greater patient engagement and more staff training is undoubtedly correct, but it is a vital first step and not a solution. In addition, as outlined above, the simplified definitions of Safety I and Safety II used in the Patient Safety Strategy risk making consistent implementation of this aspect difficult. Outcome measures are needed to assess the success or otherwise of these programmes.

Improvement, Section III, has the most metrics and more explicit financial incentives such as CQUINs and QOFs. These have the potential to incentivise behaviours, but again there needs to be a clearer link made between the proposals and a measurable outcome. The drop in C. Diff and MRSA infections demonstrate how well these programmes can work, but there needs to be consistent checking on the outcomes of these interventions so their effectiveness can be maximised.

The Patient Safety Strategy is an important step forward. However, the next evolution of the strategy has to address how this data is used to deliver improvements including far more measures of effectiveness.

---

[58] These five actions ensure best care and decrease the readmission rates. They are (1) medication review and demonstrate use of inhalers; (2) provide a written self-management plan and emergency drug pack; (3) assess and offer a referral for smoking cessation where appropriate; (4) assess suitability for pulmonary rehabilitation and refer in appropriate patients; (5) arrange a follow-up call within 72 hours of discharge.

[59] These are (1) bedhead signs, (2) availability of emergency equipment and (3) a daily care bundle.

[60] www.brit-thoracic.org.uk/quality-improvement/clinical-resources/asthma/.

[61] See www.nela.org.uk/NELA_home for further details.

5

NHS Policy on Responding to Mistakes

I. Being Open

A major driver in the shift towards greater transparency was the introduction of the *Being Open* policy first launched in 2005.[1] The *Being Open* principles were subsequently embedded in the *NHS Constitution for England*, introduced in 2009, as a pledge to patients in relation to complaints and redress. In the 2009 revision of *Being Open*[2] the National Patient Safety Agency stated:

> Being open involves:
> - acknowledging, apologising and explaining when things go wrong;
> - conducting a thorough investigation into the incident and reassuring patients, their families and carers that lessons learned will help prevent the incident recurring;
> - providing support for those involved to cope with the physical and psychological consequences of what happened.

It is important to remember that saying sorry is not an admission of liability and is the right thing to do.

The principles:

The following set of principles has been developed to help healthcare organisations create and embed a culture of Being open:

1. Acknowledgement
2. Truthfulness, timeliness and clarity of communication
3. Apology
4. Recognising patient and carer expectations
5. Professional support
6. Risk management and systems improvement
7. Multidisciplinary responsibility
8. Clinical governance
9. Confidentiality
10. Continuity of care.[3]

---

[1] *Being Open Safer Practice Notice* (National Patient Safety Agency, 2005).
[2] Being Open – Communicating Patient Safety Incidents with Patients and their Carers (National Patient Safety Agency, 2009) and the associated Patient Safety Alert NPSA/2009/PSA003.
[3] www.nrls.npsa.nhs.uk/resources/collections/being-open/?entryid45=83726.

The *Being Open* policy stated that the following should be communicated to a patient who has been harmed:[4]

– the chronology of clinical and other relevant facts;
– details of the patient's, their family's and carers' concerns and complaints;
– a repeated apology for the harm suffered and any shortcomings in the delivery of care that led to the patient safety incident;
– a summary of the factors that contributed to the incident;
– information on what has been and will be done to avoid recurrence of the incident and how these improvements will be monitored.

II. Candour and Apologies

Throughout the 2000s the bodies responsible for handling litigation in England and Wales have encouraged healthcare professionals to apologise and provide explanations to patients harmed as a result of healthcare treatment, and explain that an apology is not an admission of liability:

> It is both natural and desirable for clinicians who have provided treatment which produces an adverse result, for whatever reason, to sympathise with the patient or the patient's relatives; to express sorrow or regret at the outcome; and to apologise for shortcomings in treatment. It is most important to patients that they or their relatives receive a meaningful apology. We encourage this, and stress that apologies do not constitute an admission of liability. In addition, it is not our policy to dispute any payment, under any scheme, solely on the grounds of such an apology.

There has also long been an emphasis on encouraging both clinicians and NHS bodies to supply appropriate information whether informally, formally or through mediation.[5]

> Patients and their relatives increasingly ask for detailed explanations of what led to adverse outcomes. Moreover, they frequently say that they derive some consolation from knowing that lessons have been learned for the future.

This concurs with the longstanding professional duty of candour healthcare professionals have to be open and honest with patients if things go wrong, as is detailed in a 2019 joint statement from regulators of healthcare professionals.[6] As well as this personal duty health and social care professionals often also have a contractual duty for candour in their employment contracts.

---

[4] *Being Open: Saying Sorry When Things Go Wrong* (National Patient Safety Agency, 2009) Stage 5: Process Completion.

[5] Apologies and Explanations: Letter to Chief Executives and Finance Directors (National Health Service Litigation Authority, May 2009). Technical Note 23, Apologies and Explanations (Welsh Risk Pool, 2001, updated 2009).

[6] Joint statement on the professional duty of candour, www.pharmacyregulation.org/sites/default/files/joint_statement_on_the_professional_duty_of_candour.pdf.

A. Statutory Duty of Candour

Unfortunately, the guidelines and duties over being candid were not always adhered to, and a statutory Duty of Candour for English NHS bodies was introduced in November 2014,[7] and expanded to all CQC registered care providers in April 2015. This legislation places a duty on the entity providing the care, rather than on the individual practitioners, but the individual practitioners are required to discharge the organisational duty. A Statutory Duty of Candour was introduced in Scotland from April 2018.[8] A similar statutory duty was enacted in Wales in June 2020, but requires secondary legislation to be put into effect.[9]

While the obligations under the legislation are clear this does not guarantee they will be implemented. The patient safety charity Action against Medical Accidents (AvMA) has produced reports into the implementation of the duty. In England the CQC monitors compliance and use their inspections to monitor whether providers are safe and compliant. AvMA examined CQC inspection reports to allow us to understand how the CQC have assessed the NHS bodies' understanding and implementation of the duty of candour. In their 2018 report *Regulating the Duty of Candour: Requires Improvement*[10] AvMA found that 39 per cent of CQC inspection reports contained a detailed assessment of the way a Trust implemented the duty, 49 per cent had contained a moderate assessment, in 8 per cent of cases a superficial assessment had been undertaken, but 5 per cent of inspection reports were entirely silent on the matter.

The CQC enforces the duty of candour. This can take the form of requirement notices; urgent imposition of conditions; warning notices; cancellation of registration; and urgent suspension. In particularly egregious cases the CQC can prosecute for breach of the statutory duty. In January 2019 the CQC successfully prosecuted Bradford Teaching Hospitals NHS Foundation Trust.[11] This related to care that was provided in July 2016 to a baby who subsequently died. Although the Trust had recorded the care as a notifiable safety incident, which triggers the duty of candour requirements, the baby's parents were not informed of this, and did not receive an explanation or apology until October 2016. A fixed penalty notice of £1,250 was issued.

In September 2020 the CQC successfully prosecuted a breach of the statutory duty action by the University Hospitals Plymouth NHS Trust.[12] This related to care that was provided in December 2017 when all the professional, contractual and statutory duties had been in place for a number of years.

---

[7] Regulation 20 of the Health and Social Care Act 2008 (Regulated Activities) Regulations 2014 available at www.legislation.gov.uk/ukdsi/2014/9780111117613.

[8] Health (Tobacco, Nicotine and Care etc) (Scotland) Act 2016 asp 14 available at www.parliament.scot/parliamentarybusiness/Bills/89934.aspx and the Duty of Candour Procedure (Scotland) Regulations 2018 SSI 57 available at www.legislation.gov.uk/ssi/2018/57/made.

[9] Part 3 of the Health and Social Care (Quality and Engagement) (Wales) Act 2020 2020 asc 1 available at www.legislation.gov.uk/asc/2020/1/part/3.

[10] D Negroni, *Regulating the Duty of Candour: Requires Improvement. A Report by Action against Medical Accidents on CQC Inspection Reports and Regulation of the Duty of Candour* (October 2018) www.avma.org.uk/wp-content/uploads/Requires-improvement.pdf.

[11] www.cqc.org.uk/news/releases/bradford-teaching-hospitals-fined-failure-comply-duty-candour.

[12] www.cqc.org.uk/news/releases/care-quality-commission-prosecutes-university-hospitals-plymouth-nhs-trust-breaching.

While the CQC has taken enforcement action in some particularly egregious cases it remains to be seen how common such prosecutions will be.

Despite the increased emphasis placed on candour and implementation of a statutory duty there are still examples of failures to be open and honest following mistakes. While some of these relate to historic incidents, sadly this is not the case for all. What we do not know is how widespread a failure to be candid is and how it maps across different injury types and severity. There are some indications from the CQC prosecutions and from NHS Resolution's Early notification scheme that the duty of candour is not being applied in a substantial proportion of cases. The Early notification Scheme requires that all qualifying birth injuries are reported to NHS Resolution. These injuries are more than likely to have triggered the statutory duty of candour requirements. A report by NHS Resolution[13] on the first year of the scheme's operation found

> 77% (71/92) of families were notified by the trust that an incident had occurred, and 35% (32/92) were recorded as having been offered an apology. This low figure is concerning. All NHS organisations are required to comply with the duty of candour and urgent action is required by both the trusts and commissioners and the CQC to drive improvement in this area.

This raises significant questions over the levels of compliance with the statutory duty which need to be investigated further.

III. NHS Policy on Responding to Mistakes Conclusions

There is a clear commitment to greater openness and candour. However, rhetoric and good intentions do not always translate to actions on the ground. It is still relatively early day to judge the statutory duty of candour, but there are some concerning signs that it is not always being implemented and that further analysis is needed on why this is so and how to improve culture and openness within the pockets of the NHS that are failing to deliver full candour.

---

[13] NHS Resolution, *The Early Notification Scheme Progress Report: Collaboration and Improved Experience for Families. An Overview of the Scheme to Date Together with Thematic Analysis of a Cohort of Cases from Year 1 of the Scheme, 2017–2018* (September 2019) available at https://resolution.nhs.uk/wp-content/uploads/2019/09/NHS-Resolution-Early-Notification-report.pdf.

PART II

Raising Concerns

This part of the book will focus on the mechanisms by which patients and other members of the public are able to raise concerns about NHS care. In most of the examples reviewed (complaints, ombudsmen, Healthcare Safety Investigation Branch and complaints to professional regulators) the individual with the concern can raise it directly with the entity that determines the outcome. If acting as a litigant in person the same applies to clinical negligence claims. However, litigation is more usually carried out by lawyers on behalf of the claimants, adding an additional layer.

In the above examples anyone who meets the relevant pre-defined criteria can chose to raise a concern. Public inquiries and reviews are different. There are no fixed criteria for holding an inquiry or review. Usually, they follow campaigning which is initiated by affected or concerned individuals, they are not commissioned directly by the individuals who have concerns.

The Coroner's Court, and particularly the 'Preventing Future Deaths Reports'[1] can raise issues of concern and can make an important contribution to patient safety. However, this book will not examine the Coroner's Court. The coronial process is statutory and does not require individuals to raise a concern. Ordinarily, the interests of affected individuals and/or other concerned people are allied to the aims of a coroner's inquest, but if there is a divergence of view then a coroner's inquest will be triggered and carried out irrespective of their wishes. As such it differs from the other mechanism and will not be considered further.

---

[1] As set out in paragraphs 28 and 29 of the Coroners (Investigations) Regulations 2013, available at www.legislation.gov.uk/uksi/2013/1629/part/7/made.

6

Mechanisms for Dealing with Staff Concerns

I. Mechanisms for NHS Staff to Raise Concerns

This part of the book will focus on mechanisms for patients and members of the public to raise concerns rather than the arrangements that have been put in place to enable staff to raise concerns. However, it is worth nothing that there has been a significant change in attitudes in a relatively short space of time. It was only in 1993 that formal guidance was given to the NHS on raising concerns at work. Until 1985 deprecation of other doctors could potentially be considered misconduct.[2] Move on 30 years and this contrasts sharply with the position outlined by Sir Robert Francis in his 2015 Freedom to Speak Up review.[3] There is still work to be done on ensuring that whistle-blowers and other staff feel empowered to raise concerns, but it is important to recognise the improvements that have been made. This theme will be returned to in Part III as part of a wider look at improving culture and outcomes.

II. Resolving Concerns Raised by Staff and Employers

Where there are concerns both practitioners and employers can seek advice from the Practitioner Performance Advice Service.[4] When it was launched in 2001 it was known as the National Clinical Assessment Authority, and later changed to the National Clinical Assessment Service (NCAS). It was created to provide a support service for NHS providers who were faced with concerns about the performance of an individual.[5] Originally it only covered doctors and dentists, but its remit has been expanded subsequently to include other healthcare practitioners. It had been a part of the National Patient Safety Agency, but when the NPSA was abolished in 2010 it was decided that NCAS would become a service delivered by NHS Resolution. NCAS provide expert, impartial advice and interventions to healthcare organisations in how to effectively manage and resolve concerns raised about the practice of individual healthcare practitioners.

---

[2] K Ehrich, 'Telling Cultures: "Cultural" Issues for Staff Reporting Concerns About Colleagues in the UK National Health Service' (2006) 28 *Sociology of Health & Illness* 903–26. https://doi.org/10.1111/j.1467-9566.2006.00512.x.

[3] Sir Robert Francis, *Freedom to Speak up: An Independent Review into Creating an Open and Honest Reporting Culture in the NHS* (February 2015) available at https://webarchive.nationalarchives.gov.uk/ukgwa/20150218150512/http://freedomtospeakup.org.uk/the-report/.

[4] https://resolution.nhs.uk/services/practitioner-performance-advice/.

[5] This was in response to recommendations made by the Chief Medical Officer in two reports, *Supporting Doctors, Protecting Patients* (November 1999) and *Assuring the Quality of Medical Practice: Implementing 'Supporting Doctors Protecting Patients'* (January 2001).

7

NHS Complaints

NHS complaints processes are devolved and not UK wide. This section will briefly consider NHS complaints in the wider context of public service complaints. The approaches taken in England, Wales and Scotland will then be briefly outlined below, along with analysis of various reports and recommendations made about NHS complaint handling. Long-standing research indicates that complaining about NHS service is a fairly uncommon reaction to dissatisfaction with care.[1]

I. Public Service Complaints in England

Healthcare complaints are part of a wider trend of increases in public service complaining behaviour. In the 2004 White paper *Transforming Public Services*[2] the Department for Constitutional Affairs laid out expectations for complaints about public services

> We are all entitled to receive correct decisions on our personal circumstances; where a mistake occurs we are entitled to complain and to have the mistake put right with the minimum of difficulty; where there is uncertainty we are entitled to expect a quick resolution of the issue; and we are entitled to expect that where things have gone wrong the system will learn from the problem and do better in future.

Despite these expectations, the 2005 National Audit Office report *Citizen Redress: What Citizens Can Do if Things Go Wrong with Public Services*[3] concluded that such complaint systems were inefficient, costly and confusing. A 2005 survey found that most people using adult care services saw 'no point' in making a complaint.[4]

In 2014 the Public Affairs Standing Committee called for a general policy of encouraging more complaints by all public services, so as to fund a culture that constantly learned and improved.[5] This was followed in 2015 by a report from the National Audit Office *Public*

---

[1] L Mulcahy and JQ Tritter, 'Pathways, Pyramids and Icebergs? Mapping the Links Between Dissatisfaction and Complaints' (1998) 20(6) *Sociology of Health and Illness* 825–47.

[2] A White Paper issued by the Department for Constitutional Affairs, *Transforming Public Services: Complaints, Redress and Tribunals* (July 2004) available at https://webarchive.nationalarchives.gov.uk/20040722013223/http://www.dca.gov.uk/pubs/adminjust/adminjust.htm.

[3] National Audit Office, *Citizen Redress: What Citizens Can Do if Things Go Wrong with Public Services* Session 2004–2005, HC 21, 9 March 2005, available at www.nao.org.uk/report/citizen-redress-what-citizens-can-do-if-things-go-wrong-with-public-services/.

[4] Department of Health commissioned survey, 2005, referred to in *Listening, Responding, Improving: A Guide to Better Customer Care* (Department of Health, 26 February 2009).

[5] Public Affairs Standing Committee, *More Complaints Please!* Twelfth Report of Session 2013–14, HC 229, 14 April 2014, available at www.publications.parliament.uk/pa/cm201314/cmselect/cmpubadm/229/229.pdf.

Service Markets: Putting Things Right When They Go Wrong[6] which found that 49 per cent of people who have a problem with a public service do not complain, and when individuals do make a complaint only 31 per cent of them are satisfied with the outcome. The report described the complaints and redress landscape as complex, stating consumers found it difficult to navigate and that there are gaps in the system. It called for quicker, more effective resolution of complaints and found that there was poor central leadership when it came to improving the complaints process. They concluded that public services do not make enough use of complaints to improve services, and that, in fact, there are serious impediments to doing so.

In 2015 Citizens Advice commissioned a national survey of complaints about any public services.[7] In this survey GP services attracted the greatest reports of dissatisfaction (37 per cent), followed by local authorities (29 per cent) and then hospitals (28 per cent).[8] It is clear from this survey that poor service experiences in healthcare form the majority of poor public sector user experiences. However, only 22 per cent of those experiencing poor service from the public sector went on to make a formal complaint.

Similarly, a survey of 4,263 members of the public carried out in April 2015 on all public services under the jurisdiction of the Parliamentary and Health Service Ombudsman (PHSO) found that although most people believe you should complain if you are unhappy about a service (90 per cent), just one third of people (34 per cent) who were unhappy after using a public service in the Ombudsman's remit actually made a complaint, leaving 64 per cent who did not complain despite being unhappy.[9] The reasons why people who felt unhappy with a public service did not complain were:

- 29 per cent thought that complaining does not make a difference
- 14 per cent thought it would be more hassle than it was worth
- 9 per cent felt it would be too time consuming
- 7 per cent did not know where to go to make a complaint
- 6 per cent did not think it would be taken seriously.

These findings make it clear that formal complaints do not reflect the full gamut of dissatisfaction.

II. NHS Complaints in England

To be counted as an NHS complaint and to be dealt with under the complaints processes a grievance must be in writing. NHS complaints are, therefore, a relatively formal way for

---

[6] National Audit Office, *Public Service Markets: Putting Things Right When They Go Wrong* Session 2015–16, HC 84, 17 June 2015, available at www.nao.org.uk/wp-content/uploads/2015/06/Putting-things-right.pdf.

[7] Learning from Mistakes: How Complaints Can Drive Improvements to Public Services (Citizens Advice, 2016) 15, available at www.citizensadvice.org.uk/Global/CitizensAdvice/Public%20services%20publications/Learning-from-mistakes.pdf.

[8] ibid.

[9] *What Do People Think About Complaining?* Parliamentary and Health Service Ombudsman, July 2015, www.ombudsman.org.uk/about-us/news-centre/press-releases/2015/only-one-in-three-people-complain-to-a-public-service-when-they-are-unhappy,-according-to-new-research.

an individual to express their dissatisfaction with the NHS. Guidance[10] on how to make a complaint about the NHS in England differentiates between providing feedback and making a complaint and gives an outline of the processes and requirements. The complexity associated with making a complaint about the NHS in England is obvious even in the short guidance: complaints can be made either to the healthcare provider or the commissioner, but identifying the commissioner is not always straightforward, see Table 1.

Table 1 Potential recipients of healthcare complaints in England

Care provided	Who to complain to
Healthcare provider	
Healthcare provider	Healthcare provider
Commissioner	
Primary care – GP, dentist, optician, pharmacy etc	NHS England
Secondary/tertiary care – mental health services, out of hours and community services such as district nursing, etc	Local clinical commissioning group
Public health organizations – disease prevention, health promotion, etc	Local Authority

Complaints cover a vast range of subjects and degrees of severity. The governance of NHS complaints is set out in the Local Authority Social Services and National Health Service Complaints (England) Regulations 2009.[11] These regulations detail who can complain, time limits for making a complaint and the arrangements for handling and considering complaints.

NHS complaints are divided into 20 categories which cover both clinical and non-clinical issues.[12]

The non-clinical treatment categories are: Access to treatment or drugs; Admissions, discharges and transfers, Appointments including delays and cancellations; Commissioning Services; Communications; Consent to treatment; End of life care; Facilities Services; Integrated care; Patient care including Nutrition/Hydration; Mortuary and post-mortem arrangements; Prescribing errors; Privacy, dignity and wellbeing; Restraint; Staffing numbers; Transport (ambulances only); Trust Administration; Values and Behaviour (Staff); Waiting times; and Other.

The clinical treatment categories are: Accident & Emergency; Anaesthetics; Clinical Oncology; Dental Group; General Medicine group; Obstetrics & Gynaecology; Paediatric group; Pathology Group; Public Hospital Medicine and Community Health Services (PHM &CHS); Psychiatry group; Radiology group; and Surgical group.

---

[10] www.gov.uk/government/publications/the-nhs-constitution-for-england/how-do-i-give-feedback-or-make-a-complaint-about-an-nhs-service.

[11] The Local Authority Social Services and National Health Service Complaints (England) Regulations 2009 (SI 2009/309) available at www.legislation.gov.uk/uksi/2009/309/regulation/12/made.

[12] For a more detailed breakdown see https://digital.nhs.uk/data-and-information/publications/statistical/data-on-written-complaints-in-the-nhs/2017-18.

There is potential overlap between some categories. The issues raised fall within a category are not necessarily homogenous, for example, the 'communications' category can contain events that range from those without any implication for physical health, such as addressing the patient by the wrong title or not using their preferred form of address, to failing to communicate appointments for cancer screening or the need for follow-up tests, which has the potential to have profound implications on the patient's physical health.

Not all complaints will involve physical harm to the complainant, not least because in many cases complaints are made on behalf of someone else. However, it goes without saying, that all issues that are complained about have the potential to be distressing and to impact on mental health of the complainant and/or the patient.

The motivation of individuals to make a complaint was examined in the Clwyd and Hart review of the NHS hospitals complaints system in 2013. They found the following key points, from their review of 2,500 letters and emails from the public and carers, on why people complain:[13]

- Lack of information – patients said they felt uninformed about their care and treatment.

    … We formed the impression that this sense of confusion caused by lack of information made people fear that they or their relative had not received the right care. As a result, they were more likely to question the treatment or make a formal complaint.

    Compassion – patients said they felt they had not been treated with the compassion they deserve.

    Dignity and care – patients said they felt neglected and not listened to.

    … We did not form the impression that patients were generally making unreasonable demands or exaggerating minor inconveniences. People were, by and large, describing significant lapses in the standards of care they were entitled to and that hospital managers, clinicians and carers should feel proud to provide.

    Many people said that staff frequently did not (or could not) make time to speak to patients in a friendly or concerned way. This was not what they expected from staff providing their care. As a result, minor needs or concerns that could have been resolved promptly or courteously, might be neglected until they turned into major problems or formal complaints.

    A common theme was that those who could not speak up for themselves were most likely to suffer a lack of dignity and care. However, there were also examples of articulate and assertive patients being neglected or treated badly.

- Staff attitudes – patients said they felt no one was in charge on the ward and the staff were too busy to care for them.
- Resources – patients said there was a lack of basic supplies like extra blankets and pillows.

A. Support and Advocacy Services for Complainants

Although it has long been recognised that making a complaint can be stressful, services to provide support and advocacy have not always been effective. Community Health Councils (CHCs) took over the complaint support functions which had previously been held by

---

[13] A Clwyd and T Hart, *A Review of the NHS Hospitals Complaints System. Putting Patients Back in the Picture* (Department of Health, 2013).

regional hospital boards in 1974 in England and Wales and from 1975 in Scotland.[14] The role of CHCs was described by Mrs Janet Smith in the fifth report into Harold Shipman:

> Community Health Councils (CHCs) provided advice and support for persons wishing to pursue a complaint. Before 1996, the CHC would correspond with the FPC [Family Practitioner Committee] or FHSA [Family Health Service Authorities] on the complainant's behalf, would advise on the preparation of the complaint for a MSC [Medical Services Committee] hearing and would accompany the complainant at the hearing, acting as adviser throughout. From 1996, the CHC would, on request, assist in lodging a complaint or requesting an independent review. It would also correspond with the HA/PCT [Health Authority/Primary Care Trust] making the arrangements for an IRP [Independent Review Panel] hearing and would attend and support the complainant at the hearing. Evidence received by the Inquiry suggests that many CHCs did this work well and that their work was greatly appreciated.

In December 2003 CHCs were replaced by two organisations; the Independent Complaints Advisory Service (ICAS)[15] and Patient Advice and Liaison Service (PALS).

ICAS was established in England with outlets at most hospitals.[16] It was intended to provide general help, support and information to patients, including with complaints. From 1 April 2013 ICAS services were replaced by Independent Advocacy Services which operate outside the NHS and are commissioned directly by each English local authority.[17] Similar arrangements are in place in Scotland. The format that these services take varies; in some areas the service is provided by organisations such as Healthwatch or Citizens Advice, in other areas local authorities provide the services either for their individual area or some-times by grouping together and providing the service on a regional basis. Wales retained CHCs until very recently. There are over 150 entities providing this service in the different regions across the UK, which can make it difficult for users to identify where they should go.

PALS is located in every Trust, provides a point of contact for patients, families and carers, offering confidential advice, support and information on health-related matters.[18] Specifically PALS can offer advice on the NHS complaints procedure and where individuals can go to get independent help with making a complaint as well as providing information on support groups.

While there are arrangements in place for secondary care since the abolition of CHCs primary care has not had such formal structures, which can be particularly difficult as the GP is the first point of contact for a patient.

B. Complaints and Healthcare Staff

It must be remembered that complaints can impact not just on patients, but also on staff. Mulcahy's extensive analysis of the early development and state of NHS complaints provides

---

[14] Section 9 of the NHS Reorganisation Act 1973 c.32 1973 available at www.legislation.gov.uk/ukpga/1973/32/enacted and section 20 of the National Health Services Act 1977 c.49 available at www.legislation.gov.uk/ukpga/1977/49/section/20.

[15] www.pohwer.net/how_we_can_help/independent.html.

[16] A Clwyd and T Hart, *A Review of the NHS Hospitals Complaints System. Putting Patients Back in the Picture* (Department of Health, 2013). It was found that some hospitals combine this with complaints management, and also that loss of a national brand was causing confusion.

[17] Health and Social Care Act 2012.

[18] See www.nhs.uk/nhs-services/hospitals/what-is-pals-patient-advice-and-liaison-service/.

useful background and highlights a number of critical issues.[19] First, complaints reverse the usual direction of the doctor-patient exchange.[20] This can lead to perceptions of complaints as a challenge to the professional competence of an individual professional and a symbolic challenge to the wider healthcare group.[21]

Second, doctors have continuously resisted losing control of the complaints process, and how it is handled. Professional bodies have lobbied hard to retain control over the initial stages of complaint handling, and over all stages of clinical complaint handling.[22] In contrast, managers have been more likely to adopt a conciliatory approach than doctors.[23]

Third, doctors have exerted a claim to autonomy and self-regulation that was successful for some decades. However, shifts occurred from no professional regulation to self-regulation,[24] imposition of managerial controls,[25] to recent – and contested – imposition of formal regulation of professionals, organisations and facilities. Professional autonomy has been whittled away to impose external accountability, but this has not been straightforward and some sectors of the medical professionals remain unhappy over the perceived compromise in relationships.

Fourth, Mulcahy identified a systemic distortion of meaning in the interactions between doctors, patients and managers, in which each had differing and mis-matched conceptions of what constituted appropriate care.[26] Patients root their stories in moral and caring identities. In contrast, doctors respond to what are perceived as attacks on professional competence with defensive reactions based on a culture of expertise and reputation. Mulcahy noted doctors' resentment at what they perceived as an attempt by lawyers to invade their culture in ways they saw as unhelpful and an affront to their medical expertise and achievement. In many cases the lawyers were highlighting that the system does not deliver quality emotional care and support: this is unsurprising as the system did not prioritise or seek to deliver these aspects. She noted a clear need to support health professionals in coping with the aftermath of mishaps, complaints and legal claims.[27]

C. Complaints Processes

i. English NHS Complaints Processes and Parameters[28]

The breadth of issues raised and range of potential consequences means that there are a wide range of potential approaches which could be used for NHS complaint handling.

---

[19] L Mulcahy, *Disputing Doctors: The Socio-legal Dynamics of Complaints About Medical Care* (Open University Press, 2003).

[20] ibid, 1 and ch 6.

[21] ibid, 6.

[22] ibid, 28.

[23] ibid, 7.

[24] R Klein, *The Politics of the NHS* 2nd edn (Longman, 1989) 57; J Allsop, *Health Policy and the NHS* (Longman, 1995) 33.

[25] Ministry of Health, First Report of the Joint Working Party on the Organisation of Work in Hospitals (London, HMSO, 1967) (the Cogwheel Report); Press release-More Open Complaints Procedures (Department of Health and Social Security, 1983).

[26] L Mulcahy, *Disputing Doctors: The Socio-legal Dynamics of Complaints About Medical Care* (Open University Press, 2003).

[27] ibid, 104–21, 148.

[28] Some of the following is derived from CJS Hodges, *Law and Corporate Behaviour: Integrating Regulation, Enforcement, Compliance, Culture and Ethics* (Oxford, Hart Publishing, 2015).

As Mulcahy highlighted, the historical shifts in healthcare complaint handling, briefly detailed below, reflect general developments in administrative justice and complaints against the state and public sector.[29] A shift occurred from judicial procedure to a tribunal-type procedure, but the latter was still adversarial and formal. These shifts also paralleled the spread of the concept and language of consumerism, procedural fairness and managerial responsibility for complaint handling, but according to Mulcahy 'the rhetoric of account-ability was not applied with such vigour to complaints about clinical care as it was to other complaints'.[30]

ii. 1960s to 1980s

NHS procedures for handling complaints evolved relatively slowly. By the 1960s, complaints against NHS doctors were heard by a local Medical Service Committee, which applied the statutory terms of service, using the legal standard of care (Bolam test)[31] and operated like a public sector tribunal. In 1966 a non-binding attempt at standardisation of local complaint handling practices within hospitals was made,[32] but it took until 1985 before it was made compulsory for a procedure to exist.[33] Even after that point the approach to NHS complaint handling was heavily determined by the local NHS organisation.

External controls were asserted with the creation of the Health Service Commissioner in 1973,[34] although that remit was restricted for over 20 years to non-clinical complaints. The 1973 Davies Committee established management responsibility for handling complaints by applying principles to investigate complaints properly, undertaking a fair review or eval-uation of the complaint, and taking remedial action or a reasoned explanation as to why this was not appropriate.[35]

iii. 1990s to 2000

After the government's general 1991 *Citizen's Charter* in relation to citizens' rights in respect of general public services, the Wilson Report proposed a managerial model, resolving griev-ances at local level with appeals only in exceptional circumstances to a convener who has power to decide whether an Independent Review Panel (IRP) should be established.[36] The subsequent 1996 NHS complaints procedure was not prescriptive about process, but placed emphasis on principles of good practice including openness, flexibility, fairness and under-standing what complainants want.

---

[29] L Mulcahy, *Disputing Doctors: The Socio-legal Dynamics of Complaints About Medical Care* (Open University Press, 2003) 23.

[30] ibid, 36, 37.

[31] *Bolam v Friern Hospital Management Committee* [1957] 1 WLR 583; *Bolitho v City and Hackney Health Authority* [1997] 3 WLR 1151.

[32] *Health Memorandum (HM(66)15)* (Department of Health and Social Security, 1966); *Health Circular (HC(81)5)* (Department of Health and Social Security, 1981).

[33] The Hospital Complaint (Procedure) Act 1985. Guidance in *Health Circular (HC(88)37)* (Department of Health and Social Security, 1988).

[34] NHS Reorganisation Act 1973.

[35] *Report of the Committee of Inquiry into Whittingham Hospital* (Department of Health and Social Security, 1973) (Davies Committee).

[36] *Being Heard: Report of the Review Committee on NHS Complaint Procedures* (Leeds, National Health Service Executive Committee, 1994).

Complaining about the NHS had historically been a complex business, and the shift that occurred in 1996 following the Wilson Report was described as shifting slowly from the 'prosecutory-disciplinary model' to the 'consumer orientated/learning model'.[37] As set out in *Being Heard*, the first stage of this procedure was to attempt local resolution. Complainants who were dissatisfied with the response from the initial local resolution had 28 days, to request an independent review panel to be set up by the appropriate Trust, health authority or board.

Each Trust, health authority or board had to appoint a 'convener'[38] who received all such complaints. The convener's role was very important, he or she had the power to refer the complainant back for further attempts at local resolution, to convene an independent review panel (and to determine its terms of reference) or to determine that there was no further means of resolving the complaint. If an independent review panel was established it had three members: the convener; an independent lay member (who acted as Chairman); and a representative of the purchaser of the care. For complaints related to clinical matters the panel had to be advised by at least two independent clinical assessors. While the composition of panels ensured representation of lay members, panels were only held at the behest of the convener. There was recourse to the Health Service Ombudsman for dissatisfied complainants either if a convener refused to create an independent review panel or if the complainant was dissatisfied with the outcome of such a panel.

Despite these reforms research found concerns with both the local resolution stage and the IRP process, such as over lack of impartiality, fairness of the process and the attitude of complaint handlers and the inadequacy of outcomes.[39]

A 1999 review of complaints highlighted another area of concern; that the wealth of information available reported that data from complaints was a largely underused resource.[40] This has been, and remains, a consistent theme.

iv. 2000 to 2020

A 2003 government review of NHS complaints recorded that patients and staff felt that

(a)   it is unclear how to raise complaints and concerns, and difficult to do so,

(b)   there is often delay in responding to complaints and concerns,

(c)   too often complaints receive a negative response,

(d)   complainants do not seem to get a fair hearing,

(e)   patients do not get the support they need when they want to complain,

---

[37] J Allsopp and L Mulcahy, *Regulating Medical Work: Formal and Informal Controls* (Open University Press, 1996).

[38] Usually a non-executive director of the NHS body, or for primary care services, the health authority or board with whom the practitioner had contracted to provide services.

[39] R Kyffin, G Cook and M Jones, *Complaint Handling and Monitoring in the NHS: A Study of 12 Trusts in the North West Region* (University of Liverpool Institute of medicine, Law and Bioethics, 1997); H Wallace and L Mulcahy, *Cause for Complaint: An Evaluation of the Effectiveness of the NHS Complaints Procedure* (Public Law Project, 1999); *Handling Complaints: Monitoring the NHS Complaints Procedures, England 2000–01* (Department of Health, 2001).

[40] K Walshe, 'Medical Accidents in the UK: A Wasted Opportunity for Improvement?' in MM Rosenthal, L Mulcahy and S Lloyd-Bostock (eds), *Medical Mishaps. Pieces of the Puzzle* (Open University Press, 1999) 68.

(f)   the Independent Review stage does not have the credibility it needs,
(g)   the process does not provide the redress patients want, and
(h)   there does not seem to be any effective way of learning from complaints in order to bring about improvements.[41]

The Health and Social Care (Community Health and Standards) Act 2003 provided for the replacement of the Commission for Health Improvement (CHI) with the Commission for Healthcare Audit and Inspection (CHAI). CHAI was often known as the Healthcare Commission (HCC). The 2003 Act abolished Community Health Councils in England and replaced them with PALS. In July 2004 the National Health Service (Complaints) Regulations 2004[42] came into force. The regulations set out the complaints process and specified that if a complainant was dissatisfied with the result of a complaint they could refer it to the Healthcare Commission.[43] If the complainant was still dissatisfied after the HCC had considered the matter it could be referred to the Ombudsman. The 2004 regulations removed the requirement for a convener to review all complaints.

A 2005 Report by the Health Service Ombudsman highlighted the problems faced by people using NHS services in getting a satisfactory response to a complaint and the failure of the NHS to learn lessons from complaints.[44] A major causative issue noted was the fragmentation of complaints systems across the NHS, private healthcare and social care. This, combined with a failure to focus on patient needs, poor leadership and lack of capacity and competence in complaint handling, was said to have led to a system which made it difficult for patients to have things put right where they had gone wrong.

There followed a survey that found that most people using adult care services saw 'no point' in making a complaint,[45] a National Audit Office Report on health and care services that asserted that people found making a complaint too complex and that many complaints took too long to resolve,[46] and a Healthcare Commission review that found that many NHS complaints related to the fundamentals of good healthcare, such as effective communication with patients, the attitude of staff, record-keeping, privacy and dignity, plus in 19 per cent of cases a problem with the way in which a complaint was handled.[47]

In January 2009 the NHS constitution[48] was first published.[49] The constitution set out the principles and values of the NHS in England, as well as providing information on how

---

[41] NHS Complaints Reform: Making Things Right (Department of Health, 2003). Summary taken from A Clwyd and T Hart, *A Review of the NHS Hospitals Complaints System. Putting Patients Back in the Picture* (Department of Health, 2013).

[42] The National Health Service (Complaints) Regulations 2004 SI 2004/1768 available at www.legislation.gov.uk/uksi/2004/1768/contents/made.

[43] Established under the Health and Social Care (Community Health and Standards) Act 2003.

[44] *Report: Making Things Better? A Report on Reform of the NHS Complaints Procedure in England* HC 413 2004–2005 (HMSO, March 2005). See previously H Wallace and L Mulcahy, *Cause for Complaint: An Evaluation of the Effectiveness of the NHS Complaints Procedure* (The Public Law Project, 1999); *Being Heard* (Department of Health, 1994) (the Wilson Report); *Cause for Complaint* (Public Law Project, 1999).

[45] Department of Health commissioned survey, 2005, referred to in *Listening, Responding, Improving: A Guide to Better Customer Care* (Department of Health, 26 February 2009).

[46] *Making Experiences Count: A New Approach to Responding to Complaints* (Department of Health, 2007).

[47] *Feeding Back? Learning from Complaints Handling in Health and Social Care* (National Audit Office, 2008).

[48] See www.gov.uk/government/publications/the-nhs-constitution-for-england.

[49] It was given full effect later that year in the Health Act 2009 c 21 available at www.legislation.gov.uk/ukpga/2009/21/contents.

to make a complaint about NHS services. In relation to complaints and redress, the 2015 edition of the NHS Constitution states that any individual has the right to:[50]

- have any complaint you make about NHS services dealt with efficiently and have it properly investigated.

- discuss the manner in which the complaint is to be handled, and to know the period within which the investigation is likely to be completed and the response sent.

- be kept informed of progress and to know the outcome of any investigation into your complaint, including an explanation of the conclusions and confirmation that any action needed in consequence of the complaint has been taken or is proposed to be taken.

- take your complaint to the independent Health Service Ombudsman if you are not satisfied with the way your complaint has been dealt with by the NHS.

- make a claim for judicial review if you think you have been directly affected by an unlawful act or decision of an NHS body or local authority.

- compensation where you have been harmed by negligent treatment.

Under the constitution NHS organisations were subject to legal,[51] contractual[52] and professional[53] obligations to provide an accessible and suitably responsive complaints procedure for service users. In order to facilitate this in 2009 a common approach to handling complaints across both the NHS and adult social care services was introduced.[54] All organisations were requested to review their systems 'so as to be able to respond flexibly to complaints, concerns and complements and feed the resulting lessons into their work on learning from patients' feedback to improve services'.[55] The policy was to 'encourage a culture that seeks and then uses people's experiences to make services more effective, personal and safe'.[56]

---

[50] The Health Act 2009 places a duty on NHS organisations (including contractors) to 'have regard to the NHS Constitution'.

[51] The Local Authority Social Services and National Health Service Complaints (England) Regulations 2009/308.

[52] From April 2009, all Primary Care Trusts (PCTs) are required to be registered with the Care Quality Commission, under the Health and Social Care Act 2008. As a condition of registration, a PCT is required to ensure that 'there are systems in place to ensure that patients, their relatives and carers:

- have suitable and accessible information about, and clear access to, procedures to register formal complaints and feedback on the quality of services

- are not discriminated against when complaints are made

- are assured that organizations act appropriately on any concerns and, where appropriate, make changes to ensure improvements in service delivery.' (Core standard C14, Standards for Better Health).

[53] For doctors: 'Patients who complain about the care or treatment they have received have a right to expect a prompt, open, constructive and honest response including an explanation and, if appropriate, an apology. You must not allow a patient's complaint to affect adversely the care or treatment you provide or arrange.' *Good Medical Practice* (General Medical Council).

[54] The Local Authority Social Services and National Health Service Complaints (England) Regulations 2009 (SI 2009/309) available at www.legislation.gov.uk/uksi/2009/309/regulation/12/made.

[55] *Listening, Improving, Responding: A Guide to Better Customer Care*, Letter from J Saddler, National Director of Patient and Public Affairs (Department of Health, 2009).

[56] *Listening, Responding, Improving: A Guide to Better Customer Care* (Department of Health, 2009) at http://webarchive.nationalarchives.gov.uk/+/www.dh.gov.uk/en/publicationsandstatistics/publications/publicationspolicyandguidance/dh_095408.

The 2009 common approach adopted the Health Service Ombudsman's six Principles of Good Complaint Handling:[57]

- getting it right
- being customer focused
- being open and accountable
- acting fairly and proportionately
- putting things right
- seeking continuous improvement.

The common approach specifies two stages in making complaints.[58] Stage 1 is local resolution with the local healthcare provider. The GP, or hospital, or whoever the complaint is about should provide a copy of their complaints procedure, on request. Many of these complaints procedures will include some form of conciliation or mediation. There is usually a time limit of six months from the date when the action complained about happened. Stage 2 involves taking the complaint to the relevant ombudsman service, which can investigate poor treatment and poor service by any NHS healthcare provider. The NHS complaints procedure does not provide compensation – it aims to discover whether something has gone wrong with the treatment of the complainant, and to offer an explanation or an apology to the complainant. If court proceedings are instituted, the NHS complaint procedure is not available.

In 2019 PHSO were invited by the House of Commons Select Committee on Public Administration and Constitutional Affairs to explore the 'state of local complaint handling' across the NHS and UK Government Departments.[59] In 2020 PHSO published *Making Complaints Count – Supporting Complaints Handling in the NHS and Government Departments.*[60] This report was clear on the need for more consistent processes for complaint handling. In an attempt to standardise complaint handling the NHS Complaint Standards Framework[61] was consulted on and introduced in 2020 after a long period of development. This recognises that complaint handling is a skill and staff handling complaints need a clear framework and appropriate training. The Framework sets out a single set of standards for staff to follow when they handle complaints. It aims to provide a clear and consistent set of expectations for complaint handlers to follow, rather than references to 'good practice'. This should provide both complainants and those complained about with greater certainty and clarity because it clearly sets out what they can expect to see throughout the complaints process. It also sets out how organisations can best capture and act on the learning from

---

[57] *Spotlight on Complaints: A Report on Second-stage Complaints about the NHS in England* (Healthcare Commission, 2009). See earlier, *Principles of Good Administration* (March 2007) and *Principles for Remedy* (October 2007).

[58] *Listening, Responding, Improving: A Guide to Better Customer Care* (Department of Health, 26 February 2009).

[59] https://publications.parliament.uk/pa/cm201719/cmselect/cmpubadm/1855/185508.htm#_idTextAnchor028.

[60] *Making Complaints Count: Supporting Complaints Handling in the NHS and UK Government Departments.* PHSO 15 July 2020 HC 390, available at www.ombudsman.org.uk/sites/default/files/%28HC%20390%29%20-%20Making%20Complaints%20Count-%20Supporting%20complaints%20handling%20in%20the%20NHS%20and%20UK%20Government%20Departments.pdf.

[61] www.ombudsman.org.uk/organisations-we-investigate/complaint-standards-framework/about-complaint-standards-framework.

complaints, including providing support for staff who are complained about so that the complaint is viewed as a learning opportunity as opposed to a '*finger-pointing exercise*'.

v. Overview of English Complaints Data

From 1 April 2019 to 31 March 2020 there were 113,241 new written complaints about NHS Hospital and Community Health Care Services (down from 116,247 the previous year).[62] During 2019–20 110,060 complaints were resolved. Of these 31 per cent were upheld, 32.9 per cent were partially upheld and 36.1 per cent were not upheld.

The majority, around three in four, of complaints are in the 'non-clinical' categories, see Table 2.[63] Of the non-clinical complaints the three categories which have consistently had the most complaints in are Communications; Patient care including nutrition/hydration; and Values and Behaviours of Staff. The categories used to define complaints are as clear as they could be, for example the boundary between a 'clinical' complaint about patient care and a 'non-clinical' complaint about patient care is not always obvious. That said these figures indicate that patients express more dissatisfaction about the non-clinical aspects of their care. This may in part reflect the fact that patients are relatively more comfortable voicing concerns about non-clinical aspects than they are about raising concerns over clinical care.[64]

Of the clinical complaints the three categories which consistently had more complaints were General Medicine; Surgical group; and Accident and Emergency.

Table 2 Breakdown of total NHS complaints into clinical and non-clinical 2015–20

	2015–16	2016–17	2017–18	2018–19	2019–20
Complaints excluding clinical treatment	68.0%	73.3%	73.8%	72.5%	72.9%
Clinical Treatment Complaints	32.0%	26.7%	26.2%	27.5%	27.1%

D. Reviews and Reports Considering NHS Complaint Handling

i. Dr Harold Shipman

Harold Shipman, a general medical practitioner, committed multiple murders and it is alleged other serious criminal acts throughout his professional career. From 1974 until 1998 it is thought he killed over 215 patients, making him one of the most prolific serial killers.

In spring 2002 a public inquiry chaired by Dame Janet Smith commenced and subsequently issued a sequence of six reports from 2002 to 2005 on different aspects of concern.[65]

---

[62] https://digital.nhs.uk/data-and-information/publications/statistical/data-on-written-complaints-in-the-nhs/2019-20-quarter-4-ns.

[63] ibid.

[64] L Mulcahy, *Disputing Doctors: The Socio-legal Dynamics of Complaints About Medical Care* (Open University Press, 2003).

[65] See https://webarchive.nationalarchives.gov.uk/ukgwa/20090808155005/http://www.the-shipman-inquiry.org.uk/home.asp, starting with The Shipman Inquiry; Chairman: Dame Janet Smith DBE, *First Report. Volume One. Death Disguised* (2002).

Amongst the very many matters Dame Janet identified were a lack of fair procedures, failure to investigate complaints properly, failure to give adequate explanations and lack of impartiality in organisations investigating their own conduct.[66] Recommendation 16 of the fifth report was for a single portal for complaints.

> In order to ensure that, so far as possible, complaints about healthcare can reach the appropriate destinations, there should be a 'single portal' by which complaints or concerns can be directed or redirected to the appropriate quarter. This service should also provide information about the various advice services available to persons who are considering whether and/or how to complain or raise a concern. Advice must be provided for persons who are concerned about the legal implications of raising a concern.

ii. The Three Inquiries

In 2001 three independent inquiries were launched into the conduct and competence of four doctors, two inquiries were into Clifford Ayling, a GP, and Richard Neale a gynaecologist, the third inquiry jointly looked into the conduct of two psychiatrists (William Kerr and Michael Haslam). Ayling and Neale were both accused of negligent treatment, with Ayling also accused of overtly sexual behaviour, including indecent assault, of female patients; Kerr and Haslam of engaging in sexual relationships with vulnerable mentally ill women. The terms of reference of the three inquiries all covered similar themes including how the local NHS dealt with the complaints and concerns that were raised over the conduct of these doctors.

The Kerr-Haslam Inquiry outlined that

> The NHS should, jointly with the appropriate National Standards body, produce a standardised complaints system to be implemented in all Trusts/organisations providing services to NHS patients.[67]

They felt this could be similar to the published guidance on consent.

Both the Neale Inquiry and the Kerr-Haslam Inquiry made recommendations on the appropriate level of training for complaint staff. The Neale Inquiry recommendation 23 was that 'The head of the unit dealing with complaints should be an appropriately trained manager'.

The Kerr-Haslam Inquiry recommended[68] that PALS and complaints staff should be middle management level, and also that they should have direct access to a line manager at board level and to senior medical staff. Interestingly the Kerr-Haslam Inquiry also took a very patient-focussed approach to the classification of complaints, which was a significant departure from the requirements that complaints needed to be in writing.

> The revised regulations should require that all formal complaints should be directed to designated complaints managers in PCTs and NHS Trusts. Formal complaints should be interpreted as any matter which the complaints would like to be treated as formal.

---

[66] Fifth Report of the Shipman Inquiry, 2004, available ibid.
[67] Page 30 of *The Kerr/Haslam Inquiry Report Volume*, Cm 6640-1 (TSO, August 2004).
[68] Page 31 of *The Kerr/Haslam Inquiry Report Volume*, Cm 6640-1 (TSO, August 2004).

iii. Robert Francis QC: Mid-Staffs Independent Inquiry 2010

The events at Mid Staffordshire NHS Foundation Trusts were horrifying with many deaths due to appalling failings in healthcare. Estimates on exactly how many people died at Mid-Staffs between January 2005 and March 2009 are disputed, but are understood to run into the hundreds. An independent inquiry, chaired by Robert Francis QC, was commissioned. This focussed on the quality of care at Mid-Staffs. It found that complaints were poorly investigated, remedial action was often not applied, appraisal and professional development were accorded a low priority, the focus of the Board was on processes not outcomes and its reaction to criticism was individually and collectively one of denial instead of searching self-criticism.

His report[69] made 18 recommendations. Recommendation 6 focussed on complaints and incident reporting. It reads

> The Board should review the Trust's arrangements for the management of complaints and incident reporting in the light of the findings of this report and ensure that it:
> - provides responses and resolutions to complaints which satisfy complainants;
> - ensures that staff are engaged in the process from the investigation of a complaint or an incident to the implementation of any lessons to be learned all part of the recommendation
> - minimises the risk of deficiencies exposed by the problems recurring; and
> - makes available full information on the matters reported, and the action to resolve deficiencies, to the Board, the governors and the public.

iv. Health Select Committee 2011

In 2011 the Health Select Committee made a series of recommendations.[70] First, it supported the existing two-tier system (local handling of complaints followed by the Ombudsman) but noted that it had not been fully implemented across the NHS. Second, it noted the importance of PALS for many complainants, and expressed concerns about the visibility of advocacy services to complainants. Third, it recommended there should be a single point of access for the entire local resolution of a complaint and this could be provided by integrated complaints and advice teams. A fourth recommendation, that a single organisation should be responsible for maintaining an overview of complaints handling in the NHS, setting and monitoring standards, supporting change and analysis of complaints data, was rejected by the government.

v. Robert Francis QC: Mid-Staffs Public Inquiry 2013

Following a change of government a public inquiry was launched into the events at Mid-Staffs. This was also chaired by Robert Francis QC. The public inquiry had a wider

---

[69] *Independent Inquiry into Care Provided by Mid Staffordshire NHS Foundation Trust January 2005-March 2009 Volumes I and II. Chaired by Robert Francis QC*, HC375-I and HC375-II, 24 February 2010 available at www.gov.uk/government/publications/independent-inquiry-into-care-provided-by-mid-staffordshire-nhs-foundation-trust-january-2001-to-march-2009.

[70] Health Select Committee, *Complaints and Litigation*, Sixth Report of Session 2010–11, HC 786-1, 22 June 2011, available at https://publications.parliament.uk/pa/cm201012/cmselect/cmhealth/786/786i.pdf.

remit than the initial inquiry, it looked at the system-wide failures to detect and correct the poor care at Mid-Staffs. In this report Francis's list of recommendations was more extensive, detailing 290 separate recommendations. He made 14 recommendations on the handling of complaints, which made clear it that he did not feel the two tier complains system was fit for purpose.[71] He identified the following the key themes:

– The reluctance of patients and those close to them to complain, in part because of fear of the consequences. This and other barriers prevented organisations receiving complaints

– Support for complainants, whether or not they are specifically vulnerable, with advice and advocacy still requires development.

– The feedback, learning and warning signals available from complaints have not been given a high enough priority.

– Information about the content of complaints should, where permissible, be made available to and used by commissioners and local scrutiny bodies; the CQC should use material from complaints more widely.

– There was a case for independent investigation of a wider range of complaints.

vi. Berwick 2013

In response to the events in Mid-Staffordshire the government commissioned Professor Don Berwick to distil for Government and the NHS the lessons learned, and to specify the changes and reforms that were needed to drive improvements. His 2013 review of patient safety in the NHS strongly urged the adoption of a learning and no blame culture across the NHS in order to put patient care and safety above all other aims.[72] He set out seven problems including:

2. NHS staff are not to blame … the vast majority of staff wish to do a good job, to reduce suffering and to be proud of their work. Good people can fail to meet patients' needs when their working conditions do not provide them with the conditions for success.

…

5. Responsibility is diffused and therefore not clearly owned … When so many are in charge, no-one is.

6. Improvement requires a system of support … the NHS needs a considered, resourced and driven agenda of capability-building in order to generate the capacity for continuous improvement. The most important single change in the NHS in response to this report would be for it to become, more than ever before, a system devoted to continual learning and improvement of patient care, top to bottom and end to end. (original emphasis)

7. Fear is toxic to both safety and improvement.

---

[71] *Report of the Mid Staffordshire NHS Foundation Trust Public Inquiry. February 2013 Chaired by Robert Francis QC*, HC947, available at www.gov.uk/government/publications/report-of-the-mid-staffordshire-nhs-foundation-trust-public-inquiry.

[72] *A Promise to Learn – A Commitment to Act Improving the Safety of Patients in England* (August 2013) available at www.gov.uk/government/publications/berwick-review-into-patient-safety.

To address these issues the system must:

1. Recognise with clarity and courage the need for wide systemic change.
2. Abandon blame as a tool. Trust the goodwill and good intentions of the staff ...
3. Reassert the primacy of working with patients and carers to set and achieve health goals
4. Use quantitative targets with caution
5. Recognise that transparency is essential and expect and insist on it at all levels and with regard to all types of information
6. Ensure that responsibility for functions related to safety and improvement are vested clearly and simply
7. Give the people of the NHS career-long help to learn, master and apply modern methods for quality control, quality improvement and quality planning.
8. Make sure pride and joy in work, not fear, infuse the NHS.

The eight solutions set out in his report remain just as valid now as they were a decade ago. Professor Berwick very clearly sets out his view that

> In the end, culture will trump rules, standards and control strategies every single time, and achieving a vastly safer NHS will depend far more on major cultural change than on a new regulatory regime.

vii. Clwyd and Hart 2013

The government responded to the Allitt[73] and Shipman scandals, and the findings of the Public Inquiry into Mid-Staffs about complaint handling by commissioning a more general report into NHS complaint handing.[74] Clwyd and Hart's 2013 report recorded the following key points on how the system should operate, based on their findings on 'what it feels like to complain':

–   Information and accessibility – patients want clear and simple information about how to complain and the process should be easy to navigate.

–   Freedom from fear – patients do not want to feel that if they complain their care will be worse in future.

–   Sensitivity – patients want their complaint dealt with sensitively.

–   Responsiveness – patients want a response that is properly tailored to the issue they are complaining about.

–   Prompt and clear process – patients want their complaint handled as quickly as possible.

–   Seamless service – patients do not want to have to complain to multiple organisations in order to get answers.

–   Support – patients want someone on their side to help them through the process of complaining.

–   Effectiveness – patients want their complaints to make a difference to help prevent others suffering in the future.

---

[73] Beverley Allitt was a nurse who was convicted of killing various patients while working in the children's ward at Grantham and Kesteven Hospital, Leicestershire in 1991.

[74] A Clwyd and T Hart, *A Review of the NHS Hospitals Complaints System. Putting Patients Back in the Picture* (Department of Health, 2013).

–   Independence – patients want to know the complaints process is independent, particularly when they are complaining about a serious failing in care.

Clwyd and Hart noted that complaints came to hospital Trusts through a variety of routes, for example, directly to the Chief Executive, through to a clinical colleague or made through the Complaints' Manager. They supported a system in which the first step should be to discuss a concern with the healthcare professional(s) involved so as to resolve problems quickly. They noted that immediate appropriate action can help avoid an issue escalating into a more serious problem. They said that reported concerns need to be noted in writing by the staff concerned along with any action taken and the outcome.[75]

In relation to the criterion of 'effectiveness' listed above, Clwyd and Hart commented:

> Many people who complain felt that nothing had been learned or achieved as a result of their complaint. They were disappointed about this because this had been one of their reasons for complaining in the first place. Many people said that an early acknowledgement of fault and a genuine apology would have satisfied them; but that having suffered through a lengthy and taxing complaints system, they wanted the hospital to acknowledge their responsibility and for staff to face appropriate sanctions where necessary. …
>
> **What patients want**: Patients want to know that their complaints make a difference. The prime desired outcomes are usually the admission of responsibility, an apology, the reassurance that lessons will be learned and – where appropriate and where individuals are clearly at fault – some form of sanction. This is particularly important if staff have attempted to cover up their failings. Patients want openness and to know that where staff have done something wrong they will not be allowed to remain anonymous.

Clwyd and Hart also noted a number of difficulties faced by NHS organisations in responding to complaints, largely flowing from the system's complexity and changing structures. Significantly, their recommendations focused first on improving the quality of care and communicating with patients. In relation to improvements in the way complaints are handled, they recommended:

a)   … development of professional behaviour in the handling of complaints. This includes honesty and openness and a willingness to listen to the complainant, and to understand and work with the patient to rectify the problem.

b)   Staff need to record complaints and the action that has been taken and check with the patient that it meets with their expectation.

c)   … NHS accredited training for people who investigate and respond to complaints.

d)   Trusts should actively encourage both positive and negative feedback about their services. Complaints should be seen as essential and helpful information and welcomed as necessary for continuous service improvement. …

e)   Commissioners and regulators should establish clear standards for hospitals for complaints handling. …

f)   There should be proper arrangements for sharing good practice on complaints handling between hospitals, including examples of service improvements which result from action taken in response to complaints.

They also called for greater perceived and actual independence in the complaints process, including offering a truly independent investigation where serious incidents have occurred,

---

[75] ibid, 11–12.

ensuring the true independence of the clinical and lay advice and advocacy support offered to the complainant in initial conversations, keeping patient services and patient complaints support separate, and ensuring Board level scrutiny of complaints, regularly involving lay representatives.

viii. PHSO's 2015 Review of Complaints

An academic review carried out at one hospital found that most complaints and medico-legal claims are not associated with a prior clinical error, and also that most local complaints are not upheld.[76] However, in December 2015 the Parliamentary and Health Service Ombudsman (PHSO, whose role is discussed in the next section) published a review of 150 NHS complaints investigations where avoidable harm or death was alleged, and a survey of over 170 NHS complaints managers.[77] Her factual findings are summarised in Table 3, revealing significant failings in the *process* and culture, and hence missed opportunities for learning and giving trustworthy explanations to patients. The Ombudsman said:[78]

> When things go wrong with NHS care, it can have devastating consequences for patients and their families. People want answers, to understand what happened and why, and to know that action is being taken to prevent the same thing happening again to others. But our research has cast a question mark over the current ability of NHS organisations to conduct effective investigations where it is alleged that someone may have been harmed, or died, avoidably. We have found that NHS trusts are not always identifying patient safety incidents and are sometimes failing to recognise serious incidents. When investigations do happen, the quality is inconsistent, often failing to get to the heart of what has gone wrong and to ensure lessons are learnt.
>
> …
>
> Avoidable harm spans everything from minor to moderate harm, to unexpected or avoidable death and incidents that may cause widespread public concern resulting in a loss of confidence in healthcare services. Where the consequences of these failures to patients, families and carers, staff or organisations are so significant or the potential for learning is great, cases should be investigated as serious incidents.[79]

The Ombudsman stated that whether or not the event was significant enough to warrant being labelled a serious incident or a patient safety incident, people have a right to know that

---

[76] P Goldsmith, J Moon, P Anderson, S Kirkup, S Williams and M Gray, 'Do Clinical Incidents, Complaints and Medicolegal Claims Overlap?' (2015) 28(8) *International Journal of Health Care Quality Assurance* 864. This study at Newcastle Hospitals NHS Foundation Trust in 2013/14 found 1.5 million discrete patient encounters, around 32,000 contacts with the Patient Advisory and Liaison Service, 702 formal complaints. of which 29 were taken to the Ombudsman and only three were upheld. In only 58 cases could matches in the names of patients be made in incidents common to the database of 13,266 internal incident reports and 443 complaints recorded in seven months in 2014. Of those, only 17 (3.8% of 443 complaints) was the incident related to the complaint, and in 20 (3.4%) there was a single reported incident but the complaint was unrelated.

[77] *A Review into the Quality of NHS Complaints Investigations Where Serious or Avoidable Harm Has Been Alleged* (Parliamentary and Health Service Ombudsman, 2015).

[78] ibid, 2.

[79] Serious incidents are defined as 'unexpected or avoidable death, unexpected or avoidable injury resulting in serious harm – including those where the injury required treatment to prevent death or serious harm, abuse, Never Events, incidents that prevent (or threaten to prevent) an organisation's ability to continue to deliver an acceptable quality of healthcare services and incidents that cause widespread public concern resulting in a loss of confidence in healthcare services.' NHS England (March 2015) Serious Incident Framework. Available at www.england.nhs. uk/wp-content/uploads/2015/04/serious-incidnt-framwrk-upd.pdf.

their complaint has been taken seriously and investigated thoroughly. She expected Trusts to be measuring and improving people's experience of complaining by using *My Expectations*[80] when assessing the performance of their complaints service and to what extent this is meeting the needs of the public. The Ombudsman noted that a new Independent Patient Safety Investigation Service (IPSIS, noted further below) was to be established from April 2016, and called on IPSIS and the NHS to collaborate strongly to 'make a decisive difference to how the NHS improves the way it investigates in the future'.

Table 3 Extracts from Findings of PHSO Review into the Quality of NHS Complaints Investigations

---

1. The process of investigating is not consistent, reliable or good enough.

We found that 40% of investigations were not adequate to find out what happened. Not only are trusts not identifying failings, they are also not finding out why the failings happened in the first place. [19% of investigations had relevant evidence (medical records, statements and interviews) missing when they were conducted.] For example, trusts did not find failings in 73% of cases in which we found them, and in over a third of cases [36%] where failings were found, trusts did not find out why something went wrong. This is in marked contrast to the perception of 91% of NHS complaints managers who were confident an investigation could find out what had gone wrong.

Serious incidents are not being reliably identified by trusts; we judged 28 of the [150] cases we looked at to be serious enough to lead to a serious incident investigation, but only 8 had been treated as such by the NHS. [We found that identification often relied on either clinicians to spot an incident or on a central risk team flagging incidents. In almost a fifth of investigations medical records, statements and interviews were missing, making it difficult for trusts to arrive at what went wrong and why.] ….

We are concerned that there is no national guidance for patient safety incident investigations which make clear:

• who should investigate and how independent of events they should be;
• the level of training an investigator should have for any particular type of investigation;
• broad requirements for the specific evidence needed. For example, statements, interviews or independent clinical reviews;
• how investigations should be independently quality assured;
• what general outcomes any good investigation should aim to achieve.

2. Staff do not feel adequately supported in their investigatory role

There is no national, accredited training programme to support investigators and/or complaints staff in their role. Cultural issues can often be a barrier to getting to the heart of why something has happened.

Common reasons cited during our visits to trusts included a lack of respect; not being provided with protected time to investigate, and the lack of an open and honest culture despite the introduction of the duty of candour in November 2014.

(continued)

---

[80] PHSO, *My Expectations: A User-led Vision for Raising Concerns and Complaints* (November 2014) available at www.ombudsman.org.uk/__data/assets/pdf_file/0008/28817/My-expectations-for-raising-concerns-and-complaints-summary-leaflet.pdf.

Table 3 *(Continued)*

3. There are missed opportunities for learning. Many complain because they do not wish the same thing to happen to somebody else. Therefore it was worrying to find that 25% of complaints managers were unsure that sufficient processes existed to prevent a recurrence of an incident, and a further 10% believed sufficient processes were not in place. … Action is needed in order for learning to take place and this requires people working together in a joined up way. … [4. Failure to Explain to Patients] In 41% of cases inadequate explanations were given to complainants for what went wrong and why.

The PHSO also published a report into why older people are afraid or reluctant to complain about the NHS despite accessing its services more than other groups of people.[81] The report revealed that people over the age of 75 often lack the knowledge and confidence to complain, and worry about the impact complaining might have on their future care and treatment; many fearing that complaining will simply make matters worse for them. The report found that:

- Over half (56 per cent) of those aged 65 and over who had experienced a problem but not complained, were worried about the impact that complaining might have on their future treatment.
- Nearly one in five (18 per cent) people over the age of 75 did not know how to raise a complaint about the NHS or a social care provider.
- Among those over the age of 65 who were unhappy with a service, but who didn't complain, over a third (32 per cent) felt that complaining would not make a difference.
- Less than a third of the older people surveyed could recall being offered support to make a complaint.

The Ombudsman said:

> These are barriers which can dissuade or prevent anyone from making a complaint regardless of age. However, for older people there are often many additional factors – such as ongoing reliance on NHS care or living alone – which can make these barriers even harder to overcome. In order to overcome these barriers, change needs to happen. Our report makes a number of recommendations to improve older people's experience of the complaints system.

The report made a series of recommendations that NHS and social care providers to assist making older people aware of how to complain; to point them to the support that is available to them; to make it absolutely clear that their future care will not be compromised if they complain; and to use the framework contained in 'My expectations for raising concerns and complaints', which sets out what good complaint-handling looks like from the perspective of patients and service users, and which can be used to measure how effectively complaints are being handled.

---

[81] *Breaking Down the Barriers* (PHSO, 2015).

When the PHSO's *Review into the Quality*[82] was considered by the Public Administration and Constitutional Affairs Committee in early 2016,[83] Mike Durkin, the National Director for Patient Safety for NHS England, accepted that the approach to clinical investigation varied across the 250 or so trusts in England,[84] and the most important task was to establish an exemplar model of clinical investigation.

ix. *Southern Health Review (Stage I) 2021*

The Southern Health Review was chaired by Nigel Pascoe QC on behalf of NHS Improvement. The first stage of the review[85] looked into the circumstances of the deaths of five patients[86] of Southern Health NHS Foundation Trust. The Trust provides services for patients with mental health issues and learning disabilities. The deaths occurred between October 2011 and November 2015. The first stage report was published in February 2020. It found that failings in care, failings to investigate the death and failures to communicate with families have caused lasting harm. The report cited 'disturbing insensitivity and a serious lack of proper communication with family members' which caused deep hurt to families.

A Stage II review looking at more general policy issues at Southern Health NHS Trust,[87] also chaired by Nigel Pascoe QC, followed which focussed on five key policy areas, one of which was complaint handling processes. The original families declined to take part in the Stage II review citing concerns that the independent panel members all had links to the NHS. The Stage II report cited a 2016 internal thematic report[88] carried out by Southern Health Trust which found that

> 21% of patients and service users stated that they may be prevented from speaking up as they worry that care would be even worse as an outcome' and '26% of patients and service users indicated that they were unsure who they should go to if they had concerns about their care.

The Stage II report noted that the Trust had made improvements in complaint handling.

x. *Baroness Julia Cumberlege: IMMDS 2020*

The Independent Medicines and Medical Devices Safety Review considered three medical interventions: hormone pregnancy tests, the impact on the child of sodium valproate use

---

[82] *A Review into the Quality of NHS Complaints Investigation Where Serious or Avoidable Harm Has Been Alleged* (PHSO, 2015).

[83] Public Administration and Constitutional Affairs Committee, Oral evidence: Follow-up to Public Health Service Ombudsman's report on Clinical Investigations, HC 792, 2 February 2016.

[84] Ben Gummer MP, Parliamentary Under Secretary of State for Care Quality, described the variation as 'very patchy'; Q18. The scale of the problem was revealed by the fact that 27 trusts had been put into special measures in two and a half years; 11 had come out, 16 remained in: Q28.

[85] Nigel Pascoe QC, *Stage 1 Independent Review into Southern Health NHS Foundation Trust* (February 2020) available at www.england.nhs.uk/south-east/publications/ind-invest-reports/southern-health/.

[86] Five patient deaths were considered by the review, but only four patient stories are featured in the report as one family did not wish to be included in the publication.

[87] Nigel Pascoe QC, *'Right First Time': Stage 2 Independent Review into Southern Health NHS Foundation Trust* (September 2021) available at www.england.nhs.uk/south-east/publications/ind-invest-reports/southern-health/.

[88] Complaints, Compliments and Concerns: A Thematic Peer Review, June 2016.

during pregnancy and the use of mesh in the pelvis. The use of these interventions spanned many years from the 1950s to date. A number of the individuals affected by these interventions told the IMMDS review of their experiences of the complaints process. The IMMDS report, *First Do No Harm*,[89] published in July 2020 found that

> Patients struggle to navigate the complaints system and it may take some time to find the correct organisation to complain to. All the while patients are still living with the complications that led to the original complaint, and may have had further upsetting experiences including surgeons dismissing their pain and other complications – patients described being 'broken' by this journey.

They were concerned about the disconnect between the NHS and private healthcare complaints mechanisms and they recommended

> Patients across the NHS and private sector must have a clear, well-publicised route to raise their concerns about aspects of their experiences in the healthcare system.

They also recommended reversing one of the change brought in by the 2004 Regulations

> All organisations who take complaints from the public should designate a non-executive member of the board to oversee the complaint-handling processes and outcomes, and ensure that appropriate action is taken.

xi. Ockenden Reports 2020 and 2022

The quality of complaints handling was a key theme in both the interim and final Ockenden reports,[90] specifically the disingenuous and deeply insensitive way in which complaints were handled[91]

> There is evidence that complaint responses lacked transparency and honesty, especially with regards to clinical care. The review team has identified families where care was sub-optimal, where different management would likely have made a difference to the outcome, however the complaint responses justified actions, delays and omissions in care. In addition, they often lacked compassion and in a number of responses it was implied that the woman herself was to blame.

The Final Report detailed a lack of senior oversight into complaint handling, a serious lack of openness and transparency and a failure to take actions from the complaints trend analysis. The reports made a number of local action points to improve complaint handling at the Trust, as well as the following essential action that applied across all maternity services in England.

> All maternity services must involve service users (ideally via their MVP[92]) in developing complaints response processes that are caring and transparent.

---

[89] J Cumberlege, *First Do No Harm: The Report of the Independent Medicines and Medical Devices Safety Review* (2020) available at www.immdsreview.org.uk/Report.html.

[90] Ockenden Review, *Emerging Findings and Recommendations from the Independent Review of Maternity Services at the Shrewsbury and Telford Hospital NHS Trust – Our First Report following 250 Clinical Reviews* HC 1081, 10 December 2020, available at www.gov.uk/government/publications/ockenden-review-of-maternity-services-at-shrewsbury-and-telford-hospital-nhs-trust and Ockenden Review, *Findings, Conclusions and Essential Actions from the Independent Review of Maternity Services at the Shrewsbury and Telford Hospital NHS Trust – Our Final Report* HC 1219, 30 March 2022, available at https://assets.publishing.service.gov.uk/government/uploads/system/uploads/attachment_data/file/1064302/Final-Ockenden-Report-web-accessible.pdf.

[91] Final report, ibid.

[92] Maternity Voices Partnership – a team of women and their families, commissioners and providers (midwives and doctors) working together to review and contribute to the development of local maternity care.

III. NHS Complaints in Wales

A. Welsh Public Service Complaints

As with other UK jurisdictions in the early 2000s there were a range of sector-specific complaint handling frameworks in Wales. In order to improve complaints handling systems a standardised *All Wales Model Concerns and Complaints Policy* for all public services (except health) was proposed. This policy was developed by the Complaints Wales Group chaired by the Public Services Ombudsman for Wales. The policy,[93] originally published in 2011, contained proposals for simplifying public service complaints handling processes and making it easier for individuals to complain. In particular the policy developed by the group stated that complaints processes should be:

– accessible and simple;
– fair and impartial;
– timely, effective and consistent;
– accountable; and
– should deliver continuous improvement.

The published *Policy and Guidance* noted that there are differences between public service providers, but was clear that public service providers should have regard to the guidance when developing their complaints handling services and that the 'guidance will be suitable for most organisations'. The intentions was not to be overly prescriptive 'Variations can be introduced to take account of the size or operational requirements of organisations, but must not impact on people's experience of a common approach in complaint handling by public service providers.'

In a parallel development in April 2011 the Welsh Government introduced new arrangements for the management of healthcare concerns: *Putting Things Right*. *Putting Things Right* followed the same principles that were contained in the *All Wales Model Concerns and Complaints Policy*.

The approach to concerns and redress in the NHS in Wales was extended in August 2014 into a general framework for handling complaints and representations by local authority social services in Wales.[94] The general principles for dealing with complaints are set out in Table 4. The procedure focuses on a first stage of local resolution of complaints, where all complainants are offered a discussion to resolve the matter, and a second stage involving a formal investigation with independent scrutiny. Every local authority is required to appoint a Complaints Officer to manage the procedures for handling and considering complaints and representations, including maintaining a pool of Independent Investigators and Independent Persons. In stage two, an investigation is to be carried out by an Independent Investigator, who compiles a formal written record, which is sent to the complainant, and

---

[93] Welsh Government, *Model Concerns and Complaints Policy and Guidance*, 2011.
[94] The Social Services Complaints Procedure (Wales) Regulations 2014 and the Representations (Wales) Regulations 2014. See *A Guide to Handling Complaints and Representations by Local Authority Social Services* (Welsh Government, 2014).

a full written response sent normally within 25 working days. The investigation will be planned to respond to the circumstances of the case and the needs and circumstances of the complainant. An Independent Person is appointed in every case, from being involved in early discussions about the approach to be taken, and to provide a brief report that appropriate procedures have been followed. The formal report should:

- be evidence based with contributions from all the people involved;
- be as clear as is possible about the facts in each aspect of the complaint;
- be written concisely and clearly, avoiding jargon and easily understandable;
- distinguish between fact, feelings and opinion;
- reach clear conclusions;
- make recommendations for resolving the complaint; and
- make recommendations for improving the service so that other service users do not have cause to make the same complaint.

The local authority must determine whether or not the complaint is upheld and what action is to be taken as a consequence. Its response should be signed by the Director of Social Services, and must satisfy various criteria. If the matter is not resolved, a further complaint may be made to the Public Services Ombudsman for Wales. It is intended that complaints and representations should be used to monitor the local authority's compliance with regulations, improve its service delivery, and increase its effectiveness.[95]

Table 4 General principles for dealing with social services complaints in Wales[96]

(i) Accessible and Simple
Well publicised.
Easy to find, understand and use – both for public and staff.
Bi– lingual and reflecting More than just words.
Simple and clear instructions for the public about how to make a complaint.
Has flexibility to meet the different needs of different people, ensuring that those who face challenges in access are not excluded.
Provides information on advocacy and support services.
The stages in the complaint handling process are kept to a minimum.
(ii) Fair and Impartial
Concerns are dealt with in an open– minded and impartial way.
Complainants are assured that making a complaint will not adversely affect their future dealings and contacts with the body concerned.
Ensures that complainants get a full response and that decisions are proportionate, appropriate and are fair.
The staff complained about are treated as fairly as complainants.

(continued)

[95] *A Guide to Handling Complaints*, ibid, para 113.
[96] ibid, para 30.

Table 4 *(Continued)*

(iii) Timely, Effective and Consistent

Within the parameters of what is appropriate and possible, frontline staff themselves should seek to resolve complaints.

"Investigate Once, Investigate Well" – when a complaint requires formal investigation, this should be done thoroughly to establish the facts of the case.

Dealt with as quickly as possible.

Consistent so that people in similar circumstances are treated in similar ways.

Concerns involving more than one public service provider are dealt with in such a way that the complainant's experience is of one system.

(iv) Accountable

Provides honest, evidence– based explanations and gives reasons for decisions.

Information is provided in a clear and open way.

When concerns are found to be justified, as appropriate, local authorities:
 -     acknowledge mistakes;
 -     apologise in a meaningful way;
 -     put matters right; and
 -     provide prompt, appropriate and proportionate redress.

Follow up to ensure any decisions are properly and and promptly implemented.

Where appropriate, the complainant is told about the lessons learnt and changes made to the service, guidance or policy.

Ensures that complainants are informed of their right to complain to the Public Services Ombudsman for Wales (or of other appropriate routes open to them, for example, the Welsh Language Commissioner in respect of complaints about compliance with Welsh Language Schemes, Equality and Human Rights Commission).

(v) Delivers Continuous Improvement

Lessons learnt from complaints are gathered and feedback is used to improve service design and delivery.

Systems are in place to record, analyse and report on the learning from concerns.

The leadership of the local authority (which includes the Director of Social Services):
 -     takes ownership of the complaints and representations process;
 -     regularly reviews and scrutinises its effectiveness;
 -     receives regular monitoring reports;
 -     demonstrates what the organisation has done to improve service delivery as a result of complaints and representations.

Directors of Social Services should report regularly to Cabinet on these matters

Local authorities must publish an Annual Report on these matters.

Regulators have an important role in ensuring that lessons learnt from concerns are implemented satisfactorily and sustained.

In 2019 the requirements on the Public Services Ombudsman for Wales (PSOW) were codified in the Public Services Ombudsman (Wales) Act 2019.[97] This Act required PSOW to publish a statement of principles concerning the complaint handling procedures of specified authorities and gave PSOW the authority to publish Model Complaint Handling Procedures (MCHPs).[98] The Act also required that PSOW monitor complaint handling practice, identify trends, promote best practice and encourage co-operation and sharing of best practice among listed authorities. PSOW set up an internal unit, the Complaints Standards Authority,[99] to deliver these duties.

B. Welsh NHS Complaints Overview

Putting Things Right, introduced in 2011, created a single integrated approach to the management of complaints, incidents and claims. The intention was that there should be a unified effective process: 'investigate once, investigate well'. It was underpinned by a comprehensive set of Regulations[100] and supporting guidance and policies. The main focus of this was to make it easier for patients and carers to raise concerns; to be engaged and supported during the process; to be dealt with openly and honestly; and for bodies to demonstrate learning from when things went wrong or standards needed to improve.[101]

The 2011 Regulations establish the general principles which must be followed when handling and investigating concerns under the Regulations, which are set out in Table 5.[102] Some concerns could be dealt with 'on the spot' without further ado, others require more investigation.

Table 5 General principles for the handling and investigation of concerns, NHS Wales

Any arrangements set up under these Regulations for the handling and investigation of concerns must be such as to ensure that–
(a) there is a single point of entry for the submission of concerns;
(b) concerns are dealt with efficiently and openly;
(c) concerns are properly investigated;
(d) provision should be made to establish the expectations of the person notifying the concern and to seek to secure their involvement in the process;
(e) persons who notify concerns are treated with respect and courtesy;

(continued)

[97] Part 4 of the Public Services Ombudsman (Wales) Act 2019, 2019 ANAW 3, available at www.legislation.gov.uk/anaw/2019/3/contents/enacted.

[98] See www.ombudsman.wales/wp-content/uploads/2020/08/2-CSA-Model-Concerns-and-Complaints-Policy.pdf.

[99] www.ombudsman.wales/complaints-standards-authority/.

[100] Contained in The National Health Service (Concerns, Complaints and Redress Arrangements) (Wales) Regulations 2001 (2011 No 704 (W 108)) available at www.legislation.gov.uk/wsi/2011/704/contents/made.

[101] www.wales.nhs.uk/sites3/home.cfm?orgid=932.

[102] ibid, reg 3.

Table 5 *(Continued)*

(f)   persons who notify concerns are advised of–
(a)   the availability of assistance to enable them to pursue their concern;
(b)   advice as to where they may obtain such assistance, if it is required; and
(c)   the name of the person in the relevant responsible body who will act as their contact throughout the handling of their concern;
(g)   a Welsh NHS body must give consideration to the making of an offer of redress in accordance with Part 6 where its investigation into the matters raised in a concern reveal that there is a qualifying liability;
(h)   persons who notify concerns receive a timely and appropriate response;
(i)   persons who notify concerns are advised of the outcome of the investigation;
(j)   appropriate action is taken in the light of the outcome of the investigation; and
(k)   account is taken of any guidance that may be issued from time to time by the Welsh Ministers.

C. Welsh NHS Complaints Processes and Parameters

The regulations refer to 'concerns' which is to be interpreted broadly. Concerns may be raised orally[103] or in writing either by email or letter.[104] Any patient can raise a concern, this includes children who should be supported if they want to raise concerns for themselves.[105] In appropriate situations concerns can be raised by representatives, the regulations set out more detail on this.[106] Interestingly the regulations also permit staff members to bring complaints about the care of patients.[107] If concerns raised by staff are about a patient who the initial investigation concludes has suffered moderate harm, severe harm or death then the patient or their representative must be informed of the concerns, save where the body considers that it would not be in the interests of the patient to do so.[108]

The time limits for notifying a concern are 12 months from the incident or 12 months from the patient becoming aware of the incident providing this is not more than 24 months after the incident occurred.[109] There is some discretion on these time limits, but there is a longstop of three years from the incident or from the complainant becoming aware of it.[110]

The first stage of the process is an attempt at local resolution. If this is not successful then the second stage is to raise the issue with the Public Services Ombudsman for Wales.

Concerns can be raised directly with the organisation where the concern arose.[111] In addition, concerns about a primary care provider can be raised with the local health

---

[103] If an oral complaint is resolved locally within one day the regulations do not apply.

[104] The National Health Service (Concerns, Complaints and Redress Arrangements) (Wales) Regulations 2001, reg 11. A concern may be withdrawn at any time by the person who notified the concern, in writing, electronically or verbally: reg 16.

[105] ibid, reg 12(4).

[106] ibid, reg 12.

[107] This does not include complaints related to the staff member's employment or contract.

[108] The National Health Service (Concerns, Complaints and Redress Arrangements) (Wales) Regulations 2001, reg 12(6), (7) and (8).

[109] ibid, reg 15.

[110] ibid, reg 15(3).

[111] ibid, reg 13.

board. The local health board will then consider if it would be more appropriate for the primary care provider to consider the complaint.[112] A reasoned decision by the local health board should be notified to both the complainant and the primary care provider within five working days.

Local resolution of complaints which involve more than one responsible body require that the responsible bodies cooperate and provide a coordinated response.

Each hospital or practice should have a responsible officer and a senior investigations manager.[113] The responsible officer oversees the arrangements for dealing with concerns and implementing actions for improvement.[114] The senior investigations manager is responsible for the investigation and consideration of concerns. It must also ensure that its staff receive appropriate training to enable them to comply with the requirements.[115]

Concerns must be acknowledged within two working days.[116] For concerns that are raised orally a written record of the concern must be given to the complainant. The organisation must offer to discuss how the investigation will be conducted and the likely timescale for the investigation and for the provision of a full response as well as what advocacy services are available. When a complainant does not want to discuss these matters this information should be given in writing.[117] The organisation must also send a copy of the notification of a concern to the person who is the subject of the concern unless it is of the view that this action could prejudice its consideration of the matters raised by the concern.[118]

If an organisation is of the opinion that the concern raised relates to an excluded matter it must, as soon as reasonably practicable, notify the complainant in writing giving the reasons for this decision.[119]

The exact process for investigating the concern is not prescribed in the Regulations, rather the emphasis is on ensuring the investigation is thorough, speedy, efficient and appropriate to the particular concern raised. Investigations should be carried out in a manner which the organisation feels is the most appropriate to reach a conclusion, having regard to a series of specified matters.[120]

In general, the investigation and the full response should be sent to the complainant within 30 days of the complaint being made. If it is not possible to meet this timeframe the complainant must be informed of why this is and told when they can expect a full response. The Regulations specify the response must:[121]

(a)   summarises the nature and substance of the matter or matters raised in the concern;
(b)   describes the investigation undertaken in accordance with regulation 23;
(c)   contains copies of any expert opinions that the person investigating the concern has received during the investigation;
(d)   contains a copy of any relevant medical records, where this is appropriate;

---

[112] ibid, reg 16.
[113] ibid, regs 4 and 5.
[114] ibid, regs 6, 7 and 8.
[115] ibid, reg 9.
[116] ibid, reg 22.
[117] ibid, reg 22(4).
[118] ibid, reg 22(6).
[119] ibid, reg 14(2).
[120] ibid, reg 23.
[121] ibid, reg 24.

(e)   where appropriate, contains an apology;

(f)   identifies what action, if any, will be taken in light of the outcome of the investigation;

(g)   contains details of the right to notify the concern to the Public Services Ombudsman for Wales;

(h)   offers the person notifying the concern the opportunity to discuss the contents of the response with the responsible officer or a person acting on his or her behalf; and

(i)   is signed by the responsible officer or a person acting on his or her behalf.

Under the Regulations where there is a 'qualifying liability' the hospital/local health board have to consider whether to offer financial redress up to £25,000. This financial redress requirement does not apply to primary care providers or independent providers treating NHS patients.

Interestingly Community Health Councils remained in Wales until 2020.[122] One of the core CHC functions was to provide a free, confidential and independent complaints advocacy service for individuals who want support to raise a concern about NHS care and treatment. In June 2020 CHCs were replaced by the Citizen Voice Body for Health and Social Care,[123] which has the ability to make representations to health and social care providers and to provide advocacy services in respect of service complaints.

i. Keith Evans 2014

A 2014 review of the Welsh NHS complaints system by a leading businessman concluded that although the new approach mandated in *Putting Things Right* was the right approach, and widely welcomed by staff, implementation had fallen far short.[124] Three major reasons were highlighted for this failure. First, inadequate resources had been allocated to making the new system work. In particular, a need for staff training in the approach had not been satisfied. Second, the entire NHS organisational structure, as well as the complaints structure, was far too complex.[125] As a result, patients who wanted to complain found the multiple options confusing and impenetrable, and even staff had difficulty in explaining the system.[126] It was recommended that the complaint system should be simple, standard, slim and speedy, with excellent quality.[127] Third, the culture of the NHS needed to be completely aligned with the new approach, and this was not the case. He said that complaints need to be treated as a gift, which reflect a profound sense of response to the trust that patients put in

---

[122] There were seven regional CHCs; Aneurin Bevan; Cwm Taf Morgannwg; Hywel Dda; North Wales; Powys; South Glamorgan; and Swansea Bay.

[123] Health and Social Care (Quality and Engagement) (Wales) Act 2020 part 4 available at www.legislation.gov.uk/asc/2020/1/part/4.

[124] K Evans, *"Using the Gift of Complaints": A Review of Concerns (Complaints) Handling in NHS Wales* (Welsh Government, 2014). The author was former Chief Executive and Managing Director of Panasonic UK and Ireland, supported by Dr Andrew Goodall, Chief Executive of Aneurin Bevan University Health Board, available at www.wales.nhs.uk/usingthegiftofcomplaints.

[125] ibid, para 51 ('there are too many levels of vertical and horizontal management; it is probably the most complex matrix organisation I have ever come across and mostly of its own making ...').

[126] ibid, para 40. 'I have struggled myself always to make sense of the different and sometimes it seems conflicting roles within the complaints infrastructure. Imagine how this must feel for individual complainants without the access to the system I have had': Executive Summary, Recommendations, fifth bullet.

[127] ibid, para 27.

healthcare providers.[128] The latter should see themselves, their systems and the service they provide, through the eyes of users.

In relation to the existing culture, the author stated that 'the political debate and general blame culture is too heavy and seriously affects those working in the service'.[129]

Openness and honesty will never be forthcoming in organisations that foster blame and criticism as the tools of management. As a result the siege mentality I have observed is the highest I have ever come across. ... There are indicators that show the impact this could be having such as difficulties in recruitment, higher staff turnover, higher numbers of complaints, staff reporting concerns outside the organisation and impact on quality outcomes. It also has in some instances caused anxiety for patients who are using or expecting to use services.[130]

By contrast, the desired culture needed to be based on 'no blame' and positive mutual support:

Organisations need to carefully develop an environment built on trust with their own staff. It is important to ensure that your staff members are working in the manner in which you would wish to know that your clients, business partners or users are being treated. This practice can only start in the Chief Executive's office. The leadership of the Chief Executive and consequently the Board to the operational teams will in the end define the manner in which your customers are treated. For example, arrogance, contempt, rudeness and bullying will be experienced by your users if this is what is applied to staff members on a daily basis from the top! Conversely, honesty, cooperation, leadership and humility will also be reflected if they are the leadership stance and will be deeply appreciated by the users and those who wish to complain or voice an opinion.[131]

The list of Recommendations included the following clear prescription of a no blame culture:

Despite all temptations to do otherwise in the face of a difficult and very public environment, ensure that a no blame culture is developed and maintained at all levels. This is the key to success ...[132]

The report stated that complaints represented less than 0.1 per cent of the total activity of NHS Wales, and reported patient safety incidents totalled less than one per cent of activity, but nevertheless represented a 'vast number' of people.[133] It expressed concern at the number of complainants who actually felt dissatisfied with their experience of the Putting Things Right (PTR) process or the care they had received.[134]

The greatest numbers of complaints fell consistently across the organisations into the following areas:[135]

- Clinical care and diagnosis
- Delays/cancellations/ appointments
- Waiting times

---

[128] ibid, paras 22
[129] ibid, para 44.
[130] ibid, para 46.
[131] ibid, para 30.
[132] ibid, Executive Summary, Recommendations, ninth bullet.
[133] ibid, para 64.
[134] ibid, para 18 (the number was 'quite disturbing to see').
[135] ibid, para 73.

- Communication
- Attitudes
- Admission/ transfer/ discharge

ii. *The Once for Wales Concerns Management System*

In response to recommendations in the Evans report the Welsh Government commissioned the Once for Wales Concerns Management System project.[136] This is part of the national safety programme and provides a range of integrated functions to support patient safety and patient experience in Wales, including:

- Incidents Reporting & Investigation
- Complaints Management & Investigation
- PTR & Redress Case Management
- Claims Management
- Learning from Deaths (Mortality Reviews, link to Medical Examiner activity)
- Intelligent Monitoring & Quality Indicator Dashboards
- Safety Alerts Management & Compliance Log
- Professional Regulatory Referrals Case Management
- Safeguarding (adults & children) Referrals Log
- Serious Incident Notification & Closure Portal
- WRP Reimbursement Requests Portal
- Healthcare Risk Management (Risk Register, Board Assurance Framework)

It is hosted by the Welsh Risk Pool and supported by the Welsh Government. The complaints and concerns management project aims to bring consistency to the digital complaints management tools used by Welsh NHS bodies, this includes the development of: a common code-set for complaints categorisation, process outcomes for complaints categorisation, and harm code-set for complaints categorisation.[137]

IV. NHS Complaints in Scotland

A. Scottish Public Service Complaints

In June 2006, Scottish Ministers commissioned Professor Lorne Crerar to evaluate the systems of regulation, audit and inspection, and complaints handling in Scottish public

---

[136] https://nwssp.nhs.wales/all-wales-programmes/once-for-wales-concerns-management-system/.
[137] See https://cwmtafmorgannwg.wales/Docs/Quality%2C%20Safety%20and%20Risk%20Committee/04%20August%202005%202019/3.4.1%20Appendix%201%20Concerns%20Data%20Submissions%20QSR%205%20Aug%202019.pdf.

services. His report, *The Crerar Report*, was published in September 2007.[138] *The Crerar Report* considered complaints handling as a strand of external scrutiny. It included proposals to improve complaints handling systems giving the public better access to redress and scrutiny. A key recommendation was a standardised complaints handling system for all public services, which would be implemented and overseen by the Scottish Public Services Ombudsman (SPSO).

A short-life working group was established, the Fit for Purpose Complaint System Action Group chaired by Douglas Sinclair, to set out the Government's response to *The Crerar Report*.[139] The Action Group's report (*The Sinclair Report*), published July 2008, contained proposals for simplifying public service complaints handling processes and streamlining the complaints handling landscape, including amalgamation of some complaints handling bodies.

In order for SPSO to deliver the standardised complaint handling procedures recommended in the *Crerar* and *Sinclair* reports legislation was needed. The Public Services Reform (Scotland) Act 2010[140] required SPSO to publish a statement of principles concerning the complaint handling procedures of specified authorities and gave SPSO the authority to publish Model Complaint Handling Procedures (MCHPs). The Act also required that SPSO monitor complaint handling practice, identify trends, promote best practice and encourage co-operation and sharing of best practice among listed authorities. SPSO set up an internal unit, the Complaints Standards Authority, to deliver these duties.

Various MCHPs were published over the next few years. In 2012 Further Education; Higher Education; Local Authority; and Registered Social Landlords MCHPs were published. In 2013 the Scottish Government, Scottish Parliament and associated public authorities MCHP was published. In 2013 the Social Work MCHP was published. The NHS was the last MCHP to be published in 2017. The NHS MCHP was developed using a partnership approach, led by a Steering Group involving the Scottish Public Services Ombudsman (SPSO) and representatives from across NHS Scotland including territorial boards, the Scottish Health Council, NHS Education for Scotland, NHS National Services Scotland, the National Prisoner Healthcare Network, primary care and the NHS Complaints Personnel Association Scotland (NCPAS). The independent Patient Advice and Support Service (PASS) and Healthcare Improvement Scotland public partners were also actively involved.

In 2018–19 all the MCHPs except the NHS one were reviewed and revised. In 2020 the Social Work MSP and the Local Authority MCHP were combined into one MCHP, the Local Authority MCHP.[141]

---

[138] Professor Lorne D Crerar, *THE CRERAR REVIEW The report of the Independent Review of Regulation, Audit, Inspection and Complaints Handling of Public Services in Scotland* (September 2007) available at www.gov.scot/binaries/content/documents/govscot/publications/independent-report/2007/09/crerar-review-report-independent-review-regulation-audit-inspection-complaints-handling/documents/0053093-pdf/0053093-pdf/govscot%3Adocument/0053093.pdf.

[139] See www.gov.scot/publications/crerar-review-government-response/.

[140] The Public Services Reform (Scotland) Act 2010, 2010 ASP 8, available at www.legislation.gov.uk/asp/2010/8/contents.

[141] If a complaint relates to a social work decision made by an Integrated Joint Board then the Integrated Joint Board should follow the MCHP for the Scottish Government, Scottish Parliament and Associated Public Bodies.

B. Scottish NHS Complaints Overview

Rights to make a complaint or provide feedback about NHS services in Scotland are grounded in the Patient Rights Act (Scotland) 2011 and subsidiary legislation,[142] which introduced the Charter of Patient Rights and Responsibilities.[143] The Charter provides a high-level summary of rights and responsibilities. In March 2012 the Scottish Government published *Can I Help You? Guidance for Handling and Learning from Feedback, Comments, Concerns or Complaints About NHS Health Care Services*,[144] which provides guidance on day to day complaint handling. The aim of the 2011 Act and supporting legislation was two-fold. First, to consolidate and codify the rights of patients to give feedback, raise concerns and to complaint. Second, to place a responsibility on the NHS in Scotland to encourage, monitor, take action and share learning derived from the information they receive from patients. To facilitate these aims the 2011 Act established the Patient Advice and Support Service (PASS)[145] to provide patients and the public with advocacy and support services and to raise awareness among patients and the public of their rights and responsibilities contained within the Charter. The Charter encourages not just complaints, other forms of feedback are encouraged, for example the Care Opinion website[146] is an independent, not-for-profit organisation where individuals can post anonymous stories about the healthcare received.

C. Scottish NHS Complaints Processes and Parameters

The procedure for making a complaint about the NHS in Scotland is laid out on the NHSinform website.[147] If a complaint is about a GP then the requirements of the National Health Service (General Medical Services Contracts) (Scotland) Regulations 2018/66[148] should be incorporated into the complaints procedure. Briefly, complaints can be made by a patient/former patient, anyone who is affected or is likely to be affected, by an act or omission of the NHS in Scotland, a parent/guardian on behalf of a child,[149] a person acting on

---

[142] Patient Rights (Scotland) Act 2011, 2011 asp 5, available at www.legislation.gov.uk/asp/2011/5/contents; Patient Rights (Complaints Procedure and Consequential Provisions) (Scotland) Amendment Regulations 2016, SSI 2016 No 401 available at www.legislation.gov.uk/ssi/2016/401/introduction/made and the Patient Rights (Feedback, Comments, Concerns and Complaints) (Scotland) Directions 2017.

[143] www.gov.scot/publications/charter-patient-rights-responsibilities-2/.

[144] The Scottish Government, *Can I Help You? Guidance for Handling and Learning from Feedback, Comments, Concerns or Complaints about NHS Care* (Edinburgh, 2012) available at www.gov.scot/binaries/content/documents/govscot/publications/advice-and-guidance/2012/03/help-guidance-handling-learning-feedback-comments-concerns-complaints-nhs-health-care-services/documents/00390974-pdf/00390974-pdf/govscot%3Adocument/00390974.pdf.

[145] PASS is provided by Citizens Advice Service, see www.cas.org.uk/pass.

[146] www.careopinion.org.uk/.

[147] www.nhsinform.scot/care-support-and-rights/health-rights/feedback-and-complaints/feedback-complaints-and-your-rights.

[148] Parts 6 and 7 and Schedule 8 of the National Health Service (General Medical Services Contracts) (Scotland) Regulations 2018/66 (Scottish SI). SSSI 2018 No 66, available at www.legislation.gov.uk/ssi/2018/66/contents.

[149] If a child is in local authority care then the local authority may make a complaint.

behalf of a competent adult with that adult's consent or anyone, or if the patient is an adult who is incapable of making a complaint, a relative or 'other adult person who has an interest in their welfare' can complain on their behalf.[150]

Local resolution is the first stage. If a complainant remains dissatisfied after attempting local resolution they have recourse to PHSO. In the first instance complainants should discuss the matter with the staff involved in the care to see if it can be resolved immediately. If this is not possible then a complaint can be made either verbally to a senior member of staff/Feedback and Complaints Officer at the NHS organisation involved or in writing. Complaints should contain the name and address of the patient (and the complainant if it is a third-party complaint), details of the cause the of concern and information on what resolution is being sought.

Complaints must be made within six months of the incident or within six months of the complainant becoming aware of the incident, with a 12-month longstop. There is discretion on these time limits.

Complaints can be resolved either by Early Resolution or by Investigations and so are categorised into three groups depending upon the nature of the complaint and the action sought by the complainant.

Stage 1: Early Resolution. This process is for straightforward complaints that can be resolved to the satisfaction of the complainant within five working days. Stage 1 complaints do not require the organisation to send a written response or to carry out an investigation. If the Complaints Officer thinks it will help to resolve the complaint this period can be extended to 10 working days. Complaints handled in this way must be recorded to support organisational learning.

Stage Two: Escalated applies to complaints where early resolution has been attempted but the complainant remains dissatisfied and requests an investigation.

Stage Two: Investigation applies to claims which should progress straight to an investigation without attempting Early Resolution because the issues raised are complex and require detailed investigation or because the complaint relates to serious, high-risk or high-profile issues. Complaints which are to be investigated must be acknowledged in writing within three working days. The acknowledgement must contain: contact details for the Feedback and Complaints Officer; details of advice and support available, including PASS; contact details for SPSO and information on their role; and a statement confirming either that the complaint will be investigated withing 20 working days or an explanation of why this is not possible.

Complainants and clinicians who are the subject of a complaint should be kept informed throughout the investigation and clinicians should be given the opportunity to discuss the issues with the complainant. A full response to the complaint should be sent within 20 working days. The full response should: demonstrate that staff have looked into the complaint; reply to the points made in the complaint; offer an apology if appropriate; explain what

---

[150] In these circumstances the healthcare provider should also take account of the Adults with Incapacity (Scotland) Act 2020 (2000 ASP 4, available at www.legislation.gov.uk/asp/2000/4/contents) and the views of a welfare attorney if one has been appointed.

actions have been/will be taken to prevent reoccurrence; if there are aspects of the complaint that the NHS cannot do any more about this should be explained; and offer the chance to discuss anything in the letter that the complainant does not understand.

Where multiple NHS bodies are the subject of a complaint these bodies are expected to cooperate and coordinate to produce a joint response. Similarly, if a complaint involves the NHS and another public body they should cooperate and coordinate to produce a joint response.

NHS bodies are required to consider the use of alternative dispute resolution to resolve complaints in cases where both parties agree and ADR is considered appropriate. This usually takes the form of mediation or conciliation.

Healthcare providers have a duty to inform the health board information about their complaints every quarter. They should detail the number of complaints received, whether the response was provided within the 20-day timescale, the key themes and any action taken to improve services.

Certain types of complaints are not covered by the arrangements under the Patients Rights (Scotland) Act 2011. These are detailed in The Patient Rights (Complaints Procedure and Consequential Provisions) (Scotland) Regulations 2012.[151] They include:

– a complaint by an NHS body about another NHS body;
– a complaint by a service provider about the contractual arrangements under which that service provider provides health services;
– a complaint by an NHS employee relating to that employee's contract of employment;
– a complaint which is being or has been investigated by the SPSO;
– a complaint about an alleged failure to comply with an FOI request;
– a complaint about which the complainant has stated in writing that the complainant intends to take legal proceedings;
– a complaint about which a responsible body is taking or proposing to take disciplinary proceedings against the person who is the subject of the complaint; or
– a complaint which has previously been investigated.

While NHS bodies are not required to apply the complaints framework in these cases there is some flexibility. Where the complainant has indicated they intend to take legal action, an NHS body may still decide to investigate the complaint if they feel it would be helpful.

i. Overview of Scottish Complaints Data

From 1 April 2018 to 31 March 2019 there were 31,849 complaints made to NHS Scotland.[152] The majority, 80.9 per cent, of stage one complaints are fully closed within five days. For claims that are Stage 2 – Escalated only 57.2 per cent are fully closed within the required timeframe of 20 days. Similarly, just 55.1 per cent of Stage 2 – Investigation claims are fully

---

[151] Part 3 Regulations 7 of The Patient Rights (Complaints Procedure and Consequential Provisions) (Scotland) Regulations 2012 SSI 2012 No 36, available at www.legislation.gov.uk/ssi/2012/36/regulation/7/made.
[152] www.isdscotland.org/Health-Topics/Quality-Indicators/NHS-Complaints-Statistics/Complaints-2019.asp.

closed within 20 days. The outcomes for complaints are given in Table 6, which shows the breakdown per stage.

Table 6 Scottish NHS complaint outcomes 2018–19

	Upheld	Partially Upheld	Not upheld	Total
Stage 1 Early Resolution	3,588	1,819	4,922	**10,329**
Stage 2 Escalated	509	585	483	**9,699**
Stage 2 Investigation	2,862	2,798	4,039	**1,626**

V. Conclusions: Complaints

The recurrent themes outlined above of the difficulty and complexity of complaining about NHS care in England go back years. A 2018 report by the Behavioural Insights Team found that almost half, 34 per cent of those who had made a claim against the NHS were unaware of how to make an official NHS complaint.[153] A 2007 National Audit Office Report on health and care services asserted that people found making a complaint too complex and that many complaints took too long to resolve,[154] and a 2008 Healthcare Commission review found that while many NHS complaints related to the fundamentals of good health-care, such as effective communication with patients, the attitude of staff, record-keeping, privacy and dignity, in 19 per cent of cases there was also a problem with the way in which the complaint had been handled.[155]

The various reports mentioned highlight the difficulty for patients in navigating the complaints system in England. A major causative issue noted was the fragmentation of complaints systems across the NHS, private healthcare and social care. The need for a clear pathway for complaints has been consistently raised, but remains uncreated.

In 2011 the Health Select Committee recommended that there should be a single point of access, by patients in relation to complaints against the NHS, provided by integrated complaints and advice teams.[156] This was not a new idea, it had been proposed in 2005 by Dame Janet Smith in the fifth Shipman Report. In their response, *Safeguarding Patients*[157] the Department of Health were clear:

> We accept that many patients are confused about how and where to make a complaint on a health-care matter, and in particular about the role of the regulatory bodies. This has many causes: the UK healthcare system itself is complex, and media coverage of high profile GMC cases may encourage

---

[153] Behavioural Insights Team, *Behavioural Insights into Patient Motivation to Make a Claim for Clinical Negligence: Final Report by the Behavioural Insights Team* (August 2018).

[154] *Making Experiences Count: A New Approach to Responding to Complaints* (Department of Health, 2007).

[155] *Feeding Back? Learning from Complaints Handling in Health and Social Care* (National Audit Office, 2008).

[156] Health Select Committee, *Complaints and Litigation* Sixth Report of Session 2010–11, HC 786-1, 22 June 2011, available at https://publications.parliament.uk/pa/cm201012/cmselect/cmhealth/786/786i.pdf.

[157] *Safeguarding Patients. The Government's Response to the Recommendations of the Shipman Inquiry's Fifth Report and to the Recommendations of the Ayling, Neale and Kerr/Haslam Inquiries*, HMSO London, February 2007, available at https://assets.publishing.service.gov.uk/government/uploads/system/uploads/attachment_data/file/228872/7015.pdf.

patients to think that the regulatory bodies have a wider remit than is the case. In any case, most people see the NHS as a single system and assume – quite reasonably – that, once a complaint is lodged at any point, 'the system' will deal with it.

However, they rejected a portal in favour of MOUs between complaint handling bodies.

> We are therefore sympathetic to the Shipman Inquiry's proposal for a single 'portal' for submitting complaints. Experience suggests that however well such a 'portal' is advertised, patients will still continue to submit complaints by a variety of routes. What is needed therefore is a set of common standards for all healthcare and regulatory bodies to ensure that, wherever a complaint is submitted, it is promptly redirected to the appropriate body.

What is clear is that a dozen years later the IMMDS Review chaired by Baroness Julia Cumberlege found that 'Patients struggle to navigate the complaints system and it may take some time to find the correct organisation to complain to … patients described being "broken" by this journey'.

The Department of Health's preferred approach does not seem to have worked in practice. It is arguable that patients submit their complaints by a variety of routes because the system is so complex and difficult to navigate. Another potential barrier is seen in England where the rules require that complaints are made out in writing.

Even when a patient has raised a complaint there is no guarantee that it will be dealt with effectively, in their 2020 report *Making Complaints Count* PHSO sets out their expectations for effective complaints handling, and concludes

> Analysis of our casework often tells us not all organisations meet these expectations. There are many reasons for this, but a recurring theme in our research is that investigations are often carried out by staff who have limited or no training, or who lack appropriate support to carry out this important role. This often leaves them under significant pressure.

If an organisation is not delivering on its core complaint handling objectives that is likely to discourage individuals from raising a concern, as there is little point in doing so, which defeats the purpose of the system. In England the new NHS Complaints Standards Framework attempts to raise the level of poor performer and provide a consistently high level of complaint handling across the NHS. This is far too new to evaluate, but it is worth noting that this will work within the existing complaints rules, so only encompassing written complaints and putting the onus on the individual to make a formal complaint. Wales and Scotland have gone further than England by embedding a Complaints Standards Authority function within their ombudsmen so that the quality of complaint handling can be centrally monitored.

In Wales there is a significant focus on capturing concerns. The system extends complaints and personal injury claims by wrapping them into a wider structure based on 'concerns'. This is intended to provide a single and consistent method for grading and investigating concerns.[158] The focus on concerns came from the fact that concerns of patients, relatives and staff at Mid-Staffs were not picked up or were ignored. In response, Wales created a new regulatory structure to capture concerns and ensure that they are dealt with,

---

[158] A framework for grading concerns is at *Putting Things Right: Guidance on Dealing with Concerns from the 1st April 2011* (3rd Version, Welsh Government, 2013) Appendix I.

with internal and external responses. Written into the legislation was a requirement to assist those who might struggle, such as children, with raising their concerns.

The Once for Wales Concerns Management System is relatively new and it is too early to determine its effectiveness, but *prima facie* it has removed one of the obstacles to raising a complaint – identifying where to raise it. It has also done away with the requirement that a complaint must be in writing. It has shifted some of the onus onto staff to recognize and record concerns, removing potential barriers from patients. Most importantly it emphasises that complaints are a 'gift'[159] to be valued.

However, the system is not without problems in continuing to be based on tort law, and to need considerable internal expertise. The continuation of the negligence system's use of the 'responsible body of medical opinion' (*Bolam/Bolitho*) test[160] affords a relatively solid defence for clinicians against a finding of liability and as Vivienne Harpwood has said, the continued focus on the performance of the clinician, as opposed to the system as a whole, threatens efforts to encourage a culture of openness.[161]

It may be queried whether the whole Welsh structure, and the focus on concerns, results in a system that is too bureaucratic and burdensome? Well-run organisations should not need excessive bureaucracy, such as a requirement to investigate every concern to the full, and record findings in detailed writing. If the concern is with poorly run organisation, does the real remedy to the organisational culture lie elsewhere than in simply imposing considerable bureaucracy?

It remains to be seen whether the system improves learning, provides a more human face to patients, supports a better culture amongst healthcare professionals, reduces delays in responding to concerns or injuries and reduces overall cost.

The Welsh Redress system can deliver both learning and more comprehensive redress including financial redress. The Welsh Redress system aims to contribute to learning from errors. This scheme does not set out how lessons are to be fed back to organisations, managers and clinicians, but it does provide a mechanism to investigate matters of concern and to produce a report on causes and steps to be taken. Responsibility for these tasks is given to particular individuals.

Welsh Redress set out to herald a new culture of openness, in support of a policy articulated in so many policy documents of apologising when necessary for adverse outcomes and offering explanations about what had occurred.[162] At first sight, there should be advantages in the attempt to integrate redress into the complaints/concerns system. Such integration should make administrative sense by avoiding separate tracks, and hence capturing all the information that will be necessary for learning. It also provides more comprehensive response to the needs of those affected, delivering a caring response as well as financial provision.

---

[159] Ironically in German the word 'gift' means poison.

[160] *Bolam v Friern Hospital Management Committee* [1957] 1 WLR 583; *Bolitho v City and Hackney Health Authority* [1997] 3 WLR 1151.

[161] V Harpwood, 'Clinical Negligence and Poor Quality Care: Is Wales "Putting Things Right?"' in PR Ferguson and GT Laurie (eds), *Inspiring a Medico-Legal Revolution: Essays in Honour of Sheila McLean* (Ashgate, 2015).

[162] ibid. At the time, see *Interim Guidance on the Handling of Concerns in the NHS Wales Structure* (NHS Wales, 2009) 5.

However, the system is not without problems in continuing to be based on tort law, and to need considerable internal expertise. It has been pointed out that the continuation of the negligence system's use of the 'responsible body of medical opinion' (*Bolam/Bolitho*) test[163] continues to afford a relatively solid defence for clinicians against a finding of liability.[164]

The use of the *Bolam/Bolitho* test through the adversarial system has provided in many cases both a high and complex barrier for patients to overcome, and an objective robust scrutiny process. Can it be said that decisions by administrators who are employees of the very body that is to pay any liability will be, or seen to be, independent and trustworthy?[165] Will internal examination within the NHS be seen as independent and trustworthy?[166] Will decisions be biased? Will internal power games emerge between investigators and clinicians, which obstruct the truth? It has already been found that the need to train staff who are sufficiently expert in the various complexities of clinical negligence law has produced significant strains and inconsistencies in decisions. The system aims to guard against this by referring injured patients to a private sector solicitor, paid for by the NHS. But the fees for such work are restricted,[167] and it may be that the lack of detailed adversarial experience will reduce the expertise of such third parties, and their limited role and funding may prevent adequate attention being given to whether complete evidence or expert views have been deployed in the NHS body's internal investigation. The third party's role is merely to give an opinion, not to carry out such further investigations as appear necessary.

This system carries the problems that it attempts partial incremental changes to an adversarial system without creating a fully independent inquisitorial system. A more radical embrace of independent inquisitorialism might solve more problems as well as provide financial economies.

There is a particular dearth of information on the financial efficiency of complaints. It is difficult enough to establish how much the service costs per claim handled, it is much harder to ascertain the value of these services in a more holistic sense.

Various reviews and inquiries have highlighted deficiencies in the complaints process, and while the UK Ombudsmen all provide external oversight of complaint handling they do not provide any financial oversight. PHSO attribute unsatisfactory complaint handling, at least in part, to complaint handling staff having limited or no training and/or insufficient support.[168] Improving complaint handling will require considerable investment both, financial and non-financial, in complaint handling staff. However, complaint handling is a non-frontline service and given the backlog and pressures on the NHS due to COVID it seems likely that any investment will focus on front line services.

---

[163] *Bolam v Friern Hospital Management Committee* [1957] 1 WLR 583; *Bolitho v City and Hackney Health Authority* [1997] 3 WLR 1151.

[164] V Harpwood, 'Clinical Negligence and Poor Quality Care: Is Wales "Putting Things Right?"' in PR Ferguson and GT Laurie (eds), *Inspiring a Medico-Legal revolution: Essays in Honour of Sheila McLean* (Ashgate, 2015).

[165] A-M Farrell and S Devaney, 'Making Amends or Making Things Worse? Clinical Negligence Reform and Patient Redress in England' (2007) 27(4) *Legal Studies* 630.

[166] S Taylor, *Medical Accident Liability and Redress in English and French Law* (Cambridge University Press, 2015) 17.

[167] A tariff is at *Putting Things Right: Guidance on Dealing with Concerns from the 1st April 2011* (3rd Version, Welsh Government, 2013) Appendix O.

[168] PHSO *Making Complaints Count* 2020 available at read://https_www.ombudsman.org.uk/?url=https%3A%2F%2Fwww.ombudsman.org.uk%2Fpublications%2Fmaking-complaints-count-supporting-complaints-handling-nhs-and-uk-government.

8

UK Health Service Ombudsman

I. The UK Ombudsman Landscape

The growth in the administrative and regulatory powers of the state in areas such as finance, welfare, immigration, licensing, etc drove the creation of a complaint mechanism for those who felt they had not been treated fairly and competently.[1] In 1967 the Parliamentary Commissioner for Administration (PCA), more commonly known as the Parliamentary Ombudsman or PHSO was created.[2] Initially this role encompassed the entire UK. Subsequently, devolution has led to the creation of the Scottish Public Services Ombudsman (SPSO) and the Public Services Ombudsman for Wales.

II. The Parliamentary Ombudsman Background

The PHSO can investigate complaints about central government departments and other public bodies in the UK.[3] Three major impediments have hampered the effectiveness of the Ombudsman: the need for complainants to access the Ombudsman through their Member of Parliament for complaints about government departments and agencies; the jurisdiction of the Ombudsman being based on 'maladministration', which limits complaints to how decisions were reached rather than being able to review the fairness of decisions themselves;[4] and the fact that Ombudsman's recommendations are not binding.[5]

---

[1] L Webley and H Samuels, *Complete Public Law Text, Cases, and Materials* (Oxford University Press, 2009) ch 13; M Seneviratne, *Ombudsman in the Public Sector* (Open University Press, 1994). In 2009, the highest number of complaints the government departments are receiving were the Department for Work and Pensions (especially the Child Support Agency and Jobcentre Plus) and HM Revenue and Customs (especially the tax credit system): *Small Mistakes, Big Consequences* (Parliamentary and Health Service Ombudsman, 2009). A decade later in *The Ombudsman's Casework Report 2019* the four central government departments and their public-facing agencies receiving the most complaints were the Department for Work and Pensions (DWP), the Ministry of Justice (MoJ), the Home Office (HO) and Her Majesty's Revenue and Customs (HMRC).

[2] Introduced by The Parliamentary Commissioner Act 1967.

[3] www.ombudsman.org.uk/.

[4] The maladministration must have resulted in an injustice to the complainant that has not been put right. Maladministration refers to a fault in the way an organisation made a decision. Healthcare decisions also include service failure, see Section III, 'Health Service Ombudsman Background' below.

[5] The absence of an appeal from the Parliamentary Ombudsman's decisions, for example by a public authority which believes a mistake has been made, has been criticised: R Kirkham, B Thompson and T Buck, 'When Putting Things Right Goes Wrong: Enforcing the Recommendations of the Ombudsman' [2008] *Public Law* 510.

III. Health Service Ombudsman Background

The Parliamentary Ombudsman also holds the position of the Health Service Ombudsman, dealing with complaints against the health service.[6] A statutory position has existed since 1977.[7] The Health Service Commissioners Act 1993, which replaced previous legislation, set out the provisions for a Health Service Ombudsmen for England, Scotland and Wales.[8] Since devolution, separate legislation has been enacted for complaints about the National Health Service in Scotland and Wales.[9]

The 1993 Act gives the Health Service Ombudsman a wider jurisdiction than just maladministration; he is able to investigate complaints from or on behalf of someone who has suffered hardship or injustice resulting from: a failure in a service provided by a health service body; a failure of such a body to provide a service which it was a function of the body to provide; or maladministration connected with any other action taken by or on behalf of such a body. Unlike the Parliamentary jurisdiction, members of the public can lodge complaints directly with the Health Service Ombudsman.

A. Overview of PHSO's Activity

In 2018–19[10] the PHSO handled 112,262 enquiries, of these 82,998 were redirected to other more appropriate agencies and 29,841 were accepted by PHSO as complaints.[11] The vast majority of PHSO's caseload relates to healthcare complaints, of the 29,841 complaints 78 per cent were healthcare complaints. When looked at in more detail 24,183 of these complaints either were not ready for the PHSO or the PHSO could not take them forward. The PHSO reached a decision on the remaining 5,658 complaints. In 444 cases the complainant agreed that the issue had been resolved without the need for an investigation. An assessment decision was reached in 1,425 cases. These cases are closed without an investigation because there would be no benefit to an investigation, for example, this could be because an organisation has already taken actions to rectify their mistakes or there have not been any service failings in that case. An investigation was carried out in 1,617 cases. Of these investigations in 871 cases the complaint was not upheld, and in 746 cases the complaint was either fully or partially upheld. PHSO's net operating costs for 2018–19 were £27 million.

---

[6] A drawback here is that the statutory basis of each jurisdiction, and procedures, differ. In 2007 closer operational working between the Parliamentary Ombudsman, the Health Service Ombudsman and the Local Government Ombudsman was facilitated by their being permitted to share information, work jointly on cases with the complainant's consent and to issue joint reports: Regulatory Reform (Collaboration etc between Ombudsmen) Order 2007/1889.

[7] Health Service Act 1977 c 49 available at www.legislation.gov.uk/ukpga/1977/49/contents/enacted and the Health Service (Scotland) Act 1978 ch 29 available at www.legislation.gov.uk/ukpga/1978/29/contents.

[8] Health Service Commissioners Act 1993 ch 46 available at www.legislation.gov.uk/ukpga/1993/46/contents.

[9] The Scottish Public Services Ombudsman Act 2002 and the Public Services Ombudsman (Wales) Act 2005.

[10] While there are figures available from PHSO's 2019–20 Annual Report these have been affected by the COVID-19 pandemic. Therefore figures from *The Ombudsman's Annual Report and Accounts 2018–19* (Parliamentary and Health Service Ombudsman, 2019) are used here as they are more representative. Available at www.ombudsman.org.uk/sites/default/files/PHSO_Annual_Report_and_Accounts_2018-2019.pdf.

[11] These are the figures as given in PHSO's 2018–19 report *ibid*. The complaints handled in 2018–19 is a combination of complaints that carried over from previous years and new complaints recorded in 2018–19 (29,264).

In 2018–19 the PHSO closed 39 per cent of complaints within 13 weeks, 71 per cent within 26 weeks and 91 per cent within 52 weeks.[12] The average time to close a complaint was 158 days.

Table 1 Recommendations made by PHSO in 2018–19

Number	Action recommended by PHSO
510	Formal Apology
450	Service improvement
345	Payments
103	Other actions for putting things right.

Table 1 details the recommendations made by the PHSO in 2018–19. Service improvements can include actions such as changing procedures or training staff. Payments are intended to make up for financial loss or to recognise the impact of what went wrong. Payments totalled £236,038.18 from NHS organisations, and £16,435.00 from UK government departments and other UK public organisations. Other actions to put things right can include a variety of measures, for example, asking a government department to review a decision, or asking a GP practice to correct errors in medical records. As stated earlier the Ombudsman's recommendations are non-binding, but are generally adhered to.

From 30 April 2021 PHSO began to routinely publish its investigations including those cases where serious mistakes have been made and not readily admitted nor addressed. Prior to this only a selection of investigations had been published to showcase the breadth of work undertaken by PHSO. The intention behind the increased publication is to provide a learning tool for the NHS and government bodies by illustrating what has gone wrong and what needs to be addressed to prevent reoccurrence.

B. PHSO's Process for Healthcare Complaints

The procedure is contained in the 1993 Act[13] and is explained in detail on the Ombudsman's website.[14] Briefly the ombudsman can only investigate a complaint made in writing by either the aggrieved party, or if the individual is deceased or unable to act for himself by his personal representative, a member of his family or a suitable body or person. Complaints must be related to service failure or maladministration. Generally, the ombudsman cannot investigate cases where the complainant has not exhausted the NHS complaints process or where the complainant has a right to take an action in a Tribunal or Court of Law. Complaints should be brought to PHSO within a year of the individual becoming aware of the issue that is being complained about, though there is some discretion over this time limit.

PHSO are responsive only, they cannot instigate an investigation on their own initiative. This contrasts with the situation in Northern Ireland and Wales where the national

---

[12] ibid.

[13] Sections 4, 9, and 11 of the 1993 Health Service Commissioners Act.

[14] www.ombudsman.org.uk/__data/assets/pdf_file/0003/1011/Bringing-a-complaint-to-the-Health-Service-Ombudsman.pdf.

ombudsmen have their own initiative investigatory powers. Over the past few years PHSO have proposed that they should have their own initiative posers, to date these powers have not been granted.

Following introduction of the NHS's new complaints system in 2009, the number of health enquiries received by the Ombudsman almost tripled in comparison with the previous year. The complaint statistics for 2008–09 to 2018–19 are summarised at Tables 2 and 3 (in two Tables because the details published have changed). Figures for 2019–20 have not been included in this analysis as PHSO temporarily halted NHS complaints and investigations during this time due to the COVID-19 pandemic. It will be seen that the Ombudsman accepts for investigation only a very limited number of the complaints that are received. As Tables 2 and 3 demonstrates the PHSO engaged in a five-year programme to significantly increase the number of cases it accepts, changing the criteria for investigation from 'clear evidence that something went wrong' to signs that there is a case to answer.[15]

Table 2 Health complaints received and accepted by the NHS Ombudsman 2008–13

	2012–2013		2011–2012		2010–2011		2009–2010		2008–09	
Number of complaints:	received	accepted	received	accepted	received	accepted	received	accepted	received	accepted
NHS hospital, specialist and teaching trust	8,086	229	7,403	222	6,924	177	6,304[16]	195[17]	2,142[18]	80[19]
GP	3,319	86	2,951	82	2,581	66	2,419	57	891	15
Primary care trusts	2,071	30	2,247	28	2,714	54	2,411	30	810	16
Mental health, social care and learning disability trusts	1,839	28	1,560	26	1,356	20	1,393[20]	26[21]	510[22]	15[23]
Strategic health authorities	193	8	175	2	240	6		16		

(continued)

[15] *RESOLVE: News from the Ombudsman Service* (PHSO, December 2015); *The Ombudsman's Annual Report and Accounts 2014-15* (Parliamentary and Health Service Ombudsman, 2015) HC 570. The number of cases assessed (looked at in depth) by the PHSO increased in two years from 400 to over 4,000.

[16] Foundation trusts 2,672; non-foundation trusts 3,632.

[17] Foundation trusts 69; non-foundation trusts 126.

[18] Foundation trusts 813; non-foundation trusts 1,329.

[19] Foundation trusts 34; non-foundation trusts 46.

[20] Foundation trusts 798; non-foundation trusts 595.

[21] Foundation trusts 14; non-foundation trusts 12.

[22] Foundation trusts 232; non-foundation trusts 278.

[23] Foundation trusts 6; non-foundation trusts 9.

Table 2 *(Continued)*

	2012–2013		2011–2012		2010–2011		2009–2010		2008–09	
General dental practitioners	1,236	13	1,037	16	707	0	659			
Other	1,225[24]	64[25]	963[26]	24[27]	544[28]	6[29]	1,243[30]	22[31]	731[32]	10[33]
Healthcare commission			1		36				1,696	153
Total	17,969	426	16,337	400	15,066	329	14,429	346	6,780	289

Table 3 Inquiries and investigations by PHSO into NHS complaints 2013–19

	2018/19	2017/18	2016/17	2015/16	2014/15	2013/14
Healthcare Inquiries received by PHSO	23,293	24,664	22,965	21,406	20,109	17,964
Total number of NHS investigations carried out by PHSO	1,722	2,232	3,297	3,346	3,472	3,075
Completed NHS investigations	*	2,355	3,715	3,185	3,275	1,778

* This information is not given in PHSO's 2018/19 annual report

In December 2015 the PHSO reported that 'too many unresolved complaints are being brought to us which could be resolved by public services locally' and 'People bring their unresolved complaints to us because they want an explanation, an apology and for the service to improve for others'.[34] This remains a consistent theme, as can be seen in Table 3 the number of inquiries is far in excess of the number of investigations PHSO pursues.

[24] Ambulance Trusts 347, Care Trusts 257, Independent providers 415, Opticians 37, Other health Authorities 18, Pharmacies 86, Special Health Authorities 57, Unknown 8.

[25] Ambulance Trusts 3, Care Trusts 7, Independent Providers 19, Optician 1, Other Health Authority1, Pharmacy 1, Special Health Authorities 0, Unknown 0.

[26] Ambulance Trusts 262, Care Trusts 235, Independent providers 272, Opticians 32, Other health Authorities 21, Pharmacies 91, Special Health Authorities 49, Unknown 1.

[27] Ambulance Trusts 7, Care Trusts 2, Independent Providers 12, Optician 1, Other Health Authority 1, Pharmacy 1.

[28] Ambulance Trusts 226, Pharmacies, 97, Care Trusts 88, Special Health Authorities 79, Healthcare Commission 36, Opticians 18.

[29] Ambulance Trusts 4, Care Trusts 2.

[30] Ambulance Trusts 216, General dental practitioners, Pharmacies 62, Healthcare commission 531, Strategic health authorities 300, Special health authorities 85, Opticians 18, Care Trusts 31.

[31] Ambulance Trusts 12, General dental practitioners 9, Pharmacies 1, Healthcare commission 0, Special health authorities 0, Opticians 0, Care Trusts 0.

[32] Strategic health authorities 321, General dental practitioners 276, Ambulance Trusts 64, Special health authorities 37, Opticians 15, Care Trusts 12, Pharmacies 6.

[33] Strategic health authorities 5, General dental practitioners 3, Special health authorities 1, Care Trusts 1, Ambulance Trusts 0, Opticians 0, Pharmacies 0.

[34] *RESOLVE: News from the Ombudsman Service* (PHSO, December 2015).

C. A Unified Public Services Ombudsman for England

In 2015, following parliamentary[35] and civil service reports,[36] the Government announced its intention to create a single Public Service Ombudsman, embracing the remits of the Parliamentary Ombudsman, the Health Service Ombudsman, the Local Government Ombudsman and the Housing Ombudsman.[37] In his earlier report on reform, Robert Gordon suggested that a new Public Service Ombudsman could provide an 'open door' into the complaints system by taking receipt of any compliant and finding the right home for it, which was what the Public Service Ombudsman Wales was trying to achieve with Complaints Wales.[38] In response to all these reports, the Minister, Oliver Letwin, began his Foreword by stating

> Too often public services regard complaints as a nuisance. They are nothing of the sort. Rapid, effective redress does an enormous amount to restore the confidence of the individual user in the service about which he or she has complained. And intelligent analysis of patterns of complaints can do an equally enormous amount to identify and locate systemic defects in public services – and hence to prompt repair of these defects. When something goes wrong, our customers deserve not just an apology, but also action from the organisations concerned to repair the problem and to learn from the mistake.[39]

This view was reinforced by the Ombudsman in 2015 in one of the periodic reports the PHSO issues that give summaries of resolved cases and illustrate the types of issues that arise,[40] she commented:

> These cases show the impact that service failure can have on individuals and their loved ones. These case studies – which are a snapshot of our work – show the wide range of unresolved complaints we look at, many of which should be resolved by the organisations locally, without people having to refer the complaint to us. Good complaint handling has to start from the top, and leaders will recognise the valuable opportunities complaints provide to really improve the service they are delivering. Many people complain about public services to enable lessons to be learnt because they don't want the same thing to happen to somebody else.[41]

---

[35] Public Affairs Standing Committee, *Time for a People's Ombudsman Service*, Fourteenth Report of Session 2013–14, HC 655, 28 April 2014, www.publications.parliament.uk/pa/cm201314/cmselect/cmpubadm/655/655.pdf.

[36] R Gordon, *Better to Serve the Public: Proposals to Restructure, Reform, Renew and Reinvigorate Public Services Ombudsmen* (Cabinet Office, 2014).

[37] *A Public Service Ombudsman: Government Response to Consultation (Cabinet Office, 2015). See earlier A Public Service Ombudsman. A Consultation* (Cabinet Office, 2015).

[38] R Gordon, *Better to Serve the Public: Proposals to Restructure, Reform, Renew and Reinvigorate Public Services Ombudsmen* (Cabinet Office, 2014) para 80.

[39] ibid.

[40] *Report on Selected Summaries of Investigations by the Parliamentary and Health Service Ombudsman. October to November 2014* (Parliamentary and Health Service Ombudsman, 2015); *Report on Selected Summaries of Investigations by the Parliamentary and Health Service Ombudsman. December 2014 and January 2015* (Parliamentary and Health Service Ombudsman, 2015); see also *The Ombudsman's Annual Report and Accounts 2013–14. A Voice for Change* (Parliamentary and Health Service Ombudsman, 2015).

[41] Comment on the launch of the *Report on Selected Summaries of Investigations by the Parliamentary and Health Service Ombudsman. October to November 2014* (Parliamentary and Health Service Ombudsman, 2015 avaialble at www.ombudsman.org.uk/news-and-blog/news/ombudsmans-report-highlights-poor-complaint-handling-and-service-failures-across.

In response to the proposal for a unified public services ombudsman, the Parliamentary Ombudsman proposed that the design principles that should apply to a new Public Ombudsman Service should be those set out in Table 4.[42]

Table 4 Principles proposed by PHSO for a new Public Ombudsman Service

Independent, impartial and authoritative

- provides expert advice, insight and evidence to the Westminster Parliament in order to help it hold the executive to account
- independent of those subject to its jurisdiction
- sits at the apex of public service complaints systems.

Easily accessible

- simple to understand for the citizen and for those providing public services
- bridges the gap between central and local services, for example, health and social care, Defra and local authorities on sewage and land use, Ministry of Justice and local authorities on supporting victims of crime.

Comprehensive and coherent

- covers all UK public services accountable to the Westminster Parliament and all public services in England
- able to follow the public pound regardless of the status of the provider (that is, public, private, or third sector)
- provides a common approach to the investigation of complaints, ensuring that service providers do not get different adjudications from different ombudsmen.

Accountable

- modern and robust governance structure
- accountability model reflects the devolution settlement
- scrutiny of strategy and budget by the Westminster Parliament.

Better value for money

- best value for the public pound in terms of its own operations (for example, through avoiding duplication of functions between multiple ombudsmen and giving increased flexibility to meet shifting demand)
- best value for the public pound through the impact the service has on the delivery of public services as a whole
- simple and transparent funding arrangements that do not create perverse incentives for service providers.

While these proposals have been welcomed by PHSO and the Local Government Ombudsman there has been limited concrete progress. A draft Public Service Ombudsman Bill[43] was published in December 2016, but to date has not been taken further.

---

[42] Letter by Dame J Mellor to the Cabinet Office, 'Cabinet Office Consultation: A Public Service Ombudsman' (16 June 2015) at www.ombudsman.org.uk/__data/assets/pdf_file/0018/32652/2015-06-16-PHSO-response-to-Cabinet-Office-Ombudsman-Consultation.pdf.

[43] www.gov.uk/government/publications/draft-public-service-ombudsman-bill.

IV. Scottish Public Services Ombudsman (SPSO) Background

SPSO was created by an Act of the Scottish Parliament in 2002.[44] SPSO replaced three existing statutory bodies, the Scottish Parliamentary Ombudsman, the Health Services Ombudsman and the Local Government Ombudsman for Scotland. SPSO also absorbed the role of the non-statutory Housing Association Ombudsman for Scotland. A key aim of the creation of SPSO was to create a unified 'one stop shop' Public Services Ombudsman in Scotland. Subsequently SPSO has acquired two additional functions; they carry out independent reviews the Scottish Welfare Fund (decisions that councils make on community care and crisis grants) and they are the Independent National Whistleblowing Officer (the final stage in the process for those raising concerns about the NHS in Scotland).

A. Overview of SPSO's Activity

In 2018–19[45] the SPSO handled 1,707 enquiries which included general enquiries, enquiries about organisations that were not within jurisdiction and where a complaint had not been made out to a public body. Of these enquiries, 813 were redirected to other more appropriate agencies. In 2018–19 SPSO received 4,188 complaints and carried forward 595 complaints from previous years. The largest category of SPSO's caseload relates to healthcare complaints, of the 4,188 complaints 1,451 were healthcare complaints, see Table 5. In the previous year Local Authority complaints had been the largest category.

SPSO have a three-stage process. The initial stage is assessment, where SPSO check the claim is within jurisdiction, has completed the local complaint handling process and that they have sufficient information to take the matter forward. In 2018/19 3,285 of the 4,188 complaints SPSO received were closed after the initial assessment either because they were not ready for SPSO or SPSO could not take them forward. Of these 798 cases were premature, they had not exhausted the local complaint handling process. Claims must be made within one year of the person becoming aware of the issue, though there is some discretion.

Investigation follows the initial assessment and is split into two components: proportionality and investigation. An investigation can only proceed if it would be proportional to do so, so the first stage of the investigation phase is a proportionality assessment. If SPSO consider there would be no significant benefit to the complainant or the outcome desired is unachievable the case will be closed on the basis of proportionality. If a case is closed in this way SPSO do make some enquiries, but these fall short of a full investigation. These enquiries include checking that a public body delivers on any action that has been agreed to. In 2018/19 900 cases were closed after a proportionality assessment.

---

[44] Scottish Public Services Ombudsman Act 2002, 2002 ASP 11, available at www.legislation.gov.uk/asp/2002/11/contents.

[45] While there are figures available from SPSO's 2019–20 Annual Report these have been affected by the COVID-19 pandemic. Therefore figures from *SPSO's Annual Report and Accounts 2018-19* are used here as they are more representative. Available at www.spso.org.uk/sites/spso/files/communications_material/annual_report/SPSOAnnual%20Report2018-19PerformanceReport.pdf.

In cases where it would be proportional a full investigation follows. Complaints subject to investigation can be closed either by letter to the parties or by a full public investigation report if the case meets SPSO's public interest criteria. When closed by letter a provisional decision is sent to the parties, setting out our provisional views and inviting comments before reaching a final decision. For cases closed by a full public report both parties receive a draft for comment on factual accuracy before SPSO issue a final decision.

Either party can ask SPSO to review a decision closed by letter if they can show that either the decision was based on inaccurate facts, or that new and relevant information has become available and would affect the decision SPSO came to.

In 2018–19 SPSO closed 670 cases after full investigations.[46] From these investigations SPSO have an uphold rate of 58 per cent.[47] SPSO's net operating costs for 2018–19 were £4.9 million.[48]

Table 5 Complaints received by SPSO by sector in 2018–19

Sector	2018–19
Health (including prison health)	1,451
Local Authority	1,301
Housing Associations	323
Scottish Prison Service	313
Joint Health & Social Care	209
Scottish Government & Devolved Admin (excluding Scottish Prison Service)	181
Universities	164
Water	164
Other	50
Colleges	32
Total	**4,188**

In 2018–19 the SPSO met their complaints performance indicator 1 (PI-1) –100 per cent of advice stage complaints were handled within 10 working days. They did not quite achieve PI-2 – that 95 per cent of early resolution complaints should be decided or moved to complex investigation stage within 70 working days – their performance was at 89 per cent. The final performance indicator (PI-3) – that 95 of complaints investigations should be completed within 260 working days – was also narrowly missed, 97 per cent were completed within this timeframe.

---

[46] If provisional decisions are included (technically these are not counted as 'closed' cases) then 711 investigations were completed.

[47] This uphold figure includes provisional decisions, see n 46 above.

[48] See SPSO's Annual Accounts for 2018–19 available at www.spso.org.uk/sites/spso/files/communications_material/annual_accounts/SPSO2018-19AnnualReportAndAccounts.pdf.

Table 6 Recommendations made by SPSO in 2018–19

Recommendation type	Number
Complaint Handling	130

Individual recommendations (total)
    Breakdown
    – individual apology   – 342
    – individual financial   – 8
    – individual other   – 36
	386

Learning and improvement	644
Total	**1,160**

SPSO monitor compliance with their recommendations, compliance by sector is set out in Table 7 below, taken from their 2018/19 Annual Report. As stated earlier the SPSO's recommendations are non-binding, but are generally adhered to as can be seen from Table 7.

Table 7 SPSO recommendations compliance timescales

Authority Sector	Completed – Within Target	Completed – Over Target – under 3 months	Completed – Over Target – over 3 months	Total	% Within Target	% Within Target or within 3 months of target
Colleges	6	1	0	7	86%	100%
Health	467	478	54	999	48%	94%
Housing Associations	9	8	0	17	53%	100%
Joint Health and Social Care	40	15	9	64	63%	86%
Local Authority	131	57	10	198	66%	95%
Scottish Government & Devolved Administration	37	19	0	56	66%	100%
Universities	18	10	3	31	58%	90%
Water	2	1	2	5	40%	60%
Total	**710**	**589**	**78**	**1,377**	**52%**	**94%**

SPSO have set out in their 2018 Support and Intervention Policy[49] the follow-up support and interventions for organisations under their jurisdiction.

---

[49] www.spso.org.uk/news-and-media/support-and-intervention-policy.

V. The Public Services Ombudsman for Wales (PSOW) Background

The PSOW was created by the Public Services Ombudsman (Wales) Act 2005.[50] PSOW replaced four existing bodies, the statutory Welsh Administrative Ombudsman,[51] the Health Services Commissioner for Wales, the Social Housing Ombudsman for Wales and the Commissioner for Local Administration in Wales.[52] The Public Services Ombudsman (Wales) Act 2005 has been repealed and replaced by the Public Services Ombudsman (Wales) Act 2019 (PSOW 2019) which came into force on 22 May 2019.[53]

PSOW has two major functions: first, to consider complaints about public services providers in Wales; second, to consider complaints that members of local authorities have broken the Code of Conduct. The Public Services Ombudsman (Wales) Act 2019 gave PSOW the power to investigate on their own initiative.[54] Where the Ombudsman decides that the criteria for investigation are met[55] then he may undertake two types of investigations:

–   Extended Investigation: The extension of a matter already under investigation
–   Wider Investigation: A stand-alone investigation which does not relate to a complaint made by an individual

The trigger for PSOW involvement is maladministration: unless there has been delay, bias, neglect, turpitude etc on the listed authority's part, the Ombudsman cannot question that decision. The exception to this rule relating to health and social care complaints is set out in section 15(1) of the 2019 Act. It allows the Ombudsman to question the merits of a decision taken without maladministration if the decision is taken in consequence of the exercise of professional judgement which appears to the Ombudsman to be exercisable in connection with the provision of either health care or social care.

A. Overview of PSOW's Activity

In 2018–19[56] the PSOW handled 4,627 enquiries which included general enquiries, enquiries about organisations that were not within jurisdiction, and where a complaint had not been made out to a public body. In 2018–19 PSOW received 2,489 complaints and carried forward 557 complaints from previous years. These comprised 2,207 Public Body

---

[50] Public Services Ombudsman (Wales) Act 2005, 2005 c 10, available at www.legislation.gov.uk/ukpga/2005/10/contents.

[51] The Government of Wales Act 1998, 1998 c 38, available at www.legislation.gov.uk/ukpga/1998/38/contents.

[52] The Commission for Local Administration in Wales included the office of the Local Commissioner for Wales.

[53] Public Services Ombudsman (Wales) Act 2019, 2019 ANAW 3, available at www.legislation.gov.uk/anaw/2019/3/contents/enacted.

[54] Part 3, Section 4 of the Public Services Ombudsman (Wales) Act 2019, 2019 ANAW 3, available at www.legislation.gov.uk/anaw/2019/3/contents/enacted.

[55] The Criteria for Own Initiative investigations are available from the PSOW website, see www.ombudsman.wales/wp-content/uploads/2020/08/Document-1-OI-Criteria.pdf.

[56] While there are figures available from PSOW's 2019–20 Annual Report these have been affected by the COVID-19 pandemic. Therefore, figures from *PSOW's Annual Report and Accounts 2018-19* are used here as they are more representative. Available at www.ombudsman.wales/wp-content/uploads/2019/07/Annual-Report-and-Accounts-2018-2019-Final-ENG.pdf.

Complaints and 282 Code of Conduct Complaints.[57] The largest category of Public Body complaints by some margin were healthcare complaints at 41 per cent, Housing was the next largest group at 12 per cent.

PSOW have a three-stage process. The initial stage is assessment by the Complaints Assessment Team, who check the claim is within jurisdiction, that an alternative route of appeal or litigation is not an option, that it has completed the local complaint handling process, that it is within time and that there is merit in investigating the complaint and that resolution is possible. Some complaints are resolved by early resolution. If PSOW consider that the organisation being complained about could quickly take action to resolve the complaint then PSOW will contact them. If the organisation agrees to take that action forward then once either the action has taken place or it has been agreed to, PSOW will write to the complainant and close the case. In 2018/19 1,604 of the 2,207 Public Body complaints PSOW received were closed after the initial assessment. A further 322 were settled voluntarily, including 302 early resolutions.

Investigation follows the initial assessment. Complaints subject to investigation can be closed either by letter to the parties or by an investigation report. If PSOW consider it would be in the public interest then the report will be published. For cases closed by a full report both parties will generally receive a draft for comment on factual accuracy before PSOW issue a final decision.

Complainants can ask PSOW to review a decision closed by letter within 20 days of receiving it if they can show that PSOW failed to take proper account of the information provided or that new and relevant information has become available to consider.

In 2018–19 PSOW discontinued 12 investigations and closed 313 cases after full investigations. From these investigations PSOW have a full or partial uphold rate of 65 per cent (if settled cases are included as well as upheld cases the figure rises to 67 per cent).

Overall PSOW received 2,235 public services complaints in 2018/19, of which 532 (24 per cent) were either resolved or upheld. PSOW's net operating costs for 2018–19 were £4.2 million.[58]

PSOW have the targets set out in Table 8, which includes PSOWs 2018–19 performance against these targets. They did not hit any of their target measures, and have shown a downturn in performance compared to the previous year.

Table 8 PSOW's Complaint handling targets and performance for 2018–19

	Target maximum timeframe	Achieved 2018/19	Achieved 2017/18
Decision on whether complaint within jurisdiction/premature	3 weeks	83%	92%
Decision on whether or not to investigate, following detailed assessment	6 weeks	84%	89%
Where decision to seek early resolution without need to investigate, resolution achieved	9 weeks	85%	91%
Date sufficient information is received to Investigation start date	6 weeks	55%	74%

[57] Code of Conduct complaints are not particularly relevant to this chapter so will not be explored further. More details on these complaints can be found on the PSOW website and in the annual reports.
[58] See PSOW's *Annual Report and Accounts for 2018-19* available at www.ombudsman.wales/wp-content/uploads/2019/07/Annual-Report-and-Accounts-2018-2019-Final-ENG.pdf.

PSOW monitor compliance with their recommendations. As stated earlier the PSOW's recommendations are non-binding, but are generally adhered to. PSOW may decide to issue a public interest report including cases where there are wider issues from which others can learn; where what went wrong is significant or is ongoing and the investigation has highlighted systemic problems; the failures identified are ones that PSOW has identified previously and lessons haven't been learned or when a public body has refused to agree to PSOW's recommendations. During 2018/19 just 14 public interest reports were issued. In addition, PSOW may issue a Special Report under section 22 of the PSOW Act 2019 if a body fails to satisfactorily implement any recommendations made in a PSOW report, or fails to comply with the terms of a settlement. In 2018/19 PSOW issued one Special Report.

B. PSOW's Healthcare Complaints

Healthcare complaints make up the largest category of PSOW's Public Service complaints, and are increasing. Complaints about Welsh NHS Bodies increased by 9 per cent on the previous financial year – 1,007 in 2018/19 compared to 924 in 2017/18. This is the first time that the number of complaints about NHS bodies exceeded 1,000 in one year.

In the 2017/18 Annual report the Ombudsman reported that healthcare complaints are around five times more likely to require investigation than other public service complaints. This remained the case in 2018/19, and is attributed to the fact that PSOW are less likely to be able to resolve a complaint or reach a decision without securing additional information, including medical records. The Ombudsman describes these complaints as: 'they can be complex and time-consuming to investigate because, since I am able to consider professional judgement in health complaints, I frequently need to seek professional clinical advice to inform my decision making'.[59] This neatly illustrates the difference between the remit of the Ombudsman with relation to health care/social care complaints and other public service complaints.

Table 9 gives a breakdown of the complaints received and closed in 2018/19 for the seven health boards. It also details the number and proportion of complaints that were closed with a PSOW intervention. Interventions include both upholding a complaint and settling a complaint. Overall 39 per cent of healthcare complaints that were closed were either resolved or upheld, which is considerably higher than the 24 per cent that were resolved/upheld across all public service complaints.

Table 9 PSOW healthcare complaints by Health Board 2018/19

	Complaints received 2018/19	Complaints closed 2018/19	Complaints closed with a PSOW intervention	% intervention
Abertawe Bro Morgannwg University Health Board	139	139	54	39%
Aneurin Bevan University Health Board	134	128	49	38%

(continued)

[59] ibid.

Table 9 *(Continued)*

	Complaints received 2018/19	Complaints closed 2018/19	Complaints closed with a PSOW intervention	% intervention
Betsi Cadwaladr University Health Board	194	210	86	41%
Cardiff & Vale University Health Board	102	107	37	35%
Cwm Taf University Health Board	75	82	27	33%
Hywel Dda University Health Board	109	115	48	42%
Powys Teaching Health Board	26	17	10	59%
Powys Teaching Health Board – All-Wales Continuing Health Care cases		16	7	44%
Total	**779**	**814**	**318**	**39%**

* Powys Teaching Health Board figures exclude complaints relating to All-Wales Continuing Health Care cases which are shown separately.

VI. The Northern Ireland Public Ombudsman Services (NIPSO) Background

The NIPSO functions started in 1969 under the Commissioner for Complaints Act (Northern Ireland) 1969.[60] Subsequent amendments were detailed in the Commissioner for Complaints (Northern Ireland) Order 1996[61] and The Ombudsman (Northern Ireland) Order 1996.[62] These statutes have been replaced by the Public Services Ombudsman Act (Northern Ireland) 2016 which consolidated the previous duties and came into force on 19 February 2016.[63]

NIPSO has three major functions: first, to consider complaints about public services providers in Wales; second, to consider complaints that members of local authorities have broken the Northern Ireland Local Government Code of conduct for Councillors; third to consider complaints from applicants for judicial appointments of alleged maladministration by the Northern Ireland Judicial Appointments Commission or their committees.

---

[60] The Commissioner for Complaints Act (Northern Ireland) 1969 c 25 (NI).

[61] Commissioner for Complaints (Northern Ireland) Order 1996 1996/1287 (N.I. 7) available at www.legislation.gov.uk/nisi/1996/1297/contents.

[62] The Ombudsman (Northern Ireland) Order 1996, 1996/1298 (N.I. 8), available at www.legislation.gov.uk/nisi/1996/1298/contents.

[63] Public Services Ombudsman Act (Northern Ireland) 2016, c 4 2016, available at www.legislation.gov.uk/nia/2016/4.

NIPSO has a wide remit to consider complaints about public services providers in Northern Ireland including:[64] education, local authorities, central government, social housing and health and social care. The Public Services Ombudsman Act (Northern Ireland) 2016 gives the power to investigate on their own initiative.[65] Where the Ombudsman decides that the criteria for investigation are met[66] then he may undertake an investigation, the procedure for investigations is at the discretion of the Ombudsman.[67]

For non-health and social care claims the trigger for NIPSO involvement is maladministration.[68] The exception to this relates to health and social care complaints and is set out in sections 15(2), 16(2) and 17(2) of the 2016 Act. It allows the Ombudsman to question the merits of a decision taken without maladministration if the decision is taken in consequence of the exercise of professional judgement which appears to the Ombudsman to be exercisable in connection with the provision of either health care or social care.

A. Overview of NIPSO's Activity

In 2018–19[69] the NIPSO's Advice, Support Service and Initial Screening Team (ASSIST), who screen all the contacts and enquiries, classified 762 enquiries as warranting further analysis. The breakdown of the 762 enquiries is shown in Table 10, with Health and Social Care being by some margin the largest group.

Table 10 Breakdown of NIPSO enquiries by sector 2018/19

Sector	Number of Complaints	Percentage
Health and Social Care	310	40%
Government Departments and Agencies	143	19%
Education	90	12%
Local Councils	76	10%
Housing	74	10%
Other	69	9%
Total	**762**	**100%**

---

[64] See schedule 3 of the Public Services Ombudsman Act (Northern Ireland) 2016, c 4 2016, available at www.legislation.gov.uk/nia/2016/4.

[65] Section 29 of the Public Services Ombudsman Act (Northern Ireland) 2016, c 4 2016, available at www.legislation.gov.uk/nia/2016/4.

[66] See sections 14–18 of the Public Services Ombudsman Act (Northern Ireland) 2016, c 4 2016, available at www.legislation.gov.uk/nia/2016/4.

[67] Section 30 of the Public Services Ombudsman Act (Northern Ireland) 2016, c 4 2016, available at www.legislation.gov.uk/nia/2016/4.

[68] Section 23 of the Public Services Ombudsman Act (Northern Ireland) 2016, c 4 2016, available at www.legislation.gov.uk/nia/2016/4.

[69] While there are figures available from NIPSO's more recent Annual Report these have been affected by the COVID-19 pandemic. Therefore, figures from *NIPSO's Annual Report and Accounts 2018–19* are used here as they are more representative. Available at https://nipso.org.uk/site/wp-content/uploads/2019/07/Ombudsmans-Report-2018-19.pdf.

NIPSO have a three-stage process: initial assessment; assessment; investigation. The first two stages are dealt with by the ASSIST Team, the third stage by the Investigation Team.

Initial assessment. Enquiries would not be investigated further if they were not within NIPSO's jurisdiction, for example enquiries about organisations that were not within jurisdiction; those where a complaint had not been made out to a public body; those where more than six months had elapsed from the end of the complaints process, etc. This stage was completed in 10 working days in 93 per cent of cases.

Assessment. This stage involves the ASSIST team obtaining further information on the complaint, this may be from the complainant or the organisation concerned. This information will be used to determine if there is a prima facie case of maladministration. Some suitable complaints can be resolved by informal resolution known as settlement. Settlement could be an apology, an acknowledgement that something has gone wrong, a commitment to improve a service or reimbursement of expenses. If NIPSO consider that the organisation being complained about could quickly take action to resolve the complaint then the ASSIST team will contact them. In 2018/19 42 public body complaints NIPSO received were settled after the initial assessment. If settlement is not appropriate the assessment process will decide if an investigation would be proportionate, in the public interest and able to bring about a practical outcome.

Investigation. Investigation follows the initial assessment. In 2018/19 98 cases were referred for investigation and 73 investigations were completed. Investigations are carried out in private. A draft report is shared with complainant and the organisation for comment. If NIPSO consider it would be in the public interest then the report will be published in an anonymised form so complainant's cannot be identified. In 2018/19 27 investigation reports were published.

In 2018/19 NIPSO reported on 117 separate issues of complaint. 70 per cent were upheld or partially upheld, with 30 per cent not upheld.

NIPSO have the targets set out in Table 11, which includes NIPSO's 2018–19 performance against these targets. They hit or were close to all of their target measures in 2018/19.

Table 11 NIPSO's complaint handling KPIs and performance for 2018–19

Key Performance Indicator (KPI)	Target 2018/10	Achieved 2018/19
KPI 1 – measures how quickly NIPSO make a decision on whether they can accept a complaint for further assessment. NIPSO aim to inform the complainant within 2 weeks or less of their complaint being received in 90% of cases	90%	93%
KPI 2 – measures how quickly NIPSO decide on what action they can take on a complaint which has been accepted for assessment. They aim to complete this assessment and inform the complainant of the decision within 10 weeks of their complaint being received.	70%	70%
KPI 3 – measures how quickly NIPSO reach a decision on the investigation of a complaint and share the draft report with the body and the complainant. They aim to complete this within 50 weeks of the decision at KPI 2 being made.	70%	68%

B. NIPSO's Healthcare Complaints

Health and social care complaints make up the largest category of NIPSO's Public Service complaints. Table 12 gives a breakdown of the complaints received and determined in 2018/19. The 2018/19 Annual report shows that health and care complaints are more likely to require investigation than complaints about other Public Services, see Figure 1.

Table 12 NIPSO health and social care complaints by organisation and stage 2018/19

	Brought forward at 01/04/2018	Complaints received 2018/19	Determined at initial assessment	Determined at assessment	Determined at investigation	Carried forward at 31/03/2019
Health & Social Care trusts	104	242	105	84	41	116
Health Service providers	8	36	18	5	5	16
Independent Health & Social Care providers	3	5	2	0	1	5
Not Specified HC body	0	2	2	0	0	0
Public Health Agency	0	1	0	1	0	0
R H&S Care Board	3	4	3	2	2	0
RQIA	2	3	1	2	0	2
Private Nursing/Care Home	6	12	7	4	2	5
Business Services Organisation	0	5	4	0	0	1
Total	126	310	142	98	51	145

Figure 1 NIPSO determination profiles in 2018/19 by complained about sector

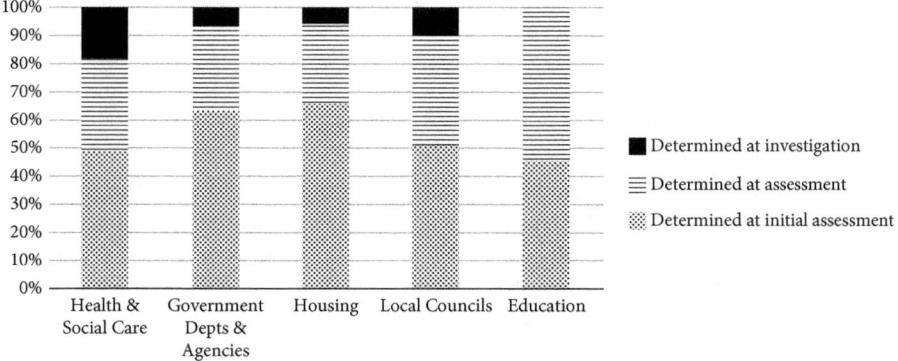

VII. Conclusions: Ombudsmen

The current two-stage model (local complaint handling as the first stage with an ombudsman as the second stage) has been subject to significant criticism. It is notable that a very large proportion of issues raised with ombudsmen are rejected, many of them because the individual has not been through the local complaints process. In his investigations into Mid-Staffs Sir Robert Francis found examples of barriers to people raising complaints. These included complaints being ignored or where they were prevented from raising issues for fear of provoking adverse consequences in the care delivered. These initial barriers then prevented the individual from raising their concerns with PHSO. As a consequence, HealthWatch was set up, its primary purpose is to provide a way to incorporate service users' voices into healthcare commissioning and delivery, as part of this remit, in conjunction with Citizens' Advice, they provide practical help for those making complaints. While greater support and signposting for those raising complaints is a positive development it needs to be supplemented by a change in attitudes so that those receiving the complaints also ensure that complaints are recorded and properly investigated. If the first stage is not working then a complainant is unable to progress. There is a risk that the eligibility criteria mean that rather than providing independent oversight the ombudsman acts to reinforce any deficiencies in the first tier complaint handling.

For patients who meet the requirements for an investigation by an ombudsman this can provide all of the desired outcomes that good complaint handling can provide including apologies, clarity on what happened and why, admissions of responsibility and the reassurance that improvements will be made. As the second tier complaint handler these outcomes can apply to both the healthcare provider and to their complaint handling staff. In addition, ombudsmen are able to provide financial redress. This serves two purposes, first to compensate the affected individual and second to act as a form of sanction on the organisation. In actuality the value of the compensation awarded by the UK Ombudsmen is minimal in comparison to the value of compensation awarded by clinical negligence litigation. In 2018–19 financial compensation awarded as a result of 345 recommendations made by PHSO totalled £252,473. Similarly, SPSO made only eight financial recommendations during 2018–19 from across their sectors.

A. Scotland and Wales

PHSO produce insight reports drawing on their findings on system failings related to specific topics, which are laid before parliament. What is less clear is the impact that these reports have. There is a clear difficulty for the PHSO as set out by their Chief Executive in an oral hearing before the Public Administration and Constitutional Affairs Select Committee as part of their scrutiny of the PHSO in 2018–19.[70]

> Once we have reported, we follow up with those bodies and see whether they have followed through with those recommendations. For some things like apologies or financial payments, we

---

[70] Question 39 Public Administration and Constitutional Affairs Committee: Oral Evidence: Parliamentary and Health Service Ombudsman Scrutiny, 2018–19, HC117, Monday 18 May, available at https://committees. parliament.uk/oralevidence/397/default/.

can check that those have happened. Where people are putting in place a long-term programme of change activity or service improvements, it is not our role. We are not a regulator. We are not able to go in and determine whether those have been followed through. We provide copies of our recommendations to the Care Quality Commission, and the Care Quality Commission has the opportunity in its inspections of those bodies, if they are health bodies, to see whether recommendations that are more systemic in nature and long-term have been followed through.

Compliance with ombudsman recommendations is generally high. PHSO's published compliance information demonstrates that the vast majority of recommendations they make are complied with; of the 1,266 recommendations closed in 2018–19 just 11 were not complied with. These included recommendations for formal apologies, financial recompense, service improvements such as changing procedures or training staff and other actions to put things right. SPSO also publish compliance information and 94 per cent of health recommendations were complied with in 2018–19. A similar picture is seen in Wales, where during 2018/19 just 14 public interest reports were issued when previously identified lessons haven't been learned or when a public body has refused to agree with PSOW's recommendation. In 2018/19 PSOW issued one Special Report under section 22 of the PSOW Act 2019 which are used if a body fails to satisfactorily implement any recommendations made in a PSOW report, or fails to comply with the terms of a settlement.

If the complaints process worked perfectly there would not be any need for oversight as second-tier complaint handlers, but this is clearly not the case. External oversight of PHSO is provided by the Public Administration and Constitutional Affairs Select Committee, and part of the annual appraisal considers PHSO's value for money. In 2018 PHSO's chief ombudsman commissioned an independent value for money study.[71] This study was clear that cost per case was an unsophisticated measure of value for money and that value really needed to be addressed in context including advice, signposting and support work as well as wider systemic work to improve public services. Between 2015 and 2018 as part of the austerity cuts PHSO reduced its budget by 24 percent, indicating that there was some slack in the system prior to this point. The 2018 value for money report was clear that the statutory limits on PHSO prevent it from operating more efficiently and in a way that delivers wider benefits for public service delivery.

PHSO's value for money relative to other UK ombudsmen in 2018–19 has been strongly questioned in evidence[72] submitted to the Public Administration and Constitutional Affairs Select Committee's Parliamentary and Health Service Ombudsman Scrutiny 2018–19 Inquiry,[73] however, the resulting inquiry report did not reflect these concerns.

---

[71] P Tyndall, C Mitchell and C Gill, *Value for Money Study: Report of the Independent Peer Review of the Parliamentary and Health Service Ombudsman* (12 November 2018) available at www.ombudsman.org.uk/sites/default/files/Value_for_Money_report_final.pdf.

[72] Written Evidence submitted by Nicholas Wheatley (HOS 25) to the Public Administration and Constitutional Affairs Committee Parliamentary and Health Service Ombudsman Scrutiny 2018–19 Inquiry available at https://committees.parliament.uk/writtenevidence/2516/pdf/.

[73] Public Administration and Constitutional Affairs Committee Parliamentary and Health Service Ombudsman Scrutiny 2018–19 Inquiry HC117 (30 June 2020) available at https://committees.parliament.uk/publications/1733/documents/16787/default/.

9

Clinical Claims Against the NHS

I. Clinical Negligence Litigation as a Compensation Mechanism

Although medical liability is currently entirely familiar, it was largely unknown in England and Wales until the latter part of the twentieth century[1] and is a relatively new phenomenon in many European jurisdictions.[2] Factors that have been identified in driving this change include the massive expansion in medical science and technology, the number of people and conditions addressed, the general development of tort law,[3] the movement towards patients' rights,[4] a collapse in a culture of deference towards doctors[5] and the expansion of legal services providers in providing specialist intermediary skills.

The picture for claims against the NHS is complex. There are different jurisdictions, for example Scotland is separate from England and Wales. The effects of devolution means that even within the same jurisdiction different rules may apply, for example claims are handled differently in Wales to the way the same claim would be handled in Wales. The processes will be outlined below.

This section will focus on the how liability is judged in clinical negligence and how these thresholds could help or hinder the development of an open culture where mistakes are reported.

A. Liability and the Thresholds Used to Assess Individuals

Clinical negligence for NHS hospitals operates under the principle of vicarious liability, a case is brought against the hospital or trust, not against an individual practitioner. However, when liability is judged it is against the *Bolam* test, which is a test of individual performance. There may be more than one practitioner involve in a litigation case, but the behaviour of each individual will be judged as an individual. In recent years there have been some interesting developments in clinical negligence litigation which have sought to modify the standards used to judge liability in certain clinical negligence cases. The classic test used

---

[1] J Mason and R McCall-Smith, *Law and Medical Ethics* 9th edn (Butterworths, 2013).

[2] E Hondius (ed), *The Development of Medical Liability* (Cambridge University Press, 2010) 8.

[3] J Spier (ed), *The Limits of Liability: Keeping the Floodgates Shut* (Kluwer Law International, 1996) v; editions of P Cane, *Atiyah's Accidents, Compensation and the Law* 8th edn (Cambridge University Press, 2013).

[4] ibid, 9.

[5] W Swain, 'The Development of Medical Liability in England and Wales' in Hondius, n 2, citing I Kennedy, *The Unmasking of Medicine* (Granada, 1983) 151–80; H Teff, *Reasonable Care* (Oxford University Press, 1994) 100–02; S Law, 'A Consumer Perspective ion Medical Malpractice' (1986) 49 *Law & Contemporary Problems* 305.

to determine liability is the *Bolam* test:[6] 'A doctor is not guilty of negligence if he has acted in accordance with a practice accepted as proper by a responsible body of medical men skilled in that particular art'. It was devised in 1957 and, until recently, it has survived with relatively minor modifications from subsequent cases, notably *Bolitho*[7] which required that the body of medical opinion must be 'reasonable, responsible or respectable' and have a 'logical' and 'defensible' basis. Reforms in the delivery of healthcare have also had a subtle but important effect on the legal standard applied to clinical negligence claims. The introduction of prescribed approaches in clinical care pathways replaced the traditional test with what constituted a consensus of medical opinion, based on meta-analysis of what produced better outcomes.[8] Peysner describes this shift as a move from 'I do what other people do' to 'I do what works'.[9] He suggested that the shift partly reduces individual autonomy, especially to respond to individual or unusual challenging cases.[10] The *Bolam* test, as amended, has been, and remains, the predominant test for most clinical negligence litigation, but there are some exceptions.

i. Diagnosis Cases: Reasonable Care and Skill Cases

There are some circumstances in which an alternative to the *Bolam* test is used, the 'reasonable care and skill test' derived from *Penney v East Kent Health Authority*.[11] In the *Penney* case cervical smear test slides of three women had been declared to be negative for aberrant changes by screeners, but the claimants then went on to develop cervical cancer. Based on the facts the first instance court determined that *Bolam* was not appropriate and that a reasonable care and skill test should be applied. In case he was incorrect in his rejection of *Bolam* the judge also considered the *Bolitho* exception to *Bolam*, and determined that the defence experts' evidence did not stand up to logical analysis. At the appeal, which upheld the judgment, Lord Woolf giving the majority judgment did not address the rejection of *Bolam* first instance, but concurred that the court had been correct in its use of the *Bolitho* qualification. The *Muller*[12] case further evolved this area. It related to a histopathology slide of a malignant melanoma that was misdiagnosed as a benign ulcer. It was agreed that the slide did, in fact, show evidence of a melanoma. The Trust submitted that the issue was whether, when the doctor diagnosed the ulcer, her practice had been in accordance with what a competent responsible body of histopathologists would have considered proper – the

---

[6] *Bolam v Friern Health Management Committee* [1957] 1 WLR 582 (QB).

[7] Lord Browne-Wilkinson 'the court has to be satisfied that the exponents of the body of opinion relied upon can demonstrate that such opinion has a logical basis. In particular in cases involving, as they so often do, the weighing of risks against benefits, the judge before accepting a body of opinion as being responsible, reasonable or respectable, will need to be satisfied that, in forming their views, the experts have directed their minds to the question of comparative risks and benefits and have reached a defensible conclusion on the matter'. *Bolitho v City and Hackney HA* [1998] AC.

[8] A Samanta, M Mello, C Foster, J Tingle and J Samanta, 'The Role of Clinical Guidelines in medical negligence Litigation: A Shift from Bolam' (2006) 14 *Medical Law Review* 321.

[9] J Peysner, *Access to Justice: A Critical Analysis of Recoverable Conditional Fees and No-Win No-Fee Funding* (Palgrave Macmillan, 2014).

[10] However, the high rates of successful defences that continue to be reported by NHSLA and the MDU raise questions about whether this is so.

[11] *Penney & Ors v East Kent Health Authority* [2000] Lloyds Rep Med 41.

[12] *Muller v Kings College Hospital* [2017] EWHC 128 (QB).

test which should be applied was the *Bolam* test. The claimant based on *Penney* contended that it was for the court to determine firstly the objective facts on whether the slide showed evidence of melanoma, and then whether the failure to report the signs was due to a lack of reasonable care and skill. Kerr J differentiated between 'pure treatment' cases in which *Bolam* applied and 'pure diagnosis cases'[13] in which the reasonable care test should apply adopted the approach taken in *Penney*, and found for the claimant.[14]

The reasonable care and skill test has been adopted by the courts in the cases of *Lillywhite v UCL*[15] and *XXX v King's*[16] both cases involving ultrasound scan interpretation. Mr Justice Foskett set out the position at paragraph 11 of *XXX v King's*:

> There is no dispute about the legal framework for the decision. Mr Jayasinghe's actions have to be judged by determining whether he acted with reasonable care according to the standards of the reasonably competent and well-informed sonographer on the basis of what contemporary standards required in July 2011. Ms Elizabeth-Anne Gumbel QC, for the Claimant, referred me to Penney v East Kent Health Authority [2000] Lloyd's Rep Med 41, where issues of a comparable nature were considered.

ii. Consent Cases

The 2015 Supreme Court judgment[17] on the Scottish case of *Montgomery v Lanarkshire Health Board* has had the most profound impact on the use of the *Bolam* test. Mrs Montgomery was an insulin-dependent diabetic of short stature. Diabetic mothers are likely to have babies that are larger than average, and have an elevated risk, agreed to be 9–10 per cent, of shoulder dystocia. Shoulder dystocia is where the baby's head is delivered, but the shoulders wedge behind the mother's pelvic bones trapping the baby in the birth canal and preventing the delivery of the rest of the baby. Shoulder dystocia requires either that physical manipulations are used to free the baby's shoulders to enable vaginal delivery or that surgery, usually an emergency caesarean section, is performed. It is an obstetric emergency for the mother, with potentially serious adverse consequences for the baby.

Mrs Montgomery was told at the 36-week scan to assess foetal size and growth that she was having a larger than average baby. Mrs Montgomery expressed concern about the size of her baby to the obstetrician, but she did not ask 'specifically about exact risks'. In the absence of such specific questioning the doctor did not warn Mrs Montgomery of the risk of shoulder dystocia. In fact, Mrs Montgomery's doctor specifically said during the trial that it was her practice not to discuss or advise of the risk of shoulder dystocia because she believed she considered the risk to be very slight, and if she mentioned it most diabetic expectant

---

[13] It is slightly curious that *Penney* was described as a 'pure diagnosis case' as the screening of smear tests is preventative rather than diagnostic.

[14] Although Kerr J found for the claimant on the issue of negligence he also found that at the point the slide was examined in November 2011 it was more likely than not that the claimant's cancer has already metastasised, so the negligence had little impact on the claimant's outcome.

[15] *Lillywhite & Another v University College Hospital's NHS Trust* [2005] EWCA Civ 1466, available at https://www.bailii.org/ew/cases/EWCA/Civ/2005/1466.html. At paragraph 33 Lord Justice Latham states: 'As in the case of Penny (supra) which was a case involving the evaluation of smear tests, the real question was the extent to which a reasonable sonologist, given the information provided by the ultra-sound, could with reasonable care and skill have come to the conclusion that he did.'

[16] *XXX v King's College Hospital NHS Foundation Trust* [2018] EWHC 646 (QB).

[17] *Montgomery v Lanarkshire Health Board* [2015] AC 1430 available at www.bailii.org/uk/cases/UKSC/2015/11.html.

mothers in a similar situation would opt for caesarean section. She expressed the view that caesarean sections were not in the maternal interest.

Mrs Montgomery was induced and while attempting to deliver her baby vaginally, shoulder dystocia occurred. There was a 12-minute lag between the baby's head appearing and him being delivered, during this time he was deprived of oxygen which caused cerebral palsy in all four of his limbs. Mrs Montgomery litigated on two grounds, the first of which was that she ought to have been given advice about the risk of shoulder dystocia occurring during a vaginal birth, and of the alternative possibility of delivery by elective caesarean section. Judgment in the Supreme Court was given by Lords Kerr and Reed, with Lords Neuberger, Clarke, Wilson and Hodge in agreement. The judgment stated

> An adult person of sound mind is entitled to decide which, if any, of the available forms of treatment to undergo, and her consent must be obtained before treatment interfering with her bodily integrity is undertaken. The doctor is therefore under a duty to take reasonable care to ensure that the patient is aware of any material risks involved in any recommended treatment, and of any reasonable alternative or variant treatments. The test of materiality is whether, in the circumstances of the particular case, a reasonable person in the patient's position would be likely to attach significance to the risk, or the doctor is or should reasonably be aware that the particular patient would be likely to attach significance to it.

Under the traditional *Bolam* perspective informed consent was focussed on what a reasonable doctor would do. In contrast, Montgomery, which was retrospectively applied, requires the doctor to have provided information on any risk that would be significant to that patient (or a reasonable person in that patient's position). The focus has shifted from the doctor to the patient. Montgomery is not without its critics. For example, Montgomery and Montgomery[18] contend that although, on the facts, justice was done, and that it brought the legal position into line with the existing guidance,[19] the judgment was flawed and 'calls into question the competence of the courts to adjudicate on matters of clinical judgement'.

iii. Liability Thresholds

These cases illustrate that the *Bolam* test, while still good law, is by no means the only test in clinical negligence. *Bolam* is still the test used for the majority of clinical negligence cases, but as the law evolves the scope of the *Bolam* test is being altered.

B. Institutional Non-delegable Duties of Care

One particularly interesting development has been the approach taken by the Supreme Court in *Woodland v Essex County Council* in 2013[20] to the duty of care owed by schools and hospitals. This chapter will give a very brief overview[21] and will adopt the terminology

---

[18] J Montgomery and E Montgomery, 'Montgomery on Informed Consent: An Inexpert Decision?' (2016) 42(2) *Journal of Medical Ethics* 89–94. doi: 10.1136/medethics-2015-102862. PMID: 26811487.

[19] General Medical Council, *Consent Guidance: Patients and Doctors Making Decisions Together* (GMC, 2008).

[20] *Woodland v Essex County Council* [2013] UKSC 66 available at www.supremecourt.uk/cases/docs/uksc-2012-0093-judgment.pdf.

[21] For an excellent and far more comprehensive description see P Giliker, 'Non-delegable Duties and Institutional Liability for the Negligence of Hospital Staff: Fair, Just and Reasonable?' (2017) 33(2) *Tottel's Journal of Professional*

used by Giliker of a 'hospital non-delegable duty'. This area of law is particularly pertinent to healthcare as NHS entities may choose to contract out service provision to external organisations (both NHS and private). This outsourcing potentially prevents claimants from making tort-based claims grounded in the well-established doctrine of vicarious liability. The imposition of a non-delegable duty provides these potential claimants with a route to recover damages grounded in the tort of negligence.[22]

The appellant in *Woodland* had been a pupil at Whitmore Junior School, which was the responsibility of Essex County Council. When she was aged 10 she suffered a severe brain injury after getting into difficulties during a school swimming lesson. The school had a responsibility to provide these swimming lessons, which it had delegated by arranging for the swimming lessons to be provided by a private contractor. The Appellant claimed against various parties including Essex County Council. The Supreme Court had to determine whether the Essex County Council owed the claimant a non-delegable duty of care that would make it potentially liable for the negligence of the private contractors it had delegated the provision of swimming lessons to.

The Supreme Court found for the claimant, and concluded that a non-delegable duty existed. Five 'defining features' were laid out by Lord Sumption which would typically trigger a non-delegable duty.[23] In essence they were:

1)   the claimant is a patient or child or some otherwise vulnerable or dependent person;
2)   there is an antecedent relationship between the claimant and the defendant which puts the claimant in the care of the defendant and from which it is possible to assign to the defendant a positive obligation actively to protect the claimant from harm (as opposed to a duty simply to refrain from harmful conduct);
3)   the claimant has no control over how the defendant chooses to perform those obligations;
4)   the defendant has delegated some part of its function to a third party, and the third party is exercising, for the purpose of the function delegated to it, the defendant's custody or care of the claimant and the element of control that goes with it; and
5)   the third party has been negligent in the exercise of that delegated function.

However, even if all the five defining features are met Lord Sumption's judgment is clear that a non-delegable duty of care should be imputed to schools only so far as it would be fair, just and reasonable to do so.

The practical implication of this judgment on healthcare as it is currently delivered is likely to be fairly insignificant as NHS Resolution have long indemnified most care undertaken by private providers on behalf of the NHS[24] and from April 2013 private providers have been allowed to join its Clinical Negligence Scheme for Trusts (CNST).[25] However,

---

Negligence 109–27 available at https://research-information.bris.ac.uk/ws/portalfiles/portal/111316458/Giliker_2017_JPN_final.pdf.

[22] The actual extent of the application of vicarious liability, and therefore the impact of a hospital non-delegable duty is the subject of some debate, see Giliker, ibid and para 5.24 of GT Laurie, SHE Harman and G Porter, *Mason and McCall Smith's Law and Medical Ethics* 10th edn (Oxford University Press, 2016).

[23] Paragraph 23 of *Woodland v Essex County Council* [2013] UKSC 66, available at www.supremecourt.uk/cases/docs/uksc-2012-0093-judgment.pdf.

[24] https://assets.publishing.service.gov.uk/government/uploads/system/uploads/attachment_data/file/212814/guidance-note-for-use-of-the-CNST-cover.pdf.

[25] https://resolution.nhs.uk/services/claims-management/clinical-schemes/clinical-negligence-scheme-for-trusts/.

under the new integrated care arrangement this could become far more relevant to clinical negligence litigation.

The potential impact on other sectors, such as education, cared for children and care home residents is likely to be greater as these sectors do not have arrangements comparable to CNST. However, what is really interesting is the intention of the Supreme Court and their willingness to depart from the traditional fault-based approach to liability; in *Woodland* Lord Sumption acknowledged the non-delegable institutional is 'inconsistent with the fault-based principles on which the law of negligence is based'.[26]

II. Threshold Conclusions

Tort litigation is not a fixed quantity, as Lady Hale eloquently stated in *Woodland*:[27]

> The common law is a dynamic instrument. It develops and adapts to meet new situations as they arise. Therein lies its strength. But therein also lies a danger, the danger of unbridled and unprincipled growth to match what the court perceives to be the merits of the particular case. So it must proceed with caution, incrementally by analogy with existing categories, and consistently with some underlying principle.

The tests used today may remain broadly the same for years or they may be modified or developed so they are more suitable for contexts which the court finds itself deciding upon. One of the limitations of precedent-based litigation as a mechanism for holding account is that the courts have no control over the issues raised in the cases brought before them. The courts cannot proactively amend thresholds, they must wait for a case with suitable facts to be brought before them and even then they 'proceed with caution, incrementally ...'. In a field that develops as quickly as medical treatments, this can be limiting.

All of the tests in use today for clinical negligence focus on an individual:

– Did that individual treat the patient in a way that was in line with what is known to work?

– Did that individual use reasonable care and skill when treating that patient?

– Did the doctor give the patient information that would be significant to them when making their decision?

This has been the traditional approach. While it may have been appropriate when decisions were made by a single doctor in charge of that patient's care it is difficult to see how, and why, this approach can be sustained given the predominance of shared decision-making in MDTs, etc. As we move towards a position where there is a greater use of algorithms to make diagnostic and treatment decisions this individual approach becomes less tenable. Reform seems inevitable and a move away from individual culpability towards a test framed around the service provided would be more appropriate and would remove the fear of blame, which inhibits open disclosure by healthcare professionals.

---

[26] Para 22 of *Woodland v Essex County Council* [2013] UKSC 66, available at www.supremecourt.uk/cases/docs/uksc-2012-0093-judgment.pdf.

[27] ibid.

III. Clinical Claims Against the NHS in England

England is part of a combined legal jurisdiction with Wales. However, there are distinct differences in how clinical negligence cases are approached in these two countries.

A. NHS Clinical Negligence Claims in England Overview

Since 1996 clinical negligence claims against all NHS bodies in England have been handled under the Clinical Negligence Scheme for Trusts (CNST), a voluntary agreement under which costs are pooled.[28] Claims against NHS institutions are administered by NHS Resolution, which until 2017 was known as the National Health Service Litigation Authority (NHSLA).[29] NHS Resolution handles various schemes,[30] primarily the Clinical Negligence Scheme for Trusts, which pools litigation risk amongst all NHS Trusts, Foundation Trusts and Primary Care Trusts.[31] NHS Resolution has a panel of defence solicitors. The system is intended to provide better quality claims handling, earlier admission of liability, encourages apologies, explanation and mediation, and so to result in legal costs being reduced.

Concern has existed for many years over the phenomenon of claims handling and litigation in relation to the NHS in England.[32] There are also significant concerns over the size and value of the clinical negligence market; the number of claims and amounts paid has increased greatly over the years. The Medical Defence Union estimated that medical

---

[28] The Clinical Negligence Scheme for Trusts, at www.nhsla.com/claims/Documents/CNST%20Rules.pdf. The CNST was established by Regulations originally made pursuant to the National Health Service and Community Care Act 1990 s 21 and subsequently the National Health Service Act 2006 s 71 as amended by the Health and Social Care Act 2012. See also *Risk Management in the NHS* EL(93)111 (London, Department of Health, 1993).

[29] NHSLA is established under the National Health Service Act 2006, s 71: National Health Service Litigation Authority (establishment and Constitution) Order 1995, SI 1995/2800; National Health Service Litigation Authority Regulations 1995, SI 1995/2801. It was first established under the NHS Act 1977, s 11.

[30] NHS Resolution manages five clinical negligence schemes, detailed below:
  – Clinical Negligence Scheme for Trusts (CNST), which covers clinical negligence claims for incidents occurring on or after 1 April 1995.
  – Existing Liabilities Scheme (ELS) is centrally funded by DHSC and covers clinical negligence claims against NHS organisations for incidents occurring before 1 April 1995.
  – Ex-Regional Health Authority Scheme (Ex-RHAS) is a relatively small scheme, centrally funded by DHSC, covering clinical negligence claims against former Regional Health Authorities abolished in 1996.
  – DHSC clinical covers clinical negligence liabilities that have transferred to the Secretary of State for Health and Social Care following the abolition of any relevant health bodies.
  – Clinical Negligence Scheme for General Practice (CNSGP), is a relatively new scheme which covers clinical negligence claims for incidents occurring in general practice on, or after, 1 April 2019.

In addition they manage three non-clinical schemes:

  – Liabilities to Third Parties Scheme (LTPS).
  – Property Expenses Scheme (PES), both covering non-clinical claims where the incident occurred on or after 1 April 1999.
  – DHSC non-clinical which covers non clinical liabilities that have transferred to the Secretary of State following the abolition of a relevant health body.

[31] It is not an insurance arrangement and so not subject to insurance regulatory capital requirements.

[32] P Pleasence, NJ Balmer, H Genn, A Buck and A O'Grady, 'The Experience of Clinical Negligence Within the General Population' (2003) 9 *Clinical Risk* 211–17; L Mulcahy, 'Can Leopards Change Their Spots? An Evaluation of the Role of Lawyers in Medical Negligence Mediation' (2001) 8(3) *International Journal of the Legal Profession* 203–24.

negligence claims doubled between 1975 and 1985[33] and this upward trajectory has largely continued. The cost of the initial scheme (CICS) was £190 million in 1996–97, and administration accounted for 8.8 per cent of total costs. By 2002, the estimated expenditure was £10 billion.[34] The cost of compensation to the NHS in 1974/1975 was £6.33 million in 2000 prices, and by 2001/2002 it had increased to £446 million.[35]

i. National Audit Office Report 2001

In their 2001 report, *Handling Clinical Negligence Claims in England*,[36] the NAO concluded that that the quality of clinical negligence solicitors was improving. They found the number and value of claims continued to rise. Claims were taking a long time to settle; on average claims (excluding cerebral palsy and brain injuries) were taking five and a half years. Nearly half of claims resulted in more paid in legal fees than was paid in damages, for claims under £50,000 over 65 per cent of cases resulted in a larger legal bill than damages payment. Over 20 years later, and the number of claims, expense of claims, slow timeframes and disproportional legal costs continue to be discussed today.

ii. Marsh Report 2011

In 2011 the increased trend in scheme liabilities prompted the Department of Health to commission a private sector review of the NHSLA carried out by Marsh Ltd. Their report concluded that NHS risk pooling remained a valid concept but there were various operational problems, including significant delays in Trusts reporting claims to the NHSLA, limitations on the ability of the NHSLA to leverage improved risk management by Trusts such as through imposition of penalties, the absence of a service driven culture and limited NHSLA role in improving patient safety.[37] Interestingly they also recommended a personal injuries assessment board, based on the Irish model to quantify claims where liability was not in issue.

In their response government accepted most of the recommendations, but did not accept that there was the need for a rebrand of NHSLA; cap expert fees; or accept the personal injuries assessment board proposals. Stronger links and more emphasis were put on safety.

iii. National Audit Office Report 2017

A 2017 NAO report into the rising costs of clinical negligence[38] concluded the Department of Health and NHS Resolution's proposed actions to contain the rising cost of clinical

---

[33] *Medical Defence Union Annual Report* (London, MDU, 1986).

[34] J Broughton, B Gravelsons, C Hensman et al, *The Cost of Compensation Culture* (London, Institute of Actuaries, 2001).

[35] *Making Amends: A Consultation Paper Setting Out Proposals for Reforming the Approach to Clinical Negligence in the NHS*. Report by the Chief Medical Officer (Department of Health, 2003) 9 and 60.

[36] *NAO Handling Clinical Negligence Claims in England* (May 2001) available at www.nao.org.uk/report/handling-clinical-negligence-claims-in-england/.

[37] *Department of Health NHS Litigation Authority Industry Report* (March, 2011) available at www.gov.uk/government/publications/nhs-litigation-authority-industry-review-department-of-health-response.

[38] NAO, Managing the Costs of Clinical Negligence in Trust (September 2017) available at www.nao.org.uk/report/managing-the-costs-of-clinical-negligence-in-trusts/.

negligence claims, including fixed recoverable cost and the early notification scheme for birth injuries, were unlikely to stop this growth. They reported that the government lacked a coherent cross-government strategy, underpinned by policy to address the rising cost of clinical negligence. They concluded that many of biggest factors influencing costs fell across the remits of more than one government department or largely outside the health system's control. They include developments in the legal market and the increasing level of damages awarded for high-value claims. As at May 2022 a cross-departmental response has yet to be published, but a consultation is expected.

iv. Civil Justice Council Report into Fixed Recoverable Cost in Lower Value Clinical Negligence Claims

The 2019 report into fixed recoverable costs for lower clinical negligence claims[39] came from a long history of concern over the disproportionate costs on lower value claims. The NAO report found that in 2016–17, the claimant's legal costs exceeded the damages awarded in 61 per cent of successful claims, with the greatest disparity being found in lower value awards. The proposed policy solution was fixed recoverable costs in lower value clinical negligence cases, following the FRC model applied to other personal injury cases. The Civil Justice Council reached an impasse on this issue and failed to reach an agreement. At the time of writing there is a government consultation on fixed recoverable costs. If enacted these provisions would apply to England and Wales, but are unlikely to have a significant impact on Wales due to Welsh Redress.

v. Health and Social Care Select Committee Inquiry into NHS

The 2022 Inquiry into NHS litigation reform[40] looked at clinical negligence claims.[41] It delivered a comprehensive rejection of the current litigation system, stating:

> Maintaining a costly and adversarial litigation system is evermore at odds with our understanding of how the NHS should respond to failures in care. England's system of clinical negligence stands in stark contrast to international best practice in terms of patient safety. In other countries, gains are made by careful system-wide analysis rather than an insistent search for individual error.

The report's major recommendation was moving away from litigation and adopting an administrative scheme that awards compensation based on system performance rather than individual error. Other recommendations included removing the requirement to pay compensation at private care and discount the availability of NHS care; basing loss of earnings claims for children on average earnings rather than estimates of the child's earnings based on family socio-economic status. The recommendation was that the administrative scheme should be brought in incrementally, starting with birth-related brain injuries. During this transition phase various recommendations were made to improve the clinical negligence process including compulsory ADR at an early stage.

---

[39] Report of the Civil Justice Council Working Group *Fixed Recoverable Costs in Lower Value Clinical Negligence Claims* (October 2019) available at www.judiciary.uk/related-offices-and-bodies/advisory-bodies/cjc/archive/fixed-recoverable-costs-in-lower-value-clinical-negligence-claims/.

[40] Health and Social Care Select Committee, *NHS Litigation Reform*, Thirteenth Report of Session 2021–22, HC 750, 28 April 2022, available at https://committees.parliament.uk/publications/22039/documents/163739/default/.

[41] Sonia Macleod acted as a Special Advisor to the Committee.

vi. Overview of NHS Resolution's Clinical Claim Handling Activity

In the past NHS Resolution provided CNST for secondary and tertiary care providers. Primary care was not included and GPs, etc, were required to take out insurance/indemnify themselves appropriately. From 1 April 2019 NHS Resolution took on GP practice indemnity as well.

a. The Filtering and Funding of Potential Clinical Negligence Claims in England

NHS Resolution is a defence organisation, it is not usually the first stage in a potential claimant's litigation journey, which will ordinarily be when an individual approaches a clinical negligence solicitor about their concern. The vast majority of concerns raised with solicitors are rejected; the Society of Clinical Injury Lawyers estimate that only 3 per cent of claims are deemed actionable and therefore proceed through this filtering stage.[42] As a mechanism for raising a concern clinical negligence litigation is therefore seriously limited before the process even starts.

The exception to this is litigants in person, for whom NHS Resolution may be their first port of call, though they may have contacted other sources of advice and support, such as Citizens Advice.

Claimants considering litigation need to establish how this will be funded. Self-funding of clinical negligence is relatively rare where a lawyer is used. It is more common for litigants in person. This presents a potential barrier to litigation for individuals.

Another potential funding option might be legal aid. In practice the availability of legal aid for clinical negligence has in effect been removed for almost all clinical negligence cases, the only exception being brain injured babies. This was driven by the Legal Aid, Sentencing and Punishment of Offenders Act 2012 (LAPSO). LAPSO significantly changed the way clinical negligence litigation is funded, shifting cases which might previously have been eligible for legal aid towards Conditional Fee Agreements (CFAs or 'no win no fee').

LAPSO also dramatically impacted the way CFAs and litigation funding operated. Prior to LAPSO coming into effect in April 2013, a claimant could enter into a CFA and purchase an After the Event (ATE) insurance policy. If the individual lost their case the CFA meant they did not have to pay their solicitor and the ATE policy covered the defendant's legal costs. It was not uncommon for the payment of the premium used to purchase the ATE policy to be deferred and contingent on success, meaning that the policy pays out while a losing claimant did not actually have to pay the premium. This was a totally risk-free position for the claimant.

Claimants who won their case recovered damages, their own legal costs, a success fee and the cost of the ATE premium from the NHSLA. Because NHS clinical negligence litigation was funded by the NHSLA they did not benefit from the positive attributes of CFAs. This was felt to be unbalanced and to place excessive cost burdens on NHSLA (and downstream the tax payer who funds them) so was reformed under LAPSO. Key points for CFA agreements entered into after 1 April 2013[43] are:

- Success fees are taken out of the claimant's compensation. Success fees cannot exceed 100 per cent of legal base costs, and additionally cannot exceed 25 per cent of the

---

[42] See the Access to Justice section of www.scil.org.uk/campaign.

[43] Full requirements are detailed in s 44, s 46 and s 48 of LASPO 2012; Arts 1–6 of Conditional Fee Arrangements Order 2013; s 58 of Courts and Legal Services Act 1990; The Recovery of Costs Insurance Premiums in Clinical Negligence Proceedings Regulations 2013 and part 48.2 of the Civil Procedure Rules.

compensation awarded for general damages and past losses (except for appeals where the cap is 100 per cent of the compensation).

- Pre-LASPO the whole value of the insurance premium for legal costs insurance (either before the event, BTE, or after the event, ATE) could be recovered from the losing side. LASPO changed this and in clinical negligence litigation the premium is now partially recoverable – the portion of costs insurance premium relating to expert report fees is recoverable.

- Qualified One-way Cost Shifting (QOCS) applies to clinical negligence cases. QOCS protects a losing claimant because, in the majority of circumstances, the unsuccessful claimant is not liable to pay the defendant's costs. QOCS were introduced so that claimants would not need to purchase ATE legal costs insurance, and therefore would not be disadvantaged by not being able to fully recover the premium.

- In clinical negligence cases successful claimants will have a 10 per cent uplift applied to their general damages for non-pecuniary loss (ie pain and suffering, loss of amenity, etc) to make up for the loss of recoverability and the fact that the success fee (of up to 25 per cent) is taken from their damages.

These reforms protect claimants from liability for NHS Resolution's costs and mean that an individual awarded compensation from successful clinical negligence litigation using a CFA will not recover the full value of the slightly higher damages awarded.

If a claimant can find a solicitor willing to take on their case using a CFA they have nothing to lose and no financial barriers to entry. The risk in this relationship sits with the claimant solicitor, who risks not be paid for time invested in a losing case, and that may go some way to explaining the very high rejection rates seen when claimant solicitors filter claims.

b. The Handling of Clinical Negligence Claims in England

Those claims that pass through the filtering process then progress into the clinical negligence process. Data will be taken from annual reports up to and including the 2018/19 annual report to avoid fluctuations due to the impact of the pandemic.[44]

Since 1999 clinical negligence claims have followed a very standard litigation process, including steps to enable the dispute to be settled without recourse to the courts, as set out in the pre-action protocol for the resolution of clinical disputes.[45] This protocol includes set timeframes for the letter of claim and letter of response; timeframes and costs for obtaining medical records; and a requirement that parties consider alternative dispute resolution. Non-compliance with the protocol can result in adverse costs awards.

The current protocol for clinical negligence claims, which includes all claims against hospitals, GPs, dentists and other healthcare providers, both NHS and private, taken from Annex J of the Civil Justice Council Report into Fixed Recoverable Costs[46] is outlined in Figure 1. Briefly,[47] the general scheme is that a claimant should request medical records

---

[44] NHS Resolution *Annual Report and Accounts 2018/19*, available at https://resolution.nhs.uk/wp-content/uploads/2019/08/NHS-Resolution-Annual-Report-2018-19.pdf.

[45] Available at www.justice.gov.uk/courts/procedure-rules/civil/protocol/prot_rcd.

[46] Appendix I of the Report of the Civil Justice Council Working Group *Fixed Recoverable Costs in Lower Value Clinical Negligence Claims* October 2019, available at www.judiciary.uk/related-offices-and-bodies/advisory-bodies/cjc/archive/fixed-recoverable-costs-in-lower-value-clinical-negligence-claims/.

[47] See Pre-Action Protocol for the Resolution of Clinical Disputes for full details.

(usually from a prospective defendant), which should be supplied within 40 days; the claimant sends a Letter of Notification outlining the nature of the claim, injuries and heads of damage claimed; the parties consider what steps should be taken to promote rehabilitation;[48] the claimant then sends a more detailed Letter of Claim and the defendant sends a Letter of Response, both generally in accordance with official templates; the parties consider whether the matter can be resolved without further recourse to the court; they then seek to narrow issues in dispute and to agree the chronology and key facts before taking the matter further in civil proceedings.

Figure 1 The current clinical negligence process

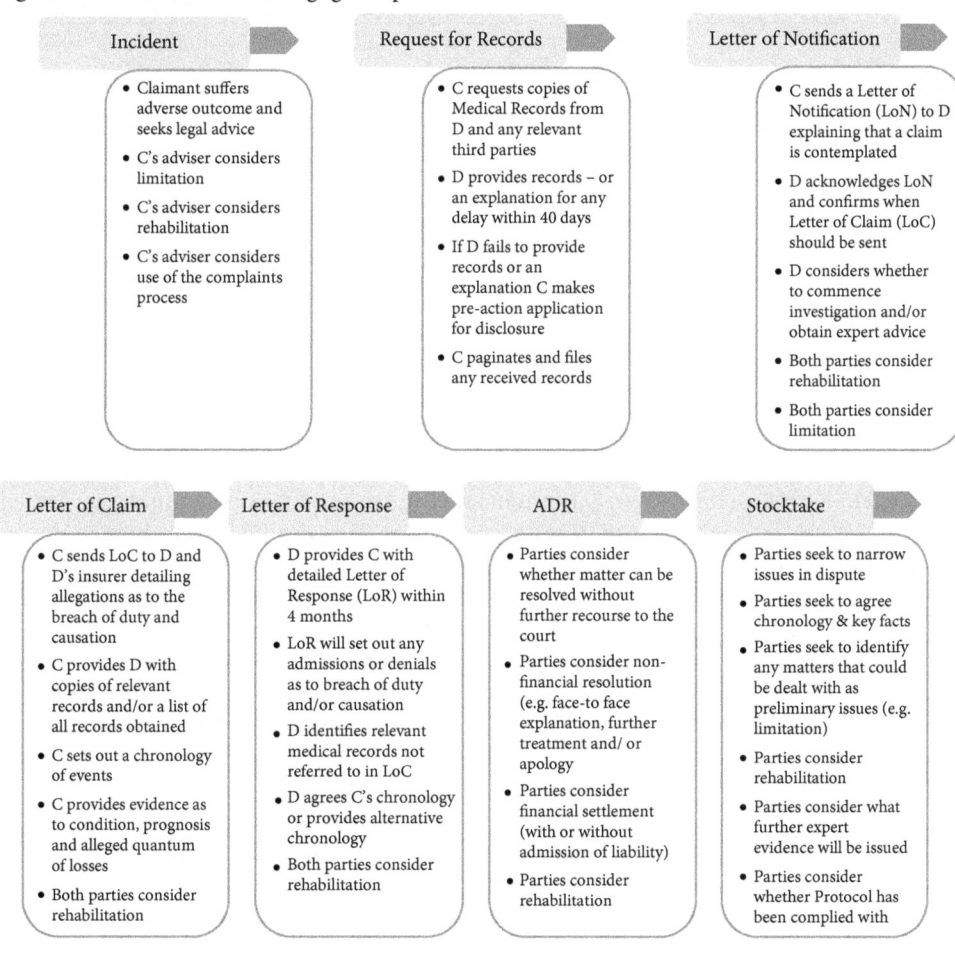

The total number of clinical and non-clinical claims reported, and the total expenditure and costs paid on claims, for 2012 to 2019 are at Table 1. Clinical claims have risen rapidly: from

---

[48] In accordance with the *Rehabilitation Code*, issued by the International Underwriting Association of London Limited 2013, at www.iua.co.uk/IUA_Member/Publications. The aim of the code is to promote the use of rehabilitation and early intervention in the compensation process so that the injured person makes the best and quickest possible medical, social and psychological recovery.

6,652 in 2009/10 to 10,678 in 2018/19. The high point in claims numbers seen in 2013/2014 is likely to be due to solicitors bringing claims under the more profitable pre-LAPSO rules.

In 2018/19 total expenditure on clinical claims was £2,360 million, of which 75 per cent (£1,778 million) was on damages and 25 per cent was on legal costs (19 per cent, £442.3 million, being for claimants and 6 per cent, £139.6 million, on defence costs), to which should be added administrative costs.[49] In that year, total NHS Resolution administration costs were £25.8 million.

Table 1 NHS Resolution claims and costs 20012/13 to 2018/19

Year	2012/13	2013/14	2014/15	2015/16	2016/17	2017/18	2018/19
Clinical Claims reported	10,129	11,945	11,497	10,965	10,686	10,673	10,678
Damages paid (£m)	£907.5	£840.7	£774.4	£950.4	£1,083.0	£1,632.0	£1,778.0
Claimant legal costs (£m)	£274.8	£259.2	£291.9	£418.0	£498.5	£466.6	£442.3
Defendant legal costs (£m)	£76.5	£92.5	£103.2	£120.1	£125.7	£128.9	£139.6
Total Legal costs (£m)	£351.3	£351.7	£395.1	£538.1	£624.2	£595.5	£581.9
Total Expenditure (damages, costs, interim payments) £m	£1,259.0	£1,193.0	£1,223.0	£1,488.5	£1,707.2	£2,228.0	£2,360.0
Total administration costs* £m	£13.4	£20.3	£20.5	£19.0	£20.3	£23.0	£25.8

The vast majority of claims are settled without proceedings, see Figure 2 created using data contained in NHS Resolution's 2018/19 annual report. Of the 15,655 claims that were settled in 2018/19 damages were paid in 56 per cent of cases. This can be further broken down; before proceedings were issued damages were paid in 45 per cent of cases; once proceedings had been issued damages were paid in 83 per cent of cases; for cases that reached trial damages were paid in 35 per cent of cases, see Figure 2. This is likely to reflect the discovery process. If the objective of the litigation process is to obtain damages then the overall probability of succeeding of 56 per cent is only slightly in the claimants' favour. However, given the year on year rise in claims reported this does not seem to deter potential claimants.

Figure 2 NHS Resolution 2018/19 clinical claims settlement profile

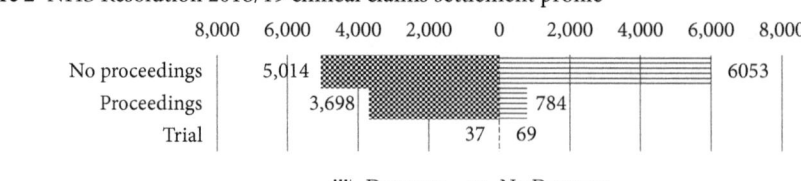

Given that litigation is a slow, adversarial process where obtaining damages is by no means certain the breakdown of cases received by NHS Resolution in 2018/19 by value shown in

---

[49] NHS Resolution administrative costs are given as a total figure and include claims handling (both clinical and non-clinical) and other workstreams.

Figure 3 is interesting. Just over 40 per cent of cases are valued by NHS Resolution at less than £25,000. The cases valued at zero are potentially surprising as the function of litigation is to provide compensation, and there is a professional obligation on solicitors not to bring claims that do not have a reasonable prospect of success the number of claims in this band should be very small. It is not: in 2018/19 it was 12 per cent of the cases received by NHS Resolution. It would be interesting to know the proportion of claims received in each tranche that are made by litigants in person, who are not under any obligation not to undertake claims which do not have a reasonable prospect of success and who will not incur legal costs.

Figure 3 2018/19 clinical claims received by NHS Resolution by estimated value tranche

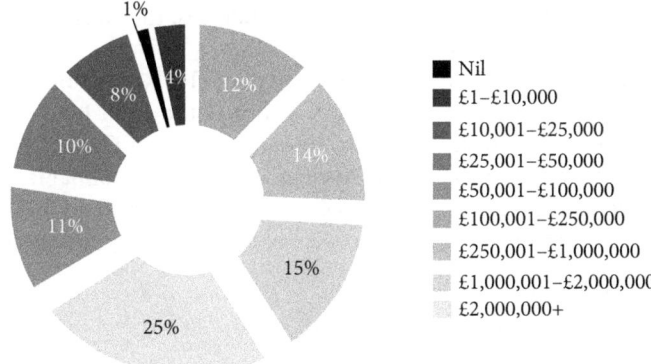

The percentages of claims received in 2018/19 by number and value are shown in Table 2. The cost of obstetrics claims is a notable outlier, and this is due to the value of support paid to neonates who are damaged at birth. The number of such claims has remained fairly even over the past decade, but their value has risen inexorably.

Table 2 NHS Resolution claims received by specialty in 2018/19

Specialty	Percentage of claims received	Value of claims received
Orthopaedic Surgery	12%	4%
Emergency Medicine	13%	8%
Obstetrics	10%	50%
General Surgery	9%	3%
Gynaecology	5%	–
General Medicine	5%	2%
Radiology	4%	2%
Urology	3%	–
Psychiatric/Mental Health	3%	2%
Gastroenterology	2%	4%
Paediatrics	–	7%

(continued)

Table 2 *(Continued)*

Specialty	Percentage of claims received	Value of claims received
Neurology	–	3%
Ambulance	–	2%
Other (54 aggregated specialties)	34%	13%

– = figure not individually detailed in the report, these numbers will be within the 'other' category.

NHS Early Notification Scheme

The devastating nature of birth-related brain injuries and their huge financial impact on the damages paid has led NHS Resolution to develop strategies, the early notification scheme and the maternity incentives scheme.

The early notification scheme originally required that NHS Resolution was automatically notified of a qualifying incident (an incident which met the Each Baby Counts criteria). Each Baby Counts was the Royal College of Obstetricians and Gynaecologists' (RCOG) national quality improvement programme to reduce the number of babies who die or are left severely disabled as a result of incidents occurring during term labour. Babies who meet the Each Baby Counts criteria are those who were at least 37 weeks gestation and suffered

– an intrapartum stillbirth
– an early neonatal death (within the first week of life)
– a severe brain injury defined as a baby who was

   ° diagnosed with grade III hypoxic ischemic encephalopathy (HIE); or
   ° therapeutically cooled; or
   ° had a decreased central tone, was comatose and had seizures

COVID has meant that since 1 April 2020 the notification to ENS has been dropped and instead the Trust must inform HSIB, who effectively 'triage' these cases for NHS Resolution. From 1 April 2021 further changes to reporting were implemented. First, that NHS Resolution would not start an investigation until an HSIB investigation was completed. Second, that the remit of the ENS scheme would be narrowed to only considering cases where there is a hypoxic brain injury, ordinarily babies who have an abnormal MRI scan where there is evidence of changes in relation to intrapartum hypoxic ischaemic encephalopathy. This is to allow NHS Resolution to focus on the highest value cases.

These arrangements create an unusual dynamic; the investigation into potential litigation is not instigated by the claimant and there is no family involvement in the ENS investigation process.

NHS Resolution's Mediation Panel

Despite having been recommended in the pre-action protocol for many years previously the NHS Resolution's mediation service was finally launched in December 2016. This followed a pilot mediation service run by NHSLA which had run from 31 July 2014.[50] The adoption

---

[50] *Report and Accounts 2014/15* (NHS Litigation Authority, 2015), 24 available at https://assets.publishing.service.gov.uk/government/uploads/system/uploads/attachment_data/file/454320/NHS_LA_Annual_Report_and_Accounts_2014-15.pdf.

of mediation lagged behind other sectors and it differs from standard mediations in which the parties jointly agree on a mediator. In NHS Resolution's mediations the mediator can only be selected from a panel of firms chosen by NHS Resolution. There are currently two independent accredited mediation firms on the panel, the Centre for Effective Dispute Resolution (CEDR) and Trust Mediation Ltd.

From December 2016 to 31 March 2019 a total of 606 mediations had been completed. The vast majority of these were in later years as uptake was slow to start with.[51] In 2018/19 380 clinical cases were mediated and 10 non-clinical cases. There were also seven costs mediations. The majority of mediations took place prior to proceedings being issued. Almost three quarters (74 per cent) of cases settle either on the day of the mediation or within 28 days. NHS Resolution always funds mediation in full for litigants in person. However, litigants in person are less likely to settle at mediation; 45.5 per cent of unrepresented claimants do not settle compared to 18.5 per cent of represented claimants. The reasons for this are not clear.

B. Claims Against the NHS in England Conclusions

The rising number (and costs) of clinical negligence litigation have long been a concern for policymakers. The year-on-year increase in claims numbers combined with the extensive rejection rate from the filtering done by claimants' solicitors indicates that people are willing to litigate, this should not be a surprise – litigation is the only realistic option to obtain compensation[52] and there is an entire claimant solicitor industry built around attracting and supporting people to make a legal claim. The odds of obtaining damages are not high: of the small proportion of claims (circa 3 per cent) that make it through the filtering by solicitors just over half (56 per cent) will actually result in a payment of damages.

The impact of proposed reforms to the litigation process will be discussed in Part III of this book.

IV. Clinical Claims Against the NHS in Scotland

A. NHS Clinical Negligence Litigation in Scotland Overview

Scotland is a separate legal jurisdiction and although there are many common aspects, including a shared Supreme Court, see Figure 4, there are distinct differences in how civil cases generally and clinical negligence cases specifically are approached. There are a variety of procedures which can be used to bring a claim depending on the court chosen and the complexity and/or potential value of the claim. A personal injury claim for under £100,000 can be initiated in either the local sheriff court or the All Scotland Personal Injury Court. Actions over £100,00 can be initiated in either of these courts or they can opt to go to the

---

[51] *NHS Resolution Mediation in Healthcare Claims – An Evaluation 2020*, available at https://resolution.nhs.uk/wp-content/uploads/2020/02/NHS-Resolution-Mediation-in-healthcare-claims-an-evaluation.pdf.

[52] PHSO can offer compensation, but it is far more restrictive and is capped.

Court of Sessions Outer House. It is for the pursuer (claimant) to decide where the claim is initiated.

In 2018–19 39 per cent of clinical negligence cases were initiated in the Sheriff Personal Injury Court, 35 per cent in the Court of Sessions and 27 per cent in local sheriff courts (8 per cent of these were under the summary cause procedure (under £5,000) and 19 per cent used the ordinary procedure (over £5,000)).[53]

Figure 4 Schematic of the Scottish civil court structure for handling personal injury claims

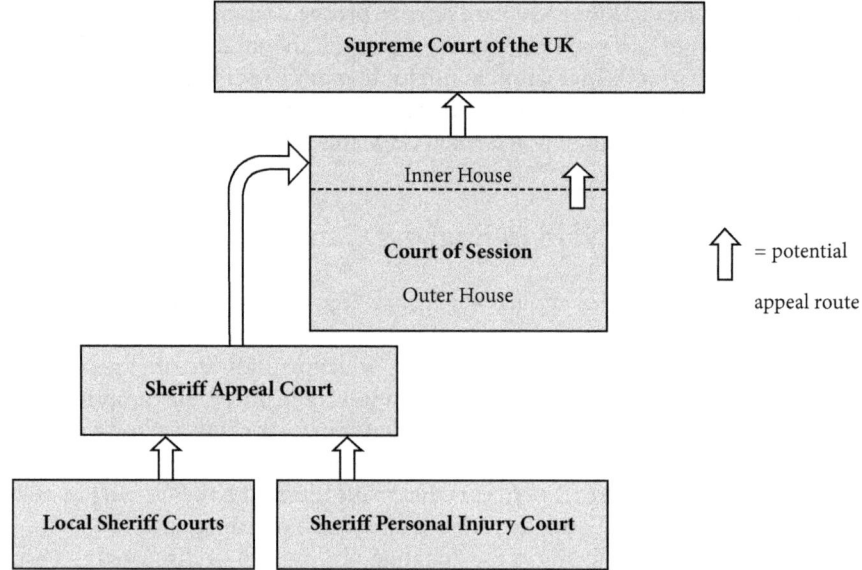

B. CNORIS and the Central Legal Office

Clinical negligence claims against all Scottish NHS boards are handled under the Clinical Negligence and Other Risks Indemnity Scheme (CNORIS),[54] a mandatory agreement established by statute in 2000,[55] under which costs are pooled. Private contractors such as dentists and GPs are outside the scheme, though GPs may be covered where there is a direct employment contract, for example when providing out of hours care. The scheme was expanded from April 2015 to allow Integration Joint Boards and Local Authorities to join.[56]

CNORIS has an agreed deductible of £25,000 with members paying all claims costs up to this value from their own budgets. Each year the Scottish Government Health and Social

---

[53] Civil Justice Statistics Scotland 2018–19, available at: gov.scot/publications/civil-justice-statistics-scotland-2018-19/pages/1/.

[54] https://clo.scot.nhs.uk/our-services/cnoris.aspx.

[55] The National Health Service (Clinical Negligence and Other Risks Indemnity Scheme) (Scotland) Regulations 2000 (Regulations (SSI 2000 No.54).

[56] Public Bodies (Joint Working) (Scotland) Act 2014 asp 9 available at www.legislation.gov.uk/asp/2014/9/contents/enacted.

Care Directorate fund all losses that exceed the CNORIS deductible. At the end of the financial year contributions are collected from members to repay the deficit accrued in the year by the Scottish Government. Contributions are based on a member's proportion of the overall risks assessed using clinical and non-clinical risk profiles.

Since September 2013[57] CNORIS has been managed by the National Health Service Scotland (NSS) with the Central Legal Office providing legal advice and guidance to members. The system is intended to provide better quality claims handling, earlier admission of liability, encourages apologies, explanation and mediation, and so to result in legal costs being reduced.

i. Overview of CNORIS

a. The Filtering and Funding of Potential Clinical Negligence Claims in Scotland

As a defence organisation, CLO is not usually the first stage in a potential claimant's litigation journey, which will ordinarily be when an individual approaches a clinical negligence solicitor about their concern.

Claimants considering litigation need to establish how this will be funded. Self-funding of clinical negligence is relatively rare where a lawyer is used. It is more common for litigants in person.

Another potential funding option might be legal aid.[58] In Scotland the availability of legal aid for clinical negligence is still in place, subject to eligibility criteria.[59] For civil cases, including clinical negligence legal aid is automatically available to individuals who receive or who are included in their partner's claim for the following benefits:

- Income support
- Income based jobseekers allowance
- Income based Employment and Support Allowance
- Universal Credit

For those who do not automatically qualify there are assessments of net annual income, annual outgoings and total disposable capital. All cases that apply for legal aid will also be checked to establish if there is a 'probable cause', if it is a reasonable use of public money and if funding could be found from elsewhere, such as a trade union or insurer. A contribution may be required for individuals who have assets above a certain threshold and clawbacks may be applied to winning litigants. There is a prohibition on solicitors combining legal aid funding with the use of a success fee in the same claim.[60]

The ways in which Scottish clinician negligence litigation could be funded underwent substantial changes in 2020, following the coming into force of the Civil Litigation

---

[57] Prior to September 2013 the scheme was managed by Willis Limited.

[58] Governed by The Legal Aid (Scotland) Act 1986 and associated commencement orders, The Civil Legal Aid (Scotland) Regulations 2002, The Civil Legal Aid (Scotland) (Fees) Regulations 1989, the Act of Sederunt (Civil Legal Aid Rules) 1987.

[59] An eligibility assessment tool is available on the Scottish Legal Aid Board website, see www.slab.org.uk/new-to-legal-aid/eligibility-estimators/estimator-civil-legal-aid/.

[60] S 32(a) of the Legal Aid (Scotland) Act 1989.

(Expenses and Group Proceedings) (Scotland) Act 2018.[61] This Act arose from two major reviews of civil litigation, the 2009 Scottish Civil Courts Review chaired by Lord Gill[62] and the 2013 Review of Expenses and Funding of Civil Litigation in Scotland carried out by Sheriff Principal James Taylor.[63] These reviews considered legal processes and funding. The Taylor Review aimed to address the significant concerns about an 'excluded middle' group of claimants who were inhibited from litigating as they over the threshold for eligibility for legal aid and were not wealthy enough risk being liable for costs (theirs and their opponents) in any action they undertook. The result of this was a consultation which resulted in the 2018 Act, some details of which will be outlined below.

The 2018 Act significantly changed the options for civil litigation funding in Scotland, including altering the way clinical negligence actions can be funded. It should be noted that these reforms were carried out in against a background of concerns about a lack of access to justice and no evidence of a compensation culture. The major recommendations were:

- Prior to the Act coming into force Scottish solicitors could enter into Speculative Fee Agreements (SFAs), which are a form of 'no win, no fee'. If the cases is lost a solicitor does not generally receive a fee from the client. If the case is won the solicitor's costs (base costs) are recoverable from the losing party. A success fee, usually an uplift on the base costs, is paid by the client. The maximum uplift was previously set at 100 per cent of the base costs.[64]

- Under a Damage Based Agreement (DBA) no fee is payable if the case is lost; it is another type of no win, no fee agreement. If the case is won then the base costs are recovered from the losing side and a success fee is taken out of the claimant's compensation. The success fee is an agreed percentage of the damages. Prior to the 2018 Act solicitors and advocates could not enter into DBAs with clients, but claims management companies could. The 2018 Act enabled solicitors to enter into DBAs with clients.

- The success fees for personal injury actions, including clinical negligence cases, are capped.[65] They cannot exceed 100 per cent of legal base costs, and additionally cannot exceed: 20 per cent of the compensation awarded for general damages and past losses up to £100,000; 10 per cent of the compensation awarded for general damages and past losses between £100,000 and £500,000; and 2.5 per cent of the compensation awarded for general damages and past losses over £500,000.

- The 2020 Regulations[66] also provide consumer protection and specify the form and content an agreement between a solicitor and client must include for it to be valid.

---

[61] Civil Litigation (Expenses and Group Proceedings) (Scotland) Act 2018 asp 10 available at www.legislation.gov.uk/asp/2018/10/contents/enacted.

[62] Report of the Scottish Civil Courts Review (2009) available at www.scotcourts.gov.uk/docs/default-source/civil-courts-reform/report-of-the-scottish-civil-courts-review-vol-1-chapt-1---9.pdf?sfvrsn=4.

[63] Sherrif Principal James A Taylor, *REPORT OF THE REVIEW OF EXPENSES AND FUNDING OF CIVIL LITIGATION IN SCOTLAND* (Edinburgh, 2013) available at www.webarchive.org.uk/wayback/archive/20160105185842/http://www.gov.scot/About/Review/taylor-review.

[64] Act of Sederunt (Fees of Solicitors in Speculative Actions) 1992.

[65] S2. The Civil Litigation (Expenses and Group Proceedings) (Scotland) Act 2018 (Success Fee Agreements) Regulations 2020, available at www.legislation.gov.uk/ssi/2020/110/regulation/2/made.

[66] ibid.

- Qualified One-way Cost Shifting (QOCS) was introduced in Scotland and applies to clinical negligence cases. QOCS protects a losing claimant because, in the majority of circumstances, the unsuccessful claimant is not liable to pay the defendant's costs. QOCS were introduced as an 'equality of arms' measure so that claimants would be able to litigate against a defendants with 'deep pockets'.

These reforms protect claimants from liability for CLO's costs and mean that an individual awarded compensation from successful clinical negligence litigation using a DBA will not recover the full value of the damages awarded due to the success fee.

Fees in Scotland are fixed and transparent. Fees are recoverable from the losing party and are calculated based on a statutory fixed table of charges, which regulates the expenses that the successful party can claim. These are updated annually by statute. The winning party can opt either to calculate their fees on the basis of fixed statutory 'inclusive charges' for particular periods of the litigation/types of work done or by charging for the work carried out by reference to set statutory 'detailed charges'. Most cases opt to use 'inclusive charges'. The paying party cannot challenge the choice of the successful party as to the basis for calculating their expenses. Separate tables of charges exist for the Court of Session (and the sheriff court).

If a claimant can find a solicitor willing to take on their case using a no win, no fee agreement they have nothing to lose and no financial barriers to entry. The risk in this relationship sits with the claimant solicitor, who risks not being paid for time invested in a losing case. These reforms are very new and the impact on claims rates will not be known for some time.

b. The Handling of Potential Clinical Negligence Claims in Scotland

There is a statutory pre-action protocol for personal injuries valued at under £25,000 heard in the sheriff court,[67] which expressly excludes clinical negligence claims.[68] There is not a specific clinical negligence protocol, but there are various voluntary protocols, including a voluntary protocol for professional negligence[69] and a voluntary protocol for disease claims (this is widely constructed and is not limited to industrial or workplace diseases).[70] The protocols all vary, but broadly they aim to establish a framework for the early exchange of information to facilitate investigations into liability and the identifying of the issues in dispute, to resolve issues without the need for litigation, and to set out good practice making it easier for parties to obtain and rely upon information required. The personal injury and professional protocols include the requirement to consider ADR and limitation on the entitlement to fees for cases that are settled without recourse to litigation. They are aimed at cases valued at under £25,000. This is the agreed CORIS deductible.

---

[67] www.scotcourts.gov.uk/rules-and-practice/rules-of-court/sheriff-court---civil-procedure-rules/ordinary-cause-rules.

[68] Schedule 1 of the Act of Sederunt (Sheriff Court Rules Amendment) (Personal Injury Pre-Action Protocol) 2016 SI 2016/215, available at www.legislation.gov.uk/ssi/2016/215/schedule/1/made.

[69] www.lawscot.org.uk/members/rules-and-guidance/rules-and-guidance/section-f/division-d/advice-and-information/pre-action-protocol-in-professional-negligence-cases/.

[70] www.lawscot.org.uk/members/rules-and-guidance/rules-and-guidance/section-f/division-d/advice-and-information/pre-action-protocol-in-disease-cases/.

Since 2003 the rules[71] for the handling of personal injury claims in the Sessions Court have been set out in Chapter 43 of the Court of Session Rules (sometimes also known as the 'Coulsfield' Rules). The Chapter 43 rules which aim to eliminate unnecessary delay and expense and to make efficient use of the Court and Judge's time. Parallel provisions for the sheriff courts were brought in 2006.

The aim of swift early resolution in these pre-action protocols seems to be achieved. The vast majority of clinical negligence claims in Scotland settle before proof (trial).

The total number of clinical claims paid by CNORIS,[72] and the total expenditure paid on clinical claims, for 2012/13 to 2018/19 are at Table 3. Clinical claims have risen from 160 in 2013/14 to 10,678 in 2018/19, the high point in claims numbers is seen in 2016/2017. This is very low in comparison with England.

Table 3 CNORIS claims and costs 20012/13 to 2018/19

Year	2012/13	2013/14	2014/15	2015/16	2016/17	2017/18	2018/19
Clinical Claims paid	168	160	193	235	342	260	265
Value of payment from CNORIS on clinical claims £m	£33.13	£34.87	£36.96	£49.70	£38.29	£32.00	£37.54

The percentages of claims received in 2018/19 by number and value are shown in Table 4. Of the 300 payments made in 2018–19, there were six payments of over £1 million and 21 payments (related to 16 claims) where the total value of the claim value was in excess of £1 million.

Given the annual claim numbers are relatively low a breakdown of the three financial years (2016–17, 2017–18 and 2018–19) provides a more balanced view. Throughout these three years obstetrics claims account on average for only 21.7 per cent of the number of claims, but they account on average for 37.4 per cent of the total value of claims over these years. The cost of obstetrics claims is the most expensive, and this is due to the value of support paid to neonates who are damaged at birth. However, unlike England where obstetrics claims represent an increasing and disproportionate percentage of the total claims value, Scottish obstetrics and gynaecology claims are actually a decreasing percentage of the value, see Figure 5. It should be remembered that that these figures are net of deductibles, so removing the sub £25,000 claims which should increase the impact of high value claims.

The largest category over the three years is the 'other <£250k' category, which covers 48 different specialities where there was less than £250k of claims in each of those three years. During this time there was a total of 342 claims valued at £22.56 million.

[71] www.scotcourts.gov.uk/rules-and-practice/rules-of-court/court-of-session-rules.
[72] Figures taken from CNORIS Annual reports available from https://clo.scot.nhs.uk/our-services/cnoris/frequently-asked-questions.aspx.

Table 4 CNORIS claims received by speciality in 2018/19

Speciality	Percentage of claims received	Value of claims received
Trauma and Orthopaedic Surgery	4.3%	2.1%
Emergency Medicine	3.7%	4.5%
Obstetrics and Gynaecology	22.3%	30.5%
General Surgery	7.0%	4.2%
General (Acute) Medicine	3.7%	2.5%
Neurology	3.3%	11.1%
Neurosurgery	3.7%	2.0%
Medical Oncology	7.7%	11.0%
Clinical Other	13.7%	11.7%
Cardiology	1.0%	3.9%
Slips, trips and falls	4.0%	2.6%
Other (aggregated, <£250K per specialty)	25.7%	13.8%

Figure 5 CNORIS claims values for Obs & Gyn, other clinical and non-clinical claims 2009–19

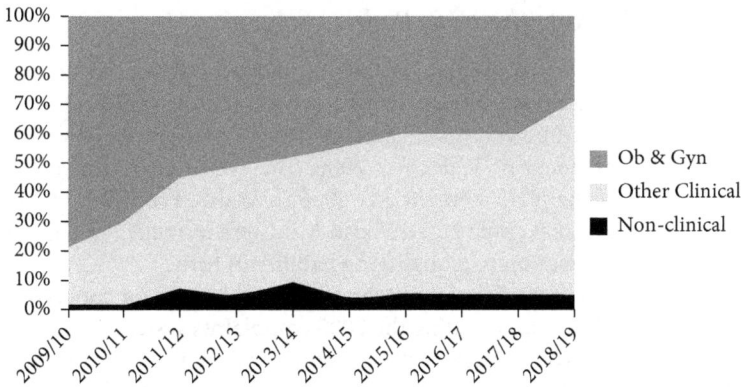

Clinical claims can take many years to conclude, the majority of payments related to claims settled more than five years after the incident occurred, with some settlements taking considerably longer. For claims paid in 2018–19, where dates are provided, the average period between the incident date and the date the claim was received by CLO was 2.74 years, with an average of 4.50 years between CLO receiving the claim to payments being reclaimed by health boards.

C. Claims Against the NHS in Scotland Conclusions

Clinical negligence claiming in Scotland is quite distinct from the patterns seen in England. From a claimant perspective the recent changes to the ways of funding litigation provides more certainty and the introduction of QOCS de-risks the process for the pursuer. It remains to be seen if the move towards a more English funding model will result in higher levels of litigation as is seen south of the border.

V. Clinical Claims Against the NHS in Wales

A. NHS Clinical Negligence Claims in Wales Overview

In 2001 the Auditor General for Wales highlighted that although the annual cost of clinical negligence to the NHS in Wales was considerable and rising, reducing the funds available for patient care, there was little administrative attempt to tackle the underlying causes or the cost issues.[73] In response, a pilot project was introduced in Wales in 2005 entitled *Speedy Resolution*, dealing with claims valued between £5,000 and £15,000. It encouraged NHS bodies to provide explanations to patients who had expressed concerns about their care, and apologies where appropriate, and recommended the use of action plans as a means of learning from mistakes and reducing the number of future claims. An evaluation of the scheme by stakeholders in 2008 found that it had proved beneficial in some respects to both claimants and defendants but the problem of delay remained.[74]

i. Claims under £25,000: The NHS Redress Scheme

Wales is unusual in that it has a unified complaints and legal claims process for claims of £25,000 or less, the NHS Redress Scheme (also known as the Putting Things Right scheme). The NHS complaints procedure was established in 2003.[75] Wales received various devolved powers under the Government of Wales Act 2006. The Welsh Government took steps to implement the policy of the NHS Redress Act 2006 in Wales. From 9 July 2008 the NHS Redress (Wales) Measure 2008 empowered Welsh Ministers to make regulations in respect of NHS redress arising in relation to a qualifying liability in tort.

The Welsh Government introduced its integrated arrangements for concerns, complaints and redress as of 1 April 2011, superseding the 2003 complaints system.[76] The system is built around the notification to Welsh NHS bodies of 'concerns' about health services they have provided, which trigger a duty on the receiving body to investigate the matter through a standing administrative system and respond appropriately, see chapter seven, Section III,

---

[73] *Clinical Negligence in the NHS in Wales* (National Audit Office, 2001). In 1999–2000, over 700 patients or relatives of patients made claims against Welsh trusts and health authorities for alleged clinical negligence. At March 2000 there were over 1,600 open (unresolved) claims for clinical negligence against the NHS Wales, with a total potential value of over £400 million. In 1999–2000 cash payments made by the NHS Wales on clinical negligence cases totalled £26.9 million. It took on average nearly two years for patients to make a claim against the health body after the incident of negligence occurred, and two and a half years for trusts to settle those claims that they received.

[74] *Evaluation of the Speedy Resolution Scheme* (2008), at www.wales.nhs.uk/sites3/Documents/420/WAG%20 Speedy%20Resolution%20Scheme%20-%20July%202008.pdf.

[75] In Directions to Local Health Boards and NHS Trusts in Wales, and in guidance *Complaints in the NHS – A Guide to Handling Complaints in Wales* (2003).

[76] The National Health Service (Concerns, Complaints and Redress Arrangements) (Wales) Regulations 2011, No 704 (W.108) ('2011 Regulations'). See AL Ferguson and E Braithwaite, 'Putting Things Right in Wales' (2012) 18 *Clinical Risk* 6.

'NHS Complaints in Wales'. The body must also consider whether the notification includes an allegation that harm has or may have been caused, and, if so, conclude whether it has a 'qualifying liability', in which case it must produce a written response leading to an offer of redress. The basis of the 'qualifying liability' remains tort law. The redress that can be offered is wider than just financial compensation. A general description of the arrangements follows.

The redress elements of the Regulations do not apply to primary care providers or independent providers.

ii. Claims Over £25,000

Claims for more than £25,000 are dealt with by the courts as clinical negligence cases. Funding and court structures are the same as in England.

Since 2019 clinical negligence claims against NHS Trusts and Health Authorities in Wales have been reimbursed by the Welsh Risk Pool (WRP).[77] The WRP covers risks above a £25,000 threshold[78] which arise from NHS activities, except for business interruption and motor insurance. The reimbursement of claims by the Pool is managed by the Welsh Risk Pool Committee comprising representatives from NHS trusts, local health boards and the Welsh Government.[79] The WRP is administered by the NHS Wales Shared Services Partnership (NWSSP), hosted by the Velindre NHS Trust.

The Welsh Government provides the NWSSP with two distinct funding stream in respect of the WRP:

i.   Departmental Expenditure Limit (the DEL) to meet in year costs associated with settled claims arising within Health Boards and Trusts, eg a lump sum or periodic payment order.
ii. Annually Managed Expenditure (the AME) to meet the costs of accounting for the long term liabilities of claims, ie the provision for the future costs of claims.

In the event that the annual revenue allocation from the Welsh Government is not sufficient to meet the value of the forecast in year expenditure, that is, the DEL, then the service bears the risk of any variation from the estimate and the excess will be subject to an agreed risk sharing agreement with the NHS Wales member organisations.

The WRP risk sharing model is calculates weighted risks for each organisation according to performance in five key areas, see Table 5.[80]

---

[77] Prior to this they were handled by the Welsh Government.
[78] The £25,000 threshold does not apply to GP claims handled under the General Medical Practice Indemnity scheme.
[79] The Clinical Negligence Scheme for Trusts, at www.nhsla.com/claims/Documents/CNST%20Rules.pdf. The CNST was established by Regulations originally made pursuant to the National Health Service and Community Care Act 1990 s 21 and subsequently the National Health Service Act 2006 s 71 as amended by the Health and Social Care Act 2012. See also *Risk Management in the NHS* EL(93)111 (Department of Health, 1993).
[80] Taken from NWSSP Legal and Risk Services including the Welsh Risk Pool, *Impact and Reach Report*, November 2020, available at ttps://cwmtafmorgannwg.wales/Docs/Quality,%20Safety%20and%20Risk%20 Committee/14%20NOVEMBER%2018%202020/2.8c%20Impact%20and%20Reach%20Report%202020%20 final%20QSC%2018%20November%202020.pdf.

Table 5 Welsh Risk Pool risk sharing model categories and weightings

	Area	Weighting
A	Hospital and Community Health Services and Prescribing Allocation	30%
B	Claims History	20%
C	New claims passed to Legal and Risk Services for Litigation	10%
D	Claims potentially affecting next years' spend: i. cases with estimated cash flows within a year ii. Periodic payment orders	25%
E	Management of concerns and learning from events.	15%

From 1 April 2019 the NWSSP also administer the General Medical Practice Indemnity (GMPI), a discretionary state-backed scheme providing indemnity for providers of GP services in Wales for compensation arising from clinical negligence claims relating to the care, diagnosis and treatment of a patient following incidents on or after 1 April 2019.[81]

NWSSP's key purpose is:

- to provide a comprehensive in-house legal and risk service to NHS Wales that is recognised as approachable, responsive and reliable; and

- to support health bodies in learning lessons from things that go wrong.

B. NHS Redress Arrangements

A Welsh NHS body that receives notification of a concern that includes an allegation that harm has, or may have, been caused must determine whether or not an offer of redress should be made to a patient, where there is, or may be, a qualifying liability.[82] Where the qualifying liability arises, the Regulation 24 duty to prepare a written response described in chapter seven, Section III does not apply, and instead an interim report under regulation 26 must be prepared. Where the body decides that there is no qualifying liability and the redress arrangements in Part 6 will not be triggered, it must provide reasons for that view.[83]

The interim report:[84]

- summarises the nature and substance of the matter or matters notified in the concern;

- describes the investigation undertaken in accordance with regulation 23;

- describes why, in the opinion of the Welsh NHS body, there is or there may be a qualifying liability;

- contains a copy of any relevant medical records;

---

[81] There is also a Wales Existing Liabilities Scheme for details see https://nwssp.nhs.wales/ourservices/legal-risk-services/areas-of-practice/general-medical-practice-indemnity-gmpi/.

[82] The National Health Service (Concerns, Complaints and Redress Arrangements) (Wales) Regulations 2011, No 704 (W.108) ('2011 Regulations') reg 25.

[83] ibid, reg 24(3).

[84] ibid, reg 26.

- explains the availability of access to legal advice without charge in accordance with the provisions of regulation 32;
- explains the availability of advocacy and support services which may be of assistance;
- explains the procedure which will be followed to determine whether or not a qualifying liability exists and the procedure for making an offer of redress if such a qualifying liability is found to exist;
- confirms that, when prepared, a copy of the investigation report referred to in regulation 31 will be made available, in accordance with the provisions of that regulation, to the person who is seeking redress;
- contains details of the right to notify the concern to the Public Services Ombudsman for Wales;
- offers the person who is seeking redress the opportunity to discuss the contents of the interim report with the responsible officer or a person acting on his or her behalf; and
- is signed by the responsible officer or a person acting on his or her behalf.

The duty to consider redress under Part 6 only applies to Welsh NHS bodies, which are defined in regulation 2 as Local Health Boards and National Health Service Trusts managing a hospital or other establishment or facility wholly or mainly in Wales. It does not apply to primary care providers or independent providers.

The form that redress may take is:[85]

- the making of an offer of compensation in satisfaction of any right to bring civil proceedings in respect of a qualifying liability;
- the giving of an explanation;
- the making of a written apology; and
- the giving of a report on the action which has been, or will be, taken to prevent similar cases arising.

The compensation that may be offered can take the form of entry into a contract to provide care or treatment or of financial compensation, or both.[86] Guidance sets out a tariff for general damages.[87]

There is a limit of £25,000 on the financial compensation element of redress in relation to special and general damages.[88] If, on investigation, it transpires that the financial quantum of the claim exceeds £25,000, redress must not be offered in accordance with the Regulations.[89] However, regulation 29(3) provides that if the financial limit will be exceeded, a Welsh NHS body may give consideration to making an offer of settlement outside the

---

[85] ibid, reg 27.

[86] ibid, reg 27(2).

[87] A tariff is at *Putting Things Right: Guidance on Dealing with Concerns from the 1st April 2011* (3rd version, Welsh Government, 2013) Appendix Q. The guidance states that responsible bodies should 'avoid settling cases of doubtful merit, however small, purely on a "nuisance value" basis': para 8.22.

[88] The National Health Service (Concerns, Complaints and Redress Arrangements) (Wales) Regulations 2011, No 704 (W.108) ('2011 Regulations'), reg 29.

[89] ibid, reg 29.

provisions of the Regulations, assessing the value of any compensation on the common law basis.[90] The Welsh Ministers also have the power to issue a compensation tariff.

Redress is not available in relation to a liability that is or has been the subject of civil proceedings and if civil proceedings are issued during the course of a Welsh NHS body's consideration of redress, the Welsh NHS body's consideration of redress must stop and the person who notified the concern must be so advised.[91]

Limitation periods are suspended during the period in which a liability is the subject of an application for redress under the Regulations.[92]

Where a Welsh NHS body has determined that a qualifying liability exists or may exist it must ensure that legal advice is available, on prescribed matters, free of charge to the person who notified the concern, from a lawyer who is a member of one of two defined groups that specialise in clinical negligence.[93] It must also ensure that if medical experts need to be instructed, they are instructed jointly by the Welsh NHS body and the person who notified the concern.[94]

C. Welsh Risk Pool Claims Handling[95]

Soon after the NHS Redress scheme was introduced in 2011, early statistics indicated an increase in complaints about healthcare throughout Wales of up to 60 per cent, many accompanied by solicitors' letters and requests for redress.[96] Patients and their relatives initiated concerns and complaints in almost equal numbers, but the Community Health Councils also played a part in the process.[97] Legal reforms in 2013–14 led to further claim volume increases, but the volume of open cases being managed by the Welsh Risk Pool has been steadily declining, with the volume of cases opened annually dropping from 1,168 (2013–14) to 854 (2017–18). The value of claims has been rising, see Table 6, which is in part due to changes in the PIDR.

Clinical negligence claims make up the vast majority of the WRP payments by value, consistently between 92–97 per cent from 2014–19. The WRP data does not include claims under £25,000, these claims are included in the total clinical negligence figures in Table 6 and Figure 6. As can be seen in Figure 6 the WRP claims make up the vast majority of the value of the total clinical negligence claims paid despite being the minority of claims made, as would be expected. Part of the increase in the value of clinical negligence claims seen in Figure 6 is attributable to the changes in the Personal Injury Discount Rate (PIDR) from 2.5 per cent to minus 0.75 per cent in March 2017. Another knock-on from the changes in

---

[90] ibid, reg 29(3).
[91] ibid, reg 28.
[92] ibid, reg 30.
[93] ibid, reg 32.
[94] ibid.
[95] Taken from the NHS (Wales) Summarised Accounts 2014–15, 2015–16, 2016–17, 2017–18, 2018–19 and the Velindre University NHs Trust Annual accounts 2018–19.
[96] V Harpwood, 'Clinical Negligence and Poor Quality Care: Is Wales "Putting Things Right?"' in PR Ferguson and GT Laurie (eds), *Inspiring a Medico-Legal Revolution: Essays in Honour of Sheila McLean* (Ashgate, 2015).
[97] ibid.

PIDR has been for claimants to ask for more of their settlement to be delivered in the lump sum and less paid as periodical payments (PPOs). This emerging trend has not been reversed by the announcement made by the Lord Chancellor in July 2019 to changes the PIDR from minus 0.75 per cent to minus 0.25 per cent.[98]

Table 6 Welsh Risk Pool and total Welsh clinical negligence claims paid and values 2014–19

	2014/15	2015/16	2016/17	2017/18	2018/19
Value of WRP Clin Neg claims paid (£m)	£58.182	£41.02	£54.12	£77.121	£96.489
Number of WRP Clin Neg claims paid	324	327	298	363	375
Total value of Clin Neg claims paid (£m)	£67.931	£56.59	£71.754	£91.378	£103.697
Total number of Clin Neg claims paid	702	686	759	792	985

Figure 6 Number and value of Welsh clinical negligence claims

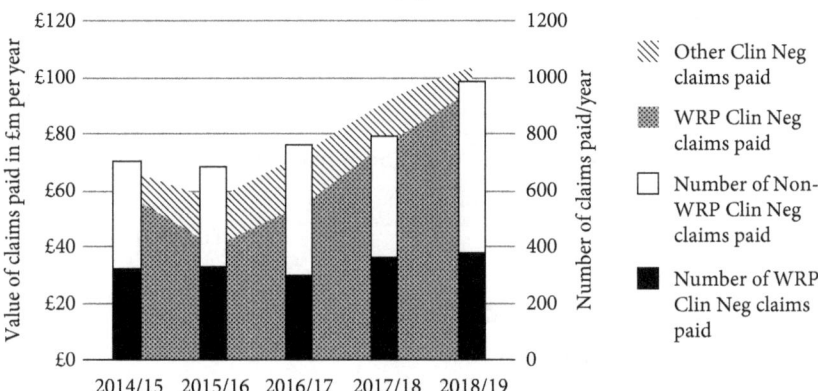

The number of higher value claims paid by the WRP has increased slowly since 2014, see Table 7 which details claims worth over £300,000, though it is difficult to confirm a statistically significant upsurge as these are relatively low numbers, there does seem to be a trend. However, the values of these claims have increased substantially over the same time period. This is likely to be due in part higher life expectancies and the changes in the PIDR.

Table 7 Clinical negligence claims over £300,000 in Wales 2014–19

	2014/15	2015/16	2016/17	2017/18	2018/19
Number of Clin Neg claims paid	47	48	57	50	62
Value of Clin Neg Claims paid £m	£39.561	£31.887	£44.312	£61.088	£70.125

---

[98] Page 20 of NWSSP Legal and Risk Services including the Welsh Risk Pool *Impact and Reach Report* (November 2020) available at https://cwmtafmorgannwg.wales/Docs/Quality,%20Safety%20and%20Risk%20 Committee/14%20NOVEMBER%2018%202020/2.8c%20Impact%20and%20Reach%20Report%202020%20 final%20QSC%2018%20November%202020.pdf.

As is seen in other nations of the UK maternity incidents are very expensive to compensate, see Figure 7 which shows 2019/20 expenditure over £500,000 as at March 2020.

Figure 7 WRP 2019/20 expenditure over £500,000 as at March 2020

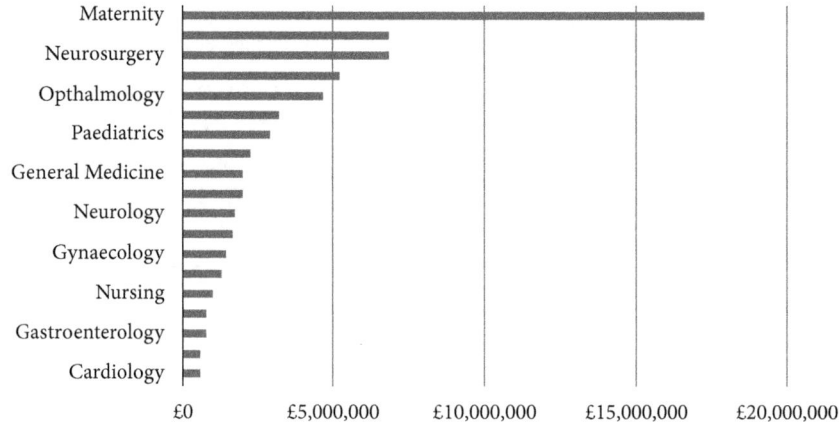

As at 1 April 2020 the following provisions had been made for the WRP.[99]

Clinical Negligence lump sum payments	
– Secondary care	£675,550
– Primary Care	–
– Redress Secondary Care	£3,375
Personal Injury lump sum payments	£5,144
Defence legal fees and other administration	£8,688
Structured settlements	£441,063
Total	**£1,133,820**

Provisions for claims are accounted for according to their probability of settlement, see Table 8.

Table 8 Provisions made for different classifications of claims by WRP

Classification	Probability of settlement	Provisions made
Remote	0–5%	None – contingent liability
Possible	6%–49%	Defence fee – all other expected expenditure classed as a contingent liability and no provision is made
Probable	50%–94%	Full provision
Certain	95%–100%	Full provision

[99] NHS (Wales) Summarised Accounts Local Health Boards, NHS Trusts and Special Health Authority in Wales 2020–21 available at https://senedd.wales/media/odndmexj/agr-ld14491-e.pdf.

The breakdown of provisions set aside by the WRP by case classification for 2018/19 and 2019/20 is set out in Table 9.[100] The majority of cases are in the certain category so are expected to be realised. The average value of provisions for probable and certain cases was around one million pounds per case (£.0987 million in 2018/19; £1.034 million in 2019/20). This is a very high value.

Table 9 Closing provisions for claims made by WRP in 2018/19 and 2019/20

	2018/19		2019/20	
	Numbers of cases	**Provision made £m**	**Numbers of cases**	**Provision made £m**
Probable	123	£103.387	130	£73.335
Certain	544	£555.538	540	£619.567
Total probable & certain cases	**667**	**£658.925**	**670**	**£692.902**
Contingent liabilities	1,126		1,004	
Total cases	**1,793**		**1,674**	

D. Learning from Events

Under the redress process each responsible body must ensure that it has processes in place to ensure that any deficiencies in its actions or service provision that are identified as part of an investigation of a concern are acted upon and monitored.[101] It must keep a record of any actions taken in order to monitor the operation of the arrangements for dealing with concerns under the Regulations,[102] and must prepare an annual report on such matters.[103]

The process of learning from claims and redress cases has become known as the Learning from Events process and is overseen by WRP.

i. Learning from Litigated Cases

Learning from claims has been well established for many years. However, an internal review of the Learning from Events process revealed that the submission of a learning plan was often late in the claims process, reducing the potential for learning, so a new process was developed, see Figure 8.

---

[100] Page 20 of NWSSP Legal and Risk Services including the Welsh Risk Pool *Impact and Reach Report* (November 2020) available at https://cwmtafmorgannwg.wales/Docs/Quality,%20Safety%20and%20Risk%20Committee/14%20NOVEMBER%202018%202020/2.8c%20Impact%20and%20Reach%20Report%202020%20final%20QSC%2018%20November%202020.pdf.

[101] The National Health Service (Concerns, Complaints and Redress Arrangements) (Wales) Regulations 2011, No 704 (W.108) ('2011 Regulations') reg 49.

[102] ibid, reg 50.

[103] ibid, reg 51.

Figure 8 Old and new processes for learning from claims

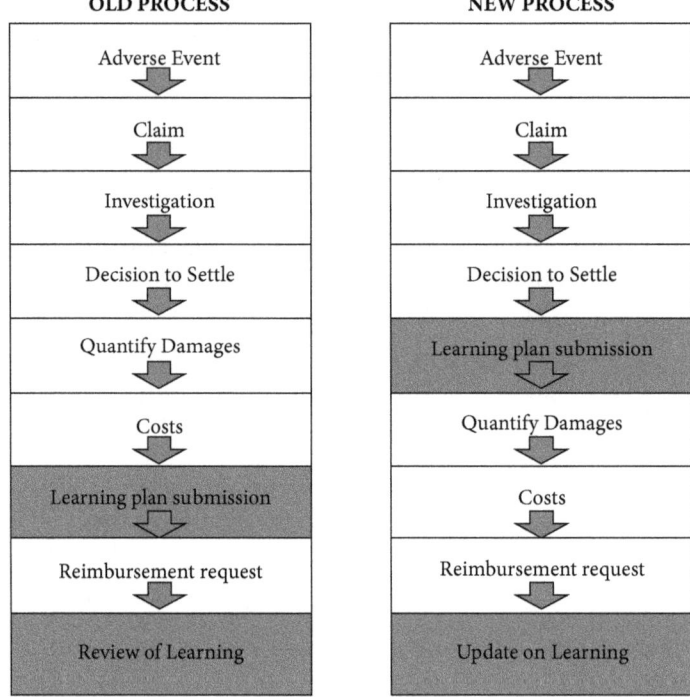

Causal factors are identified during the analysis of the claim. Generic causal factors tend to fall into three categories: communication issues, documentation issues and/or escalation issues.

Using the reviews of causal factors and lessons learned the WRP is able to identify specific themed areas that require improvement and changes in clinical and/or organisation practice. These have included:

– Maternity services – specifically looking at communication issues and analysis, recording and responses to CardioToco Graph (CTG) monitoring of the baby. Practical Obstetric Multi-Professional Training (PROMPT) Wales programme has been implemented and identified as having a positive impact on communication issues.

– Access to Regional Services – such as referral to and acceptance by regional specialist services like neurosurgery and vascular services.

– Radiological Investigations – a 2018/19 review of Welsh radiological services identified that while all radiology services have discrepancy review processes to monitor and learn from errors in image interpretation there is limited sharing of learnings from these discrepancy reviews, either locally or nationally. Delays in acting on unexpected and incidental findings on radiology reports was also identified as a common theme. Until the national electronic solution to share findings and ensure they are acted upon is available resources need to be made available. WRP follow ups include another review and updates on actions taken by organisations.

- Consent to examination and treatment – this is complex and WRP created a national team to drive the consent agenda across all services. Highlighted actions include ensuring that consistent information is provided to all Welsh patient using the EIDO consent system by refusing to reimburse claims where the EIDO patient leaflets are not used.
- Pressure ulcers – analysis of claims identified direct and indirect causal factors, usually due to deficits in basic nursing care. A Causal Factor table on the Datix system enables organisations to map the effectiveness of their pressure ulcer strategy both across and within the organisation.

ii. *Learning from Redress Cases*

A key driver for the transfer of responsibility for the reimbursement of redress cases from Welsh Government to WRP in 2019 was the need to implement scrutiny of the learning from each case. It was felt that despite the intentions in the Regulations the redress process needed to move from a purely financial reimbursement model into a more learning model. To provide support to health bodies in this process WRP Safety and Learning Advisors were deployed to assist organisations analyse their redress case investigation findings and to link learning and improvement actions to these.

Since 2019 hundreds of redress cases have been scrutinised and in the majority of cases examined there had been learning assurance. The objective going forward is to ensure the provision of more structured consistent learning information. This has broadly been viewed as a positive development by claims handling teams within hospitals and Trusts as it provides leverage for them to encourage healthcare professionals and departments to provide the necessary information and to implement any resulting action plans.

An additional level of oversight of learning from redress cases has been added by the creation of a peer-review panel. This panel is formed of junior leadership clinicians from around Wales, the peer-review group shares the learning from all redress cases and makes recommendations to the Welsh Risk Pool Committee about whether the learning information is suitable and sufficient.

E. Conclusions on the Welsh Scheme

Various features of the Welsh NHS redress scheme are notable. First, it introduces the concept of redress into the formal duties of NHS bodies, thereby attempting to provide a better pathway for providing redress than through legal claims backed by litigation. Second, it integrates complaints and redress into a unified system. This provides a single point of entry for patients and means that patients do not have to consider whether they want to raise a formal written complaint or initiate litigation, a verbal concern can be enough to initiate the process. This is very different to the other UK jurisdictions and should create a much easier route for patients to obtaining compensation.

It aims to produce consistent responses, save overheads and enable learning by creating a unified database of information. In their 2020 Impact and Reach Report the Share Services Partnership Legal and Risk Services state 'Effective use of the Redress process has a direct impact on the litigation costs for each organisation, with average savings of over £30k in claimants' costs'. However, concerns have been raised about delays to the way concerns with qualifying liabilities are investigated and a lack of oversight from this.[104]

VI. Clinical Claims Against the NHS in Northern Ireland

A. NHS Clinical Negligence Claims in Northern Ireland Overview

Civil cases in Northern Ireland which are valued at less than £30,000 are initiated in the County Court. The County Court has a fairly predictable costs trajectory as both solicitor and barrister costs are scaled or fixed.[105] This allows a litigant to know in advance how much they will be liable to pay should they lose the case.

Clinical negligence cases valued at over £30,000 are heard in the High Court. This is where the majority of Northern Irish clinical negligence claims are heard. In a consultation in 2021[106] on the jurisdiction of the County Court the Government asked if clinical negligence claims should be reserved as High Court actions. The Government response to the consultation in November 2021 summarised the responses and concluded that there should be no change to the existing arraignments which allow County courts to hear lower value clinical negligence claims. The consultation response also noted the development of a protocol for Clinical Negligence claims in the High Court.

i. *The Filtering and Funding of Potential Clinical Negligence Claims in Northern Ireland*

A potential claimant's litigation journey will ordinarily start when that individual approaches a clinical negligence solicitor about their concern.

Claimants considering litigation need to establish how this will be funded. Self-funding of clinical negligence is relatively rare where a lawyer is used, it is more common for litigants in person.

Another potential funding option might be legal aid.[107] In Northern Ireland the availability of legal aid for clinical negligence is still in place, subject to very strict eligibility criteria based on disposable income and disposable capital. Claimants who fall below the lower limits will receive their legal aid and no contribution is required, claimants who fall

---

[104] M Rosser, 'The Welsh NHS Redress Arrangements – Are They Putting Things Right for Welsh Patients?' (2014) 20(6) *Clinical Risk* 144–49, DOI: 10.1177/1356262214566700; www.itv.com/news/wales/2018-12-18/more-than-half-of-nhs-wales-complaints-not-resolved-within-target-time.

[105] The current scales can be found in the County Court (Amendment) Rules (Northern Ireland) 2017, NISR 2017/19, available at www.legislation.gov.uk/nisr/2017/19/contents/made.

[106] Consultation on increasing the jurisdiction of the county courts available at www.justice-ni.gov.uk/consultations/consultation-increasing-jurisdiction-county-court.

[107] Legal Aid is administered by the Legal Services Agency Northern Ireland (LSA NI) which was established under the Legal Aid and Coroners' Courts Act (NI) 2014 c 11, available at www.legislation.gov.uk/nia/2014/11/contents.

between the lower and upper limits will be required to make a contribution. In personal injury cases the current lower limit for disposable income is £3,355; the upper disposable income limit is £10,955. The disposable capital lower limit is £3,000, the upper limit is £8,560. These limits have remained unchanged from 6 April 2009.

Technically no win, no fee arrangements are not permitted in Northern Ireland.[108] The second part of the Report on Access to Justice chaired by Colin Stutt[109] described various funding mechanisms for personal injury litigation including

> specialist personal injury practitioners who deal with large volumes of cases and have established ATE insurance arrangements covering all their clients … Other funding options include trade union support. For smaller firms however more informal practices are used. My understanding is that most claims are pursued 'on spec' on the express or implied understanding that the solicitor will not pursue the client for costs if the claim is unsuccessful, although the client will usually be expected to fund the disbursements if they can afford to do so.

As the report acknowledged many personal injury cases in Northern Ireland operate under what are in practice conditional fee agreements, although they are not recognised as such.

Another significant difference is that QOCS are not applied in litigation in Northern Ireland. This means that there is a risk to potential litigants. QOCS have been discussed in the Stutt report, but have not been implemented to date.

ii. The Handling of Potential Clinical Negligence Claims in Northern Ireland

Unlike the other UK jurisdictions there is no centralised defence body like NHS Resolution, CNORIS or WRP. Claims are handled by the defendant health body.

Cases are handled according to standard clinical negligence proceedings, as set out in Practice Direction No 2 of 2021.[110] The 2021 clinical negligence protocol objectives include:

i.   Early communication between patients and healthcare providers of any perceived concerns about medical care or treatment.

ii. The development by healthcare providers of early reporting and investigation systems.

iii. Disclosure of sufficient information so as to enable patients and healthcare providers to understand the issues and encourage early resolution.

iv. The timely provision of relevant medical records by healthcare providers to patients or their legal representatives.

---

[108] Section 58 of the Courts and Legal Services Act 1990 c 41 available at www.legislation.gov.uk/ukpga/1990/41/contents, did not extend to Northern Ireland (see s 123 of the Act) and s 58(3)(b) expressly provided that a conditional fee agreement 'must not relate to proceedings which cannot be the subject of an enforceable conditional fee agreement'. Although Part III of the Access to Justice (Northern Ireland) Order 2003 2003 No 435 (N.I. 10), available at https://www.legislation.gov.uk/nisi/2003/435/contents, made provision for conditional fee agreements, these articles were never commenced. In the case of *Baranowski v Rice* [2014] NIQB 122 Mr Justice Stephens held that fees under a conditional fee agreement were irrecoverable under Northern Irish law unless sanctioned by statute.

[109] The Report of Access to Justice, *A Strategy for Access to Justice* (September 2015) available at www.justice-ni.gov.uk/sites/default/files/publications/doj/access-to-justice-review-part-2-report.pdf.

[110] Practice Direction No 2 of 2021 Protocol for clinical negligence in the High Court and Practice Direction for Experts effective from 1 October 2021, available from www.judiciaryni.uk/judicial-decisions/practice-direction-0221.

v.   Placing the parties in a position where they may be able to resolve cases fairly and early without litigation together with the consideration of mediation and/or other forms of Alternative Dispute Resolution, where appropriate.

vi.   The promotion of an overall "cards on the table" approach to litigation in the interests of keeping the amount invested by the participants in terms of money, time and stress to a minimum, consistent with the requirement that the issues be resolved in accordance with the accepted standards of fairness and justice for both parties.

What is particularly interesting is that objective ii. sits entirely outside the remit and scope of the civil courts.

The protocol specifically draws attention away from litigation at points 13 and 14.

Health Service Complaints Procedure

13. Attention is drawn to the complaints procedures that exist with the healthcare providers. These procedures are designed to provide patients with an explanation of what happened and an apology, if appropriate. They are not designed to provide compensation for cases of negligence. However, patients might choose to use these procedures if their only, or main, goal is to obtain an explanation, or to obtain more information to help them decide what other action might be appropriate.

Alternative Dispute Resolution

14. The parties might inform their clients of the options available to resolve disputes by alternative dispute resolution and in particular that it is voluntary, confidential and impartial. A form of alternative dispute resolution might be more suitable than litigation, and if so the parties may consider which form to adopt and pursue in a timely manner.

Although there is no centralised claims handing as happens in the other UK jurisdictions the Department of Health publishes annual clinical negligence statistics.[111]

Table 10 Northern Irish claims and costs 20012/13 to 2018/19

Year	2014/15	2015/16	2016/17	2017/18	2018/19
Clinical Claims opened	752	686	667	744	704
Damages paid (m)	£30.1	£16.3	£19.7	£26.3	£21.2
Claimant legal costs (m)	£6.7	£7.4	£6.3	£6.1	£5.8
Defendant legal costs (m)	£4.5	£2.9	£2.6	£3.3	£2.1
Total Legal costs (£m)	£11.2	£10.3	£8.9	£9.4	£7.9
Total Expenditure (damages, costs) £m	£41.3	£26.6	£28.5	£35.7	£29.2

Despite not having a centralised claims handling facility there is relatively little difference between the breakdown of expenditure by damages and legal fees seen in Northern Ireland

[111] www.health-ni.gov.uk/articles/clinical-negligence-statistics.

compared to other UK jurisdictions, see Table 11. There is somewhat more variability year to year in Northern Ireland, which may be due to the relatively low claims numbers.

Table 11 Breakdown of clinical negligence expenditure by damages and costs

	2014/15	2015/16	2016/17	2017/18	2018/19
Damages as a % of total expenditure	73%	61%	69%	74%	73%
Claimant legal cost as a % of total expenditure	16%	28%	22%	17%	20%
Defendant legal costs as a % of total expenditure	11%	11%	9%	9%	7%
Legal Costs as a % of total expenditure	27%	39%	31%	26%	27%

The Northern Irish reports tend to use open cases as their reference point, that is cases where an official letter of notification of intention to proceed with the case has been received and the case has not been settled of closed by the end of the year in question. As at 31 March 2019 2,995 cases remained open. Settled cases are those where an agreement to settle has been reached, but the case had not been closed in that year. As at 31 March 2019 211 cases were settled. Closed cases refers to: (i) a case where the decision has been made to withdraw or not proceed with no money being awarded; or (ii) a case where all monies awarded have been paid, and there is no longer any activity. A case is officially closed when the Directorate of Legal Services (DLS) issue a letter stating that the case has been closed. 789 cases were closed during 2018/19. What is clear from these numbers is that the majority of claims are taking a considerable time to resolve the average time a case had been open for in 2018/19 was 2.8 years. For cases that were closed in 2018/19 around two thirds had been open for less than five years. For a third of the cases which closed in 2018/19 the legal process (this is from notification, not from the incident) had lasted for more than five years. This is hardly speedy dispute resolution.

During 2018/19 a total of £138.3 was paid out on 3,995 cases which had been open at some point in 2018/19. Of these the PPO cases make up a very small percentage of the cases, but a considerable part of the value, which is simply a reflection of the type of cases where a PPO is used.

Table 12 Breakdown of clinical negligence expenditure by PPO and non-PPO cases

	Cases numbers	% of total case numbers	Payments made in 2018/19	% of total payments made
Non-PPO cases	3,962	99%	66.3	48%
PPO Cases	33	1%	72	52%
Total	3,995	100%	138.3	100%

14.9 per cent of the monies paid out in 2018/19 was on the 789 cases closed in those years. 502 (63.6 per cent) cases were closed without any damages being paid. Of these cases where no damages were awarded 63 cases (8 per cent) had legal fees paid, which totalled

£0.2 million. 287 cases were closed with payments, totalling £20.6 million. In 152 cases (53 per cent) the legal costs paid exceeded the amount of damages paid; for these cases £1.3 million was paid in damages and £2.6 million was paid in legal fees.

The percentages of claims open in 2018/19 by speciality are shown in Table 13. Obstetric claims make up 18 per cent of the claims, but over half of the amounts paid (£77.7 million, 56.2 per cent of amounts paid on open claims in 2018/19). The cost of obstetrics claims is a notable outlier, see Figure 9, and this is due to the value of support paid to neonates who are damaged at birth.

Table 13 Open cases by speciality in 2018/19

	2018/19	**Percentage**
Accident & Emergency	670	17%
Anaesthetics & Pain Mgt.	50	1%
Burns, Plastic & Max. Surgery	28	1%
Cardiac Surgery	23	1%
Cardiology	47	1%
Children & Young People	114	3%
Dentistry	21	1%
Ear, Nose & Throat	43	1%
General Medicine	209	5%
General Surgery	413	10%
Gynaecology	259	6%
Mental Health Acute	71	2%
Neurology	107	3%
Neurosurgery	27	1%
Obstetrics	712	18%
Oncology	43	1%
Ophthalmology	51	1%
Paediatrics	91	2%
Radiology	60	2%
Trauma & Orthopaedics	369	9%
Urology	66	2%
Other	459	11%
Unknown	62	2%
Total	**3,995**	**100%**

Figure 9 Payments on the 10 largest specialties in 2018/19

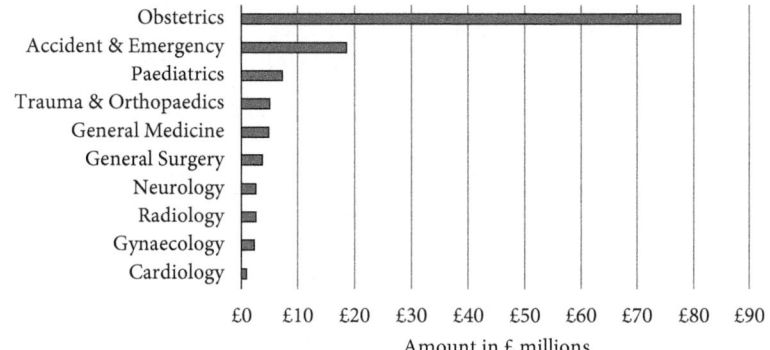

Amount in £ millions

B. Northern Ireland Clinical Negligence Conclusions

Cases in Northern Ireland seem to progress along broadly similar lines to those in England and Scotland. Of particular interest are the figures for legal fees as a percentage of damages which seem to be consistent between Northern Ireland and those seen in England. Given that NHS Resolution handles more claims and has centralised ability to contract defence solicitors and to counter excessive claimant fees this equivalence seems potentially surprising. The time litigation takes does appear to be longer. Interesting the number of PPOs also appears to be low.

VII. Conclusions: Clinical Negligence

A. Clinical Negligence Litigation in the Home Nations

While they are all unified in the tests for, and thresholds used to establish, clinical negligence there are also significant differences between the four home nations. They all have quite distinct approaches to clinical negligence litigation, for example there are marked contrasts in funding mechanism (in particular legal aid) and fees for lawyers. Wales has taken a strikingly different approach, and has a definition of Redress that is far wider than the financial compensation offered by litigation.

Focussing just on litigation rather than redress, there are striking differences seen between litigation rates and costs in the different home nations. This was highlighted in data in the Government's evidence to the Health and Social Care Select Committee's 2022 Inquiry into NHS Litigation Reform,[112] see Table 14.

---

[112] Page 145 of Health and Social Care Select Committee, *NHS Litigation Reform*, Thirteenth Report of Session 2021–22, HC 750, 28 April 2022, available at https://committees.parliament.uk/publications/22039/documents/163739/default/.

Table 14 Clinical Negligence litigation rates and spends in the home nations

Country	Population (millions)	Claims/ 100,000	Cost per capita (£)	% GDP	% Health Spend
England	56	19	42.1	0.1%	2%
Wales	3.1	14	29.2	0.1%	1%
Scotland	5.4	9	6.9	0.02%	0.3%

Figures for England and Scotland use 2018/19 data, Wales uses 2017 data.

From the perspective of a potential claimant the funding mechanisms are likely to be significant in a decision to pursue litigation. Scotland and Northern Ireland have more generous legal aid provisions than England and Wales, and have had much more limited CFAs. It is interesting that the assumption in Scotland and Northern Ireland is that as they don't have a compensation culture, moving towards a modified English model would be appropriate. The extent to which the English funding model drives the compensation culture remains to be seen.

Another very striking difference in the four nations is the value of the Personal Injury Discount Rate. This is set independently and varies, see Table 15 for the values as at the end of January 2022.

Table 15 UK personal injury discount rates as at 31 January 2022

England & Wales[113]	Scotland[114]	Northern Ireland[115]
−0.25 per cent	−0.75 per cent	−1.75 per cent

While this will not impact on the claiming process per se it will affect the overall value of the damages which successful claimants obtain. Prior to July 2017 the Personal Injury Discount Rate in England and Wales was set at 2.5 per cent, it then dropped to −0.75 per cent from 27 February 2017 until 15 July 2019 when it was changed to −0.25 per cent. In Northern Ireland the PIDR changed from 2.5 per cent to −1.75 per cent from 31 May 2021. Table 16, taken from the NI government consultation, highlights how much the PIDR impacts the value of the settlement, which in turn may impact the form of the settlement that a claimant wishes to take. The Welsh Risk Pool indicate that they think that negative discount rate has prompted more claimants towards lump sums rather than PPOs, which is potentially not surprising.

[113] As of 15 July 2019, see www.gov.uk/government/news/lord-chancellor-announces-new-discount-rate-for-personal-injury-claims, prior to this it had been at −0.75%.

[114] Last reviewed by the Government's Actuary in his *The Personal Injury Discount Rate – Review and Determination of the Rate in Scotland by the Government Actuary* (30 September 2019) see www.gov.uk/government/publications/the-personal-injury-discount-rate-review-and-determination-of-the-rate-in-scotland-by-the-government-actuary.

[115] As of 31 May 2021, see www.justice-ni.gov.uk/news/personal-injury-discount-rate-set-change.

Table 16 Worked examples of the effect of different PIDRs on an annual care award of £100,000 for the rest of the claimant's life for two scenarios[116]

Discount rate	Total award	
	40-year-old male with normal life expectancy	10-year old female with normal life expectancy
2.5%	£2,652,000	£3,475,000
1%	£3,611,000	£5,557,000
−0.25%	£4,876,000	£9,128,000
−0.75%	£5,566,000	£11,470,000
−2%	£8,005,000	£21,932,000

It is difficult to ascertain the impact of any individual variable on litigation, but what is clear is that the home nations have very different approaches and vastly disparate spends. The move towards an English model by Scotland and Northern Ireland looks as though it has the potential to increase both claim numbers, which is part of the objective where there are concerns about lack of access to justice. Table 14 demonstrates England also has a substantially higher cost per capita than Scotland, this cannot be attributed to the PIDR as both nations had a PIDR of −0.75 when these figures were collected. It is too early to say if similar increases in spend will be seen in Scotland and Northern Ireland.

B. Litigation for Clinical Negligence

In their evidence to the Health and Social Care Select Committee inquiry into NHS Litigation Reform[117] the Bar Council said that to suggest that clinical negligence should generate learning 'is to misunderstand the purpose of tort law which is to compensate the victim and not to punish or prevent recidivism by the tortfeasor'.

Litigation is outside the NHS. Raising a concern with a solicitor does not mean that the NHS will become aware of this concern; this will only happen if the case is proceeded with. According to the Society of Clinical their members filter around 100,000 contacts per year, and only circa 3 per cent of these contacts are deemed actionable.[118] The information contained within the 97 per cent of cases that are rejected is spread across the claimant lawyer market, it is lost to the NHS. All the pre-action protocols suggest that claimants should be informed of the NHS complaints system, but this is somewhat closing the stable door after the horse has bolted as the majority of those who tried to raise a concern have been filtered out before a pre-action protocol is engaged. The effectiveness of this requirement in the

---

[116] Taken from the Northern Irish Department of Justice, *The Personal Injury Discount Rate: How Should It Be Set?* (2020) p 8, available at www.justice-ni.gov.uk/sites/default/files/consultations/justice/Personal%20Injury%20 Discount%20Rate%20-%20How%20Should%20It%20Be%20Set%20a%20Consultation.pdf.

[117] Health and Social Care Select Committee, *NHS Litigation Reform* Thirteenth Report of Session 2021–22, HC 750, 28 April 2022 report is available at https://committees.parliament.uk/publications/22039/documents/163739/ default/ and the Bar Council evidence is available at https://committees.parliament.uk/writtenevidence/40565/ pdf/.

[118] See the Access to Justice Section of the SCIL Campaign available at www.scil.org.uk/campaign.

pre-action protocol is questionable, as 52 per cent of claims are made without a complaint attached, 10 per cent of claims have no complaints information and 7 per cent are unclear.[119] Given the high rate of filtering litigation is not an effective mechanism for a potential claimant to raise a concern nor does it work to alert the NHS to concerns.

The courts determining clinical negligence simply have no direct mechanism to deliver changes to the NHS. However, there have long been concerns that the fear of litigation can cause changes in the way healthcare is provided to guard against the possibility of being sued, so called defensive medicine.[120] This premise has been disputed.[121]

While the courts cannot force an NHS organisation to apologise the vast majority will. While any negligence action *ought* to compel an NHS institution to examine what went wrong, the legal system cannot *compel* this. NHS Resolution can encourage, but this is not a function of litigation per se and there is no requirement to demonstrate to the individual who has suffered harm that any change have been made. Despite this learning from claims is held up as a key part of NHS Resolution's functions and is outlined in the Long Term Plan. This is all the more surprising as litigation is slow and the litigation process can take years. As well as being distressing for the claimant this can reduce opportunities for learning as the legal outcome lags some years behind the incident, by which time staff may have moved on and practices changed. Maternity cases in particular can have a considerable lag between an incident occurring and a final settlement.[122] In 2017 the average gap between birth and a litigation settlement was 11.5 years.[123] Efforts to reduce this and promote early admissions of liability have led to the development of a specific Early Notification Scheme for Birth Injuries. Brain injuries at birth are particularly important as they have devastating consequences for the individuals affected, but also carry a significant cost to the NHS. Individual settlements can top £30 million[124] and birth injuries accounted for 59 per cent per cent of the compensation paid out in 2021. Learning from these injuries and preventing reoccurrence is a priority, however the major thrust of the learning appears to come from the HSIB investigation, rather than the early notification scheme.

As the Bar Council rightly outline the function of clinical negligence litigation is financial compensation – in actuality there are no other remedies available. For those who have suffered money can used provide for care, both health and social care. Compensation awarded by the courts is intended to put the individual back to the position they would have

[119] Behavioural Insights Team, *Behavioural Insights into Patient Motivation to Make a Claim for Clinical Negligence* (August 2018) available at https://resolution.nhs.uk/wp-content/uploads/2018/10/Behavioural-insights-into-patient-motivation-to-make-a-claim-for-clinical-negligence.pdf.

[120] For example see M Ennis and C Vincent, 'The Effects of Medical Accidents and Litigation on Doctors and Patients' (1994) 16(2) *Law and Policy* 97.

[121] C Ham, R Dingwall, P Fenn and D Harris, *Medical Negligence: Compensation and Accountability* (Centre for Socio-Legal Studies and London, King's Fund Institute, 1988).

[122] This relates to final settlements, interim payments could be used while waiting for diagnostic clarity on the extent of a child's injuries.

[123] Page 19 of the Rapid Resolution and Redress Scheme for Severe Avoidable Brain Injury at Birth Impact Assessment available at https://assets.publishing.service.gov.uk/government/uploads/system/uploads/attachment_data/file/597390/RRR_Impact_Assessment_a.pdf.

[124] Helen Vernon, CEO of NHS Resolution, Oral Evidence to the Health and Social Care Select Committee's Maternity Safety Inquiry (3 November 2020) transcript available at https://committees.parliament.uk/work/1518/nhs-litigation-reform/.

been in but for the negligence. Included within this is a right to utilise private healthcare and not rely on the NHS.[125]

Litigation will usually provide claimants with a greater understanding of what happened through the disclosure process and from expert evidence. However, given the time frames of litigation this may not be until many years after the original incident. Where negligence is found there is a judgement (though not always an acceptance) of liability. Given that litigation examines the actions of individuals claimants may not always obtain an understanding of the system-wide factors that were involved in the harm they suffered.

There is also evidence of remaining dissatisfaction by claimants who had been through the litigation process not just because they might not have received monetary compensation but also because of a failure to supply 'softer' remedies.[126] Mediation or ADR as a part of a litigation process have a greater scope to provide alternative remedies, such as apologies or assurances of service improvements. Mediation is offered free of charge by NHS Resolution to litigants in person, removing a potential barrier to some claimants.

i. Clinical Negligence: Financial Aspects

The greatest criticisms of clinical negligence tend to focus on the spiralling associated costs. The financial efficiency of clinical negligence litigation needs to be contextualised within the funding of civil litigation more widely.

For the majority of the second half of the twentieth century, virtually all medical negligence[127] and product liability[128] claims were funded by legal aid. As its cost to the public purse grew, legal aid was increasingly restricted by the government from around 1990, and privatised means of funding litigation were introduced. An experiment with conditional fees and after-the-event insurance from 1995 to 2013 was regarded as unsuccessful and was significantly retrenched, as noted below.

ii. Woolf: Mediation and Pre-Action Protocols

A review of civil procedure was undertaken by Lord Woolf in 1995–96, which led to radical reforms. The major features that were introduced in 1999 were, first, a streamlined and simplified set of Civil Procedure Rules that gave judges strong case management powers, second, an approach to litigation that encouraged settlement, especially by pre- or during-action mediation or other alternative dispute resolution (ADR) means. ADR is a generic term that covers a number of possible techniques, such as mediation, arbitration, early neutral evaluation and mini-trial. Many commercial disputes have for many years been resolved through arbitration, whether administered by permanent arbitration structures or ad hoc arrangements, rather than through state courts. Disputants have always been able

---

[125] Section 2(4) of the Law Reform (Personal Injuries) Act 1948.

[126] L Mulcahy, 'Mediation of Medical Negligence Actions: An Option for the Future?' in MM Rosenthal, L Mulcahy and S Lloyd-Bostock (eds), *Medical Mishaps. Pieces of the Puzzle* (Open University Press, 1999) 158.

[127] National Audit Office, *Handling Clinical Negligence Claims in England*, Report by the Comptroller and Auditor General, Session 2000-2001, HC 403, 3 May 2001, p1.

[128] C Hodges, *Multi Party Actions* (Oxford University Press, 2001).

to negotiate directly, and it is a short hop to the involvement of a neutral third party as a mediator or conciliator. In the UK, mediation has also been enshrined in particular areas, such as a mandatory first step in disputes involving public sector bodies,[129] tax disputes with the state,[130] family disputes[131] and employment disputes.[132]

Lord Woolf's review observed that, since parties settle most disputes, the function of a state dispute resolution facility should be to encourage such settlement rather than to be directed towards the very rare occasion when courts decide the outcome of a case.[133] Accordingly, parties are required to attempt to settle and 'litigation is to be avoided wherever possible'.[134]

The Woolf-inspired CPR therefore made the following reforms. Mediation was introduced as a formal and integral part of English civil procedure as of 1999.[135] In order to assist parties to be able to negotiate, sets of pre-action protocols were introduced that established norms for the information that parties should exchange before starting court proceedings, including: giving the other side all the relevant information at an early stage, trying to negotiate an early settlement, and considering mediation.[136] A survey of over 100 users of the Clinical Negligence protocol up to September 2001 found that it achieved the main objectives of better communication, better exchange of information, earlier investigation by defendants and improved opportunities for settlement.[137]

In July 2005 the private ADR body CEDR launched a Clinical Negligence Mediation Scheme for to all parties in clinical negligence cases where the value of the claim was £150,000 or less. The NHSLA launched a pilot mediation scheme for selected claims in August 2014,[138] which developed into the existing mediation scheme offered by NHS Resolution. This was some 15 years after the Woolf reforms integrated mediation into civil litigation. Uptake of mediation was initially very slow, but has increased in recent years.

[129] *The Dispute Resolution Commitment: Guidance for Government Departments and Agencies.* In the context of disputes involving the Government itself, this states that 'it is government policy that litigation should usually be treated as the dispute resolution method of last resort', para 1.4.

[130] See *Resolving Tax Disputes. Practical Guidance for HMRC Staff on the Use of Alternative Dispute Resolution in Large or Complex Cases* (HMRC, 2012) at www.hmrc.gov.uk/practitioners/adr-guidance-final.pdf.

[131] Legal aid is not available unless the parties have attempted mediation. See also D Norgrove, *Family Justice Review. Final Report* (Ministry of Justice, 2011).

[132] Under the Enterprise and Regulatory Reform Act 2012 all prospective claimants are required to notify ACAS before instituting proceedings.

[133] Lord Woolf, *Access to Justice: Final Report* (HMSO, 1996), available at http://webarchive.nationalarchives.gov.uk/+/http://www.dca.gov.uk/civil/final/contents.htm.

[134] ibid, Introduction, para 9.

[135] The overriding objective of dealing with cases justly inherently involves use of mediation where appropriate (CPR1.1(2)), and parties may be penalised in costs for unreasonably refusing to adopt ADR (CPR Part 44.3(5)). The Allocation Questionnaire that a party has to complete at the start of the procedure includes confirmation on whether ADR has been attempted (CPR 26.4); ADR is listed as an agenda item in Guides for Case Management Conferences (eg CAT Rule 44 (3)); solicitors have a professional duty to advise on outcome options (Code of Conduct 2011, O(1.12)).

[136] See www.justice.gov.uk/courts/procedure-rules/civil/protocol. For the *Pre-Action Protocol for the Resolution of Clinical Disputes Clinical Disputes Forum*, see www.justice.gov.uk/courts/procedure-rules/civil/protocol/prot_rcd.

[137] *Further Findings: A Continuing Evaluation of the Civil Justice Reforms* (Lord Chancellor's Department, 2002), available at http://webarchive.nationalarchives.gov.uk/+/http://www.dca.gov.uk/civil/reform/ffreform.htm.

[138] See www.cedr.com; *Mediating Claims in the NHS* (NHS Litigation Authority, 2014).

Since 2014, where both parties to a non-clinical claim worth under £10,000 tick a mediation box on the Directions Questionnaire,[139] the claim is referred to a free Small Claims Mediation Service managed at the Bulk Centre. Mediation is provided by a team of only 15 mediators, who are former court back office managers, operating by telephone for one hour, usually from home. They carry out four or five mediations a day, but are only able to service about 35 to 40 per cent of the national demand. If the case has not been settled within 28 days of referral it is sent as a defended case to the local hearing centre.[140]

However, ADR and mediation are not without strong critics.[141] A study of two mediation pilots in the Central London County Court between 2004 and 2006 concluded that the motivation and willingness of parties to negotiate and compromise is critical to the success of mediation, and found persistent rejection of mediation in personal injury cases.[142]

Mediation and settlement continue to be encouraged in place of litigation, as evidenced by the following statement by Lord Neuberger, President of the Supreme Court, in May 2015:

> I think that there must also be a lot to be said in favour of the Department of Health encouraging mediation pretty promptly after any medical procedure goes wrong in a relatively minor way. Very often in such a case, an apology, simply saying sorry, may be all the patient or the patient's family, want. Without a formal mediation, the doctors will be reluctant even to say sorry because of a fear that it will be construed as an admission of negligence.[143]

iii. Litigation Funding, Costs and Successive Reforms

Litigation incurs cost for the parties. In England and Wales, a claimant has to pay court fees, and all parties have to fund their lawyers and any experts that they instruct. In most cases, much (but not all) of the winning party's costs are reimbursed by the losing party. Major defendants will purchase insurance, and hence pool their risk on payment of damages and legal costs. Individual claimants will need access to significant funds to launch clinical negligence litigation. If a claimant loses, he or she will either need to hold insurance against the liability to pay costs, or must have some other form of protection. Few people ever purchased before the event (BTE) litigation insurance. Various ways of funding litigation, and rules on shifting of costs between the parties, have been permitted at different times. A number of experiments have been tried, some of which have been unsuccessful and produced unintended adverse consequences.[144]

---

[139] A Directions Questionnaire must be completed by the parties, in cases in which a defence is filed, to assist the court in deciding on which management track to allocate the case: Civil Procedure (Amendment) Rules 2013 (SI 2013/262), rule 22. Separate questionnaires apply for the small claims track (Form N180) and the fast track or multi-track (N181).

[140] Lord Justice Briggs, *Civil Courts Structure Review: Final Report* (Judiciary of England and Wales, 2016); *Early Progress in Transforming Courts and Tribunals* (National Audit Office, 2018); *HMCTS Response to Public Accounts Committee Report on Court Reform Programme*, 20 July 2018, at https://www.gov.uk/government/news/hmcts-response-to-public-accounts-committee-report-on-court-reform-programme, para 2.30.

[141] H Genn, *Judging Civil Justice. The Hamlyn Lectures 2008* (Cambridge, 2010).

[142] H Genn, P Fenn, M Mason, A Lane, N Bechai, L Gray and D Vencappa, *Twisting Arms: Court Referred and Court Linked Mediation Under Judicial Pressure* (Ministry of Justice, 2007), Ministry of Justice Research Series 1/07.

[143] Lord Neuberger, 'Keynote Address: A View From On High', Civil Mediation Conference 2015, para 24, www.supremecourt.uk/docs/speech-150512-civil-mediation-conference-2015.pdf.

[144] The following account draws on various pieces by Professor John Peysner, especially, J Peysner, *Access to Justice: A Critical Analysis of Recoverable Conditional Fees and No-Win No-Fee Funding* (Palgrave Macmillan, 2014).

The Legal Aid Act 1949 introduced state-funded legal aid that covered many claimants. The normal cost-shifting rule was also in practice not applied against legally-aided claimants. Hence, both claimants and the Legal Aid Board were protected from adverse decisions. This one-way cost shift situation was unpopular with defendants of legal aid claimants and referred to as 'legal aid blackmail', as it was said to induce settlements by defendants of unmerited claims, or at an over-value of what claims were worth. However, over succeeding decades, the total cost grew and legal aid was successively restricted. This left a large segment of the population without access to justice (known from the 1970s as middle income not eligible for legal aid, or MINELAs). Legal aid was in practice not available for clinical negligence claims under £10,000 if the Legal Services Commission believed that the NHS complaints procedure would be more appropriate, even if the claimant was eligible.[145]

The removal of legal aid continued alongside the facilitation of private finding of litigation, from 1995 of a regulated form of 'no win, no fee' funding was introduced as the 'conditional fee'. Under the conditional fee agreement (CFA), a winning claimant's lawyer was permitted to increase the normal fee, calculated on an hourly rate basis, by adding a success fee up to 100 per cent of the base fee, which could be deducted from damages collected.[146] The intention was that lawyers would fund cases on a CFA basis and success fees would encourage them to take some risk on cases. The level of success fee was supposedly required to be related to the risk of the case, but the ex post method of regulating this was far from effective.

Claimants who used a CFA were exposed to the normal risk of liability for opponents' costs if they lost. In order to cover this risk, after-the-event (ATE) insurance products were created. At this point, in 1998, the government's view was that 'The present civil justice system falls woefully short of the ideal. It is too complex, takes too long to deal with cases and it is too costly.'[147] Early research found that the level of ATE insurance premiums was modest, in the range of £92–£155.[148] A study of the CFA and ATE regime found that initial fears of abuse had not materialised: success fees were 50 per cent or less, the average uplift was 43 per cent, and lawyers held a strong code of ethics.[149]

As noted above, the Woolf reforms were introduced in 1999. Peysner's analysis is that Woolf believed that procedural reform alone would solve cost problems, but that defied the research evidence.[150] Peysner concluded that the Woolf reforms possibly assisted early settlement, but front-loaded parties' litigation costs.[151]

From 2000 until 2013, in the funding of money damage claims, largely personal injury claims, the CFA success fee and the ATE premium were made *recoverable* from the settling or unsuccessful defendant. This removed the need for the client to pay the premium *in any event*, reflecting the high success rate of this type of case. Peysner has described this

---

[145] Peysner, ibid.
[146] Courts and Legal Services Act 1990.
[147] *Consultation Paper: Access to Justice with Conditional Fees* (Lord Chancellor's Department, 1998).
[148] ibid, paras 2.3, 2.4, 2.5.
[149] S Yarrow, *The Price of Success: Lawyers Clients and Conditional Fees* (Policy Studies Institute, 1997).
[150] JS Kakalik, T Dunworth, LA Hill, DF McCaffrey, M Oshiro, NM Pace and ME Vaiana, *Implementation of the Civil Justice Reform Act in Pilot and Comparison Districts* (RAND Corporation, 1966). See J Peysner, *Access to Justice: A Critical Analysis of Recoverable Conditional Fees and No-Win No-Fee Funding* (Palgrave Macmillan, 2014).
[151] Peysner, ibid.

experiment in attempting to devise a 'magic bullet' for personal injury claims as creating consequences that were worse than the 'problem' that was solved.[152] Removing the need for a claimant to pay a normal premium introduced moral hazard, since claimants were indifferent to costs, and fees paid by lawyers to third parties to refer cases to them could be hidden. A new industry of claims management companies sprang up, who were highly successful at advertising for claimants, and extracting referral fees from law firms, but whose quality control on cases was lax. Some operated schemes of questionable legality.

The increase in costs payable by defendant insurers (the base costs were increased by a multiplier *plus* the ATE premium),[153] uncontrolled increases in ATE premiums (up to £1315 per case) and the increasing numbers of claims generated by claims management companies[154] led to institutional revolt, known as the 'Costs War' over recoverability. Insurers argued that insurance was unnecessary until they had had an opportunity to consider merits of a case. The delay in paying law firms that ensued whilst the courts deliberated on the regime caused firms serious cash flow consequences, and some insolvencies.

iv. Jackson: Costs Controls and Management

In recent years, claimants' lawyers are typically financed by a conditional fee agreement (CFA: no win, no fee), with an ATE insurance to cover the risk of having to pay defendants' costs. If the claimant wins, the CFA, its success fee and the ATE premium would all be paid by the defence. Until April 2013, the CFA success fee uplift was routinely 100 per cent of the level of base costs.[155]

A further major attempt at reform was initiated in 2009 after concerns amongst the senior judiciary and the government. The Jackson Review of Litigation Costs noted that the vast majority of personal injury claims were either resolved in favour of the claimant or were dropped before issue of proceedings.[156] He therefore sought to speed up the settlement of what were thought to be overwhelmingly meritorious claims. As a result, a series of reforms were introduced in 2013.

The main components of the package brought in under the Legal Aid Sentencing and Punishment of Offenders Act 2012 (LASPO) were as follows.

First, there would be a new process for personal injury claims, and the small claims limit was supposed to be raised to £25,000. In the event, it was raised to £10,000 but remained at £1,000 for person injury claims.

Second, for agreements made from 1 April 2013, only the base CFA fee was recoverable from a paying defendant, whereas neither the success fee nor the ATE premium was recoverable.[157] The exception was in clinical negligence cases, for which an ATE covering

---

[152] ibid, 36.

[153] Research found that lawyers increase work according to the value of the case: P Fenn and N Rickman, 'Fixing Lawyers' Fees Ex Ante: A Case Study in Policy and Empirical Legal Studies' (2011) 8(3) *Journal of Empirical Legal Studies* 533.

[154] Peysner found that Claims Direct was taking on 1500 cases a week.

[155] *Report and Accounts 2013/14* (NHS Litigation Authority, 2014), paras 4.13–4.15.

[156] R Jackson, *Review of Civil Litigation Costs: Preliminary Report* (TSO, 2009) 224. Over 90% of road traffic and over 70% of employers' liability claims succeed: 227.

[157] Legal Aid, Sentencing and Punishment of Offenders Act 2012, ss 44 and 46, amending the Courts and Legal Services Act 1990, s 58.

the cost of the claimant's experts' reports remained recoverable, on the basis that without such cost most claimants would not have the resource to investigate cases.[158]

Third, regulated contingency fees (referred to as damages based agreements, or DBAs) were introduced.[159]

Fourth, a rise of 10 per cent in general damages (to give headroom for introduction of contingency fees).[160]

Fifth, referral fees were banned.[161] This back-handed arrangement was thought to have fuelled the ability of claims intermediaries to dominate the legal services market, and be anti-competitive, but also to have undesirable effects on market prices and the independence of lawyers.

Sixth, judicial cost management (budgeting) was introduced.[162]

Seventh, a qualified one-way costs shifting (QOCS) rule was introduced for personal injury claimants.[163]

Eighth, private (third party) litigation funders were encouraged.

In implementing the Jackson reforms in 2013,[164] the government's primary consideration was to aid economic recovery by saving public expenditure and by promoting 'quicker, cheaper alternative dispute resolution where appropriate'.[165] However, as will appear below, the reforms produced a series of unintended consequences. Peysner's assessment of the Jackson changes is that – as with all of the successive changes in policy on procedure, funding and costs noted above – there was an almost complete absence of prior wide-ranging research, or attempts to investigate and predict the potential unintended consequences of change through pilot studies.[166] He saw the major problem likely to emerge as the ethical dimensions of the changed relationship between claimants and lawyers when recoverability is replaced by contingency fees.[167]

The QOCS rule is important in relation to personal injury cases.[168] The effect of QOCS is to reduce the financial risk for the claimant, and hence reduce the need for many claimants

---

[158] The Recovery of Costs Insurance Premiums in Clinical Negligence Proceedings Regulations 2013 No 92; repealed and replaced by The Recovery of Costs Insurance Premiums in Clinical Negligence Proceedings (No. 2) Regulations 2013 No 379. The rationale for this exception was that without this protection, claimants would be unable to finance investigation of and bringing claims.

[159] Courts and Legal Services Act 1990 s 58AA; The Damages-Based Agreements Regulations 2013, SI 2013/ 609.

[160] *Simmons v Castle* [2012] EWCA Civ 1039.

[161] Legal Aid, Sentencing and Punishment of Offenders Act 2012, ss 56–61, and Criminal Justice and Courts Act 2015, defining an inducement. See *Claims Management Regulation: Approach and Enforcement of the Referral Fee Ban* (Ministry of Justice, 2012); *The Prohibition of Referral Fees in the Legal Aid, Sentencing and Punishment of Offenders Act 2012 (LASPO) Sections 56–60* (Solicitors Regulation Authority, 2013).

[162] Amendments to the Civil Procedure Rules.

[163] R Jackson, *Review of Civil Litigation Costs, Final Report* (TSO, 2009) 88; Legal Aid, Sentencing and Punishment of Offenders Act 2013, s 44.

[164] R Jackson, *Review of Civil Litigation Costs: Preliminary Report* (TSO, 2009); R Jackson, *Review of Civil Litigation Costs: Final Report* (TSO, 2010). See the Legal Aid, Sentencing and Punishment of Offenders Act 2012.

[165] Consultation paper CP6/2011, *Solving Disputes in the County Courts: Creating a Simpler, Quicker and More Proportionate System. A Consultation on Reforming Civil Justice in England and Wales* (Ministry of Justice, 2011).

[166] J Peysner, *Access to Justice: A Critical Analysis of Recoverable Conditional Fees and No-Win No-Fee Funding* (Palgrave Macmillan, 2014).

[167] J Peysner, 'Tail Wags Dog: Contingency Fees (and Part 36 and Third Party Funding)' (2013) 231 *Civil Justice Quarterly* 1.

[168] For the policy on which the Rules are based see Written Ministerial Statement: Implementation of Part 2 of the Legal Aid, Sentencing and Punishment of Offenders Act 2012: Civil Litigation Funding and Costs (Ministry of Justice, amended 17 July 2012). Jackson also suggested that protection could apply in other types of cases (judicial review claims; defamation claims; housing disrepair claims; actions against the police; and professional negligence

to take out ATE insurance.[169] Jackson further noted that the vast majority of personal injury claims were road traffic claims, which should be straightforward, and insurers should be encouraged to settle them as swiftly as possible.[170] That may have been true of the majority of road traffic, employment and 'slips and trips' claims under the regime that then prevailed. But clinical negligence cases can be complex, in relation to both verification of facts and proof of negligence,[171] and the statistics available to Jackson did not distinguish between cases settled or dropped.[172] Under the Jackson regime, *all* personal injury claimants are protected by QOCS, unless the claimant acts unreasonably,[173] and claimants who lose pay their own costs and any success fee, but do not pay the winner's costs, and all losing defendants would pay the winner's base costs. Claimants would only have to pay defendants if:

(a)   the claim is found to be fraudulent on the balance of probabilities;
(b)   the claimant has failed to beat a defendant's 'Part 36' offer to settle; or
(c)   the case has been struck out where the claim discloses no reasonable cause of action or where it is otherwise an abuse of the court's process (or is otherwise likely to obstruct the just disposal of the proceedings).

However, the effect of the QOCS rule may simply encourage some personal injury and product liability claims to be brought that have lower merits, or without full investigation of merits, as was the situation under both of the earlier 'pre-Jackson' and 'Jackson' regimes.

In early 2016 a strenuous attack was made by the think tank Civitas on conditional fee agreements and contingency fees, together with human rights legislation, which it was said had permitted a vast increase in lawyer-driven litigation, producing 'a corrupting effect on the legal profession and have promoted the politicisation of the judiciary', and which should be repealed.[174] The author argued that the time had come to challenge a self-serving elite in the legal profession which 'is encouraging a claims culture based on gaining sectarian advantage'. He called for major reform:

> We should cancel contingency fees based on lawyers taking a share of the civil damages, including the new … DBAs … CFAs … should also be cancelled to reduce the number of cases that are primarily driven by the desire of lawyers for financial gain.[175]

---

claims) but the government was 'not persuaded' to extend QOCS: Ministry of Justice, *Reforming Civil Litigation Funding and Costs in England and Wales – Implementation of Lord Justice Jackson's Recommendations The Government Response CM 8041* (Ministry of Justice, 2011) 'Jackson response', para 27 available at: //assets.publishing.service.gov.uk/government/uploads/system/uploads/attachment_data/file/228974/8041.pdf.

[169] Ministry of Justice Consultation paper CP13/2010, *Proposals for Reform of Civil Litigation Funding and Costs in England and Wales Implementation of Lord Justice Jackson's Recommendations CM 7947* (Ministry of Justice, 2010) 'Jackson Consultation', paras 85 and 132 available at https://assets.publishing.service.gov.uk/government/uploads/system/uploads/attachment_data/file/238368/7947.pdf.

[170] R Jackson, *Review of Civil Litigation Costs: Final Report* (TSO, 2009) ch 19, para 1.3.

[171] Significantly, Jackson found that clinical negligence cases did not usually settle during the pre-action period: ibid, para 4.7.

[172] See R Jackson, *Review of Civil Litigation Costs: Preliminary Report* (TSO, 2009) ch 6. The 2007/08 claims noted were 2,837 clinical negligence claims funded by the then Legal Services Commission that were unsuccessful or partially successful, of which 2,184 were dropped or settled before issue; with 525 dropped or settled between issue and trial: para 2.4. A further 1,526 clinical negligence claims were funded that were successful: para 2.7.

[173] Jackson Consultation, para 136. For implementation policy see Written Ministerial Statement: Implementation of Part 2 of the Legal Aid, Sentencing and Punishment of Offenders Act 2012: Civil Litigation Funding and Costs (Ministry of Justice, 2012).

[174] DG Green, *Democratic Civilisation or Judicial Supremacy?* (Civitas, 2016).

[175] ibid, 83.

v. *Further Funding Cuts*

The Coalition Government from 2010 and the Conservative Government from 2015 instituted major cuts in public expenditure. Under this policy, further restrictions in the availability of legal aid were imposed. Legal aid is currently only available for personal injury cases involving children with brain (neurological) injuries resulting in severe disability, which arises during pregnancy, childbirth or up to eight weeks' postnatal (not all injuries are covered). Significant increases were made in court fees. Attempts were made to constrain claims management companies (CMCs) by regulation[176] and fees.[177]

Since clinical negligence was not covered by fixed costs rules imposed in 2013 on most personal injury claims up to £25,000,[178] there was discussion on whether to introduce fixed legal costs for clinical negligence claims valued up to £250,000, on a tariff system. Deliberations proved predictably difficult, given the complexity and variability between cases of this type of case.[179] In December 2015 the Chancellor proposed to end the right to compensation for minor injuries and raise the upper limit for personal injury claims in the small claims track from £1,000 to £5,000, effectively removing lawyers from the process.[180] These changes were in response to concerns over the costs of clinical claims and road traffic whiplash claims.[181] The anticipated consequential fall in road traffic claims were said to have the potential to save £1 billion from the cost of motor insurance policies,[182] provided claims were perceived as uneconomic by lawyers and CMCs.

In October 2014 the Ministry of Justice cut fees for whiplash medical reports, in order to tackle what the insurance industry had claimed to be a phenomenon of fraudulent motor vehicle claims.[183] A presumption was also introduced that medical evidence would be

---

[176] In 2014/15 there were 1,752 authorized CMCs, with an industry turnover of £772 million, and the regulator received 10,106 new consumer contacts, investigated 93 CMCs, cancelled the authorisation of 105 CMCs, issued warnings to 296 CMCs.

[177] Legal Aid, Sentencing and Punishment of Offenders Act 2012, Sch 1, Part 1; The Legal Services Act 2007 (Claims Management Complaints) (Fees) Regulations 2014/3316); The Legal Services Act 2007 (Claims Management Complaints) (Fees) (Amendment) Regulations 2016 No 92; The Civil Legal Aid (Merits Criteria) Regulations 2013/104. See The Public Accounts Committee, *Implementing Reforms to Civil Legal Aid*, 4 February 2015, HC 808 2014-5; National Audit Office, *Implementing Reforms To Civil Legal Aid*, 20 November 2014, HC 784 2014-15; *Briefing Paper: Changes to Civil Legal Aid in England and Wales since 2013: The Impact on Clients – Briefing Paper* (House of Commons Library, 2015).

[178] Civil Procedure Rules, Part 45, introduced by 65th update as of 31 July 2013.

[179] Queen's Bench Master Cook called the proposal 'profoundly worrying': R Rothwell, 'Judge Labels Clin Neg Fixed Costs "Profoundly Worrying"' *Gazette* (25 February 2016). There were, of course, objections from lawyers: C Dixon, 'Costs and Clinical Negligence' *Gazette* (21 August 2015); see also N Rose, 'Government Working on Fixed Costs Extension, Says Faulks, as Clinical Negligence Debate Hots Up' *Gazette* (5 May 2016) (in which the proposal to introduce fixed recoverable costs up to £250,000 was described as 'truly shocking' in relation to clinical negligence).

[180] *Spending Review and Autumn Statement 2015: Key Announcements* (HM Treasury, 2015), 25 November.

[181] In 2011 nearly 1200 whiplash claims were made each day, involving a total annual cost of £2 billion and a significant number of fraudulent claims: *Tackling the Compensation Culture: The Legal Aid, Sentencing and Punishment of Offenders Bill. Improving Systems for All* (Association of British Insurers, 2011); House of Commons Transport Committee, *Cost of Motor Insurance: Whiplash* Fourth Report of Session 2013–14; *Whiplash Reform Programme: Ministry of Justice Response to Consultation on Independence in Medical Reporting and Expert Accreditation* (Ministry of Justice, 2014).

[182] P Rogerson, 'Whiplash Curbs Could Hand Insurers £1bn-plus Profit Boost' *Gazette* (18 January 2016).

[183] It was said that were around half a million whiplash claims a year, adding an estimated £90 to the average motor insurance policy. Fees of up to £700 had been charged, and a fixed fee of £180 was imposed. Press release 'Fee Cut for Whiplash Medical Reports' (Ministry of Justice, 2014). The Association of British Insurers claimed that 59,900 dishonest motor insurance claims were identified in 2013, an increase of 34 per cent on 2012, with a

limited to a single report, unless a clear case was made, and allowing defendants to give their account of the incident direct to the medical expert, where appropriate.

vi. Clinical Negligence: Financial Efficiency

The 2017 NAO report was clear that the cost of clinical negligence claims in England was unsustainable. This was attributed to the rising numbers of claims, increased value of damages payments (including the 2017 PIDR changes) and increased claimant legal costs.

Table 17 Legal fees as a percentage of expenditure, England and Northern Ireland 2014–19

	2014/15	2015/16	2016/17	2017/18	2018/19
England – Damages as a % of total expenditure	66%	64%	63%	73%	75%
NI – Damages as a % of total expenditure	73%	61%	69%	74%	73%
England – Claimant legal cost as a % of total expenditure	25%	28%	29%	21%	19%
NI – Claimant legal cost as a % of total expenditure	16%	28%	22%	17%	20%
England – Defendant legal costs as a % of total expenditure	9%	8%	7%	6%	6%
NI – Defendant legal costs as a % of total expenditure	11%	11%	9%	9%	7%
England – Legal costs as a % of total expenditure	34%	36%	37%	27%	25%
NI – Legal costs as a % of total expenditure	27%	39%	31%	26%	27%

Table 17 shows there are remarkably similar profiles between England which has a centralised defence organisation (NHS Resolution) and Northern Ireland where claims are handled by the Trusts themselves. This is despite the 2017 PIDR changes seen in England and Wales not being mirrored in Northern Ireland making claims there much less expensive, though there are few PPO awarded in Northern Ireland which may partially explain these findings. This suggests that centralised defence organisations may not be the key to containing claimant legal fee costs.

The 2017 NAO report into the rising costs of clinical negligence[184] was clear that the costs are unsustainable and that the Department of Health and NHS Resolution's proposed actions to contain the rising cost of clinical negligence claims, including fixed recoverable cost and the early notification scheme for birth injuries, were unlikely to stop this growth.

---

value of £811 million: *Criminal Justice and Courts Bill. Fact Sheet 'Personal Injury Claims Involving Fundamental Dishonesty'* (Ministry of Justice, 2014).

[184] NAO, 'Managing the Costs of Clinical Negligence in Trust' (September 2017) available at www.nao.org.uk/report/managing-the-costs-of-clinical-negligence-in-trusts/.

a. Fixed Recoverable Costs for Clinical Negligence

There have long been considerable concerns over the disproportionality between costs and damages in relation to claims against the NHS, especially those of small or modest value. In 2014/15 the NHSLA recorded that, for claims resolved for less than £100,000 damages, the percentage of claimant costs has increased from just over 30 per cent to 50 per cent over the previous 10 years and, as an absolute figure, increased almost threefold.[185] This prompted considerable work into fixed recoverable costs, culminating in the 2019 Report of the Civil Justice Council Working Group *Fixed Recoverable Costs in Lower Value Clinical Negligence Claims* which failed to reach a consensus on this issue.[186] Despite this in January 2022 a government consultation on FRCS was launched.[187] The proposals put forward by the government mean that for standard track cases settled at stage one (the earliest stages up to the stocktake) if the damages are less than £6,875 then more will be paid in legal fees than will be paid to the claimant in damages. If the case is funded by a CFA, as the vast majority are, there is the potential for a success fee to be taken from the damages. This creates a situation whereby the lawyer working under a CFA with a standard 25 per cent success fee will be better off than the winning claimant for standard track cases settled at stage one if the damages are less than £18,300. In the Fixed Recoverable Costs consultation, Sir Rupert Jackson stated 'the holy grail pursued by every civil justice reformer is a system in which the actual costs of each party are a modest fraction of the sum in issue and the winner recovers those modest costs from the loser'. The FRC consultation might offer an improvement over the current position, but it clearly does not deliver this; and the more fundamental question is whether litigation is the correct vehicle to achieve this.

There has been a long history of trying to constrain the costs of civil litigation and improve the efficiency of the court processes. The rise in claims numbers noted above under the Jackson/LAPSO regimes suggest various conclusions. Intermediaries' behaviour is significantly affected by funding and costs rules, and such service suppliers are savvy commercial operators who will seek to maximise their own profits, that is absolutely what should be expected. Attempts to constrain the volume and cost of clinical negligence litigation have not prevented both increased claim numbers and the cost of damages and legal costs paid by the NHS are continuing to rise to very significant proportions.

In 2016 Report on developing an online court Lord Justice Briggs accepted that the Jackson Reforms, even when supported by costs budgeting and costs management, have

> not produced the result that the legal costs incurred in small and moderate value personal injury litigation (including clinical negligence) are now proportionate, particularly in the small minority of claims that go all the way to trial. On the contrary, wildly disproportionate expenditure still occurs, albeit not at the claimant's risk. In those cases, the adverse consequences of that disproportionality lie not in impeding access to justice, but rather in increasing motor and employers' liability insurance premiums, and in an increased litigation burden on the National Health Service

---

[185] *Report and Accounts 2014/15* (NHS Litigation Authority, 2015) 11.

[186] Report of the Civil Justice Council Working Group, *Fixed Recoverable Costs in Lower Value Clinical Negligence Claims* (October 2019) available at www.judiciary.uk/related-offices-and-bodies/advisory-bodies/cjc/archive/fixed-recoverable-costs-in-lower-value-clinical-negligence-claims/.

[187] www.gov.uk/government/consultations/fixed-recoverable-costs-in-lower-value-clinical-negligence-claims.

in most clinical negligence cases. Thus, the disproportionality remains a weakness of the civil justice system, but of a different kind.[188]

It will be interesting to see the impact of moving towards the English and Welsh litigation model on claims in Scotland and Northern Ireland. This may help to shed light on which factors are most causal.

VIII.   Conclusions on Litigation

There are a number of difficulties with litigation, potentially the most totemic of which is access to litigation. The above overview demonstrates how funding can dramatically impact on the numbers of cases brought. However, the number of cases brought are only a fraction of the true picture. Claimant lawyers in clinical negligence act as a filter; according to the Society for Clinical Injury Lawyers of all of the contacts made with clinical negligence lawyers about potential claims only circa 3 per cent of these contacts are deemed actionable.[189] The information contained within cases that are rejected is spread across the claimant lawyer market, it is not in any centralised repository so is, in effect, lost to the healthcare system. These individuals are unable to raise their concerns in a meaningful way; they do not receive any redress, and there is also no learning from their concerns. This is not a handful of people, it is 97 per cent of those trying to raise a concern.

For those who do manage to litigate, the evidence reviewed above leads to the following findings. In response to suffering personal adversity as a result of NHS care, people desire explanations and apologies, assurance that lessons will be learned so that the same things do not happen to others, and to receive care and help to continue with their lives. In short, they ask for a caring response. They only need money in so far as it funds necessary care and support. These consistent responses display striking altruism.

These are objectives that the legal system is not designed to deliver, and could not deliver. The traditional legal approach to responding to personal injury is to assume that there is a *right* to *compensation*, which requires a court to enforce the right by ordering that the person who has breached the right and caused the harm to the victims should pay damages that will, so far as possible, place the victim whose rights have been breached, in the position she would have been if that breach had not occurred, so far as money can achieve this. The test of eligibility (trigger) for who pays or receives (full) compensation and who does not is based on a finding that an individual carer was legally at fault.

There is a fundamental difference between the essentially forward-looking *healthcare* system and the essentially backward-looking *legal* system. The legal system cannot provide a caring and supportive personal response. It can only essentially provide prospective injunctions or retrospective orders for money to be paid. Money is, therefore, used as the currency of the legal system, as a surrogate for more direct activity, in 'putting people in the position that they would have been if the breach of duty had not occurred'. Damages are used as proxy for other deliverables, such as care, information, apologies, control of behaviour, and

---

[188] Lord Justice Briggs, *Civil Courts Structure Review: Final Report* (Judiciary of England and Wales, 2016); *Early Progress in Transforming Courts and Tribunals* (National Audit Office, 2018) para 5.46.
[189] See the Access to Justice Section of the SCIL Campaign available at www.scil.org.uk/campaign.

improvement of performance. What people might want is a more direct and immediate personal response and to receive swift care, support and the knowledge that lessons would be learnt so that improvements in practice would ensure that similar misfortunes would be less likely to happen to others in future. What litigation delivers is money, usually some time after the event. Money is paid for two reasons: first, because it is the only relevant remedy that the legal system can provide, and second, the theory has been that money can both pay for care and can affect ongoing behaviour (on the theory of deterrence). Money is, therefore, to a significant extent a surrogate for care and affecting change.

The desire of victims to see that lessons are learned is also not a goal that the legal system is well-designed to achieve. The desire for vindication through the legal system has developed as one of the only mechanisms through which people can respond to a failure to tell them what happened, in a way they can trust, and to provide care and the belief that the same thing will not happen to others. The principal historical theory is that the outputs of legal system (adverse publicity, damages, and convictions) provide deterrence, which affects future behaviour. There is very limited empirical evidence that such effects on future behaviour are produced by legal outputs. Indeed, the legal system positively impedes learning and hence improvement in performance.

The focus of the legal system on whether individuals are culpable inhibits open disclosure by healthcare staff. A fault-based system positively impedes the flow of the information that is vital for learning. A more system based assessment would potentially reduce barriers to staff disclosure.

Calls for reform of litigation have been mounting and it is difficult to see how the current status quo could be maintained.

10

Public Inquiries and Reviews

Despite the enormous delivery of effective healthcare in the NHS on a consistent basis, even a cursory look into the history of the NHS reveals that many serious problems have been identified in a seemingly endless series of inquiries into major incidents. Inquiries were held throughout the 1960s and 1970s into poor quality in hospitals at Ely,[1] Fairleigh,[2] Whittingham[3] and Normansfield.[4] In their 2002 article[5] analysing NHS Inquiries Walsh and Higgins were clear that: 'Many inquiry reports highlight similar sorts of failures, suggesting that lessons are not always learnt' and that 'Often these failures are organisational and cultural, and the necessary changes are not likely to happen simply because they are prescribed in a report'.

What is painfully obvious is that failures have continued to occur decade after decade, despite being identified in reports. Sadly, this pattern has continued into this century and there have been a number of reviews and inquiries into a series of particularly shocking events.[6] The respective reports set out detailed descriptions of events and resultant recommendations. This chapter could do justice to them all, and it does not set out to do so. Instead, it focusses on specific findings from selected reviews and inquiries published since 2000, see Table 1. These cover actions of individual practitioners (Ledward, Shipman and Paterson), particular specialities within a hospital (BRI and Morecombe Bay, Mid Staffs and Abertaw Bro Morgannwg); specific hospitals or Trusts (Keogh Hospitals Review) and particular products (IMMDS Review).

---

[1] Department of Health and Social Security, *Report of the Committee of Inquiry into Allegations of Ill-Treatment of Patients and Other Irregularities at the Ely Hospital, Cardiff* (London, HMSO, 1969) Cmnd 3975.

[2] Department of Health and Social Security, *Report of the Fairleigh Hospital Committee of Inquiry* (London, HMSO, 1971) Cmnd 4557.

[3] Department of Health and Social Security, *Report of the Committee of Inquiry into Whittingham Hospital* (London, HMSO, 1972) Cmnd 4861.

[4] Department of Health and Social Security, *The Normansfield Hospital Enquiry* (London, HMSO, 1978) Cmnd7357.

[5] K Walshe and J Higgins, 'The Use and Impact of Inquiries in the NHS' (2002) 325(7369) *BMJ* (Clinical research edn) 895–900.

[6] This is by no means an exhaustive list of all the inquiries and reviews during this period. For example, we have focused on concerns related to patient care, so we have not included the inquiry into organ retention at Alder Hay Hospital. This is not a judgment on the seriousness of the practices there, nor the harm done to affected individuals, it is simply a reflection of the fact that the concerns were about post-mortem actions.

Table 1 Selected major inquiries and reviews published 2000–22

Where/Who	Areas of concern/investigation	When	Report date
Rodney Ledward	Gynaecological surgery	1989–96	2000
Bristol Royal Infirmary (BRI)	Paediatric cardiac surgery	1984–95	2001
Harold Shipman	Murdering patients, fraud, theft	1974–98	2002–05
Ayling Inquiry	Sexual assault on patients	Mid1980s–2000	2004
Neale Inquiry	Gynaecological surgery	1977–2000	2004
Kerr/Haslam Inquiry	Sexual assault on patients	1965–88	2005
Mid Staffs Independent Inquiry	Systemic failures in (older) patient care	2005–09	2010
Winterbourne View hospital	Adults with learning disabilities	2008–11	2012
Keogh Hospitals review	14 trusts with high mortality rates	2013	2013
Mid Staffs Public Inquiry	Systemic failures in (older) patient care	2005–09	2013
Morecombe Bay	Failures in maternity services	2004–13	2015
Abertawe Bro Morgannwg	Systemic failures in (older) patient care	2012–14	2014
Gosport War Memorial Hospital	Systematic over-use of morphine hastening the deaths of many (older) patients	1987–2001	2018
Paterson	Surgeon Ian Paterson	2003(?)–11	2020
IMMDS Review	Hormone Pregnancy Tests; Valproate use in pregnancy & pelvic mesh	1953–2020	2020
Ockenden Review	Maternity Services at Shrewsbury and Telford Hospital Trust	1973–2000, mostly 2000–19	2022

Despite the fact that these reports span over two decades and cover subjects from individual practitioner's actions to issues with an entire class of medical devices used world-wide there is a theme that consistently emerges from all these inquiry reports – the importance of culture. The following narrative picks out the references to the importance of culture and how it interacts with the systems that are meant to keep patients safe and ensure the smooth running of the NHS, as highlighted by the succession of inquiries.

I. Rodney Ledward

In March 1999 the then Minister for Health Frank Dobson announced an independent inquiry into Rodney Ledward, a consultant obstetrician and gynaecologist, whose extensive poor practice over many years had harmed a large number of women. This was not the full public inquiry that patients had called for, but a less formal private inquiry chaired by Jean Richie QC.[7] Initially the scope of the inquiry was limited to looking at Ledward's NHS practice and not his private work, but the chair wrote to the Secretary of State in June 1999 to inform him that they would also consider the scope of Ledward's private practice.

Superficially Rodney Ledward appeared a very successful and well-regarded consultant obstetrician and gynaecologist. In 1980 he was appointed as a consultant to the William Harvey Hospital, Ashford, Kent. The Inquiry report[8] describes how he was seen as young blood with a strong academic and professional record and how the speed of his surgery was acclaimed; he was considered to be a breath of fresh air. Over the next 16 years Ledward continued to work at the hospital as well as at other private hospitals, despite a number of complaints about his competence being raised by patients and some of those working with him harbouring serious concerns. Even after the accusations against him gathered momentum it is clear Ledward still had a cohort of loyal supporters, including his secretaries, some of the junior doctors he had supervised and some others who had worked with him, who considered the accusations to be unjustified. After investigations Ledward was suspended from his post at the William Harvey Hospital in 1996 and struck off by the GMC in 1998.

In 2000 the Inquiry report was published. The inquiry was critical of the management at the William Harvey Hospital. While she was clear in her report that Rodney Ledward bore the greatest responsibility for the failures in his practice, Jean Ritchie QC concluded that better NHS management should have picked up the problems earlier.

The inquiry gave a detailed account of a disturbing culture where surgeons were considered god-like and beyond question and other staff feared retribution if they did raise concerns

> Consultants who worked alongside Rodney Ledward in the Trust and who gave evidence against him in the Disciplinary proceedings or before the GMC, or both, were left in no doubt by some of their eminent colleagues that if the case against Rodney Ledward did not succeed they would find themselves ostracised. They also told us that they knew they would not, in those circumstances, be able to continue to be employed in their present positions and indeed might find it difficult to find an alternative post. We are very concerned that a climate of fear and retribution was engendered consciously or unconsciously by senior members of the profession.

In her report Jean Richie QC called for an open culture and the creation of a confidential hotline to allow healthcare professionals and patients to blow the whistle on incompetent doctors.

II. Bristol Royal Infirmary

In 1998 an investigation was set up into children admitted into the Bristol Royal Infirmary (BRI) between 1984 and 1995, for complex cardiac surgery. All too often these children

---

[7] https://publications.parliament.uk/pa/cm200304/cmselect/cmpubadm/606/4111109.htm.

[8] Department of Health, *The Report of the Inquiry into Quality and Practice Within the NHS Arising from the Actions of Rodney Ledward* (London, HMSO, 2000) available at https://webarchive.nationalarchives.gov.uk/ukgwa/20130123204140/http://www.dh.gov.uk/en/Publicationsandstatistics/Publications/PublicationsPolicyAndGuidance/DH_4093337.

were let down. The mortality rates at the BRI were far higher than would be expected; for example, for five out of the seven years from 1988 to 1994 the mortality rate for open heart surgery on children under a year old was double that of other centres in England.[9] It is thought that over 30 children who died in Bristol following complex heart surgery would have survived had they been operated on elsewhere. In addition to excess deaths there were also a number of children who suffered brain damage after cardiac surgery.

Prior to 1988 there were concerns raised outside the BRI, both within the health service and publicly in a BBC Wales programme *Hearth Surgery – The Second Class Service*.[10] In 1989 Dr Stephen Bolsin joined the BRI as a consultant anaesthetist. He identified that operations were lengthier than those he had seen in his previous post and suspected death rates were higher. In a letter to Dr John Roylance, the chief executive, dated 7 August 1990 he stated that the mortality for open-heart surgery for under-ones was 'one of the highest in the country, and the problem should be addressed'. It was not acted upon, the inquiry report found it was doubtful whether the message Dr Bolsin claimed he intended to signify in his letter was sufficiently clear and strong. Dr Bolsin states that there were consequences from his letter; he was called into the office of Mr Wisheart, the head of the paediatric cardiac team and rebuked for taking information about the team to 'outsiders'.

Dr Bolsin set about compiling an audit of the excess deaths and set about trying to improve outcomes. He did not engage with either of the cardiac surgeons, Mr James Wisheart or Mr Janardan Dhasmana, in this task, though other clinicians, hospital management and department of health representatives were all made aware of it at various points. There were also unattributed reports in *Private Eye* magazine and other media.

On 11 January 1995 a clinical meeting was held to discuss the treatment of an 18-month old baby, Joshua Loveday. All those present except Dr Bolsin agreed to proceed with the switch operation. Joshua was operated on the next day, but he did not survive the operation. At this point the chief executive Dr Roylance was involved and advised to set up an independent inquiry. Mr Wisheart, in his role as medical director, was asked to set up this external independent inquiry.

Complaints were subsequently made to the GMC about Mr Wisheart, Mr Dhasmana and Dr Boylance. In the hearings that followed in 1998 they were found guilty of serious professional misconduct; Drs Wisheart and Roylance were struck off, Mr Dhasmana had conditions imposed that he would not operate on children for three years.

A group of parents formed a support group and started to call for a public inquiry. On 18 June 1998 the then Secretary of State Frank Dobson announced that there would be an independent inquiry chaired by Sir Ian Kennedy. The inquiry found a catalogue of serious system failures both in the cardiac unit that had a 'club culture' with members of the club not only denying problems but wilfully turning a blind eye, and in the hospital more widely with flagrant failures to be open and transparent when things had gone wrong and responding by closing ranks.

> Problems arise in all institutions. But it is incumbent on senior management to devise systems which respond quickly and effectively to these problems. What was unusual about Bristol was that

---

[9] *The Report of the Public Inquiry into Children's Heart Surgery at the Bristol Royal Infirmary 1984–1995: Learning from Bristol*, 2001, www.bristol-inquiry.org.uk/final_report/report/index.htm, www.gov.uk/government/uploads/system/uploads/attachment_data/file/273320/5363.pdf.

[10] Broadcast on 16 June 1987.

the systems and culture in place were such as to make open discussion and review more difficult. Staff were not encouraged to share their problems or to speak openly. Those who tried to raise concerns found it hard to have their voice heard.[11]

The Chair of the Inquiry, Professor Sir Ian Kennedy, set out a wide ambition:[12]

> to build a new culture, of trust not blame, within the NHS – a health service where there is greater partnership between patients and professionals; where lines of accountability are clear and where there is openness about mistakes; where services are designed from the patient's point of view and where safety for patients always comes first.

The Inquiry's report concluded:

> it will not be possible to achieve an environment of full, open reporting within the NHS when, outside it, there exists a litigation system the incentives of which press in the opposite direction. We believe that the way forward lies in the abolition of clinical negligence litigation, taking clinical error out of the courts and the tort system. It should be replaced by effective systems for identifying, analysing, learning from and preventing errors, along with all other sentinel events. There must also be a new approach to compensating those patients harmed through such events.[13]

In response to the Inquiry the government accepted the findings on 'the flaws and failures of the organisation and culture, not only at the BRI in the years in question, but of the wider NHS at that time'. This does not mean they accepted the recommendations in the report.

Dr Bolsin has not worked in the NHS since he acted as a whistleblower.

III. Dr Harold Shipman

Harold Shipman, a general medical practitioner, committed serial murders and it is alleged other serious criminal acts throughout his professional career. From 1974 until 1998 it is thought he killed over 215 patients, making him one of the most prolific serial killers.[14] The gravity of his crimes, the number of offences he committed and the length of time he was able to offend for were truly shocking. On 31 January 2000 Harold Shipman was convicted on 15 specimen counts of murder as well as one of forgery of a will. The next day the then Health Secretary, Alan Milburn, announced to the House of Commons that there would be an independent inquiry chaired by Lord Laming of Tewin.[15] The independent inquiry was to be held in private, but produce a public report. This decision to hold the inquiry in private was subsequently challenged in two jointly decided judicial review applications by Peter Wagstaff and the Tameside Families Support Group and a collective of eight major newspapers. In their judgment dated 20 July 2001, Lord Justice Kennedy and Mr Justice Jackson found for the appellant and remitted the matter back to the Secretary of State for

---

[11] *Learning from Bristol: The Department of Health's Response to the Report of the Public Inquiry into Children's Heart Surgery at the Bristol Royal Infirmary 1984–1995*, (2002) Cm 5363, www.gov.uk/government/uploads/system/uploads/attachment_data/file/273320/5363.pdf.

[12] ibid, i.

[13] ibid, 367.

[14] It is uncertain exactly how many of his patients he killed, but it is widely accepted that the number exceeds 215.

[15] Hansard HC *Harold Shipman* (1 February 2001) vol 343 col 907 available at https://hansard.parliament.uk/commons/2000-02-01/debates/dcd6eea3-4eaa-4c11-a489-0ba5b40a9e01/HaroldShipman.

redetermination of his decision.[16] He acceded, and Lord Laming's inquiry was wound out and a public inquiry led by Dame Janet Smith was held under the Tribunals of Inquiry (Evidence) Act 1921.[17]

Dame Janet Smith's inquiry commenced in spring 2002 and subsequently issued a sequence of six reports from 2002 to 2005 on different aspects of concern.[18] Amongst the very many matters Dame Janet identified were a lack of fair procedures, failure to investigate complaints properly, failure to give adequate explanations and lack of impartiality in organisations investigating their own conduct.[19]

IV. The Three Inquiries: Clifford Ayling Independent Inquiry; Richard Neale Independent Inquiry; William Kerr and Michael Haslam Independent Inquiry

A. Clifford Ayling

On 13 July 2001 three independent inquiries were announced by the then Secretary of State for Health, Alan Milburn, into the deeply disturbing behaviour of four individual doctors. These inquiries were collectively known as the three inquiries and had broadly similar terms of reference, to consider how the local NHS had handled complaints/concerns about the conduct and/or performance of doctors. None of these inquiries were to be held in public, though their reports were publicly available. This led to considerable disquiet from those affected, and jointly heard judicial reviews of the Ayling and Neale inquiries. In March 2002 Mr Justice Baker handed down his decision that it was lawful for these two inquiries to be held in private.[20]

The independent inquiry into Clifford Ayling was chaired by the Honourable Mrs Justice Pauffley QC.[21] It was held a 'modified form of private inquiry'.[22] On 15 July 2004 the inquiry's report into Clifford Ayling's conduct was published.[23]

Ayling qualified in the late 1960s, worked for some years in London on obstetrics and gynaecology, before relocating to Kent and working as a GP and a locum obstetrician and

---

[16] *R (Wagstaff) v Secretary of State for Health ex parte Associated Newspapers & Others* [2001] 1 WLT 292

[17] Tribunals of Inquiry (Evidence) Act 1921 c 7 available at www.legislation.gov.uk/ukpga/Geo5/11-12/7/section/1/enacted.

[18] See https://webarchive.nationalarchives.gov.uk/ukgwa/20090808155005/http://www.the-shipman-inquiry.org.uk/home.asp, starting with the Shipman Inquiry; Chairman: Dame Janet Smith DBE, *First Report. Volume One. Death Disguised* (2002).

[19] *Fifth Report* of the Shipman Inquiry, 2004 available at ibid.

[20] *R (Howard & Wright- Hogeland) v Secretary of State for Health* [2002] EWHC 396 (Admin) available at www.bailii.org/ew/cases/EWHC/Admin/2002/396.html.

[21] By the time of the publication of the report she had been made Dame Anna Pauffley.

[22] See Annex 6 of *Committee of Inquiry to Investigate how the NHS Handled Allegations about the Conduct of Clifford Ayling*, Cm 6298 (TSO, July 2004) https://webarchive.nationalarchives.gov.uk/ukgwa/20130123204058/http://www.dh.gov.uk/en/Publicationsandstatistics/Publications/PublicationsPolicyAndGuidance/DH_4088996.

[23] *Committee of Inquiry to Investigate how the NHS Handled Allegations about the conduct of Clifford Ayling*, Cm 6298 (TSO, July 2004) https://webarchive.nationalarchives.gov.uk/ukgwa/20130123204058/http://www.dh.gov.uk/en/Publicationsandstatistics/Publications/PublicationsPolicyAndGuidance/DH_4088996.

gynaecologist from the early 1980s. From the mid-1980s onwards numerous patients raised concerns and made complaints about what the inquiry termed 'sexualised behaviour' to other healthcare professionals, to the hospital where he worked as a locum, and to the police, but despite this no action was taken. Eventually, a police investigation was launched into complaints and Ayling was arrested by Kent Constabulary on 11 November 1998 and released on bail on the conditions that he should not:

- practice as a doctor;
- attend his surgery,
- touch any patient records, and
- neither contact nor interfere with prosecution witnesses.

He applied to the High Court to have these conditions varied, and on 23 November the High Court substituted new conditions, that he could practice, but he was not to examine a female patient without a qualified nurse being present, that he was not to access patient records except those necessary to treat patients before him, and only those records that were handed to him by a practice receptionist, and not to undertake home visits or clinical examinations for a deputising service. The effectiveness of these bail conditions was questioned by Mr Justice Barker in his judgment on the Judicial Review.[24] He asserts that Ayling

> continued to assault and traumatise women in his surgery up until his trial. It is a scandal that he was able to behave as he did for so long. There are very serious questions to be answered as to why this was so.

In December 2000 Ayling was found guilty of 13 counts of indecent assault on 10 female patients and sentenced to four years' imprisonment. On 15 June 2001 the Medical Practitioners Tribunal Service (MPTS) determined that his name should be erased from the medical register. There was a clear overlap between the criminal justice system and GMC remits, which is detailed in the inquiry report.

The inquiry conclusions on complaints have been dealt with in chapter seven above. The inquiry noted that Ayling's failings were widely known within the places he worked, with nurses referring to him as 'fingers Fred' and 'butcher', yet no action was taken. This was in part because there was not a formalised system for practitioners to raise concerns about colleagues. The Inquiry report seems confident that the defensiveness, deference and hierarchical structures that facilitated Ayling's crimes are a thing of the past.

> One particular feature of the Ayling story that the Inquiry noted was the level of knowledge about Ayling's clinical practices that generated anxiety amongst both hospital and community nurses and midwives. But the culture of the time mitigated against open discussion of this. We believe that today this silence would be broken, not only through the cultural shift away from professional hierarchies but also through processes we discuss below for raising concerns about patient safety.

---

[24] *R (Howard & Wright- Hogeland) v Secretary of State for Health* [2002] EWHC 396 (Admin) available at www.bailii.org/ew/cases/EWHC/Admin/2002/396.html.

B. Richard Neale

The second was an independent inquiry into an individual gynaecologist, Richard Neale. The inquiry into his conduct was chaired by Her Honour Judge Suzan Matthews CQ. The inquiry had some difficulties in persuading the harmed patients to come forward as a proportion of those affected boycotted the inquiry as it was not the full public inquiry they had been seeking and they were unhappy that the inquiry was being held in private. The inquiry's report was published in September 2004.[25]

Neale qualified as a doctor in 1971 in the UK, where he initially worked as a GP before moving into obstetrics and gynaecology. In 1977 he emigrated to Canada. In 1978 he undertook a hysterectomy on a high risk patient who had only one kidney against the advice of senior colleague. The patient died and concerns over his competence led to a formal investigation where he was given the choice between withdrawing from practice or undertaking further training. He took the latter option. In 1981 another patient died, a woman who had attended the Oshawa General Hospital, Ontario for an elective induction of labour, to whom he had given an unlicenced drug. An investigation and subsequent hearing (in his absence) led to Neale being struck off the Canadian medical register on 2 July 1985.

On 14 July 1984 Neale applied for the post of Consultant Obstetrician and Gynaecologist in Yorkshire covering the Friarage hospital and the Darlington Memorial Hospital. Neale did not make any mention of the Oshawa General Hospital or of the disciplinary proceedings in Canada in his application. He was appointed and in 1992 he was appointed Clinical Director of Obstetrics and Gynaecology by the reorganised Northallerton Health Services NHS Trust.

In 1991 Neale was cautioned for watching two men cottaging in Richmond, Yorkshire. Upon arrest Neale lied to the police and gave them a false name, date of birth, address and occupation.

In 1988 the police, the GMC and the Northallerton District Health Authority were made aware of the events in Canada, after an investigation described by the inquiry as neither 'appropriate or sufficient' Neale's employment continued unrestricted. By 1993 media stories began circulating about his striking off in Canada and the caution he had received from the police. In response to this publicity in December 1993 Dr Richard Peterson headed an investigation panel. In their report to the Trust Board the Peterson Panel concluding that given Richard Neale's acceptance of the correctness of the facts of the Canada events and the Richmond public toilet incident and that his employers at the time dealt with these matters, there was no basis for any further action against him on these grounds. They did recommend Neale should be demoted from his post as clinical director and offered retraining. The Trust issued a statement saying they had full confidence in Neale and he returned to work from a period of sick leave.

Following further concerns being raised about his competence the Trust decided to set up a disciplinary hearing into various allegations concerning his conduct and activities. On 17 July 1995 Neale was suspended to allow investigation of allegations of theft of Trust

---

[25] *Committee of Inquiry to Investigate how the NHS Handled Allegations about the Performance and Conduct of Richard Neale*, Cm 6315 (TSO, 18 July 2005) available at https://webarchive.nationalarchives.gov.uk/ukgwa/20130123204056/http://www.dh.gov.uk/en/Publicationsandstatistics/Publications/PublicationsPolicyAndGuidance/DH_4088995.

property, submission of fraudulent expenses claims, unauthorised absences from duty and unavailability when on call. These were not allegations about his clinical performance. Neale denied all the allegations. It was decided to negotiate a severance package, and he left the Trust's employment after a year's sabbatical with a total of up to £100,000. He was given a good reference and was subsequently employed by two hospitals in Leicester and the Isle of Wight. The inquiry report findings over this are mixed:

> We consider that the Trust was in an impossible position in the circumstances, which arose in 1995. The Trust was prevented from taking more effective action by the termination of appointment procedures laid down in Health Circular (90)9. In deciding to negotiate Richard Neale's departure from the Trust, it took the pragmatic course. We find that it was the choice of the lesser of two evils.

On the other hand the report is clear: '… the unfortunate consequence of the Trust's decision was that it looked after the interests of its *own* patients to the detriment of the protection of the wider public'.

Concerns about the clinical competence of Neale were brought into the public arena in late January 1998, when a BBC regional television programme made revelations about Neale involving women who had been treated by him in North Yorkshire. Regional Chief Medical Officer, Liam Donaldson, was alerted to these and at his and Dr Cresswell's[26] instigation on 12 June 1998, an alert letter[27] was sent out by the Northern and Yorkshire Regional Office to NHS health authority and Trust chief executives about Neale. Further concerns were raised and a GMC investigation ensued, in September 1999 Neale's registration was suspended on an interim basis. On 25 July 2000, following an investigation relating to the treatment of 14 former patients, the GMC erased Richard Neale's name from the medical register.

A police investigation into Neale's actions was commenced in 1999 and concluded in 2002 after it was felt there was a limited prospect of success. Following the publicity in the media a large number of affected women came forward.

The inquiry highlighted the pervading culture as set out in the Staff Handbook for Northallerton Health Authority, which stated under the Staff Relations and Communications heading:

> Your work in the health service will involve you in dealing with many other members of the staff. Please try always to remember the cardinal rule – go through the proper channels. If you are not sure what the proper channels are, ask your immediate supervisor or departmental manager. You will save endless confusion, friction and ill feeling if you stick to this simple rule – you must resist the temptation to do things by the back door!!

This can be viewed as an inhibiting message to staff faced with problems over a more senior member of staff and reflects a culture described by many staff of the reticence of staff to raise concerns about Richard Neale. This culture would make it extremely difficult for patients to raise concerns or complaints. It echoes a complacent comment heard in the evidence 'we have no complaints at the Friarage'.

---

[26] Dr Tricia Cresswell was a consultant in Public Health.
[27] NHS Circular HSG (97)36.

C. William Kerr and Michael Haslam

The third inquiry of the trio, chaired by Nigel Pleming QC, was the inquiry into William Kerr and Michael Haslam, both consultant psychiatrists at Clifton Hospital, York. It was published in July 2005.[28] It detailed how female patients reported over more than two decades sexual assaults by these two doctors. The inquiry found that Kerr and Haslam had abused at least 77 patients. Kerr had raped or molested at least 67 women between 1965 and 1988. Of these women, 38 complained to nurses and 11 to GPs but they were not believed and no action was taken. In 2000 Kerr was considered too ill to stand trial, but was convicted on one count of indecent assault on a trial of the facts. In 2003 Michael Haslam was jailed for three years, after being found guilty of four charges of indecent assault on three patients between 1981 and 1988. Haslam was also found guilty of rape, but this conviction was quashed on appeal in 2004, the convictions for indecent assault were also appealed but the appeal court found them to be 'safe verdicts of guilty'.

The inquiry was set up to discover how it was that these two perpetrators could have gone on offending for so long, it concluded:

> The story that has emerged is not one of a deliberate conspiracy by healthcare professionals knowingly acting to conceal sexual misdemeanours (or worse) of two of their consultant colleagues. It is mainly but not entirely a story of committed and caring doctors, nurses, psychologists and others. But, for a complex of reasons that we attempt to unravel in our Report, no matter how committed and caring they may have been, many nevertheless ignored warning bells or dismissed rumours and some chose to remain silent when they should have been raising their voices. It is also a story of management failure, failed communication, poor record keeping and a culture where the consultant was all-powerful.[29]

i. William Kerr

William Kerr took up his post in 1965. Numerous complaints were made about his incidents which generally occurred during home visits or out-of-hours consultations at isolated hospital sites. Patients reported that Kerr exposed himself and 'invited' sexual acts – often masturbation or oral sex, but in some cases full sexual intercourse. Some victims stated that he intimidated and threatened them into keeping quiet about his actions, for example by threatening to have one victim's children taken into care. The first allegation was made in 1965, the year he started at the hospital and further concerns were raised by patients over the next 18 years, but as the inquiry stated 'In the period prior to 1983, of the 30 concerns alleged to have been raised about William Kerr all but one fell on deaf ears.' The one concern that was raised about William Kerr was raised by a GP with Michael Haslam, who, unsurprisingly, did not take any further action or raise it with the health authority.

In 1983 Deputy Sister Linda Bigwood learned of a sexual relationship between Kerr and a patient, and she was not prepared to turn a blind eye. For the next five years she notified

---

[28] *The Kerr/Haslam Inquiry Report Volumes 1 & 2*, Cm 6640 -1 and Cm 6640-2 (TSO, August 2004) available at www.gov.uk/government/publications/the-kerrhaslam-inquiry-report.
[29] Page 5 of the *The Kerr/Haslam Inquiry Report Volume 1* Cm 6640 -1 (TSO, August 2004) available at www.gov.uk/government/publications/the-kerrhaslam-inquiry-report.

the hospital authorities, the District Health Authority and the Regional Health Authority, but to no avail; no investigation ever took place into Kerr's sexual abuse of patients. In the period between 1983 and his retirement in 1988 a further 10 complaints were raised against William Kerr. In 1988 Kerr retired with a letter of thanks for his services, by contrast Linda Bigwood felt she had been demoted and her career impacted for speaking out.

In February 1997 a former patient informed the police that she had been sexually assaulted by Kerr from 1982–86 and that she had told her Community Psychiatric (CPN) Nurse Carmel Duff of the indecent assaults. When the police contacted Carmel Duff she confirmed that 'dozens' of females in the Harrogate area had disclosed to their CPNs that they had been sexually assaulted by Kerr. An investigation followed, and eventually the trial on the facts when it had been established that Kerr was not fit to stand trial.

The GMC received a complaint about Kerr in June 1997. When they discovered the active police investigation they asked to be kept informed. By April 2001 eight of Kerr's former patients had complained to the GMC. At this point Kerr applied for voluntary erasure and in May 2003 this application was granted, taking into account Kerr's ill-health. This caused considerable unhappiness among Kerr's victims.

ii. Michael Haslam

Michael Haslam took up a post as a Consultant in Psychological Medicine at Clifton Hospital, York and Harrogate District Hospital. He carried out some unusual treatments, including Somlec,[30] carbon dioxide inhalation, Kirlian photography,[31] massage and hypnotherapy. Haslam groomed some of his victims, making them feel special by recruiting them for 'research' using these therapies.

The first complaint about Haslam was made in 1974. It was made to another doctor, who referred the patient out of area to a different doctor, but did not raise the issue with any authorities. The inquiry report states

> It is clear from the lack of surprise, which was the reaction of at least one consultant to whom the disclosure was made, that predating 1974 there were already rumours, at least in the consultant community, that: 'Michael Haslam's behaviour with patients was less than appropriate.'

In 1976 a solicitor's letter was received by the hospital concerning litigation over a sexual relationship between Haslam and a former patient, which he denied. In 1977 the complainant decided not to press her complaint, and no investigations took place either by the District or the Regional Health Authority.

The pattern of professional awareness coupled with inaction by the majority of colleagues continued. Despite various complaints it took 14 years until matters came to a head in 1988. Haslam was facing various allegations and the choice was given to Haslam to resign or face further investigations. He resigned, but was allowed to work out his notice, was given an honorary consultancy and was given a reference which enabled him to continue clinical

---

[30] The application of a weak electric current to the temples.
[31] Kirlian photography is the production of an image of the electromagnetic field around living tissue. The theory is that the type of pattern produced in the electromagnetic field varies and that this may be used as a diagnostic tool.

work in the private sector as the Medical Director of the Harrogate Clinic. No referral was made the GMC or the police at this point. Haslam did work in the NHS again, he was appointed as Medical Director of the South Durham NHS Trust in December 1993 – this was a non-clinical post.

Haslam's name was mentioned during the police investigation into Kerr and as a result he was suspended on 7 October 1997. The Regional Office, at the instigation of Professor Sir Liam Donaldson, set up an independent review – the Manzoor Review. The review was critical of the lack of action and support provided to the vulnerable complainants. As a result of the Manzoor report Haslam was dismissed from the South West Durham Mental Health Trust in 1998.

From 1996 complaints were made about Haslam to a GMC by consultants, the GMC started investigations. In 1998 the Manzoor report was sent to the GMC. In 1999 Haslam was invited to apply for voluntary erasure from the medical register, which he did. This caused considerable disquiet.

iii. Conclusions on Kerr/Haslam

The victims in these cases were particularly vulnerable because of their mental health issues. Particularly concerning was the evidence reported by victims being pressured into withdrawing their complaints by the perpetrator. The sheer length of time that these behaviours went unchecked for was staggering, the report was damning about the culture that enabled this.

> As a culture we can characterise it as unhealthy. Professionals were reluctant to take action against consultants, through either a misguided sense of loyalty or fear of confrontation. Administrators felt powerless, and devised mechanisms to protect themselves, rather than the patients or those who raised concerns. Responsibility for action was fragmented and unclear; policy and protocols were confusing or were incorrectly implemented, if at all. As a consequence, responses at virtually all levels were inadequate and unconvincing. Some of this paucity of response was due to lack of ability or to lack of training; some of it arose through lack of clarity on how best to proceed. Sadly, some of the failure arose because it was easier, perhaps professionally safer, to do little or nothing at all. As a consequence, patients were routinely disbelieved, were thought to have invented or exaggerated their concerns or complaints, and were treated neither fairly nor with the respect their situation required. Health professionals did not, in general, see their role as supporting patients in following through their concerns and complaints unless clear, unequivocal and incontrovertible evidence demanded it. In other words, if there was a possible 'other side', or a mere denial by the consultant, the matter did not proceed. Even if there was any forward movement, procrastination and delay helped to diminish the impact of concerns and complaints – with damaging consequences. Nor, in general, did NHS staff initiate action in support of patient safety.

The report noted that there had been significant improvements in patient safety since Kerr and Haslam were in practice.

D. Response to the Three Inquiries

In a joint response to the fifth Shipman report and three inquiries into Ayling, Neale and Kerr and Haslam the Department of Health issued *Safeguarding Patients* in February 2007.[32] It drew the common threads from these inquiries:

The Ayling, Neale, Kerr and Haslam cases illustrate the same point: there were enough clues potentially available to indicate serious problems at a much earlier stage. Yet the information was not 'joined up' and no effective action was taken. This partly reflects the then prevailing culture, in which it was almost unthinkable that health professionals would deliberately set out to harm their patients. But even more, it reflects the fact that NHS organisations did not have the systems and processes to ensure that the relevant information was brought together and critically scrutinised.

The response was to acknowledge the culture, but the emphasis was on creating systems and processes.

V. Mid Staffordshire Hospital Trust Independent Inquiry

Widespread systemic failure occurred at the Mid Staffordshire Hospital Trust in patient care and in the failure to respond to complaints by patients and families and to whistleblowing by staff. These shocking events led Julie Bailey CBE and other bereaved relatives and others to form a campaign group Cure the NHS,[33] to repeatedly call for a public inquiry.

Concerns about the hospital were raised externally, including to the Health Service Ombudsman,[34] but the true significance of the situation was only realised officially after an inspection by the Healthcare Commission in 2009,[35] after which two reviews, one by Professor Sir George Alberti of the contemporaneous A&E services and a second by Dr David Colin-Thome, of the treatment and care provided between 2002–07 were commissioned by the Department of Health.[36] Initially the Minister rejected the calls for a public inquiry and instead an independent inquiry chaired by Robert Francis QC was set up.

In his scathing 2010 Report Sir Robert described systemic failure within the hospital operation and management that had led to patients' 'appalling experiences'.[37] This sparked further significant reforms in approach.[38] Francis found that 'the culture of the Trust was not conducive to providing good care for patients or providing a supportive working environment for staff'.[39] The factors that contributed to this were: attitudes of patients and staff,[40] bullying (an atmosphere of fear of adverse repercussions in relation to a variety

---

[32] *Safeguarding Patients. The Government's Response to the Recommendations of the Shipman Inquiry's Fifth Report and to the Recommendations of the Ayling, Neale and Kerr/Haslam Inquiries* HMSO London, February 2007, available at https://assets.publishing.service.gov.uk/government/uploads/system/uploads/attachment_data/file/228872/7015.pdf.

[33] www.curethenhs.co.uk/about-cure-the-nhs/.

[34] Baroness Fritchie, DBE, *Review of the Health Service Ombudsman's Approach to Complaints that NHS Service Failure Led to Avoidable Death* (Parliamentary and Health Service Ombudsman, 2012).

[35] Investigation into Mid Staffordshire Foundation Trust, Healthcare Commission (2009).

[36] *Mid Staffordshire Foundation Trust: A Review of the Procedures for Emergency Admissions and Treatment, and Progress against the Recommendation of the March Healthcare Commission Report*, Professor Sir George Alberti (2009); *A Review of Lessons Learnt for Commissioners and Performance Managers Following the Healthcare Commission Investigation*, Dr David Colin-Thomé (2009).

[37] *Independent Inquiry into Care Provided by Mid Staffordshire NHS Foundation Trust January 2005 – March 2009. Volume I*. Chaired by Robert Francis QC, HC375-I (2010).

[38] See amongst various papers *Hard Truths: The Journey to Putting Patients First: Volume One of the Government Response to the Mid Staffordshire NHS Foundation Trust Public Inquiry* (Department of Health, 2014) Cm 8777-1.

[39] *Francis Independent Inquiry Report*, above n 37, para 43.

[40] 'Patients' attitudes were characterised by a reluctance to insist on receiving basic care or medication for fear of upsetting staff. Although some members of staff were singled out for praise by patients, concerns were expressed

of events was described by a number of staff witnesses), target-driven priorities,[41] disengagement from management, low staff morale, isolation, lack of openness, acceptance of poor standards of conduct, reliance on external assessments and denial. The accident and emergency department, which was a centre of problems, was also chronically understaffed. Incident reporting systems were inadequate. Complaints were poorly investigated, remedial action was often not applied, appraisal and professional development were accorded a low priority, the focus of the Board was on processes not outcomes and its reaction to criticism was individually and collectively one of denial instead of searching self-criticism.

Among the themes the Inquiry identified were:

- a corporate focus on process at the expense of outcomes;
- a failure to listen to those who have received care through proper consideration of their complaints;
- staff disengaged from the process of management;
- insufficient attention to the maintenance of professional standards;
- lack of support for staff through appraisal, supervision and professional development;
- a weak professional voice in management decisions;
- a failure to meet the challenge of the care of the elderly through provision of an adequate professional resource. Some of the treatment of elderly patients could properly be characterised as abuse of vulnerable persons;
- a lack of external and internal transparency;
- false reassurance taken from external assessments; and
- a disregard of the significance of the mortality statistics.[42]

In relation to managers responding to criticism, Francis said:

> A common response to concerns has been to refer to generic data or benchmarks such as star ratings, rather than the experiences of actual patients. While benchmarks and data-based assessments are important tools, these should not be allowed to detract attention from the needs and experiences of patients. Benchmarks, ratings and status may not always bring to light serious systemic failings.[43]

Francis summarised what went wrong as:

> A long-term failure; problems identified but not addressed effectively; confused view of responsibilities; a lack of urgency; figures preferred to people; a lack of risk and impact assessment; a focus on systems not outcomes; those who received care were not listened to; staff disengaged from the process of management; insufficient attention to professional standards; lack of support for staff; a weak professional voice in management decisions; a failure to meet the challenge of caring for the elderly and the vulnerable; a lack of external and internal transparency; false reassurance taken from external assessments; and a disregard for the significance of mortality statistics.[44]

---

about the lack of compassion and uncaring attitude exhibited by others towards vulnerable patients and the marked indifference they showed to visitors': ibid.

  [41] 'A high priority was placed on the achievement of targets, and in particular the A&E waiting time target. The pressure to meet this generated a fear, whether justified or not, that failure to meet targets could lead to the sack': ibid.

  [42] *Francis Independent Inquiry Report*, above n 37, para 80.

  [43] ibid, para 79.

  [44] ibid, pp 396–402.

Concerns were also raised internally, but either ignored or repressed by authoritarian staff.

> The few instances of reports by whistleblowers of which the Inquiry was made aware suggest that the Trust has not offered the support and respect due to those brave enough to take this step. The handling of these cases is unlikely to encourage others to come forward, and the responses to the investigation of the concerns raised have been ineffective.[45]

VI. Winterbourne View Hospital

Winterbourne View Hospital was a private hospital for 24 adults with learning disabilities and autism. Between 2008 and 2011 staff repeatedly mistreated, assaulted and abused patients. Whilst the documentation for procedures and operational practices was found to be 'impressive', behaviour in practice was 'shocking'. The facility's owner later acknowledged that there was insufficient senior management oversight and several NHS commissioning authorities, the Care Quality Commission and the police were criticised for failing to supervise, or to respond to concerns raised by families, mounting evidence or a whistleblowing alert.[46] The true position was exposed on national television by an undercover reporter, who broadcast shocking images.[47] Eleven people were prosecuted of whom six were sentenced to imprisonment.

The Department of Health referred to 'real management failure' at the hospital, and external agencies that repeatedly missed opportunities to pick up poor quality of care, and said that there were 'weaknesses in the system's ability to hold the leaders of care organisations to account'.[48] The Ministerial Foreword also said:[49]

> It is also about promoting a culture and a way of working that actively challenges poor practice and promotes compassionate care across the system.

> First and foremost, where serious abuse happens, there should be serious consequences for those responsible. ...

> And while stronger regulation and inspection, quality information and clearer accountability are vital, so too is developing a supportive, open and positive culture in our care system.

> I want staff to feel able to speak out when they see poor care taking place as well as getting the training and support they need to deal with the complex and challenging dilemmas they often face. For me, this is the bigger leadership and cultural challenge that this scandal has exposed – and answering it will mean listening and involving people with learning disabilities and their families more than ever before.

---

[45] ibid, para 62.

[46] See generally M Flynn, *Winterbourne View Hospital. A Serious Case Review* (South Gloucestershire Safeguarding Adults Board, 2012); *Department of Health Review: Winterbourne View Hospital. Interim Report* (Department of Health, 2012); *Transforming Care: A National Response to Winterbourne View Hospital. Department of Health Review: Final Report* (Department of Health, 2012).

[47] Panorama, *Undercover Care: the Abuse Exposed* (BBC, May 2011).

[48] *Transforming Care: A National Response to Winterbourne View Hospital. Department of Health Review: Final Report* (Department of Health, 2012) paras 1 and 2.12.

[49] ibid.

Although the abuse at the particular facility was described as 'an extreme example', an urgent review of the other 150 facilities found evidence of poor quality of care and too much reliance on restraining people.[50] The overall levels of compliance with both outcomes for care and welfare of people who use services, and for safeguarding adults from abuse, were low (48 per cent).

VII. The Keogh Hospitals Review

In the wake of the Mid-Staffs scandal on 6 February 2013, then Prime Minister David Cameron and the Secretary of State for Health, Jeremy Hunt, asked Professor Sir Bruce Keogh, NHS England Medical Director, to review the quality of the care and treatment being provided by those hospital trusts in England that had been persistent outliers on mortality statistics. Sir Bruce selected 14 trusts for this review on the basis that they had been outliers for the last two consecutive years on either the Summary Hospital-Level Mortality Index (SHMI) or the Hospital Standardised Mortality Ratio (HSMR). These two measures were intended to be a 'smoke alarm' for identifying potential issues with the quality of patient care and treatment at the trusts which required further investigation. The mortality measures were never intended to be used in isolation, a holistic review was undertaken, and no judgements were made at the start of the review about the quality of care that each Trusts was providing to its patients.

A 2013 report into the quality of care and treatment provided by these 14 hospital trusts found in every one of them pockets of excellent practice but significant scope for improvement, with each needing to address an urgent set of actions in order to raise standards of care.[51] Professor Sir Bruce Keogh, concluded that 'These organisations have been trapped in mediocrity, which I am confident can be replaced by a sense of ambition if we give staff the confidence to achieve excellence.'

The very fact that Professor Sir Bruce reviewed 14 different hospitals and found concerns in all of them makes clear that this was not a single 'rogue clinician' or 'bad apple' unit, but comprised more widespread endemic concerns. He noted that all 14 trusts faced a different set of circumstances, pressures and challenges, which included:[52]

(a)   the limited understanding of how important and how simple it can be to genuinely listen to the views of patients and staff and engage them in how to improve services;
(b)   the capability of hospital boards and leadership to use data to drive quality improvement;

---

[50] *Department of Health Review: Winterbourne View Hospital. Interim Report* (Department of Health, 2012). The Care Quality Commission inspected 71 NHS facilities, 47 Independent Healthcare providers and 32 adult social care facilities, covering 15,000 people in England who had learning disabilities or autism and behaviour that challenges. Around 3,400 people were in NHS-funded learning disability in-patient beds, and 1,200 were in hospital for assessment and treatment.

[51] *Review into the Quality of Care and Treatment Provided by 14 Hospital Trusts in England: Overview Report* (NHS, 2013).

[52] ibid.

(c) the fact that some hospital trusts are operating in geographical, professional or academic isolation, which can lead to difficulties in recruiting enough high quality staff, and an over-reliance on locums and agency staff;

(d) the lack of value and support being given to frontline clinicians, particularly junior nurses and doctors; and

(e) imbalance around the use of transparency for the purpose of accountability and blame rather than support and improvement. 'Unless there is a change in mind set then the transparency agenda will fail to fulfil its full potential. Some boards use data simply for reassurance, rather than the forensic, sometimes uncomfortable, pursuit of improvement.

Sir Bruce warned against an authoritarian reaction to the findings, as opposed to a focus on improvement:

> However, this is not a time for hasty reactions and recriminations. Any immediate safety issues we uncovered have been dealt with. It is a time for considered debate, a concerted improvement effort and a focus on clear accountability. So, I expect the carefully considered and agreed action plans to be enacted with serious consequences for failure to do so.

VIII. Mid Staffordshire Hospital Trust Public Inquiry

From 2007 onwards concerns had been raised about the care at Mid Staffs and there had been a series of reports and investigations, including the 2009 Healthcare Commissioner report which reviewed the period from 2007–09 and described 'appalling' care,[53] and the two reviews by the Department of Health.[54] Sir Robert Francis's independent inquiry published in 2010 (see above) was intended by the Labour government to be the final chapter. As the shadow Health Secretary Andrew Lansley had long called for a public inquiry, and following a change of government to the coalition between the Conservatives and Liberal Democrats said public inquiry was launched in 2010. This was also chaired by Robert Francis QC. The public inquiry had a wider remit than the initial inquiry, it looked at the system-wide failures to detect and correct the poor care at Mid Staffs.

The public inquiry report did not hold back on either criticism or recommendations.[55] It is not surprising that it made very uncomfortable reading in relation to Mid Staffs, references to the wider NHS were also unsettling.

> Unfortunately, echoes of the cultural issues found in Stafford can be found throughout the NHS system. It is not possible to say that such deficiencies permeate to all organisations all of the time, but aspects of this negative culture have emerged throughout the system.

---

[53] Healthcare Commission Investigation into Mid Staffordshire NHS Foundation Trust (March 2009).

[54] *Mid Staffordshire Foundation Trust: A Review of the Procedures for Emergency Admissions and Treatment, and Progress against the Recommendation of the March Healthcare Commission Report*, Professor Sir George Alberti (2009); *A Review of Lessons Learnt for Commissioners and Performance Managers following the Healthcare Commission Investigation*, Dr David Colin-Thomé (2009).

[55] *Report of the Mid Staffordshire NHS Foundation Trust Public Inquiry. February 2013 Chaired by Robert Francis QC*, HC947, available at www.gov.uk/government/publications/report-of-the-mid-staffordshire-nhs-foundation-trust-public-inquiry.

Volume 3 of the report contains a section on culture, and perhaps one of the most telling sections described a dysfunctional culture where patients' interest are not paramount:

> Many of the negative aspects of culture mentioned above derive from a failure to see things from the patient's perspective and to understand the effects of actions – or inaction – on them. In the maelstrom of discussions and efforts devoted to reorganisation, devising and implementing new systems and so on, the core purpose of healthcare services has all too often been overlooked. This Inquiry has seen evidence of many different examples of leaders, managers, regulators and others failing to have the interests and needs of patients at the forefront of their minds. Very few, if any, of the individuals involved have deliberately or consciously acted in this way. However, the pressures of their work and circumstances have led to this.

The report made 290 recommendations, including calling for a statutory duty of candour.

IX. Morecambe Bay

The Morecambe Bay Scandal, as it became known, referred to the unnecessary deaths of 11 babies and one mother due to failings in the maternity provision at Furness General Hospital between 2004 and 2013. The harm caused to families by substandard care was compounded by the responses of some staff, the hospital management, the NMC, the CQC, the PHSO and others, who not only failed to investigate, but in some cases actively covered up or destroyed evidence of the major failings in the care provided. The scandal only came to light because of dogged campaigning by affected families.

The first missed opportunity identified in the inquiry report was the case of Elleanor Bennett. In 2004 she died after she was born in very poor condition due to lack of oxygen during her delivery. The report found that the investigation into her death was 'rudimentary, protective of the midwife involved, and failed to identify the shortcomings in practice and approach that led to inadequate monitoring of a high-risk pregnancy and a lack of necessary obstetric assessment and intervention'. They concluded that a proper investigation in 2004 would have identified the issues and allowed the opportunity for them to be resolved. There were further cases that were clearly concerning in 2005 and 2006, but the occurrence of five serious incidents in 2008 indicated how serious the problems were. The five serious incidents comprised two maternal deaths (following one of which the baby also died), an intrapartum stillbirth, a neonatal death from sepsis and a baby damaged by the effects of shortage of oxygen (hypoxia) around the time of birth. The investigation carried out by the hospital into four of these incidents, the maternal deaths, the intrapartum stillbirth and the brain injury, concluded they were unavoidable. The Kirkup report concluded that care in each case was seriously deficient and this should have been obvious at the time.

The first case to show any unequivocal finding of clinical failure was the death of Joshua Titcombe. Joshua died from sepsis following prolonged rupture of the membranes, he should have been closely monitored as his mother had become acutely unwell shortly following delivery and had required IV antibiotics for a serious infection. His parents repeatedly raised concerns with nurses about Joshua, who was struggling to maintain his temperature and was at times hypothermic, but action was not taken. By the time it was recognised that he had an infection and he was given antibiotics it was too late. Joshua's father James made a formal complaint to the Hospital in November 2008. An external review of Joshua's care, triggered by a complaint made by James Titcombe, showed unequivocal evidence of clinical failure.[56] The contents of this external report were shared with the Titcombe family, who challenged several aspects, and it became clear that there were significant discrepancies between the accounts given by midwives and the record made by the Titcombe family shortly before Joshua died.

The Trust formally accepted liability for Joshua's death and, following referral to the NHS Litigation Authority, a settlement was reached in February 2009. However, the settlement was not the outcome the Titcombe were seeking. James Titcombe did not accept that the Trust had been fully open in responding to his complaint, and subsequently referred the matter to the PHSO and in May 2009 he wrote to the CQC.

The arrival of the letter from James Titcombe expressing his concerns to the CQC coincided with a notification from Monitor to the CQC about the 2008 cluster of five Serious Untoward incidents (SUIs). This notification was triggered as part of the Foundation trust status application, which required that Monitor was notified of SUIs. These five SUIs were referred to a CQC investigation manager, who examined them and concluded there was no need for further investigation as she didn't think they were linked. The Kirkup report notes this was a missed opportunity, followed by further failures to safeguard patients. The report is also clear that, while the CQC was 'The organisation that most clearly failed to deal adequately with the Trust was the CQC' it was by no means alone.[57]

In August 2009 the PHSO carried out an initial screening of James Titcombe's complaint to determine if it should be formally investigated. They decided not to do so, at least in part because they felt that CQC were investigating and were better placed to deal with systemic problems.

The NMC and the GMC were also both criticised by the Kirkup report for their handling of the Morecambe Bay scandal. Subsequently further stinging criticism was made of the NMC by the PSA in their May 2018 report,[58] which provides a detailed chronology and highlights the NMC's failure to act in a timely or appropriate manner, see chapter 12, Section II.F below for more detail.

The inquiry report chapter on external response concluded '... the external regulatory system of the NHS failed to get to grips with the issues that the affected families were bringing to them'. Following some difficulties over determining jurisdiction, the coroner's

---

[56] *External Investigation into Serious Untoward Incident At Furness General Hospital: Baby Joshua Titcombe* (Chandler, Hopps and Farrier Report), 2009.

[57] In 2013 the new chief executive of the CQC instructed the consultants Grant Thornton to draw up a report into the CQC's involvement in the Morecambe Bay scandal. The resulting report was explosive; it detailed the deletion of a in internal CQC memo which was critical of their handling of Morecambe Bay with this cover up being instigated from very top of the CQC. The Health Secretary gave a statement in parliament on 19 June 2013 'The independent report was commissioned by the new chief executive of the CQC, and the members of the new team that is running it have made it clear that there was a completely unacceptable attempt to cover up the deficiencies in their organisation. The report lists what went wrong over a period of many years.' Subsequently questions have arisen about the veracity of some of the claims in the Grant Thornton report after it emerged that the CQC had settled a libel case brought by its former Chief executive over the report contents.

[58] *Professional Standards Authority Lessons Learned Review: The Nursing and Midwifery Council's Handling of Concerns about Midwives Fitness to Practise at the Furness General Hospital. May 2018*, available at www. professionalstandards.org.uk/docs/default-source/publications/nmc-lessons-learned-review-may-2018. pdf?sfvrsn=ff177220_0.

inquest into Joshua's death was held in June 2011. The coroner made strong criticisms of both the clinical practice and conduct of Trust staff, including collusion in preparation for the inquest and possible destruction of evidence as Joshua's observation chart had disappeared. Following a Rule 43 letter from the coroner expressing these concerns, Cumbria Constabulary launched a police investigation in September 2011. The police investigation resulted in more families coming forward and it became clear that there were more affected families than had been thought. They had formed a group who were campaigning for an independent investigation. On 12 September 2013 the Secretary of State for Health announced in a written ministerial statement to parliament that there would be an independent investigation.[59]

In his 2015 report Bill Kirkup identified 20 major failures, including in management, and at external regulatory and ombudsman levels.[60] The report found a dysfunctional maternity unit, with a pattern of failure to recognise the nature and severity of the problem, with, in some cases, denial that any problem existed, and a series of missed opportunities to intervene that involved almost every level of the NHS. The issues were only exposed by determined efforts by patients. The report concluded that the problems comprised a 'lethal mix' of:

> … the seriously dysfunctional nature of the maternity service at Furness General Hospital (FGH). Clinical competence was substandard, with deficient skills and knowledge; working relationships were extremely poor, particularly between different staff groups, such as obstetricians, paediatricians and midwives; there was a growing move amongst midwives to pursue normal childbirth 'at any cost'; there were failures of risk assessment and care planning that resulted in inappropriate and unsafe care; and the response to adverse incidents was grossly deficient, with repeated failure to investigate properly and learn lessons.[61]

Significantly, the report stated a particular view in relation to ascribing blame to particular behaviour:

> We make no criticism of staff for individual errors, which, for the most part, happen despite their best efforts and are found in all healthcare systems. Where individuals collude in concealing the truth of what has happened, however, their behaviour is inexcusable, as well as unprofessional. The failure to present a complete picture of how the maternity unit was operating was a missed opportunity that delayed both recognition and resolution of the problems and put further women and babies at risk. This followed the earlier missed opportunities to identify underlying problems in 2004 and 2006/07.[62]

The report made an important finding on the complexity of the system in relation to administration, management, regulation, supervision, investigation and complaints, and the adverse effects of many years of organisational restructuring within the NHS:

> 1. Complexity of system. The review of external responses to the issues within our terms of reference demonstrates how many agencies had management or regulatory responsibilities that related

---

[59] *Report of the Mid Staffordshire NHS Foundation Trust Public Inquiry. February 2013 Chaired by Robert Francis QC*, HC947, available at www.gov.uk/government/publications/report-of-the-mid-staffordshire-nhs-foundation-trust-public-inquiry

[60] Dr B Kirkup CBE, *The Report of the Morecambe Bay Investigation* (Department of Health, 2015) available at https://assets.publishing.service.gov.uk/government/uploads/system/uploads/attachment_data/file/408480/47487_MBI_Accessible_v0.1.pdf.

[61] ibid, para 4.

[62] ibid, para 11.

to the issues we have examined. It was difficult for us to identify and trace through their interactions with the families and the Trust. It is not reasonable for the NHS to expect its users to face such a complex array of supervisory organisations without clear support in navigating the system and getting to the right people in a timely way.

2. A system in transition. A persistent feature of the material we have studied is that the health system was in some turmoil due to the transition to new governance or management arrangements. The NHS is a complex system with many organisations dealing with multiple agencies. Add to that a continuous set of restructuring and reorganisations, and the risk of things being missed, misunderstood and wrongly actioned increases massively. In this case, the Trust was moving to Foundation Trust status, dealing with a developing and changing authorisation process; the CQC was being established and its powers and methods of working were changing; the PHSO was changing and its responsibilities altering; Monitor was developing its ways of working; the SHAs were moving to new expanded geographies; and, as time went on, the whole system was grappling with the findings of the Francis Report. Such circumstances bring with them significant levels of risk.[63]

Overall, the report's verdict was: 'What is inexcusable, however, is the repeated failure to examine adverse events properly, to be open and honest with those who suffered, and to learn so as to prevent recurrence.'[64]

X. Abertawe Bro Morgannwg University Health Board

On 20 November 2013 Mark Drayford announced to the Welsh assembly[65] that there would be a review into the care offered to older patients by the ABM University Health Board at two of their hospitals; the Princess of Wales Hospital, Bridgend and Neath Port Talbot Hospital.

The review was chaired by Professor June Andrews and focussed on:

- how professional nursing standards are protected and delivered consistently, and how the Health Board responds to lapses in delivery of these standards;

- the culture of care, particularly focusing on the care of older patients in the medical wards;

- responding to complaints, particularly looking at how complaints are handled by the Health Board and how professionals are held to account for lapses in care identified through investigation of complaints (including POVA investigations); and,

- administration and recording of medicines, particularly looking at how medicines are administered to patients who are cognitively impaired or have other challenges in taking medicines orally.

The context for the review's 2014 report, *Trusted to Care*, is set out as

The Review operated in an environment of divisive public comment and campaigning activity. There was speculation expressed through the BBC, and other broadcast and print media, with

---

[63] ibid, 170.
[64] ibid, para 8.3.
[65] https://gov.wales/written-statement-independent-external-review-princess-wales-hospital-and-neath-port-talbot.

questions raised in the Welsh Assembly and through social media. Sensitivities around the remit of the Review were intensified by potential criminal prosecution of NHS nursing staff (a situation which was unresolved at the time of conclusion of the Review), and several public meetings in which calls for the resignation of the current Chief Executive of the ABMU Board were made. Much of this debate was formulated as being in the aftermath of the public enquiry by Robert Francis QC into the care of patients in Mid Staffordshire NHS Foundation Trust. It was framed as the question "Is ABMU 'another Stafford'"?

Trusted to Care looked into a number of concerns over quality of care and patient safety in two Welsh hospitals focused on poor and variable professional behaviour in relation to elderly patients. It reported attitudes showing a lack of respect for and involvement of patients and relatives, and disconnections between front-line staff and managers, with confusion over leadership responsibilities and accountabilities.[66] However, the report was emphatic that the situation was not another Mid Staffs, the hospitals were not an 'example of a failing system, the situation in ABMU is remediable if our recommendations are accepted and implemented'.

Amongst the report's recommendations were the need to create 'an organisational culture which enables staff to practice professionally with confidence at all times, both individually and collectively'. The review also criticised complaints processes as adversarial and slow:

> Everyone who is upset does not have a legal case. Every case that is lost is not unfair. Unfortunately, the process of investigation and redress in ABMU tends to push complainants towards believing that they definitely have a 'case' as a result of feelings that arise when they are not treated respectfully by the system which makes them feel unfairly treated.[67]

> One of the reasons for the length of time it takes to respond to complaints is the bureaucracy of the processes and the introduction of 'legalistic' concerns at the earliest stages. It seemed to the Review Team that the health system could lead the way by adopting a voluntary and confidential form of dispute resolution involving an independent impartial person helping to open and improve dialogue and empathy between the hospital and the patients and relatives who use it. The mediator would help staff and hospital service users to broaden the range of solutions to their grievances. They could help collaborate to find solutions.[68]

> At present, the process seems to be focussed on establishing whether the hospital did something 'wrong' and what the hospital is going to do to make up for it. There is an assumption that there is an objective measure of what can be expected from a hospital. The Review Team is of the view that some of the disputes arise not because the hospital did something objectively wrong, but because it fell below the expectation of the patient or relative. Given that there is no advance agreement of what it is reasonable to expect, the attempt at an adversarial resolution of these issues is often going to be time consuming and ultimately fruitless if the public expectation of a hospital is unrealistic.[69]

> The relationship of trust and confidence that a community has in its own hospital is one that comes to the fore if anyone ever proposes to close or downgrade the hospital. An uncritical faith in the power of a hospital can lead to bitter disappointment. Mediation rather than the current

---

[66] J Andrews and M Butler, *Trusted to Care. An Independent Review of the Princess of Wales Hospital and Neath Port Talbot Hospitals at ABMU* (Dementia Services Development Centre and The People Organisation, 2014). Available at https://gov.wales/sites/default/files/publications/2019-04/trusted-to-care.pdf.

[67] ibid, para 3.58.

[68] ibid, para 3.73.

[69] ibid, para 3.74.

complaints system is more likely to produce a result that is agreeable to both parties and will preserve the relationship rather than creating winners and losers. It is significant that the ABMU victims meetings are supported and attended by clinical negligence lawyers.[70]

Andrews and Bulter made an important point about the negative consequences on those working in public services of external attribution of blame by the media and politicians:

> The Review Team is concerned that this Report may be seen by some, and be reported by others, as evidence of failure and incompetence which should result in a search for 'the guilty' and for 'heads to roll'. This is the current bullying language frequently used to vilify those with responsibility for services and care in the NHS and other public services. … in every organisation providing services to the public, there will be lapses in standards and practice in some way. … It is very important to say this, in this report, which is about services provided by local people to fellow citizens in their own community. Local and national governance arrangements should provide the reassurance to the public that care and treatment issues … are routinely identified and action taken without recourse to one-off external reviews.[71]

XI. Gosport War Memorial Hospital

In 1991 Anita Tubbritt, a staff nurse at the Gosport War Memorial Hospital, rang her local Royal College of Nursing convenor expressing concerns about the inappropriate use of opioids, mainly diamorphine, and syringe drivers at the hospital's Redclyffe Annexe. These concerns were effectively shut down by the hospital in a subsequent meeting.

In 1998 complaints were made to the hospital, the coroner and the police about the death of Mrs Gladys Richards by her daughters. Similar concerns were raised by other families, whose loved ones had been admitted to the hospital and had died unexpectedly following unwarranted opioid administration and by 2001 Hampshire constabulary was investigating five deaths at the hospital. Central to these investigations was the role of Dr Barton and the administration of opioids to patients under her care. Unfortunately, the Richards family, and many other families, were dismissed and let down by the police, the CPS, the coronial system, the GMC, the NMC, the Health Service Ombudsman, their local MP Sir Peter Viggers, as well as by the hospital management. By 2014 the bereaved families had been through three police investigations and associated CPS reviews with no prosecution;[72] an investigation by the GMC which resulted in Dr Barton being allowed to continue practising as a doctor with conditions on her practice;[73] an investigation by the Commission for Health Improvement; a review and inquest by the Council for Healthcare Regulatory

---

[70] ibid, para 3.75.

[71] ibid, para 5.1.

[72] For a review see Hampshire Constabulary's summary of Operation Rochester, available at www.hampshire.police.uk/SysSiteAssets/foi-media/hampshire-constabulary/other_information/operation_rochester_investigation_overview.pdf.

[73] In 2010 the MPTS determined that Dr Jane Barton, the GP at the centre of the scandal, was fit to practice with conditions. This ran against the recommendation of the GMC, who lacked the power to appeal at this time. See www.gmc-uk.org/-/media/documents/gosport-war-memorial-hospital-report-gmcresponse_pdf-76338897.pdf for further details.

Excellence and a Department of Health clinical care audit.[74] Despite this there were significant unanswered questions, and so the Minister for Care and Support, Norman Lamb MP, set up an independent inquiry panel[75] with Bishop James Jones as chair.

The resulting panel report[76] details the catalogue of missed opportunities, errors and obstacles put in the way of the families in their search to find out the truth about what had happened to their loved ones by the professional bodies and those in authority who should have been protecting patient safety. The panel's report was the first time the true scale of the deaths had been assessed, and the report concludes that at least 450 individuals had their lives shortened in that hospital, though other estimates have been higher. In the foreword the Right Reverend James Jones gives a damning critique:

> ... during a certain period at Gosport War Memorial Hospital, there was a disregard for human life and a culture of shortening the lives of a large number of patients by prescribing and administering 'dangerous doses' of a hazardous combination of medication not clinically indicated or justified. They show too that, whereas a large number of patients and their relatives understood that their admission to the hospital was for either rehabilitation or respite care, they were, in effect, put on a terminal care pathway. They show that, when relatives complained about the safety of patients and the appropriateness of their care, they were consistently let down by those in authority – both individuals and institutions. These included the senior management of the hospital, healthcare organisations, Hampshire Constabulary, local politicians, the coronial system, the Crown Prosecution Service, the General Medical Council and the Nursing and Midwifery Council. All failed to act in ways that would have better protected patients and relatives, whose interests some subordinated to the reputation of the hospital and the professions involved.'

The report is very clear that this is not a case of a single 'bad apple' practitioner, but that multiple professions were part of accepted practice.

> The practice of anticipatory prescribing, and of administering certain drugs in circumstances and doses beyond what would have been indicated or justified clinically, involved the consultants, the clinical assistant, the nurses and the pharmacists. It was a practice that built up and continued over many years, and lives were shortened before the pattern changed significantly from 2000. Some nurses had questioned the practice in 1991, but it continued, becoming a culture and a norm for the wards involved. It became institutionalised on the wards.

However, a dysfunctional culture was not limited to these two wards, it was part of a pervading hospital-wide culture of accepting and not challenging these practices.

> Most obviously, there was the attempt by some of the nurses to raise concerns, but other individuals should also have been aware of what was happening, including consultants, other doctors, nurses and managers. Yet a striking feature of the documents is that no one attempted even to challenge these behaviours.

In addition to the inadequacies of the hospital's response to the deaths, the report goes on to describe the unsatisfactory outcomes of the police and GMC investigations as

---

[74] See the Gosport Independent Inquiry Terms of Reference available at http://data.parliament.uk/DepositedPapers/Files/DEP2014-1591/Gosport_Independent_Panel_-_Terms_of_Reference.pdf.

[75] www.gosportpanel.independent.gov.uk/.

[76] Bishop James Jones, *Gosport War Memorial Hospital: The Report of the Gosport Independent Panel* (June 2018) HC1084, available at www.gosportpanel.independent.gov.uk/media/documents/070618_CCS207_CCS03183220761_Gosport_Inquiry_Whole_Document.pdf.

at least in part due to the exclusive focus on one individual when there were significant systemic problems – as the proceedings began to reveal – as well as the length of time that had elapsed by then.

In 2019 Hampshire constabulary announced that they were reopening an investigation into the deaths, Operation Magenta, which is currently ongoing.

XII. Ian Paterson

In April 2017, Ian Paterson, a surgeon in the West Midlands, was convicted of wounding with intent, and imprisoned. He was given a 15-year term, but this was increased on appeal to 20 years as the original sentence was felt to be too lenient. Paterson had breached his patients' trust, abused his power and harmed hundreds of his former patients.

Concerns about Paterson's surgical procedures and medical practice were first raised in 2003, but it was not until 2011 that he was suspended by his employers. In December 2017, the Government commissioned an independent Inquiry chaired by Bishop Graham James to investigate Paterson's malpractice and to make recommendations to improve patient safety.

Although the majority of media coverage of Paterson referred to breast procedures on women it should be remembered that Paterson performed other procedures and also operated on men. The term 'cleavage sparing mastectomy' is mentioned in several patient accounts. The inquiry report is clear that this procedure has no definition and is not a recognised practice. Even though the term cleavage sparing mastectomy may not have been first used by Paterson, it has become associated with him.[77]

Paterson qualified in medicine in 1981. He then worked for a time in Manchester before he moving to work at the Good Hope Hospital in Sutton Coldfield. In 1996 Paterson was suspended for a time after he had harmed a patient in one of his operations. Good Hope Hospital arranged for Paterson's surgical work to be supervised until there was confidence that he could operate again without such oversight.

Paterson trained as a general surgeon, initially specialising in vascular surgery, but was appointed as a specialist breast surgeon in 1998 at Solihull Hospital, part of the Heart of England NHS Foundation Trust (HEFT). Paterson also treated patients in the independent sector at the Bupa Little Aston Hospital from 1993 and at the Bupa Parkway Hospital in Solihull from 1998. Both hospitals were taken over by Spire Healthcare (Spire) in 2007. Over time, Paterson increasingly treated most of his private patients at Spire Parkway Hospital. From 2003 concerns were raised about Paterson's clinical practice. In 2011 HEFT suspended Paterson and Spire suspended practising privileges at its hospitals later that year.

Chapter three of the Inquiry Report details accounts of treatment by Paterson from 211 former patients. It details how many patients were given incorrect diagnoses, including false cancer diagnoses; many were operated on unnecessarily; how Ian Paterson behaved

---

[77] Bishop Graham James, *Report of the Independent Inquiry into the Issues raised by Paterson* (February 2020) HC 31, available at https://assets.publishing.service.gov.uk/government/uploads/system/uploads/attachment_data/file/863211/issues-raised-by-paterson-independent-inquiry-report-web-accessible.pdf.

inappropriately including failure to obtain consent, failing to keep accurate medical records or lying in medical records, pressurising patients to have their surgery in the private sector and performing operations he was not qualified to do. It makes for sobering reading. What is particularly shocking is the number of patients and the time this went on for.

In 1993 a consultant oncologist who was a colleague of Paterson notified HEFT of concerns, this oncologist was concerned that the tissue that Paterson left behind after surgery put women at increased risk of their breast cancer reoccurring. The HEFT commissioned a report by a senior clinician at the Trust, but then failed to act on the information in this report.

In the spring of 2007 concerns were raised by a newly appointed breast surgeon and two oncologists about Paterson's conduct. Disciplinary procedures were instigated and a review of Paterson's performance was undertaken by a breast surgeon from another Trust. Paterson was asked to stop doing cleavage sparing mastectomies and shaves.[78] In December 2007 six healthcare professionals who worked alongside Paterson at HEFT wrote to the Chief Executive expressing their concerns about his clinical practice and patient safety.

The inquiry heard that there was a personal cost to the healthcare professionals who raised concerns about Paterson, with many saying they experienced bullying or aggression as a result and that they were not supported in raising concerns. To add insult to injury four of the doctors who raised concerns with the Chief Executive in 2007 were themselves subject later to investigation by the GMC, in order to determine their fitness to practise, because they had worked alongside Paterson.

Despite the concerns raised by colleagues Paterson was allowed to continue operating on patients until he was suspended in 2011 when a new Chief executive took over at HEFT. The GMC was informed. A review was commissioned to see why Paterson had not been stopped earlier. A recall of Paterson's patients was ordered. Paterson was also suspended by Spire and a recall of his private patients took place.

The GMC had previously been notified by patients as early as 2007, a patient complained in 2010. The GMC was asked to pause their investigation while the police investigation was ongoing, which they were happy to do as Paterson was suspended so not a danger to the public. The police investigation resulted in Paterson being charged and convicted in April 2017. On 25 July the MPTS found him unfit to practice and erased him from the medical register.

The lack of any action over concerns about Paterson seems remarkable, the inquiry describes it thus:

> This capacity for wilful blindness is illustrated by the way in which Paterson's behaviour and aberrant clinical practice was excused or even favoured. Many simply avoided or worked round him. Some could have known, while others should have known, and a few must have known. At the very least a great deal more curiosity was needed, and a broader sense of responsibility for safety in the wider healthcare system by both clinicians and managers alike. However, some seem to have been inhibited from complaining because they had seen colleagues appearing to get nowhere by doing so (and in some cases finding themselves under investigation). A few of Paterson's more

---

[78] A shave is where the tissue at the edges of the cavity created by a partial mastectomy is removed or 'shaved' to prevent reoccurrence.

junior colleagues commented that the unusual character of his surgical practice (compared with other breast surgeons) was well known. To a surprising degree he was 'hiding in plain sight'.

Chapter seven of the Inquiry Report deals with governance, accountability and culture. Its rather chilling conclusion is:

> From the evidence we heard, we believe the culture set from the top was one of avoiding problems by managing them as isolated incidents, with a lack of critical thinking about what the real issues were. It was convenient for Paterson to be characterised as a unique rogue by those who worked with him and those in charge – this lack of curiosity was to have far-reaching and devastating consequences.

> It is our opinion that it would be unwise to dismiss him as a one-off, given the evidence we have heard.

The opening page of the Paterson report provides a succinct summary:

> It is tempting for inquiries to recommend fresh layers of regulation. But our healthcare system does not lack regulation or regulators. The resources they possess, both human and financial, are very considerable. There is no process, procedure or regulation which can prevent malpractice on its own. This report is primarily about poor behaviour and a culture of avoidance and denial. These are not necessarily improved by additional regulation.

XIII. The Independent Medicines and Medical Devices Safety Review

In 2020 there was an inquiry into three unrelated products chaired by Baroness Julia Cumberlege.[79] These products were: hormonal pregnancy tests, most notably Primodos, which were hormone containing tablets given to women in the 1950–70s to test if they were pregnant; the impact of *in-utero* exposure to Valproate, which has been used since the 1970s predominantly as an anti-epileptic, but also as a mood-stabiliser; the use of surgical mesh in the pelvis used to treat stress urinary incontinence and pelvic organ prolapse. This review only came about after years, in some cases decades, of dedicated campaigning by the various patient groups and charities.

The fact that three unrelated products spanning many decades were reviewed gave the IMMDS Review Report, *First Do No Harm*,[80] a unique oversight and the conclusions were stark.

> We heard about a system that does not work in a joined-up fashion, and that lacks the leadership to deliver coherent and fully integrated patient safety policy directives and standards. Mistakes are perpetuated through a culture of denial, a resistance to no-blame learning, and an absence of overall effective accountability. This culture has to change, starting at ground level while being encouraged and supported from the top.

---

[79] Sonia Macleod was the lead researcher for the IMMDS Review.
[80] J Cumberlege, *First Do No Harm: The Report of the Independent Medicines and Medical Devices Safety Review* (2020) available at www.immdsreview.org.uk/Report.html.

The review identified cross-system failings.

> Put simply, the system has not been listening as it should. When it has listened, it does not always know how to respond. It does not recognise its own failings in this regard. Not surprisingly those patients affected, their family and friends want answers. When they try to escalate their concerns, whether to the local Patients Advice and Liaison Service, to their Trust management teams or to the regulators, they have found these services unresponsive – either unable or unwilling to help.

In the nine core recommendations and the more targeted actions for improvement for organisations First Do No Harm outlines how improvements could be driven. These included a Patient Safety Commissioner who 'will provide a focus for patients; they will finally know that the patient voice will count when and where it matters'.

XIV. The Ockenden Review of Maternity Services at Shrewsbury and Telford Hospital NHS Trust

In 2017 an inquiry was launched into concerns about the maternity provision at Shrewsbury and Telford Hospital NHS Trust, it was chaired by Donna Ockenden.[81] This review followed tenacious campaigning by two families whose babies had died while under care of the maternity services at the Trust. Rhiannon Davies and Richard Stanton's daughter Kate died in 2009 and Kayleigh and Colin Griffiths' daughter Pippa died in 2016. The Stanton-Davies and the Griffiths families had not been satisfied with the responses to the deaths of their newborn daughters and had carried out their own investigations to highlight the need for an independent assessment of the trust. Their efforts had led to 23 families being identified whose care was a cause for concern. They took this evidence to Jeremy Hunt, the then Health Secretary, and in response he commissioned the Ockenden review. As the Review progressed it became clear that this was far larger than the original 23 families. The true scale of the issues uncovered was shocking: by the conclusion of the review, the care of 1,486 families had been examined. Most related to care provided between 2000 and 2019, but the review considered cases as far back as 1973 and up to 2020.

Due to the scale of the task and the urgent need for change, an interim report was published in December 2020.[82] This report carried recommendations based on the first 250 clinical reviews. It contained a number of Local Actions for Learning[83] specifically intended for Shrewsbury and Telford and seven Immediate and Essential Actions[84] which were to be implemented across the NHS if they were not already in place.

---

[81] www.ockendenmaternityreview.org.uk/.

[82] Ockenden Review, *Emerging Findings and Recommendations from the Independent Review of Maternity Services at the Shrewsbury and Telford Hospital NHS Trust – Our First Report following 250 Clinical Reviews* HC 1081, 10 December 2020, available at www.gov.uk/government/publications/ockenden-review-of-maternity-services-at-shrewsbury-and-telford-hospital-nhs-trust.

[83] These recommended changes related to various aspects of care including maternity care, maternal deaths, obstetric anaesthesia and neonatal services.

[84] These were

1. Safety in maternity units across England must be strengthened by increasing partnerships between Trusts and within local networks. Neighbouring Trusts must work collaboratively to ensure that local investigations into Serious Incidents (SIs) have regional and Local Maternity System (LMS) oversight,

The final report[85] published in March 2022 concluded that at least 200 babies might have survived if they had had better care, 131 of these had been stillborn and 70 were neonatal deaths. The review also found major or significant concerns about the care provided to nine mothers who had died from childbirth related complications. In addition to the awful death tolls 94 children were avoidably harmed by poor maternity care, in some cases left with severe life-long disabilities including cerebral palsy and hypoxic brain injuries. In her letter to the Secretary of State which preceded her final report Donna Ockenden describes a Trust which 'failed to investigate, failed to learn and failed to improve'.

The Ockenden Review shone a light on some appalling failings both in the care provided and into the actions taken following an incident, which was noted to include blaming the mothers for poor outcomes, rather than the substandard clinical care which they had received. It is difficult to comprehend how such insensitivity could have developed in a hospital Trust whose core function is to care. What is clear is that within the Trust there was a culture of denial and downplaying incidents which, had they been properly acknowledged, investigated and learned from, could have prevented future harm. Actions taken by the Trust meant that it was not subject to appropriate external scrutiny, which compounded the impact of the internal culture and processes. It was found that there was

> a concerning and repeated culture at the Trust of not declaring adverse outcomes as an SI in line with the national framework. Instead, they were inappropriately downgraded and investigated by what the Trust termed a High Risk Case Review (HRCR). This method of investigating incidents, created by the Trust, was less robust, varied considerably in quality and lacked the rigour and transparency of an SI investigation. Notably, HRCRs were not reported to NHS England, the Clinical Commissioning Groups (CCGs) or the Trust Board, and therefore avoided external scrutiny.

Even when an SI investigation was carried out, both the Ockenden report and a 2017 RCOG Invited Review found that the Trust's process of SI investigations was complex, tardy and that those conducting the investigations were not appropriately resourced or trained. The Root Cause Analysis (RCA) that was carried out was often focussed on the wrong issues, was descriptive rather than ascertaining why things had happened and recommendations often focussed on individuals rather than on system-wide change. Crucially RCA

2. Maternity services must ensure that women and their families are listened to with their voices heard,
3. Staff who work together must train together,
4. There must be robust pathways in place for managing women with complex pregnancies Through the development of links with the tertiary level Maternal Medicine Centre there must be agreement reached on the criteria for those cases to be discussed and /or referred to a maternal medicine specialist centre,
5. Staff must ensure that women undergo a risk assessment at each contact throughout the pregnancy pathway,
6. All maternity services must appoint a dedicated Lead Midwife and Lead Obstetrician both with demonstrated expertise to focus on and champion best practice in fetal monitoring,
7. All Trusts must ensure women have ready access to accurate information to enable their informed choice of intended place of birth and mode of birth, including maternal choice for caesarean delivery.

[85] Ockenden Review, *Findings, Conclusions and Essential Actions from the Independent Review of Maternity Services at the Shrewsbury and Telford Hospital NHS Trust – Our Final Report* HC 1219, 30 March 2022, available at https://assets.publishing.service.gov.uk/government/uploads/system/uploads/attachment_data/file/1064302/Final-Ockenden-Report-web-accessible.pdf.

recommendations failed to generate actual learning and improvement. This was a consistent pattern, where reviews (both internal and external) including a 2017 internal review (the Ovington Report), the 2017 RCOG Invited Review and a 2018 PHSO review did recommend changes there were no records of changes actually being implemented.

External agencies and internal reviews gave a false sense of reassurance over the quality of the service provided at the Trust. The Ockenden report presents a culture where the Trust sought to paint a reassuring picture. Somehow this was sufficiently persuasive for various external bodies. In 2013 a report by two local CCGs found the maternity services were safe and good quality. The CQC ratings of the Trust's maternity provision was 'good' right up until 2018 when it was downgraded to 'inadequate'. When the RCOG carried out their Invited Review in 2017 they identified serious concerns, which they notified to the Trust, but crucially not to the CQC. Similarly, the NHS Litigation Agency/NHS Resolution consistently provided a level of reassurance, in 2014 when they awarded the Trust level 3 status, and then again in 2017/18 when they gave the Trust a rebate of its assessments on the basis of the Board self-certifying that 10 maternity safety actions had been met. These 10 actions were intended to demonstrate a Trust was providing safe maternity care. This rebate was repaid when it CQC downgraded the Trust's maternity provision to 'inadequate'. What is very clear is that effective external oversight was lacking and failed to identify the dysfunctional working relationships and poor standards of care provided.

The final Report contained a number of further Local Actions for Learning[86] specifically intended for Shrewsbury and Telford. It also contained another 15 Immediate and Essential Actions[87] to be shared across all maternity services in England as a matter of urgency to

---

[86] These recommended changes related to various factors, including: supporting families after the review is finished; improving the management of patient safety incidents; patient and family involvement; support for staff; improving complaints handling; improving audit processes; improving guidelines processes; leadership and oversight; care of vulnerable and high risk women; fetal growth assessment and management; fetal medicine care; diabetes care; hypertension; consultant obstetric ward rounds and clinical review; escalation of concerns; multidisciplinary working; fetal assessment and monitoring; actions specific to midwifery-led units and out-of-hospital births; post-natal care; maternal deaths; obstetric anaesthesia; neonatal care; staff voices – addressing the culture; hearing the staff voices.

[87] These were

1. Workforce planning and sustainability – financing a safe maternity workforce The recommendations from the Health and Social Care Committee Report: The safety of maternity services in England must be implemented. We state that the Health and Social Care Select Committee view that a proportion of maternity budgets must be ring-fenced for training in every maternity unit should be implemented.
2. Safe Staffing – All trusts must maintain a clear escalation and mitigation policy where maternity staffing falls below the minimum staffing levels for all health professionals.
3. Escalation and accountability – Staff must be able to escalate concerns if necessary. There must be clear processes for ensuring that obstetric units are staffed by appropriately trained staff at all times. If not resident there must be clear guidelines for when a consultant obstetrician should attend.
4. Clinical governance – leadership – Trust boards must have oversight of the quality and performance of their maternity services. In all maternity services the Director of Midwifery and Clinical Director for obstetrics must be jointly operationally responsible and accountable for the maternity governance systems.
5. Clinical governance – Incident investigation and complaints – Incident investigations must be meaningful for families and staff and lessons must be learned and implemented in practice in a timely manner.
6. Learning from Maternal deaths – Nationally all maternal post-mortem examinations must be conducted by a pathologist who is an expert in maternal physiology and pregnancy related pathologies. In the case of a maternal death a joint review panel/investigation of all services involved in the care must include representation from all applicable hospitals/clinical settings.

bring about positive and essential change. The government has accepted all of the recommendations in both the first and final reports.[88]

XV. Conclusions on Inquiries and Reviews

Even a cursory examination of the inquiries and reviews given above demonstrates the differences between them. The scope of an inquiry or review varies enormously, the focus may be on individual actions, actions in a particular hospital or care setting or on the impact of specific products. The format and means by which evidence is gathered partly depends on the statutory underpinnings. For example, in oral hearings held as part of a Public Inquiry, the Inquiry Rules 2006[89] stipulate that only the Inquiry Panel and Counsel to the Inquiry may question a witness, whereas in non-statutory reviews a less structured approach can be taken. This informality can enable a more responsive approach, as occurred during the IMMDS Review.[90] Baroness Cumberlege, Chair of the Review, emphasised the importance of listening to and learning from as many people as possible who have been affected.

7. Multi-disciplinary training – Staff who work together must train together. Staff should attend regular mandatory training and rotas. Job planning needs to ensure all staff can attend. Clinicians must not work on labour ward without appropriate regular CTG training and emergency skills training.

8. Complex ante-natal care – Local Maternity Systems, Maternal Medicine Networks and trusts must ensure that women have access to pre-conception care. Trusts must provide services for women with multiple pregnancy in line with national guidance Trusts must follow national guidance for managing women with diabetes and hypertension in pregnancy.

9. Preterm birth – The LMNS, commissioners and trusts must work collaboratively to ensure systems are in place for the management of women at high risk of preterm birth. Trusts must implement NHS Saving Babies Lives Version 2 (2019).

10. Labour and Birth – Women who choose birth outside a hospital setting must receive accurate advice with regards to transfer times to an obstetric unit should this be necessary. Centralised CTG monitoring systems should be mandatory in obstetric units.

11. Obstetric anaesthesia – In addition to routine inpatient obstetric anaesthesia follow-up, a pathway for outpatient postnatal anaesthetic follow-up must be available in every trust to address incidences of physical and psychological harm. Documentation of patient assessments and interactions by obstetric anaesthetists must improve. The determination of core datasets that must be recorded during every obstetric anaesthetic intervention would result in record-keeping that more accurately reflects events. Staffing shortages in obstetric anaesthesia must be highlighted and updated guidance for the planning and provision of safe obstetric anaesthesia services throughout England must be developed.

12. Postnatal care – Trusts must ensure that women readmitted to a postnatal ward and all unwell postnatal women have timely consultant review. Postnatal wards must be adequately staffed at all times.

13. Bereavement care – Trusts must ensure that women who have suffered pregnancy loss have appropriate bereavement care services.

14. Neonatal care – There must be clear pathways of care for provision of neonatal care. This review endorses the recommendations from the Neonatal Critical Care Review (December 2019) to expand neonatal critical care, increase neonatal cot numbers, develop the workforce and enhance the experience of families. This work must now progress at pace.

15. Supporting families – Care and consideration of the mental health and wellbeing of mothers, their partners and the family as a whole must be integral to all aspects of maternity service provision Maternity care providers must actively engage with the local community and those with lived experience, to deliver services that are informed by what women and their families say they need from their care.

[88] Hansard HC, *Ockenden Report* (30 March 2022) vol 771 col 817 available at https://hansard.parliament.uk/Commons/2022-03-30/debates/2E275996-67C4-466D-8BA3-31CB8508412A/OckendenReport.

[89] See 10(1) of the Inquiry Rules 2006 SI 1838/2006 available at www.legislation.gov.uk/uksi/2006/1838/made.

[90] J Cumberlege, *First Do No Harm: The Report of the Independent Medicines and Medical Devices Safety Review* (2020) available at www.immdsreview.org.uk/Report.html.

IMMDS team members visited locations across the UK to sit around a table with affected individuals and hear their experiences directly.[91]

There is a huge range in the number and structure of recommendations made, from an exhaustive 290 recommendations in the Mid Staffs Public Inquiry[92] to just nine recommendations made by the IMMDS Review. To an extent, comparing inquiries and reports seems to be comparing apples and pears, and care should be taken in so doing, but there are some overarching themes and findings.

Previous analysis by Howe has detailed that public inquiries can be held for a variety of reasons, summarised by Walshe and Higgins as:

- Establishing the facts – providing a full and fair account of what happened, especially in circumstances where the facts are disputed, or the course and causation of events is not clear.

- Catharsis or therapeutic experience – providing an opportunity for reconciliation and resolution, by bringing protagonists face to face with each other's perspectives and problems.

- Reassurance – rebuilding public confidence after a major failure by showing that the government is making sure it is fully investigated and dealt with.

- Leaning from events – and so helping to prevent their reoccurrence by synthesising or distilling lessons which can be used to change practice.

- Accountability, blame and retribution – holding people and organisations to account, and sometimes indirectly contributing to the assignation of blame and to mechanisms for retribution.

- Political considerations – serving a wider political agenda for government either in demonstrating that 'something is being done' or in providing leverage for change.

These points are not universally agreed. There is a lack of consensus on the core function of Inquiries. One view set out by the National Audit Office is that:

> Inquiries can fulfil multiple purposes, including establishing the facts, determining accountability and responsibility but not liability, learning lessons and making recommendations.

Walshe takes a more nuanced view:

> some stakeholders are likely to see the attribution of blame and fault as part of the inquiry's function, though others may regard this as unfair or unhelpful and best left to some of the other systems mentioned above (such as civil litigation, or professional regulation). By providing a definitive account of events, inquiries may contribute indirectly to the blaming process by providing evidence for other systems to use. Beyond blame, lies retribution in which individuals or organisations face punishment or must make amends in some way. Again, inquiries do not exact retribution directly (though appearing before an inquiry in the full glare of public attention may be seen by some as a form of retribution) but their results may be used indirectly in this way.

---

[91] Sonia Macleod was the lead researcher for the IMMDS Review.

[92] *Report of the Mid Staffordshire NHS Foundation Trust Public Inquiry. February 2013 Chaired by Robert Francis QC*, HC947, available at www.gov.uk/government/publications/report-of-the-mid-staffordshire-nhs-foundation-trust-public-inquiry.

What is clear is that inquiries are not intended to replace other accountability mechanisms such as professional regulation, civil or criminal liability, though they may provide evidence which feeds into these processes.

A common thread is the difficulty those affected have had in obtaining such a review. Securing such an inquiry is not for the faint-hearted, as it often requires years, if not decades, of sustained pressure. The Mid Staffs public inquiry was only because of the immense pressure, the initial more narrowly focused Mid Staffs Independent inquiry was intended to be the definitive report. Similarly, the Shipman Public Inquiry, which was to look into how the worst serial killer in British history had been able to offend on such a prolific scale seemingly unchallenged for decades, only took place because campaigners sought a judicial review of the initial decision to have a review conducted in private. The initial reluctance by the Department of Health to grant public inquiries in these cases, which represent the absolute nadirs of NHS care, coupled with the desire for a narrower review, seems surprising. However, these were not isolated decisions, as the decision to hold the Ayling, Neale and Kerr/Haslam inquiries in private, rather than in public, attests. This approach risks giving the impressions of a reluctance for full and open investigation and disclosure from the very top of the health service.

More recently, but in a similar vein, the initial proposals from the Department of Health and Social Care that it should be the sponsor for the infected blood inquiry,[93] which investigates actions taken by the Department of Health, show a lack of sensitivity to the importance of independence, both actual and perceived.

The considerable barriers that need to be overcome before an inquiry/review is ordered mean that the prospect of a public inquiry is so remote it is unlikely that staff going about their day-to-day business will be concerned about the specific risk of a public inquiry. While staff concerns are more likely to be about more immediate issues there are examples of the public inquiries entering the consciousness, for example in the Final Ockenden Report a staff member is reported as telling the review team.

> At a study day in 2016/2017, following the Kirkup report, a senior manager made the comment 'we (SaTH) are not a Morecambe Bay'. I made the comment that we absolutely were a Morecambe Bay – a trust full of unhappy staff with ineffective poor leadership, looking to hide or ignore poor care and poor management.

The way in which an inquiry is conducted will determine degree of detail that individuals will obtain. Some inquiries, such as Morecambe Bay and the Three Inquiries, will detail individual patient narratives. This can enable individuals, sometimes for the first time, to understand what happened and how this fitted into a wider picture. However, other inquiries take a very different approach and do not detail the narratives of individual patients, for example the IMMDS Review heard from hundreds of affected individuals, and while their experiences clearly informed and shaped the final report they were not individually detailed.

The type of inquiry heavily influences the way it is conducted and the legal powers to compel individuals or organisations to provide evidence.[94] More formal public inquiries are

---

[93] www.infectedbloodinquiry.org.uk/.

[94] For a summary of statutory and non-statutory inquiries see the Commons Library Briefing Paper SN06410 Cowie, Graeme Statutory public inquiries: the Inquiries Act 2005 (8 November 2021) available at https://research-briefings.files.parliament.uk/documents/SN06410/SN06410.pdf and the Commons Library Briefing Paper

held under the Inquiries Act 2005[95] and the Inquiries Rules 2006.[96] These Rules set out the procedural rules governing evidence and the conduct of inquiries. Public inquiries have a formal quasi-judicial process with the ability to compel witnesses. Other inquiries do not have the ability to compel witnesses, but this has to be balanced against the flexibility which a non-statutory inquiry can employ.

Inquiries can deliver an understanding of what happened and how this fitted into a wider picture. For some inquiries this may involve detailing events down to an individual level, for other inquiries a more systems and institution focussed approach will be taken.

Walshe described how an inquiry itself may be a therapeutic experience:

> They can bring the protagonists in the events being investigated face to face with each others' perspectives and problems. While this aspect of an inquiry may be painful for some of those involved, and is difficult to manage, it may have a therapeutic value for individuals or a community harmed by the events at the heart of the inquiry. The inquiry may offer a cathartic release, and an opportunity for reconciliation and resolution.

Inquiries can highlight and acknowledge when a wrong has been suffered and where apologies are due, all of which to those who have been harmed, particularly in cases where there has been denial of the harm they have suffered.

Public inquiries do not have a monopoly on conducting an open review, for example the IMMDS Review, which was an independent review rather than a public inquiry, took the decision not only to publish all the written evidence received (with appropriate redactions) but also to include videos of the oral hearings conducted. However, the openness of non-statutory reviews is at their discretion and the judicial reviews over plans to hold various reviews in private show that, understandably, this is a clear concern to those affected.

The timeframes associated with reviews and inquiries usually mean that the immediate problems have often been resolved or stopped, though this is not always the case. The maternity investigations in Morecambe Bay and Shrewsbury and Telford NHS Trust produced local recommendations, but also national ones which applied across maternity provision. Another example was that despite the known issues with the use of mesh for stress urinary incontinence these operations continued until the IMMDS review called for such surgery to be paused.

There are inquiry recommendations which lead directly to healthcare and rehabilitation services being provided for those who have been harmed by the NHS, for example in response to the IMMDS review's fifth recommendation there are now specialist centres set up to care for those who have been harmed by pelvic mesh. However, not all inquiries have such direct impacts, in some cases because the time taken for the inquiry means that any lessons have already been learned and implemented.

Given the public importance and the significant resource allocation (including financial cost) of such inquiries and reviews the body of research into their effectiveness at holding the healthcare system to account is surprisingly thin on the ground. This may be because of difficulties investigating this area due to the variations outlined above. What analysis there

---

SN02599 Cowie, Graeme Non-statutory public inquiries (23 November 2021) available at https://researchbriefings. files.parliament.uk/documents/SN02599/SN02599.pdf.

[95] The Inquiries Act 2005 c 12 available at www.legislation.gov.uk/ukpga/2005/12/contents.

[96] The Inquiry Rules 2006 2006/1838 available at www.legislation.gov.uk/uksi/2006/1838/made.

is doesn't wholeheartedly support the use of inquiries to drive changes. In relation to NHS Inquiries[97] specifically William and Kevern 2016[98] conclude

> They contribute to improving the quality assurance and accountability within the organisation but do not purport to do this as a standalone measure, and nor are they intended to. The Recommendations are the first part of a complex process, and rely upon the activities and inter-relationship of a variety of social and cultural institutions in order to bring about lasting change.

Similarly in their 2018 analysis of whether official inquiries hold the profession to account Manion et al were clear that inquiries were expensive and broadly ineffective.

> Moreover, the widest examination of professional failings (i.e. public inquiries), at least as presently constituted, are a weak and expensive institutional instrument for addressing failures of the regulatory apparatus. Their enduring appeal may be more symbolic than instrumental in that they allow space for public catharsis and help maintain political legitimacy for the NHS, while leaving untroubled professionally led and professionally dominated regulatory arrangements.

The key objective of many of the recommendations of these reports is to improve patient safety and preventing future similar harms; and improving NHS culture is highlighted time and time again as a part of the solution.

The complexity of the regulatory system was detailed in many of the reports. The lack of co-ordination between the different regulators and a joined up response was highlighted, for example the Morecambe Bay report by Bill Kirkup concluded:

> There was no clear leadership responsibility or structure for the coordination of regulatory activity. Although arrangements were in place for communication and liaison between organisations.

Several reports commented on the difficulties that patients have in navigating these complex system in order to raise concerns, for example the Kirkup report states:

> The review of external responses to the issues within our terms of reference demonstrates how many agencies had management or regulatory responsibilities that related to the issues we have examined. It was difficult for us to identify and trace through their interactions with the families and the Trust. It is not reasonable for the NHS to expect its users to face such a complex array of supervisory organisations without clear support in navigating the system and getting to the right people in a timely way.

Similarly, the lack of a clear transparent pathway for concerns was raised in the IMMDS report, which recommended:

> Patients across the NHS and private sector must have a clear, well-publicised route to raise their concerns about aspects of their experiences in the healthcare system. It will be for the implementation task force.

Given that these themes come up again and again there is a question as to how effective the solutions proposed by such reviews and inquiries are. It is much more straightforward to put forward a process-based solution, for example the changes to processes to provide

---

[97] An NHS Inquiry is a statutorily-constituted process initiated by the Secretary of State for Health under s 84 of the NHS Act 1977 or by Parliament under the Inquiry Act 1921 and 2005.

[98] M Williams and P Kevern, 'The Role and Impact of Recommendations from NHS Inquiries: A Critical Discourse Analysis' (2016) 2(2) *The Journal of New Writing in Health and Social Care* 1–11.

greater scrutiny of unexpected deaths that were proposed by Dame Janet in response to Harold Shipman's crimes, than to drive cultural change. However, the fact that culture comes up again and again across such different contexts indicates what an important part of the solution it is.

> Change of culture is at the heart of real change. Whatever the systems in place, if those who operate them at all levels are not focused on patient safety, then other factors, other pressures, will prevail.[99]

Culture is frequently portrayed as the problem; a failing culture, a blame culture, a culture of denial, etc. It is also proposed as the solution; a just culture, an open culture, etc. However, it is not always clear in the above reports what is meant by culture, how a positive culture is to be created and how to maintain it. Everyone agrees that culture is collective endeavour – a culture cannot exist in just one individual, it has to be part of a larger shared experience. Equally failings in culture cannot be the fault of an individual outlier. In contrast failures in ethics can, and do, occur at the individual level as was seen with Harold Shipman.[100] Discussions of both cultural and ethical problems and solutions need greater clarity and specificity on what is meant by culture and how to achieve the desired change in culture. The issues are discussed further in Part III below.

In some ways expecting inquiries to drive change is pointless as they are advisory; they can make recommendations, but they cannot implement them. Once the report is published the inquiry is over. The baton for delivering improvements and demonstrating learning passes to other agencies. There are some exceptions, usually where an interim report is issued with recommendations. There is an apparent peculiarity about a government recognising that there is an issue which needs to be examined, commissioning and sponsoring an inquiry (which investigates said issue in depth and at public expense) only for the sponsor department to reject some or all of the recommendations made. Unsurprisingly this can also cause frustration for those who conduct inquiries, as was expressed by Lady Janet Smith.

> If the success of public inquiries is judged in terms of changes in regulations and legislations then we cannot often claim to achieve that.
>
> Positive proposals can be very slow to emerge and even if they eventually do they are often diluted. It's an issue of great regret to me.[101]

In fact, according to a 2018 NAO review of 10 inquiries as part of a larger report[102] found that:

45 per cent of recommendations were accepted by the government;
33 per cent were 'accepted in principle', 'partially accepted' and 'subject to wider reform;
15 per cent did not have a have a clear response from the government, and
7 per cent were explicitly rejected.

---

[99] Kerr/Haslam Inquiry report, above n 18, at 808.

[100] Obviously, ethics can also be used to describe collective views and behaviours, medical ethics being a prime example.

[101] Lady Janet Smith quoted in A Hill, 'Soham Report Author Says Public Inquiries are Not Worth the Money' *The Guardian* (15 September 2010) available at www.theguardian.com/society/2010/sep/15/public-inquiries-ignored-lord-bichard.

[102] National Audit Office, *Investigation into Government-funded Inquiries, HC 836, session 2017–2019* (May 2019) available at www.nao.org.uk/wp-content/uploads/2018/05/Investigation-into-government-funded-inquiries.pdf.

The majority of recommendations are viewed positively by governments, but a substantial number are either not responded to or are rejected outright. Rejection can be for entirely valid reasons, for example in his blog[103] on inquiries Nick Timmins describes how recommendations can be unworkable 'Lawyers tend instinctively to reach for the law as a solution. And while they may not like this comment, they can on occasion make lawyerly recommendations that do not fit with the real world.' He goes on to describe

> Dame Janet Smith, as she then was, produced proposals in response to Shipman that would have put controls on the opiate drugs he used to kill his patients that would have been so draconian as to render pain relief for cancer and other disease in the community impossible. Alan Milburn, the health secretary of the day, had the courage to reject them.

For an inquiry to spend a substantial amount of time and resource only to deliver an unworkable proposal raises questions that are more fundamental than a lack of subsequent learning and improvement, but that is a separate issue.

The picking and choosing of which recommendations to implement means that it is unfair to expect inquiries to automatically drive change. The responsibility for delivering (or choosing not to deliver) the recommendations made by an inquiry falls to the government. As the NAO report makes clear this process is not particularly consistent

> Once inquiries have concluded, there is no central repository or responsibility across government for tracking whether recommendations have been implemented and ensuring that inquiries have an impact.

There are examples of the government accepting all the recommendations in a report and allocating funding to resolve the issues identified, most recently the Ockenden Reports, but these are not the standard.

Accepting a recommendation is not the same as implementing it, and there may be a considerable delay between these process even when the government is fully committed to implementation. Even where recommendations seem to have been taken up it is always worth considering how closely the resulting policy reflects the recommendations made in the report. After implementation there should be an assessment of the impact they have had.

Inquiries and reports can lead to substantial reforms and changes; the creation of HSIB and the statutory Duty of Candour are clear examples of inquiry driven changes. However, this does not mean that inquiries consistently deliver service improvement.

There is an obvious question of value for money from inquiries and reviews. The costs associated with an inquiry are as variable as the inquiries themselves, in his 2003 analysis of inquiries about NHS care Walshe estimated the costs of external private inquiries as medium to high at £200,000 upwards, with public inquiries considered high cost with the spend measured in millions of pounds. These were 2003 estimates of cost, and will be considerably out of date, but what they give is the relative expense of these two types of inquiry. A 2018 report by the National Audit Office examined 26 government funded inquiries, 15 of which were public inquiries carried out under the 2005 Inquiries Act. The total expenditure for all 26 was £239 million. An in-depth analysis of 10 of these inquiries revealed they varied

---

[103] N Timmins, 'Are Public Inquiries Worth the Time, Money and Resources?' (Institute for Government, 2013) available at www.instituteforgovernment.org.uk/blog/are-public-inquiries-worth-time-money-and-resources.

from £0.2 million to £24.9 million, with on average a third of the expenditure being spent on legal fees. In a stinging critiques of public inquiries[104] Sir Simon Jenkins termed them 'slow journalism for rich lawyers' and described them as 'the worst value for money in British government'.

In the Thames Safety Inquiry report on the sinking of the Marchioness[105] Lord Justice Clarke concluded that

> The purpose of a public inquiry is simply to ascertain the facts and to make recommendations for the future. A public inquiry should only be ordered in exceptional cases. Public inquiries are very expensive in terms of time and money and in very many cases the facts can be established and lessons learned without such an inquiry.

[104] Sir Simon Jenkins, 'Public Inquiries are Institutionally Corrupt, we Should Just Give the Money to Victims' *The Guardian* (17 June 2021)
[105] Lord Justice Clarke Thames Safety Inquiry Cm4558 January 2000 at para 5.8.

11

The Health Services Safety
Investigation Branch

I. HSSIB Background

In 2016 the Secretary of State for Health announced publication of a table that grades the openness and honesty of reporting cultures in English hospitals,[1] and the creation of a new Healthcare Safety Investigation Branch (HSIB) modelled on the Air Accident Investigation Branch. His aspiration was to use 'intelligent transparency' to turn the NHS into 'the world's largest learning organisation'.[2] He said:

> But if we are really to tackle potentially avoidable deaths, we need culture change from the inside as well as exhortation from the outside. A true learning culture has to come from the heart. And this means a fundamental rethink of our concept of accountability. Time and time again when I responded on behalf of the government to tragedies at Mid Staffs, Morecambe Bay, Winterbourne View, Southern Health and other places I heard relatives who had suffered cry out in frustration that no one had been 'held accountable.'

> But to blame failures in care on doctors and nurses trying to do their best is to miss the point that bad mistakes can be made by good people. What is often overlooked is proper study of the environment and systems in which mistakes happen and to understand what went wrong and encouragement to spread any lessons learned. Accountability to future patients as well as to the person sitting in front of you.

> The rush to blame may look decisive. It may seem like professionals are being held accountable. In fact, the opposite can happen. By pinning the blame on individuals, we sometimes duck the bigger challenge of identifying the problems that often lurk in complex systems and which are often the true cause of avoidable harm. …

> when we give patients an honest account of what happened alongside an apology, what is the impact? Countless academic studies have shown there is less litigation, less money spent on lawyers and more rapid closure, even when there have been the most terrible tragedies.[3]

A. The Expert Advisory Group Report

In preparation for establishing HSIB an Expert Advisory Group was set up in 2015. The aims of the Expert Advisory Group were to design a new mechanism, operating in a new

---

[1] www.gov.uk/government/publications/learning-from-mistakes-league.
[2] Rt Hon Jeremy Hunt MP, Speech at Global Patient Safety Summit, Lancaster House, 10 March 2016, www.gov.uk/government/speeches/from-a-blame-culture-to-a-learning-culture.
[3] ibid.

culture, which would deliver a number of different goals, which were not fully compatible. There were three main objectives for HSIB to deliver

- The cost objective – to provide a forum for investigation of future major problems that did not cost as much as inquiries such as the Bristol and Francis Inquiries had.

- The investigation objective – to provide an expert investigation function that would identify the root causes of failures, so that the right correctives could be put in place to reduce the risk of occurrence.

- The involvement objective – to provide a forum in which harmed families and patients were involved, reducing the need for them to campaign outside the system for expensive inquiries and to bring court cases simply to find out what had happened and to understand what had gone wrong. This aim was a forum in which patients and families would be treated with respect, honesty and dignity.[4] The drivers for this were partly simply a matter of respect between fellow human beings and partly because it was recognised that 'the way in which people are treated after adverse events can at times compound the distress and harm suffered'.[5]

In its 2016 Report[6] the Expert Advisory Group was clear that there were widespread, deep and long-standing problems in the NHS in relation to safety – and accident investigation – and they would not all be solved by the creation of a single new investigation body.[7] The Report made clear that responsibility for safety would remain with every individual NHS organisation, and that HSIB would not carry out itself the great majority of safety investigations.[8] Its primary goal would be to generate learning to support improvements in the safety of healthcare, which it would achieve by carrying out investigations into selected matters of highest risk, publishing investigation reports and making recommendations to prevent recurrence.[9] Recipients of HSIB recommendations would be required by legislation to publish a formal response setting out whether they accepted the safety recommendation or disputed it, and what actions they would take and by when.[10]

The Report was clear that the purpose and remit of the HSIB would be limited to that of[11]

> an enabler, exemplar and catalyst for learning-oriented safety investigation. It is not to provide justice, or remedy, for patients and families. Nor are its purposes to determine liability, find fault

---

[4] *Report of the Expert Advisory Group; Healthcare Safety Investigation Branch* (Department of Health, May 2016), www.gov.uk/government/uploads/system/uploads/attachment_data/file/522785/hsibreport.pdf. 7. '… the way in which people are treated after adverse events can at times compound the distress and harm suffered. We recognise the distress and pain that result from serious safety failures, and acknowledge that this this can be amplified by poorly handled responses and investigations. In future, when the Branch identifies failings, it will describe and investigate them, and will provide patients and families with all relevant information'.
[5] ibid, 6.
[6] ibid.
[7] ibid, 12.
[8] ibid, 7.
[9] ibid, 23, 24.
[10] ibid, 24.
[11] ibid, 6.

or attribute blame. Those are important functions, but they belong elsewhere in the system, and they should not be undermined or diluted.

One final point to note is that the Expert Advisory Group unanimously concluded that the HSIB must not only have a permanent and stable institutional base, but must also be *independent* of those it investigates.

II. Establishing the HSIB/HSSIB and its Statutory Framework

HSIB was established in 2017 without a statutory underpinning. It was therefore hosted by NHS England and so not truly independent. In September 2017 the draft Health Service Safety Investigations Body (HSSIB) Bill was published to give HSIB full statutory independence as per the Expert Advisory Group recommendation. This draft bill underwent the committee stage, and the government published a formal response to this in December 2018. The bill went to the second reading stage, but its progress was derailed by the December 2019 general election.

The intention to establish a Statutory Health Services Safety Investigations Body was reintroduced in part 4 of the Health and Care Act 2022.

Part 4 (clauses 93–119) of the Act establishes the HSSIB. The proposals include:

–   HSSIB being established as a body corporate.
–   Defining the purposes of HSSIB investigations as identifying risks to the safety of patients and addressing those risks by facilitating the improvement of services and practices in healthcare, and not to assess or determine blame, civil or criminal liability or whether action needs to be taken in respect of an individual by a regulator.
–   HSSIB must determine and publish investigation criteria, principles and processes for investigations including procedures and methods, and timescales, and processes for involving patients and families in ways that are easily accessible and understood.
–   Powers for the Secretary of State to direct the HSSIB to undertake investigations into particular qualifying incidents.
–   Information obtained by the HSSIB during investigations is subject to confidentiality protections through prohibition on disclosure, or 'safe space' protections, access to which can only be granted by the High Court or by the Secretary of State – with an exemption for coroners.
–   Granting HSSIB powers to compel witnesses to give evidence and for organisations to provide access to materials, equipment and records that HSSIB considers necessary for the purposes of investigating.
–   Remit to develop standards for the NHS in England on conducting patient safety investigations, and to provide advice, guidance and training for NHS and other organisations, with certain caveats.
–   The Act expands the remit of the HSSIB to encompass all healthcare, including that provided by the independent sector in England.

III. HSIB Internal Culture

HSIB emphasise that they provide a no-blame investigation. However, there have been serious concerns raised about the internal culture at HSIB, including accusations of bullying, sexism and racism and an internal culture where workers were 'named and shamed'.[12] An external report into HSIB commissioned by NHS England has been carried out by the King's Fund, but at the time of writing has not been published.

IV. HSIB Investigations

The initial remit were the national investigations broadly outlined above. However, in November 2017 the Secretary of State announced that HSIB would investigate all cases of birth injuries meeting the Each Baby Counts Criteria[13] and all maternal deaths and directions were made accordingly.[14] The addition of maternity investigations represented a significant departure from the original HSIB intentions and required a different approach and investigation framework, see Table 1 taken from the 2020/21 HSIB Annual Report.[15]

Table 1 Differences in HSIB approach to national and maternity investigations

	National Investigations	**Maternity Investigations**
Start date	April 2017	April 2018
Number of investigators	15	130
Number of investigations	c. 15 per year	c. 1,000 per year
Training for investigators	Investigators attend an intensive training programme as soon as they join. They attend regular professional development workshops throughout the year.	All investigators attend an intensive training programme. Additional training and updates are provided throughout the year.

(continued)

---

[12] Annabella Collins, 'Bullying, Sexism and Racism "Prevalent and Tolerated" at National Regulator' *Health Service Journal* (21 January 2022).

[13] Each Baby Counts was the RCOG's national quality improvement programme to reduce the number of babies who die or are left severely disabled as a result of incidents occurring during term labour. Babies who meet the Each Baby Counts Criteria are those who were at least 37 weeks gestation and suffered:

– an intrapartum stillbirth
– an early neonatal death (within the first week of life)
– a severe brain injury defined as a baby who was

    o   diagnosed with grade III hypoxic ischemic encephalopathy (HIE); or
    o   therapeutically cooled; or
    o   had a decreased central tone, was comatose and had seizures

[14] The National Health Service Trust Development Authority (Healthcare Safety Investigation Branch) (Additional Investigatory Functions in Respect of Maternity Cases) Directions 2018 available at https://assets.publishing.service.gov.uk/government/uploads/system/uploads/attachment_data/file/702938/NHS_Trust_Development_Authority__HSIB__Directions_2018.pdf.

[15] Taken from the HSIB Annual Review 2020/21 available at https://hsib-kqcco125-media.s3.amazonaws.com/assets/documents/HSIB_Annual_Review_Brochure_2020-21_FINAL.pdf.

Table 1 *(Continued)*

	National Investigations	Maternity Investigations
Referral route	Any person, group or organisation can refer a patient safety concern to HSIB through their website. HSIB also identify issues for investigation through research.	Individual NHS trusts refer incidents that meet the criteria.
Criteria for Investigations	HSIB evaluate patient safety issues against their own criteria and decide whether to go ahead with an investigation	We investigate maternity healthcare safety incidents that meet the criteria set out in Each Baby Counts and MBRRACE-UK.*
Investigation Status	HSIB investigation does not replace the local trust's investigation into the patient safety incident.	HSIB's investigation replaces the trust's investigation into the maternity incident for those investigations that meet the criteria.
Reporting	HSIB publish national investigation reports on their website.▫	Maternity investigation reports are shared with the family and trust. They are not published.
Safety Recommendations	HSIB make safety recommendations to relevant named organisations. They ask organisations to respond to the recommendations within 90 days and HSIB publish the responses on our website. HSIB may also make safety observations (where they consider their findings warrant attention but there is not enough information on which to make a recommendation) and identify safety actions that have been taken during an investigation to immediately improve patient safety.	HSIB make safety recommendations for learning to the trust. The trust is responsible for putting them into action. HSIB gather information about themes arising from our investigations to share learning across the health sector

* In April 2020 (with DHSC's agreement) HSIB made amendments to the programme criteria which remained in place as of 31 March 2021. Trusts continue to refer all cases in line with the existing criteria, and HSIB have temporarily ceased investigations of cases relating to hypoxic ischemic encephalopathy (HIE) where a baby had received cooling therapy and there was no apparent brain injury. The exception to this is if the family or trust request HSIB progress an investigation, in which case an investigation will be undertaken.

▫ During 2020/21 due to COVID-19 HSIB undertook some investigations directly for NHSE/I and DHSC which were not published.

V. HSIB Maternity Investigations

For the maternity investigations the family do not initiate contact with HSIB. After a qualifying incident the Trust must make a referral to HSIB (as well as complying with the standard requirements that the particular incident requires, such as making a serious incident report, referring to MBRRACE-UK etc). The Trust must inform the family about HSIB and ask the family if they are happy to be contacted by HSIB. HSIB then meet families and determine how much involvement the family wish to have in the investigation process. This is invariably a very difficult time for families and that may impact on how much they wish to engage with the investigation process. Some families will opt for full engagement with the investigation process and will attend interviews and discussions; for other families their involvement may stop at agreeing to share their medical records with HSIB. If families do not consent to being contacted by HSIB then the investigation reverts to the Trust involved.

Terms of reference will be agreed and sent to the family and Trust. As part of the investigation HSIB will visit the Trust, analyse the evidence, consider findings and potential safety recommendations. Families are kept informed throughout the process. A draft report is reviewed by the report panel and will be shared with the Trust, the staff involved and the family to check for factual accuracy. A final report is shared with the family, the Trust, NHS Resolution and other appropriate organisations. The Trust is obliged to share the report with its CCG. Individual maternity investigation reports are not published by HSIB.

This is a very different way of raising concerns to all the others reviewed in this book in that the contact with the family is initiated by HSIB who were not party to the incident. The final HSIB report is also sent to NHS Resolution's Early Notification Scheme, again this process is not initiated by the family.

A. Maternity Investigation Statistics[16]

HSIB maternity investigations commenced in 2018/19, but were not fully operational until March 2019, see Table 2. It is very early, and COVID has impacted during this time, but there seems to be a downward trend for families co-operating with an HSIB investigation. HSIB report that as at March 2021 fewer than 5 per cent of their maternity investigations had exceeded the designated six-month timescale.[17]

In March 2020, in line with NHS-wide efforts to reduce pressure on trusts, HSIB made amendments to the maternity investigation programme criteria. Under the amended criteria, Trusts continued to refer all cases in line with the existing criteria, but HSIB would not investigate cases relating to babies who had received cooling therapy where there was no apparent neurological injury. In these cases, if a family or trust reported concerns about care, the case would be individually reviewed, and an investigation progressed where appropriate. This reduced the overall investigation caseload by 15 per cent during 2020/21.

---

[16] Taken from HSIB Annual reports 2018/19, 2019/20 and 2020/21 available at www.hsib.org.uk/who-we-are/reports-and-publications/.

[17] HSIB, 'HSIB Maternity Programme Year in Review 2020/21: Summary of Highlights, Themes and Future Work' (August 2021) available at https://hsib-kqcco125-media.s3.amazonaws.com/assets/documents/HSIB_Maternity_programme_year_in_review_2020-21_Report_V29.pdf.

Table 2 HSIB maternity investigations 2018–21

	2018/19*	2019/20	2020/21
Referrals to HSIB	440	1,168	1,269
Cases progressed to investigation	355	867	760
Percentage of families who engaged with an HSIB maternity investigation	93%	88%	86%

* This was a roll out year with only partial coverage of Trusts during this time.

B. HSIB Maternity Investigation Conclusions

The maternity investigations were not part of HSIB's intended remit. Given they have been running for such a short time and the pandemic hit during that period it is too early to comment on how effective or otherwise they are. The trend for decreased levels of family engagement is concerning.

There has been stinging criticism of HSIB's maternity investigations from a coronial investigation into the death of a baby. The concerns raised in this case were both general, that an HSIB investigation replacing a local investigation 'effectively preventing the recognition of causes of concern and therefore being unable to undertake any immediate and necessary remedial action at the earliest opportunity to prevent future deaths', as well as case-specific concerns over the factual errors and inaccuracies in the draft report and the 18-month time-frame of that particular investigation.[18]

It has been confirmed that maternity investigations will be removed from HSIB in 2022. This would fit with the original remit of HSIB and also would solve the inherent tension between HSIB investigations offering 'safe space' and the involvement of, and knowledge given to, families during maternity investigations.

A decision was made to exclude babies who had been cooled but appeared not to have suffered brain damage. Babies usually require cooling as an intervention because they have been exposed to oxygen deprivation during labour. Under the new HSIB criteria the decision to investigate is determined by how a baby presents after cooling, rather than focusing on the quality of the treatment that led to the need for a cooling intervention. It is unclear whether there is less to learn from a case where a baby has responded well to cooling compared to a case where the baby unfortunately did not respond so well to cooling. What is very clear is that cases where there is less significant brain injury present a much lower potential compensation cost; the decision by HSIB to limit their investigations in this way raises questions of mission creep from NHS Resolution's Early Notification Scheme into HSIB.

Maternity investigations are to be moved from HSIB to a Special Health Authority (SHA) in 2022. The remit and function of the SHA and the purpose of its investigations will need to be made very clear from the outset.

---

[18] See Coroner Dr Karen Henderson's report, *The Inquest Touching the Death of Theo Benjamin Young A Regulation 28 Report – Action to Prevent Future Deaths* available at www.judiciary.uk/wp-content/uploads/2020/05/Theo-Young-2020-0094-Redacted.pdf and HSIB's response, available at www.judiciary.uk/wp-content/uploads/2020/05/2020-0094-Response-from-the-Healthcare-Safety-Investigation-Branch_Redacted.pdf.

VI. HSIB National Investigations

HSIB can investigate patient safety concerns over events where something dangerous has happened (even if this did not result in harm) or where conditions are unsafe and this could potentially cause harm. HSIB can currently only investigate events or unsafe conditions that have happened in NHS-funded care in England after 1 April 2017.[19]

Investigations span the full range of patient safety concerns, there is no focus on a particular service or speciality. Topics have included the placement of nasogastric tubes, recognition of the acutely ill infant, wrong site nerve blocks, implantation of the incorrect protheses during joint surgery, the management of chronic health conditions in prisons, the lack of timely monitoring of patients with glaucoma. The national investigations are also analysed and grouped by themes.[20]

HSIB National investigations can be triggered by:

– a referral to HSIB.

– HSIB identifying a safety issue by proactive analysis of a range of safety information including NRLS/DPSIMS/LFPSE, Coroner's reports, safety alerts from professional bodies, literature (research and lay), etc.

– Feedback from engagement activities, this can come from a variety of sources including patient safety groups, Royal Colleges, academics and others.

Referral and review. Referrals can be by a person, a group or an organisation. Referrals can be made using an online form which takes around 20 minutes to complete, or by leaving an answerphone message. Disclosures to HSIB by healthcare staff will not be treated as whistleblowing. All contacts are stored on a database to build a picture of safety concerns over time. All concerns are reviewed by HSIB's intelligence unit to see if they meet the HSIB criteria which are based on:

– Outcome impact
– Systemic risk
– Learning potential

Initial assessment. If HSIB decide that the incident could meet their criteria then they will start to gather information and develop the case in preparation for a potential investigation. This can involve research and obtaining views of those with subject specific expertise. A monthly scrutiny panel is held to assess developed cases to decide if they meet the criteria for a national investigation and who would be the right team of investigators to carry out the preliminary investigation into it. Even if the criteria are met this does not automatically mean HSIB will investigate the issue; HSIB was only ever meant to carry out a limited number of national investigations.

---

[19] The Health and Care Act 2022 expands HSIB's remit to encompass private healthcare.

[20] For example see HSIB National Learning Report, *A Thematic Analysis of HSIB's First 22 National Investigations* (September 2021) available at www.hsib.org.uk/investigations-and-reports/a-thematic-analysis-of-hsibs-first-22-national-investigations/.

Preliminary investigation. The next stage for chosen cases is a preliminary investigation. This involves investigating the incident in more depth. This incident becomes the 'reference event' that triggers the investigation. The CEO of the organisation involved will be notified. The person who made the referral, and patients, family members and carers involved in the incident will be contacted and interviewed. Members of the investigating team will also interview those involved in the incident as well as other people who could be relevant.

An internal debriefing is carried out within HSIB to ensure all investigators are aware of the findings and to facilitate learning by making links and connections between issues found in different investigations.

If there are clear safety findings or recommendations an interim bulletin will be published on the HSIB website. This will be sent to the people who referred the issue to HSIB.

Full investigation. This involves the entire national investigation team alongside staff from the organisation being investigated and other independent subject experts.

There may be a need to talk to the family again, as well as gathering documents and data, interviewing those involved. Once the information has been gathered the facts will be determined and contributory and causal factors identified. Safety issues and safety recommendations will be identified and recommendations to improve patient safety will be prepared.

The report. At the conclusion of the investigation a draft report will be prepared. The draft report will be shared with those who notified the concern and affected individuals, which could include patients, friends and carers, for their feedback and input. The safety recommendations, safety observations and safety actions from the draft report will be share with organisations they apply to. A final report will be prepared taking into account the feedback from affected individuals, and this will be published on HSIB's website.

For those whose referral is investigated they are involved throughout the process, and HSIB have an extensive family engagement strategy,[21] which they describe as

> Family engagement during investigations involves effective liaison between a family and the investigating team. It covers the whole investigation process from start to finish. Our aim is to get families involved and make sure they are central to investigations, depending on their preferences. We also make sure they are supported throughout the investigation process.

A. National Investigation Statistics[22]

HSIB national investigations commenced in 2017/18, see Table 3. It is very early, and Covid has impacted during this time, but there seems to be a consistent 85–90 per cent level of families co-operating with an HSIB investigation.

---

[21] HSIB National Learning Report, 'Giving Families a Voice: HSIB's Approach to Patient and Family Engagement During Investigations (September 2020) available at https://hsib-kqcco125-media.s3.amazonaws.com/assets/documents/hsib-national-learning-report-giving-families-voice.pdf.

[22] Taken from HSIB Annual reports 2018/19, 2019/20 and 2020/21 available at www.hsib.org.uk/who-we-are/reports-and-publications/.

Table 3 HSIB national investigations 2018–21

	2018/19	2019/20	2020/21
National investigation reports produced	8	15	22
Percentage of families who engaged with an HSIB national investigation	87%	88%	89%

* This was a roll out year with only partial coverage of Trusts during this time.

B. HSIB National Investigation Conclusions

This process allows individuals to raise concerns with HSIB, but there is no guarantee that the concern will meet the criteria for HSIB to investigate it. Given there are a very low number of investigations per year it is more than likely that most referrals will not progress. As a mechanism to raise concerns this is likely to be unsatisfactory for most of those who attempt to raise a concern.

VII. HSIB Conclusions

A consequence of Sir Robert Francis's concerns into Mid-Staffs (and of the high cost of the public inquiry that he had to undertake) was the creation of the Healthcare Safety Investigation Branch, modelled on the Air Accident Investigation Branch, where concerns could be raised to an independent external agency without having to go through a local first stage. However, given the number of national investigations undertaken by HSIB this route is unlikely to result in satisfaction for an individual who raises concerns unless they are part of a wider issue.

HSIB can establish what has happened, and presents a valuable opportunity to prevent future occurrences by making recommendations to address the issues identified. However, as a mechanism for raising concerns HSIB is limited by the fact that its remit is to carry out only a small number of national investigations. It is HSIB's national investigation function to identify and investigate large thematic issues, rather than addressing individual concerns. HSIB can provide information about what happened in an individual case in their maternity investigations. They can also shine a light on wider service failures and what needs to be done to address these. However, as the maternity function is due to be moved to a dedicated Special Health Authority (SHA) HSIB will no longer produce reports that focus on the care an individual received from 2022 onwards.

Maternity investigations are not instigated by concerned individuals, in fact there is no way for an individual affected by a birth injury, intrapartum stillbirth, early neonatal death or maternal death to raise a concern with HSIB. Once HSIB have initiated the process for these families they can choose to allow the investigation, which the vast majority do, indicating there is a desire to engage with an independent investigation. When maternity investigations are moved from HSIB to the SHA care will need to be taken to ensure families are happy to continue to be a part of such investigations.

Part of the rationale behind HSIB was to provide a mechanism for individuals affected by matters which cause public concern to establish the facts and have an impartial investigation which was much more modestly priced than the alternative option of a public inquiry. HSIB has consistently cost just shy of £20 million a year, which is not insubstantial, but is certainly not excessive when compared to the costs of a public inquiry. It is relatively early days to be judging the value for money that HSIB offers due to service improvements as they only conduct a small number of national inquiries and it will take time for changes to come through the system.

HSIB acquired its long-awaited statutory footing under the Health and Care Act 2022 and was renamed the HSSIB. There was considerable discussion on the role of safe space during the Health and Care Bill 2021's progress through parliament. To contextualise this it is worth returning to the original Expert Advisory Group report[23] which contained the blueprint for HSIB. Although these points were not highlighted, the Report contained two justifications for moving away from blaming individuals. The first justification emerged from the causes of safety incidents, and echoed the approach of civil aviation safety:[24]

> Safety issues and related incidents are often the result of complex local, organizational and system-wide processes, with similar events recurring repeatedly in different places across the healthcare system. The purpose of safety investigation is to understand the patterns of causality that produce harm, and to make recommendations that can address those causes across the healthcare system in order to improve the safety of all patients.

The second justification lay in the need to ensure that healthcare personnel openly, voluntarily and swiftly shared information about their activities, acts and omissions that might expose them to criticism. The Report contained repeated statements that a no blame culture was the goal, rather than the blaming of individuals, and its section on 'Promoting a just culture' is instructive.[25] The problem was recognised that staff would only volunteer information in a just culture, where they do not fear being blamed. It was said:[26]

> For staff, trust will depend principally on knowing that they will be treated fairly and not blamed for genuine mistakes. They must feel safe from unwarranted blame when taking part in an investigation. We are struck by work that has shown that the most effective learning takes place in conditions of psychological safety, characterised by a shared belief that participants will not be embarrassed, rejected, or punished for speaking up.

To this end the Act contains provisions on 'safe space'.[27] It is a criminal offence to disclose information obtained in HSSIB investigations. However, there are exceptions to the prohibition on disclosure. For example if an individual applies to the High Court for disclosure and the High Court determines that 'it is interests of justice'[28] or if the Chief Investigator deems

---

[23] *Report of the Expert Advisory Group; Healthcare Safety Investigation Branch* (Department of Health, May 2016), available at www.gov.uk/government/uploads/system/uploads/attachment_data/file/522785/hsibreport.pdf.

[24] ibid, 21.

[25] ibid, 25, 26.

[26] ibid, 32.

[27] Section 106 of the Health and Care Act 2022.

[28] Schedule 14 of the Health and Care Act 2022 sets out that the High Court can only order disclosure if it determines that the interests of justice served by the disclosure outweigh
  (a) any adverse impact on current and future investigations by deterring persons from providing information for the purposes of investigations, and
  (b) any adverse impact on securing the improvement of the safety of health care services provided to patients in England.

disclosure is 'necessary to address a serious and continuing risk to the safety of any patient or to the public' and they 'reasonably believes that the person is in a position to address the risk, and finally this disclosure is limited to what is necessary for that person take the requisite steps to address the risk'.

These provisions mean that 'safe space' is not all that safe. This is not news to the Government: in evidence he gave at the Committee stage of the Bill Sir Robert Francis stated 'as a lawyer, I would be very hesitant on the advice I would give to someone on the basis of the Bill as it stands, because there is no certainty that what goes into the safe space stays there'.

This legislation is very new and it is currently uncertain how they will play out in practice. However, the HSSIB arrangements as set out in underpinning legislation would *not* remove the potential for blame arising through regulatory, professional, employment or media channels. Accordingly, they inherently fail to establish the required systemic just/no blame culture, within which staff could be exempted from fear of exposure, criticism and litigation. Hence, the critical culture that would support volunteering potentially embarrassing information, or prevent incomplete record-keeping or even falsification of records, would not be generated.

The intention behind HSIB/HSSIB was a long way from the historical rhetoric of blame. However, there remain some serious problems over the approach that has been taken. First, the adoption of a just culture could not be effectively adopted by HSIB in isolation. The same approach would have to be – as the original Report realised – adopted holistically by every NHS unit across the entire NHS. The experience of civil aviation is that a just culture has to exist throughout social, operational, managerial and regulatory and public regimes if it is to provide a comprehensive feeling that a person who shares difficult information would not thereby trigger adverse consequences. In particular, there was no acceptance that the regulatory and enforcement policy of regulators such as the CQC, or compliance and discipline practices of NHS units, would have to be based on a just culture.

Second, there remains an unresolved and fundamental conflict in the proposed safe space arrangements between, on the one hand, providing information to patients and families and, on the other hand, maintaining a just (no blame) culture in which staff will volunteer information.

12

Complaints to Regulators

In the UK there are three different regulatory frameworks operating within healthcare regulation: professional regulation, entity regulation or the regulation of specified activities.

Professional regulation in the UK was the first type of healthcare regulation and involved separate regulators for different professions, for example, the General Medical Council (GMC) regulates doctors. Some regulators have evolved, for example the Nursing and Midwifery Council (NMC) has always regulated nurses and midwives, and has recently added nursing assistants to its remit. There is one multi-professional regulator, the Health and Care Professions Council (HCPC), which regulates 15 professions, see HCPC section below.

Some regulators, such as the General Dental Council (GDC) or the General Optical Council (GOC) can regulate individuals and to some degree entities and activities in their respective fields. If you take the GDC as an example, under the Dentists Act 1984[1] the GDC mandates that all dentists and dental care professionals must be on the register in order to practice.[2] They have enforcement powers to take action in relation to regulated activities[3] (such as tooth whitening) and misuse of protected titles[4] (any title or description that falsely implies the person is a registered dentist or dental practitioner). The GDC has some entity regulation aspects, under sections 41 and 43 of the 1984 Act it is an offence for an individual or company to operate the business of dentistry unless the majority of directors are GDC registrants. In practice the major thrust of the GDC regulation, including its activity and entity regulation functions, is focussed on the qualifications and actions of individuals.

The General Pharmaceutical Council (GPhC) regulates along similar lines to the GDC, but it also has a more explicit entity regulation function as it also maintains a register of registered pharmacies. Under the Medicines Act 1968[5] and the Pharmacy Order 2010[6]

---

[1] Dentists Act 1984 c. 24 available at www.legislation.gov.uk/ukpga/1984/24.

[2] Part III of the Dentists Act, ibid.

[3] See section 38 of the Dentists Act, ibid, for the prohibition of practice of dentistry by laymen. The practice of dentistry is defined at s 37 of the Act as 'the purposes of this Act, the practice of dentistry shall be deemed to include the performance of any such operation and the giving of any such treatment, advice or attendance as is usually performed or given by dentists; and any person who performs any operation or gives any treatment, advice or attendance on or to any person as preparatory to or for the purpose of or in connection with the fitting, insertion or fixing of dentures, artificial teeth or other dental appliances shall be deemed to have practised dentistry within the meaning of this Act'.

[4] Section 39 of the Dentists Act, ibid.

[5] S 74 of the Medicines Act 1968 c 67 available at www.legislation.gov.uk/ukpga/1968/67.

[6] The Pharmacy Order 2010 (SI 2010/231) available at www.legislation.gov.uk/uksi/2010/231/contents/made.

a business or organisation must register a physical premises as a pharmacy if it intends to carry out one or more of the following activities from those premises:

- sell Pharmacy medicines ('P medicines')

- supply P medicines or Prescription Only Medicines (POMs) against prescriptions, which require the product to be labelled for a specific patient as a dispensed medicinal product

- supply P medicines or Prescription Only Medicines (POMs) against prescriptions written by veterinary practitioners for the treatment of animals.

Again, the provisions for entity regulation put the onus onto the professional involved, which is hardly surprising as each regulator's jurisdiction only covers their specific professions.

The first regulator that was set up solely to undertake activity regulation was the Human Fertilisation and Embryology Authority (HFEA). Since its creation under the Human Fertilisation and Embryology Act 1990 HFEA has regulated very specific activities in fertility treatment.[7] The first in vitro fertilisation baby, Louise Brown, was born in July 1978. In response in 1982 the government asked Dame Mary Warnock to examine the social, ethical and legal implications of recent, and potential, developments in the field of human assisted reproduction. Her 1984 report,[8] the Warnock report, as it became known, formed the basis for the 1990 Act and the creation of the HFEA. To the best of the authors' knowledge the HFEA is the only regulator created based on the report of a philosopher.

The CQC regulates entities which carry out the regulated activities listed in Schedule 1 of the Health and Social Care Act Regulations 2014.[9] These cover a broad range of health and care provision, briefly defined as the provision of:

- personal care

- accommodation for people who require nursing or personal care

- accommodation for people who require treatment for substance abuse

- treatment of disease, disorder or injury

- assessment or medical treatment for persons detained under the Mental Health Act 1983

- surgical procedures

- diagnostic and screening procedures

- management and supply of blood and blood-derived products etc

- transport services, triage and medical advice provided remotely

- maternity and midwifery services

- termination of pregnancies

- services in slimming clinics (if provided under by/under the supervision of a medical practitioner)

---

[7] Human Fertilisation and Embryology Act 1990 c 37, available at www.legislation.gov.uk/ukpga/1990/37/contents as amended by subsequent legislation, most notable the Human Fertilisation and Embryology Act 1990 c 22 available at www.legislation.gov.uk/ukpga/2008/22/contents.

[8] Mary Warnock, *Report of the Committee of Inquiry into Human Fertilisation and Embryology* Cm 9314 1984. (HMSO, London July) available at www.hfea.gov.uk/media/2608/warnock-report-of-the-committee-of-inquiry-into-human-fertilisation-and-embryology-1984.pdf.

[9] Schedule 1 of the Health and Social Care Act (Regulated Activities) Regulations 2014 available at www.legislation.gov.uk/ukdsi/2014/9780111117613/schedule/1.

- nursing care
- family planning services (insertion or removal of IUDs by/under the supervision of a health care professional)

Its purpose is to make sure health and social care services provide people with safe, effective, compassionate, high-quality care and to encourage care services to improve.[10] Its role is to monitor, inspect and regulate services to make sure they meet fundamental standards of quality and safety, and to publish what it finds, including performance ratings to help people choose care. It publishes regular reports on the state of healthcare in the country.[11] Registered persons 'must have regard' to guidance issued by the CQC,[12] and it is itself required to take guidance into account in making its regulatory decisions.[13]

The remits of these different types of regulators overlap, most obviously the CQC overlaps with the professional regulators as well as potentially with the more niche regulators such the HFEA and the Human Tissue Authority (HTA).

I. Complaints to Activity and Entity Regulators

All the activity regulators will investigate complaints about individuals and bodies corporate who use protected titles or carry out regulated activities. Generally, in regulators such as the GOC who both hold a register and have an activity regulatory function two parallel complaints processes are run. The first is a fitness to practise process against individual registrants. The second process investigates alleged breaches of activities or protected titles outlined the relevant section(s) of the regulator's governing legislation[14] where the suspect[15] can be identified and is not registered with them.

Activity regulators vary in their approach to public complaints. The HTA website[16] has no dedicated section of its website for members of the public to raise a concern, just a general contact us page. Given the HTA was set up in the wake of the Alder Hay Organ retention scandal it is potentially surprising that there is no obvious mechanism for a member of the public to flag a concern.

In contrast the HFEA has a complaints process for those who are unhappy with the service (or lack of service) provided by a fertility clinic. The HFEA complaints process[17] is not based in statute, which limits the scope of their ability to investigate issues raised. They can only consider complaints made by a patient or donor which indicates a potential breach of the HFE Act, licence conditions or the guidance set out in the Code of Practice. In general, they expect a potential complainant to complaint to the treating clinic first.

The CQC will investigate unregistered providers of health and adult social care (with some potentially surprising exceptions such as opticians). It does not handle any other

---

[10] See *About us, What we Do and How we Do it* (Care Quality Commission, 2013); *Raising Standards, Putting People First. Our Strategy for 2013 to 2016* (Care Quality Commission, 2013).

[11] *The State of Health Care and Adult Social Care in England 2013/14* (Care Quality Commission, 2014).

[12] Health and Social Care Act 2008 (Regulated Activity) Regulations 2014 (as amended), reg 21.

[13] Health and Social Care Act 2008, s 25(1).

[14] In the GOC's case this will be sections 24, 25, 27 and 28 of the Opticians Act 1989 c 44 available at www.legislation.gov.uk/ukpga/1989/44/contents.

[15] Suspects can be either an individual or a body corporate.

[16] www.hta.gov.uk/.

[17] www.hfea.gov.uk/media/3311/complaint-about-a-licensed-clinic-policy.pdf.

complaints from members of the public about the services it regulates. It offers a signposting service directing those with concerns to the police, local councils and the various ways to make a complaint about NHS care.

II. Complaints to Professional Regulators

Each regulator has evolved independently and has its own rules and requirements. The General Medical Council was the first professional regulator and since then regulation has been extended to other professions, in some cases only relatively recently.

Two major reviews of healthcare professional regulation were commissioned in 2005 in response to the fifth Shipman Report. In her report Dame Janet Smith was clear that the concerns that had been raised with them about Harold Shipman's fitness to practise due to pethidine misuse could not have been reasonably expected to predict his subsequent murders. That said Dame Janet was very critical of the way in which the GMC handled concerns, and she was also scathing of the GMC's proposals for revalidation. In response to these concerns the then Health Secretary, John Reid commissioned two reports into the regulation of healthcare professionals. The review into the medical workforce was chaired by Professor Sir Liam Donaldson, Chief Medical Officer for England, and Mr Andrew Foster, Director of Workforce, Department of Health for England chaired the review into the non-medical workforce. The reviews were announced in January and March 2005 respectively. The remits of the two reviews were as follows.

The Donaldson review[18] aimed to:

- strengthen procedures for assuring the safety of patients in situations where a doctor's performance or conduct poses a risk to patient safety or the effective functioning of services;
- ensure the operation of an effective system of revalidation;
- modify the role, structure and functions of the General Medical Council.

The Foster review[19] sought to identify the measures needed to:

- strengthen procedures for ensuring that the performance or conduct of non-medical health professionals and other healthcare staff does not pose a threat to patient safety or the effective functioning of services, particularly focusing on the effective and fair operation of fitness to practise procedures;
- ensure the operation of effective systems of continuing professional development and appraisal for non-medical healthcare staff and make progress towards regular revalidation where this is appropriate;

---

[18] CMO, *Good Doctors, Safer Patients: Proposals to Strengthen the System to Assure and Improve the Performance of Doctors and Protect the Safety of Patients*, A report by the Chief Medical Officer available at https://webarchive.nationalarchives.gov.uk/ukgwa/20060719044921/http://www.dh.gov.uk/PublicationsAndStatistics/Publications/PublicationsPolicyAndGuidance/PublicationsPolicyAndGuidanceArticle/fs/en?CONTENT_ID=4137232&chk=KW63va.

[19] *The Regulation of the Non-medical Healthcare Professions: A Review by the Department of Health* (14 July 2006) available at https://webarchive.nationalarchives.gov.uk/ukgwa/20061023100201/http://www.dh.gov.uk/PublicationsAndStatistics/Publications/PublicationsPolicyAndGuidance/PublicationsPolicyAndGuidanceArticle/fs/en?CONTENT_ID=4137239&chk=zkSWnu.

- ensure the effective regulation of healthcare staff working in new roles within the health-care sector and of other staff in regular contact with patients.

These reports both contained many suggestions for improving the regulation of healthcare professionals, which led to a government consultation in the autumn of 2006. The two most significant changes, changing the standard of proof and separating the investigation and adjudication functions are briefly outlined below.

A. Separating the Investigation and Adjudication in Fitness to Practise Hearings

Both *Good Doctors, Safer Patients* and the fifth report of the Shipman Inquiry made recommendations that while the GMC should continue to investigate fitness to practise concerns the final adjudication should be done by an independent body. There followed some years of toing and froing with the Department of Health consulting on and then withdrawing plans to create an Office of the Health Professions Adjudicator.[20] Instead, the GMC received approval to create the Medical Practitioners Tribunal Service (MPTS)[21] to adjudicate on fitness to practise cases. The MPTS took over hearings from June 2012, and was placed onto a statutory footing from 2015.[22] The 2015 SI included provisions for the GMC to appeal the outcome of an MPTS decision.

B. Standard of Proof Required in Fitness to Practise Hearings

Another major change triggered by these reports was to the way fitness to practise concerns are judged. In 2008 the civil standard of proof, balance of probabilities, was adopted in all fitness to practise proceedings for all healthcare regulators.[23] Doctors were particularly vocal in their opposition to shifting from using the criminal standard, beyond reasonable doubt as they felt it posed an unwarranted threat to doctors' livelihoods.[24]

C. Fitness to Practise Procedures

Each professional regulator has a fitness to practise process, which vary slightly from each other. This chapter will outline the fitness to practise requirements for each of the regulators in Table 1, but will only give a detailed summary of the three regulators that cover the majority of NHS clinical staff; the GMC, the NMC and the HCPC.

---

[20] Part 2 of the Health and Social Care Act 2008 c 14, available at www.legislation.gov.uk/ukpga/2008/14/contents.

[21] www.mpts-uk.org/.

[22] The General Medical Council (Constitution of Panels, Tribunals and Investigation Committee) Rules Order of Council 2015 2015/1965, available at www.legislation.gov.uk/uksi/2015/1965/contents/made.

[23] S 112 of the Health and Social Care Act 2008 c 14, available at www.legislation.gov.uk/ukpga/2008/14/section/112.

[24] Clare Dyer, 'GMC Approves Change in the Standard of Proof' (2007) 335(1230) *BMJ* 1230 https://doi.org/10.1136/bmj.39426.356030.DB (published 13 December 2007).

Table 1 Health and care professional regulators in the UK

Regulator	Regulated persons/ entities	Complainants	Limitation	Objective	Outcome
GMC	UK Doctors	Patients, HCPs	Five year rule – generally the complaint should be within 5 years of the incident, with some exceptions.	Examination of fitness to practise going forward, not a retrospective examination of a particular incident.	Referral by GMC to Medical Practitioners Tribunal Service. The MPTS is a statutory committee of the GMC, but is operationally separate from the GMC's investigatory role and accountable directly to parliament. The MPTS makes a decision on removal from register and/or restrictions on practice. Interim orders can be used prior to final tribunal decisions.
NMC	UK Nurses and midwives	Anyone who feels public safety is at risk (including self-referral)	Currently on MNC register. No time limit. No geographical limit on where the incident took place.	Examination of fitness to practise going forward, not a retrospective examination of a particular incident.	NMC FTP Tribunal – decision on removal from register and/or restrictions on practice. Interim orders can be used prior to final tribunal decisions.
GDC	UK Dentists and those providing dental treatments e.g. tooth whitening in the UK, who are not registered with them. GDC also regulates entities, dental practices, on a voluntary basis.	Patient, representative or dental professional	Currently on GDC register. No time limit or geographical limit on when and where the concern arose.	Examination of fitness to practise as defined in s 27(2) of the Dentist Act 1984. Essentially a dental professional's fitness to practise is of concern when it relates to: – Misconduct – deficient professional performance – a charge, caution or conviction for a criminal offence – adverse physical or mental health.	GDC FTP Tribunal – decision on removal from register and/or restrictions on practice. Interim orders can be used prior to final tribunal decisions.

GCC	Anyone	Currently on GCC register. No time limit or geographical limit on when and where the concern arose.	Fitness to practise defined under Section 20 (1) of the Chiropractors Act 1994 as Unacceptable Professional Conduct (UPC), Professional Incompetence (PI), criminal conviction, or impairment due to ill health). Investigating Committee scrutinises complaints and passes cases where they think there may be a case to answer to a Hearing with either the Practice Committee or Health Committee determines if the registrant is fit to practice.	Registrants can be required to attend a medical examination if the complaint regards impairment due to ill health. Hearings can result in admonishment (a formal warning on file); suspension from the register; removal from register; restrictions on practice. Interim suspension orders can be used prior to final tribunal decisions.
GOsC[25]	Anyone	Currently on GOsC register. No time limit or geographical limit on when and where the concern arose.	Fitness to practise defined under Section 20 of the Osteopaths Act 1993 as Unacceptable Professional Conduct (UPC), Professional Incompetence (PI), criminal conviction, or impairment due to ill health). Investigating Committee scrutinises complaints and passes cases where they think there may be a case to answer to a Hearing (either the Practice Committee or Health Committee) to determine if the registrant is fit to practice. In some cases a complaint may be dealt with without a hearing under Rule 8 of the General Osteopathic Council (Professional Conduct Committee) (Procedure) Rules.[26]	Registrants can be required to attend a medical examination if the complaint regards impairment due to ill health. Hearings can result in admonishment (a formal warning on file); suspension from the register; removal from register; restrictions on practice. Interim suspension orders can be used prior to final tribunal decisions. Undertakings, Suspension and Conditions of practice are indicated on the register, with no further detail provided.
GOC	Anyone	Currently on GOC register or relevant business. No time limit.	Examination of fitness to practise judged as a breach of professional standards that would amount to an allegation under s13D of the Opticians Act 1989.	Removal/suspension from Register. Conditional registration. Financial penalty (up to £50,000).

(continued)

Table 1 (*Continued*)

Regulator	Regulated persons/ entities	Complainants	Limitation	Objective	Outcome
GPhC	Pharmacists, pharmacy technicians and pharmacies – UK excepting NI	Anyone	Currently on GPhC register or relevant business. No time limit.	Examination of fitness to practise judged as a breach of professional standards that would amount to an 'impairment' under Article 51 of The Pharmacy Order 2010. Threshold criteria are applied at the initial stage. If appropriate the compliant is referred to the Investigating Committee to scrutinises complaints and pass appropriate (impairment and public interest) cases to a Fitness to practise Committee for a hearing to determine if the registrant is fit to practice.	Investigations can result in case closure, informal guidance or referral to the FTP Committee. The FTP Committee can require Registrants to attend a medical examination if the complaint regards impairment due to ill health or to demonstrate proficiency in English if that is questioned. They can also impose; suspension/removal from register; and/or restrictions on practice. Interim suspension orders can be used prior to final tribunal decisions.
Pharmaceutical Council of N. Ireland	The professional services and the conduct of Pharmacists and pharmacy businesses in NI	Anyone, but the behaviour must involve a demonstration of attitudes or behaviour towards a patient, customer or prospective patient/ customer, from which that person can reasonably expect to be protected.	No time of geographical limits where/when the behaviour took	Scrutiny Committee considers concerns about a registrants fitness to practise, It must refer more serious cases to the Statutory Committee. The Statutory Committee makes judgements on whether a registrant's fitness to practise is impaired as described in their Code of Ethics[27] and the Pharmacy (1976 Order) (Amendment) Order (Northern Ireland) 2012 for reasons concerning their conduct, professional performance or health.	The Scrutiny Committee can: dismiss a case; give advice; issue warnings and agree undertakings if appropriate. The Statutory Committee can: issue formal warnings; agree undertakings; place conditions on the practice of a pharmacist; impose suspension and remove registrants from the Register. Interim suspension orders can be used prior to final decisions.

[27] Professional standards of conduct, ethics and performance for pharmacists in Northern Ireland available at www.psni.org.uk/wp-content/uploads/2012/09/22504-PSNI-Code-of-Practice-Book-final.pdf.

| HCPC | Arts therapists; biomedical scientists; chiropodists/ podiatrists; clinical scientists; dietitians; hearing aid dispensers; occupational therapists; operating department practitioners; orthoptists; paramedics; physiotherapists; practitioner psychologists; prosthetists/orthotists; radiographers; and speech and language therapists | Anyone | Registered professionals | To investigate the fitness to practise of professionals registered with them against the relevant standard.[28]

 Initial triage for eligibility, if thresholds met then formal allegation sent to Investigation Committee. Very serious allegations merit an application to the health care and professionals tribunal service[29] (HCPTS) for an interim hearing.[30] If the Investigation Committee decide there is a case to answer this will got to the relevant final Panel for a hearing.[31] Final hearings are held by the HCPTS.[32] | Final Panels may:-

 1. take no further action or order mediation;
 2. caution the registrant (place a warning on their registration for up to five years);
 3. set conditions of practice that the registrant must meet;
 4. suspend the registrant from practising (for no more than one year); or
 5. strike the registrant from the Register.

 Interim orders can be used prior to final tribunal decisions. |

[28] www.hcpc-uk.org/standards/standards-of-conduct-performance-and-ethics/.
[29] www.hcpts-uk.org.
[30] www.hcpts-uk.org/hearings/about/interimorderhearings/.
[31] www.hcpc-uk.org/concerns/how-we-investigate/the-investigation-process-flowchart/.
[32] www.hcpts-uk.org/hearings/about/finalhearings/.

D. Oversight of Professional Regulators' Responses to Public Concerns

Currently, general oversight of the professions' regulatory system is provided by the Professional Standards Authority. The addition of a meta-regulator is a relatively new development. In April 2003 the statutory[33] Council for the Regulation of Health Care Professionals was established. This evolved into the Council for Healthcare Regulatory Excellence and is now known as the Professional Standards Authority (PSA).[34]

The PSA regulates the following regulators: the GMC; the NMC; the GDC; the GPhC; the Pharmaceutical Society of Northern Ireland; the GOC; the General Osteopathic Council (GOsC); the General Chiropractic Council (GCC); the HCPC; and Social Work England.

i. Annual Reviews

PSA carries out annual reviews to assess performance against the PSA's Standards of Good Regulation. This includes five standards on fitness to practise set out in Table 2.

Table 2 PSA Standards related to fitness to practise

Standard fourteen	The regulator enables anyone to raise a concern about a registrant.
Standard fifteen	The regulator's process for examining and investigating cases is fair, proportionate, deals with cases as quickly as is consistent with a fair resolution of the case and ensures that appropriate evidence is available to support decision-makers to reach a fair decision that protects the public at each stage of the process.
Standard sixteen	The regulator ensures that all decisions are made in accordance with its processes, are proportionate, consistent and fair, take account of the statutory objectives, the regulator's standards and the relevant case law and prioritise patient and service user safety.
Standard seventeen	The regulator identifies and prioritises all cases which suggest a serious risk to the safety of patients or service users and seeks interim orders where appropriate.
Standard eighteen	All parties to a complaint are supported to participate effectively in the process.

Since 2015/16 the PSA has produced an annual review, which includes scoring the fitness to practise procedure or each regulator, see Chart 1. Between 2015/16 and 2018/19 the scores were awarded out of 10, in 2019/20 this shifted to a score out of five.

This chart shows there is considerable variation between regulators; the GMC has consistently achieved the maximum score, where the HCPC has been unable to achieve all the standards set by PSA for fitness to practise procedures.

---

[33] Part 2 of the National Health Service Reform and Health Care Professionals Act 2002, available at www.legislation.gov.uk/ukpga/2002/17/section/25/enacted as amended.

[34] As per section 222 of the Health and Social Care Act c 7 2012 available at www.legislation.gov.uk/ukpga/2012/7/contents/enacted as amended.

Chart 1 PSA fitness to practise performance review scores 2015–20

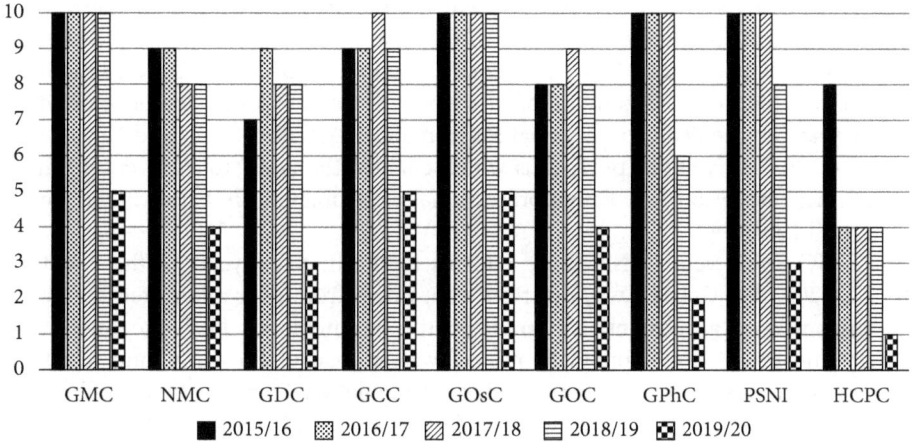

■ 2015/16   ▧ 2016/17   ▨ 2017/18   ▤ 2018/19   ▩ 2019/20

ii. *Special Reviews*

PSA also carry out special reviews where there are areas of concern, such as the reviews of the NMC fitness to practise processes mentioned later in this chapter in the NMC section.

E. The General Medical Council (GMC)

The GMC was formed in 1858,[35] prior to this there were a number of bodies, including in theory even the Archbishop of Canterbury, who could issue licences to practise as a doctor. Licences were usually geographically restricted and there was no consistency of standards between different awarding bodies. The 1841 census indicated that around one third of the doctors in England were unqualified.[36] This situation was clearly unsatisfactory and resulted in the Medical Act of 1858, which established the General Council of Medical Education and Registration of the United Kingdom. It was responsible for creating and maintaining a UK wide register or doctors, determining conduct-based or criminal fitness to practise issues, standardising medical education across the UK, and the publication of a pharmacopoeia (this was changed by the Medicines Act 1968).[37] The next substantial reforms to the GMC occurred in the 1970s following the Merrison Committee's 1975 report,[38] which recommended the addition of specialisms, including general practice, to the register, the formation of a new committee to oversee all stags of medical education, that elected members of the GMC should number more than 10 more than all other members of the

---

[35] Medical Act 1858 c 90, available at www.legislation.gov.uk/ukpga/Vict/21-22/90/enacted.

[36] See www.gmc-uk.org/about/who-we-are/our-history.

[37] In the wake of the Thalidomide disaster the copyright for the British Pharmacopoeia assigned to was the Crown by s 98 of the Medicines Act 1968, www.legislation.gov.uk/ukpga/1968/67/contents, which made the British Pharmacopoeia Commission responsible for its publication.

[38] AW Merrison, *Report of the Committee of Inquiry into the Regulation of the Medical Profession*. Cmnd 6018 London HMSO 1975, available at https://wellcomecollection.org/works/tqtncpkt.

Council, and that the GMC fitness to practise jurisdiction should be expanded to encompass cases involving a doctor's serious physical and mental ill health issues. These changes were included in the Medicine Act 1978, but the fitness to practise health procedures were not actually introduced until 1980.[39] In 1995 the first edition of Good Medical Practice was published, which set out the standard of care a patient could expect a doctor to provide. In the same year the Medical (Professional Performance) Act 1995[40] received Royal Assent. Section 1 of this act contains provisions which enabled the GMC to carry out a fitness to practise review for seriously deficient professional performance. These provisions were not enacted until 1 July 1997.[41]

The GMC underwent considerable reforms in the first few years of the twenty-first century. In 2003 the Council was drastically cut down from over a hundred members to 35 accompanied by a substantial increase in the lay members. Both the Bristol Royal Infirmary and the Shipman public inquiries were critical of the GMC and highlighted patient safety failings that had occurred under self-regulation. Some doctors vocally rejected alternatives to self-regulation, 'the General Medical Council is the crucible of our professionalism and, without it, doctors in this country would become mere technicians. Any alternative to professionally let regulation is unthinkable'.[42]

Despite opposition from some quarters a shift from self-regulation to 'professional regulation' followed. This involved some substantial changes to the way fitness to practise concerns were handled. The aim of professional regulation was that doctors would be held to a consistent set of standards, which are assessed using periodic revalidation. Revalidation had a troubled inception and did not start until 2012. In 2013 Good Medical Practice was updated.

i. Jack Adcock's Death, the GMC and Dr Hadiza Bawa-Garda's Sanctions

The death of six-year-old Jack Adcock and the subsequent litigation and fitness to practise hearings regarding Dr Hadiza Bawa-Garba have had a significant impact on the GMC. Dr Bawa-Garba was a specialist registrar in her sixth year of postgraduate training (ST6) with an impeccable record. In February 2011, Dr Bawa-Garba had recently completed a period of maternity leave and had just started at Leicester Royal Infirmary, having previously worked as a community paediatrician. On 18 February Dr Bawa-Garba arrived at work expecting to be working on the general paediatric ward, where she had been all week. At the start of shift meeting the staff were told that someone was needed to cover the children's assessment unit (CAU) as there were rota gaps. The registrar was attending a training day with no cover provided and the consultant who was meant to be in charge that day, Dr Stephen O'Riordan, hadn't released he was on call and was teaching in Warwick until the afternoon. Dr Bawa-Garda volunteered and she was single-handedly covering the CAU.

---

[39] Medical Act 1978 c 12 and The Medical Act 1978 (Commencement No 4 Order) 1980, available at www.legislation.gov.uk/uksi/1980/1524/made.

[40] Medical (Professional Performance) Act 1995 c 51 available at www.legislation.gov.uk/ukpga/1995/51/contents.

[41] The Medical (Professional Performance) Act 1995 (Commencement No 3) Order 1997 1997/1315 (c 46) available at www.legislation.gov.uk/uksi/1997/1315/contents/made.

[42] B Keighley et al, 'Letter – GMC: Approaching the Abyss. Preservation is Well Worth the Effort' (2001) 322(7302) *BMJ* 1599 available at www.ncbi.nlm.nih.gov/pmc/articles/PMC1120633/. Dr Brian Keighley and five other authors of this paper were elected/appointed members of the GMC.

At around 10.30 Jack Adcock, who had trisomy 21 and a congenital heart condition which was treated with enalapril, was brought in to the CAU with diarrhoea, vomiting and shallow breathing. He was assessed by Dr Bawa-Garda, who took bloods both for lab tests and for an acidity assessment and ordered a chest x-ray. At around quarter to 11 the blood gas test revealed Jack's blood was too acidic, and on the basis of her assessment Dr Bawa-Garda diagnosed Jack with gastroenteritis and dehydration and gave him a large bolus of fluids. At midday Dr Bawa-Garda looked for Jack's lab blood tests, but the hospital computer system was down, which delayed the blood tests. The chest x-ray became available at around 12.30pm, but Dr Bawa-Garda was treating other children until 3pm. At 3pm she checked on Jack who was sitting up in bed drinking juice and seemed much improved and she examined Jack's x-ray (she had not been told it was available before this point), which had evidence of a chest infection and she prescribed antibiotics immediately. Jack did not receive the antibiotics for an hour. At 4pm Dr Bawa-Garba chased up Jack's blood test results, which were given to her over the phone. These results indicated that Jack had kidney failure and needed antibiotics, had the computer system been working these results would have been given onscreen and the automatic alert system would have highlighted the abnormal test results. At 4.30pm in her handover to Dr O'Riordan Dr Bawa-Garda described Jack's condition and test results. Dr O'Riordan did not go and check on Jack, although he noted down that Jack's pH and lactate levels were abnormal he expected Dr Bawa-Garda to 'stress' these results to him.

At 7pm Jack was given his dose of enalapril by his mother, who had checked with a nurse prior to giving it to him and had been told it was ok for her to do so. This medication was not on his drug chart as Dr Bawa-Garba had been concerned it would drop his blood pressure too low, but she had not noted on his drug chart that it should be withheld. Jack had been moved up to a side room on ward 28 by this point. Earlier in the day the patient in the side room on ward 28 had been a boy with a terminal illness who had a do not resuscitate (DNR) order in place. At 8.20pm Dr Bawa-Garba received an emergency call as a patient in the side room on ward 28 had had a cardiac arrest. When she got to the room, despite walking past Jack's mother who was waiting outside, Dr Bawa-Garba mistakenly assumed that the patient the staff were trying to resuscitate was the boy who had been in that room earlier, and she told them to stop the resuscitation. In the ensuing confusion the team stopped work on resuscitating Jack for between 30 seconds and 2 minutes. At 09.21pm a decision was made to stop efforts to resuscitate Jack. Subsequent reports found that this cessation of resuscitation did not contribute to Jack's death. The report done by the hospital into Jack's death concluded that there were six root causes for Jack's poor care, listing 23 recommendations for improvement and 79 actions to minimise the risk of future reoccurrence.

A coronial inquest and a criminal investigation followed. In October 2015 Dr Bawa-Garba and two nurses, Theresa Taylor and Isabel Amaro, were tried for manslaughter by gross negligence. Several aspects of the trial have attracted considerable controversy. One was the cross-examination of Dr Bawa-Garba, which required her to reflect on the mistakes she had made that contributed to Jack's death, with concerns raised that the use of her reflections by the prosecution will inhibit doctors from being open about mistakes they have made. Other factors that raised concerns were the way that the system issues were felt to have been minimised, the hospital report for example was not put to the jury, and the way in which Dr O'Riordan attached the training encounter form to his witness statement. The training encounter form contained details of a conversation between Dr O'Riordan and Dr Bawa-Garba eight days after Jack's death. Dr Bawa-Garba had refused to sign this form as she did not consider it to be an accurate record, but it was nonetheless put before the court.

In November 2015 Dr Bawa-Garba and Isabel Amaro were both found guilty by the jury, they were sentenced in December and both received two years suspended.

In June 2017 the MPTS suspended Dr Bawa-Garba for a year. Mrs Adcock was angered by this and set up an online petition to see if she could appeal this decision. In fact, the GMC took up an appeal on the grounds it needed to protect the public confidence in the medical profession. Following an FOI request the GMC published the advice it received, despite the advice being subject to legal professional privilege, due to the exceptional degree of public interest in the case.[43] In January 2018 in the High Court the GMC appeal succeeded and Dr Bawa-Garba was struck off.[44] This sparked outrage from many doctors who were concerned that as a black junior doctor she had been scapegoated for a chronically understaffed, broken system and unfairly singled out for punishment by the GMC. A crowd-funding initiative raised funds to allow Dr Bawa-Garba to challenge the decision in the Court of Appeal. The case was so significant that there were a number of interveners in the case, including the British Medical Association, the Professional Standards Authority and the British Association of Physicians of Indian Origin. Dr Bawa-Garba won her appeal and was reinstated on the medical register.[45] The Court of Appeal recognised that the MPTS had not attempted to undermine the jury verdict, and that it was entitled to conduct an evaluative exercise to determine sanctions in light of future risk.

Dr Bawa-Garba returned to work, and was subject to conditions imposed by the MPTS. However, the case has raised some very important issues about openness, blame and how individual practitioners are treated in cases where there are system-wide issues, both narrowly by the GMC and more widely by the criminal justice system. It is notable that there has not been a corporate manslaughter charge against a UK hospital, just against individual practitioners.[46]

These issues were considered by Professor Sir Norman Williams in his review *Gross Negligence Manslaughter in Healthcare*, which will be considered in more detail in Part III.[47] The GMC has felt the wrath of the medical profession over their handling of the Bawa-Garba case,[48] and has professed that it has learnt a great deal from the case about supporting doctors' wellbeing.[49] Going forward the GMC set out their objectives as adopting 'a more proactive approach to regulation. And we're reducing fitness to practise investigations and building more supportive programmes.'

---

[43] www.gmc-uk.org/about/how-we-work/corporate-strategy-plans-and-impact/supporting-a-profession-under-pressure/responding-to-the-case-of-dr-bawa-garba/the-advice-that-informed-our-appeal.

[44] *General Medical Council v Dr Bawa-Garba* [2018] EWHC 76 (Admin) available at www.bailii.org/cgi-bin/format.cgi?doc=/ew/cases/EWHC/Admin/2018/76.html.

[45] *Dr Bawa-Garba v General Medical Council & Others* [2018] EWCA Civ (1879) available at www.judiciary.uk/wp-content/uploads/2018/08/bawa-garba-v-gmc-final-judgment.pdf.

[46] See Dr Jenny Vaughan's blog, 'The Long Road to Justice for Hadiza Bawa-Garba' *BMJ* (14 August 2018) available at https://blogs.bmj.com/bmj/2018/08/14/jenny-vaughan-the-long-road-to-justice-for-hadiza-bawa-garba/.

[47] Professor Sir Norman Williams, *Gross Negligence Manslaughter in Healthcare* (11 June 2018) available at www.gov.uk/government/publications/williams-review-into-gross-negligence-manslaughter-in-healthcare.

[48] Clare Dyer, 'Don't Use Our Fees to Pay Bawa-Garba's Court Case Costs, Doctors Tell GMC' (2018) 362 *BMJ* k3612, www.bmj.com/content/362/bmj.k3612.

[49] Eleanor Philpotts, 'GMC "Learnt a Great Deal" from Bawa-Garba Case, Says Chief' *Pulse* (19 January 2021) available at www.pulsetoday.co.uk/news/regulation/gmc-has-learned-lessons-from-bawa-garba-case-says-chief/.

ii. Current GMC Fitness to Practise Procedures[50]

Enquiries and concerns are screened for eligibility, do they relate to professionals on the GMC register, and if so could the case raise concerns about that individual's fitness to practise.[51] If a case meets these criteria the case is assessed to see if an interim order should be sought, if so the GMC will make a referral to the MPTS for them to consider whether to impose an interim order.

Investigations will be opened if the GMC feel that the concern (if proven) would mean they needed to restrict the registrant's practice. Upon deciding to open an investigation the GMC notifies the registrant and writes to their employer. If the concerns relate to a conviction, caution or decision by another regulatory body the GMC will automatically refer the registrant to the MPTS for an interim hearing. This does not apply to less serious convictions such as parking offences.

The GMC also investigate concerns about whether the accuracy of entry register including any potential fraud. Investigations will vary according to the concerns raises, information will be gathered which could include witness statements, expert testimony, medical assessments, performance assessments, English language assessments.

At the end of the investigation two senior decision-makers (one medical and one non-medical) will consider the evidence and decide whether to

- close the case with no further action
- issue the registrant with a warning
- agree undertakings with the registrant, or
- refer the case to the MPTS.

If the case is referred to the MPTS the GMC will provide a written decision which explains why the GMC has reached this conclusion.

The GMC does not make decisions on sanctions, that is the role of the MPTS. However, the GMC does oversee compliance with undertakings, conditions and suspensions. This includes decisions on changing, extending or removing sanctions. Generally, if an undertaking is agreed the GMC assess if it is still fit for purpose. The undertaking can be varied either by the joint agreement of the GMC and the registrant, or if agreement can't be reached then the GMC can make a referral to the MPTS. Failure to comply with an undertaking will lead the GMC to make a referral to the MPTS for a hearing. It is common practice when the MPTS impose conditions that they will also schedule a review hearing to reconsider the conditions. Should the GMC learn of failure to comply with conditions they will refer to the MPTS for an early review hearing.

a. The MPTS

The MPTS is the operationally separate statutory committee of the GMC with responsibility for delivering the fitness to practise hearings.[52] Its composition is set out in statute;

---

[50] For guidance on the GMC fitness to practise processes and thresholds see www.gmc-uk.org/concerns/information-for-doctors-under-investigation/how-we-make-decisions.

[51] This can include, for example, misconduct; poor performance; a criminal conviction or caution; physical or mental ill-health that may impact on the registrant's ability to practice medicine; a determination by another regulatory body; insufficient knowledge of English, etc, see www.gmc-uk.org/concerns/information-for-doctors-under-investigation/how-we-investigate-concerns/deciding-to-investigate-a-complaint-or-concern.

it consists of five members,[53] two of whom are medically qualified, two are also tribunal members.[54] The MPTS meets four times a year. It is accountable to parliament, for whom it must produce an annual performance report.

Cases referred by the GMC are considered by a three-person tribunal. At least one of the tribunal must be medically qualified and at least one must be a lay member. In most cases the tribunal chair will be legally qualified. The MPTS has a pool of tribunal members, currently around 300. Tribunals are sometimes supported by legal assessors, who advise them on points of law, but do not take part in the decision-making.

If the decision is made by the GMC to send the case to the MPTS committee a member of the GMC's legal team will attend the pre-hearing case management and the hearing to present the GMC's case.

After the referral by the GMC what follows is a straightforward legalistic case management process. Case management depends on the estimated length and complexity of the hearing; it may be a direct listing or it may involve a listings teleconference(s) and/or pre-hearing meeting(s) where key deadlines for the disclosure of evidence will be set and any outstanding issues can be resolved. Case managers can give legally binding directions to both the registrant and the GMC in accordance with rule 16.[55] Failure to comply with listing instructions can lead the MPTS to draw adverse inferences, refuse to admit the evidence, award costs.

Hearings comprise of three stages:

- Facts stage – this is a determination by the MPTS that the facts are proved. This can be achieved either by the registrant admitting to the facts or if the facts are contested then the GMC set out their allegations, the registrant presents their evidence in response, the parties make closing statements on the evidence and the Tribunal then decides in camera on any facts in dispute. If any facts are found proved the case progresses to the impairment stage. If the facts are not proved that is the end of the case.

- Impairment stage – this stage focuses on whether the registrant's fitness to practise is impaired by any of the facts proved in the facts stage. Both parties can call witnesses and make submissions. The Tribunal then decides in camera if fitness to practise is impaired. If they find fitness to practise is impaired the case progresses to the sanctions stage. If they find fitness to practise is not impaired that is the end of the case.

- Sanctions stage – this stage focuses on whether the MPTS should impose a sanction on the registrant. Both parties can call witnesses and make submissions. If the MPTS decides that no sanctions are appropriate, there are two possible outcomes, either the case ends with no action, or it ends with an undertaking agreed between the registrant and the GMC. If the MPTS decide to impose sanctions these can be conditions, suspension or erasure. Ordinarily any sanction cannot take place until 28 days after notice is deemed served on the registrant. In cases where the MPTS have decided to impose sanctions the GMC representative then makes representations as to whether these sanctions

---

[52] The operation and composition of the MPTS are set out in The Medical Act 1983, the GMC Fitness to Practise Rules 2004 and The General Medical Council (Constitution of Panels, Tribunals and Investigation Committee) Rules Order of Council 2015.

[53] www.mpts-uk.org/about/how-we-work/the-committee-and-their-interests.

[54] The General Medical Council (Constitution of Panels, Tribunals and Investigation Committee) Rules Order of Council 2015.

[55] www.mpts-uk.org/-/media/mpts-documents/DC4213_Case_management_procedure.pdf_51912315.pdf.

should be applied immediately and the registrant responds. The MPTS then makes a determination on this point in camera.

The outcomes from an MPTS are:

- taking no further action
- accepting undertakings offered by the doctor if these are agreed with the GMC
- voluntary removal from the register in some circumstances
- placing conditions on the doctor's registration (for a maximum of three years)
- suspending the doctor's registration (for a maximum of one year)
- erasing the doctor's name from the medical register so they can no longer practise.

Costs awards can be made by the MPTS, but they can only be made against a party that (1) has failed to comply with a relevant rule or direction and (2) has behaved unreasonably.

There is a right of appeal within 28 days of the MPTS decision or notification of the decision to the High Court in England and Wales, the Court of Session in Scotland or the High Court of Justice in Northern Ireland.

b. GMC Statistics[56]

Table 3 Fitness to practise concerns raised with the GMC 2012–19

Year	2012	2013	2014	2015	2016	2017	2018	2019
Doctors on register	252,557	259,651	267,169	273,767	280,806	288,521	298,538	311,356
Enquiries from Persons Acting in a Public Capacity	2,003	1,316	1,200	1,105	744	807	815	765
Enquiries from members of the public	6,154	6,475	6,572	6,547	6,688	5,714	5,677	5,945
Enquiries from other sources	2,190	2,075	1,852	1,766	1,714	2,025	2,081	1,944
Total enquiries	**10,347**	**9,866**	**9,624**	**9,418**	**9,146**	**8,546**	**8,573**	**8,654**

As Table 3 shows the majority of the concerns raised are raised by members of the public. The proportion of concerns raised by patients/member of the public concerns has been fairly consistent for a number of years; these were 69 per cent of the concerns in 2019, 66 per cent in 2018 and 67 per cent 2017.

The percentage of cases closed after an initial assessment is high. In 2019 73 per cent of referrals were closed after the initial assessment, which is in line with closure rates over the preceding years (in 2018 it was 73 per cent of referrals, in 2017 it was 72 per cent).

The use of interim orders tribunals remains fairly low, see Table 4.

---

[56] GMC Annual Fitness to Practise Statistics available at www.gmc-uk.org/about/what-we-do-and-why/data-and-research/medical-practice-statistics-and-reports/fitness-to-practise.

Table 4 Outcomes from GMC fitness to practise investigations 2016–20

	2016	2017	2018	2019
Suspension	58	43	48	52
Conditions	233	238	247	255
No Order made	48	71	93	81
Total	339	352	388	358

The investigation outcomes for cases that reach a case examiner have varied slightly, see Table 5. The percentage of cases that are closed has remained fairly consistent between 2015 and 2019. The percentage of referrals to the MPTS has increased year on year, having more than doubled between 2019 and 2015. By contrast the proportion of cases where the outcome from the case examine stage is advice has dropped over the same time period.

Table 5 GMC case examiner decisions 2015–19

Case examiner decision	2015	2016	2017	2018	2019
Refer to tribunal	279 (11%)	200 (11%)	200 (15%)	280 (23%)	347* (27%)
Advice	373 (15%)	333 (19%)	225 (17%)	66 (5%)	52 (4%)
Warning	135 (5%)	95 (5%)	117 (9%)	69 (6%)	85^ (7%)
Undertaking	144 (6%)	144 (8%)	106 (8%)	93 (8%)	76 (6%)
No Further action	1,635 (64%)	997 (56%)	709 (52%)	700 (58%)	719+ (56%)
Total	**2,566 (100%)**	**1,769 (100%)**	**1,357 (100%)**	**1,208 (100%)**	**1,279 (100%)**

* This figure includes three decisions where the doctor refused to accept undertakings. It does not include an additional 29 criminal conviction decisions by the registrar to refer to tribunal or six non-compliance decisions which were referred to tribunal.

^ This figure includes 15 decisions where the doctor refused to accept the warning and were confirmed by Investigation Committee (IC) or subsequently accepted by the doctor.

+ This figure includes three decisions determined by IC with no further action (NFA) but does not include an additional 55 decisions to grant voluntary erasure by case examiners.

It is very clear that there is a substantial whittling down at each state of the fitness to practise process, with only a relatively small number of cases getting to a MPTS hearing, as would be expected. Of those that do reach a hearing the outcomes remain fairly consistent from year to year, though there seems to be a trend towards suspension as opposed to erasure since 2017, see table 6.

Table 6 MPTS Fitness to Practise Panel decisions 2017–20

MPTS decision	2015	2016	2017	2018	2019
Erasure	72	70	62	65	55
	30%	31%	32%	26%	21%
Suspension	95	93	76	101	120
	40%	41%	39%	41%	47%
Conditions imposed	24	17	13	25	14
	10%	7%	7%	10%	5%
Undertakings	1	0	0	0	0
	0%	0%	0%	0%	0%
No impairment – warning	6	11	13	10	17
	3%	5%	7%	4%	7%
Impairment – no further action	2	2	4	2	4
	1%	1%	2%	1%	2%
No impairment	38	34	27	41	44
	16%	15%	14%	17%	17%
Voluntary erasure	1	2	0	3	3
	0%	1%	0%	1%	1%
Total	**239**	**229**	**195**	**247**	**257**
	100%	**100%**	**100%**	**100%**	**100%**

The time it takes from receipt of a concern to conclusion of a final hearing was 80 weeks in 2019.[57] This is down on the previous two years, which were 104 weeks in 2018 and 107 weeks in 2017. It is right that a process that can deprive a registrant of their livelihood is thorough and comprehensive, but a gap of over a year and a half reduces the potential for system-wide learning.

F. The Nursing and Midwifery Council (NMC)

There has been statutory regulatory oversight of nurses, midwives and health visitors since 1920.[58] Originally they were regulated by the General Nursing Council, which held a register (including detailing specialty areas), providing guidance to registrants. In 1921 the Disciplinary and Penal Case Committee was established to deal with fitness to

---

[57] PSA, *Performance Review 2019/20 General Medical Council*, available at www.professionalstandards.org.uk/docs/default-source/publications/performance-review---gmc-2019-20.pdf?sfvrsn=f5804920_0.
[58] Nurses Registration Act 1919 (Regnal 9 & 10 Geo 5) c 94.

practise concerns. Various evolutions followed including the addition of assistant nurses to the register in 1943,[59] the replacement of the General Nursing Council with the United Kingdom Central Council for Nursing Midwifery and Health Visiting in 1979.[60] This was replaced by the Nursing and Midwifery Council (NMC), which regulates nurses, midwives and latterly nursing associates,[61] which was formed by statute[62] in April 2002. Two years later the NMC's fitness to practise rules were codified in the Nursing and Midwifery Council (Fitness to Practise) Rules Order of Council 2004.[63] The NMC fitness to practise process has had a somewhat bumpy history, in part due to their involvement in the Morecambe Bay scandal.

i. 2008 and 2012 CHRE Reviews of NMC Fitness to Practise Procedures

From the NMC's inception there had been concerns over its fitness to practise processes. In June 2007, Mr Jim Devine MP publicly alleged[64] that the NMC appeared to be a 'fundamentally dysfunctioning organisation' and that there was 'an ingrained culture of bullying and racism'. It was also alleged that 'legal fees are paid not to address the organisation's proper purposes', that the working relationship between the Council and the executive was poor. In response the minster commissioned the CHRE report,[65] which looked at five functions – one of which was fitness to practise. The CHRE report[66] concludes that the NMC was carrying out its statutory function, but was failing to fulfil these to the standard of performance the public had a right to expect and described 'serious weaknesses' in the operation of fitness to practise processes. Specifically the report states:

> The NMC has had difficulties with the administration of fitness to practise for many years. There were real problems, including a large financial deficit, at the time of the transfer of responsibilities to the NMC from the United Kingdom Central Council for Nursing, Midwifery and Health Visiting in 2002. These were daunting challenges but, although the NMC made a difficult but necessary decision to increase registrants' fees significantly, it has not made the necessary long-term strategic investments in the infrastructure required to create a long-term solution. We are told that it is about to do so, and it must with a greater sense of urgency than it has shown so far on this matter.

Further reports followed, including a 2011 review of the progress since the 2008 report,[67] which recognised progress made, but registered concern about the seriousness of the

[59] The Nurses Act 1943 (Regnal 6 & 7 Geo.6) c 17.

[60] The Nurses, Midwives and Health Visitors Act 1979 available at www.legislation.gov.uk/ukpga/1979/36/contents.

[61] Nursing associates were added to the NMC's remit in 2019.

[62] Health Act 1999 c 8 available at www.legislation.gov.uk/ukpga/1999/8/contents and the Nursing and Midwifery Order 2001(2002/253) available at www.legislation.gov.uk/uksi/2002/253/contents/made.

[63] The Nursing and Midwifery Council (Fitness to Practise) Rules Order of Council 2004 SI 2004/1761 available at www.legislation.gov.uk/uksi/2004/1761/contents/made.

[64] Adjournment Debate was held in Westminster Hall on 11 March 2008, Hansard Hansard HC, *Nursing & Midwifery Council* (11 March 2008) vol 473 col 46WH, available at https://hansard.parliament.uk/commons/2008-03-11/debates/08031194000003/NursingAndMidwiferyCouncil.

[65] Minister of State for Health Services, Ben Bradshaw MP, in March 2008.

[66] CHRE, *Special Report to the Minister for State for Health Services on the Nursing and Midwifery Council* (11 June 2008) available at www.professionalstandards.org.uk/docs/default-source/publications/special-review-report/chre-special-report-on-the-nmc-2008.pdf?sfvrsn=f3bc7520_4.

[67] CHRE, *NMC Progress Review: A Review of the NMC's Fitness to Practise Directorate's Progress since 2008* (January 2011) available at www.professionalstandards.org.uk/docs/default-source/publications/special-review-report/nmc-progress-review-2010.pdf?sfvrsn=90477e20_2.

amount and nature of the improvements still required. Another CHRE review was commissioned in 2012. At this point the NMC had a significant backlog of fitness to practise cases. Up until this point the fitness to practise investigations had been outsourced to solicitors, from this point onwards investigations were brought in-house in an effort to save money. In this report CHRE was clear it had continually identified the need for improvement in fitness to practise. While the report acknowledged that the NMC had produced action plans and had made improvements in some areas this was not as swift or as extensive as might be expected. This report was quite critical:

> in order to carry out this regulatory role 'effectively, efficiently and economically' the NMC needs 'clear strategic direction and oversight based on reliable, meaningful information about its own performance, clear lines of accountability and decision making and sound implementation'. The fitness to practise function has floundered because it has not had this. Failure to improve and be seen to have improved has undermined confidence in it as an effective regulator and damaged its reputation.

Failures in communicating also featured heavily in the 2012 report:[68]

> The NMC is seen as ineffective in its communications and not focussed on providing a good standard of customer service … [members of the public, registrants and panel members] described an organisation that is reluctant to listen, that does not follow its own published policies or adhere to its own set timescales, that frequently misplaces documentation, that fails to respond to communications in a timely manner or present accurate responses and information that is written in plain English and presented clearly and logically.

This backdrop provides context for the NMC's involvement in the Morecambe Bay scandal.

ii. Morecambe Bay and the NMC

The events at Morecambe Bay are outlined above, but briefly failings in the maternity provision at Furness General Hospital between 2004 and 2013 led to the unnecessary deaths of 11 babies and one mother, as well as other adverse birth injuries to both mothers and babies. Table 7 indicates when the NMC were notified about concerns over midwives and when action was taken, what is very clear is for most of the midwives where a concern was raised there was a gap of several years before action was taken over. In their 2018 Lessons Learned report the PSA state that 'Further avoidable deaths occurred while the NMC were considering the complaints.'[69]

---

[68] CHRE, *Strategic Report to the Minster for State for Health Services on the Nursing and Midwifery Council -Final Report* (3 July 2012) available at www.professionalstandards.org.uk/docs/default-source/publications/special-review-report/strategic-review-of-nmc-2012.pdf?sfvrsn=85757f20_4. See also the interim report CHRE *Strategic Review of the Nursing and Midwifery Council: Interim Report* (10 April 2012) which forms Annex 2 of the final report.

[69] *Professional Standards Authority Lessons Learned Review: The Nursing and Midwifery Council's Handling of Concerns about Midwives Fitness to Practise at the Furness General Hospital* (May 2018) available at www.professionalstandards.org.uk/docs/default-source/publications/nmc-lessons-learned-review-may-2018.pdf?sfvrsn=ff177220_0.

Table 7 Fitness to practise hearing outcomes against midwives practising at Furness General Hospital 2008–16

Midwife	NMC first notified	Who notified?	Outcome	Date
1	Feb 2009	Mr A	No case to answer	Mar/Apr 2016
2	Feb 2009	Mr A	No case to answer	Mar/Apr 2016
3	Feb 2009	Mr A	**Suspended**	Sep 2016
			Judged no longer impaired – **suspension lifted**	Jan 2017
4	Feb 2009	Mr A	Interim suspension	Jun 2016
			Struck off	Oct 2016
6	Feb 2009	Mr A	No case to answer	Jan 2017
7	July 2009	Mr A	**Struck off**	June 2017
9	Nov 2012	Cumbria police	No case to answer	July 2013
11	Nov 2013	Trust	Interim Suspension	Jan 2014
			Struck off	May 2015

Briefly the NMC were first notified of concerns about the situation at Furness General Hospital when they received a complaint in February 2009 relating to the death of a baby in 2008 from an infection, referred to in their reports as Baby A. A root cause analysis, carried out by midwife 7 (one of the midwives at Furness General Hospital), was completed in January 2009; it was shared with the family who were deeply unhappy with it. The root cause analysis did not identify any significant concerns about the care that had been provided. An independent review of the root cause analysis was then commissioned, this did not identify any issues with the root cause analysis. However, the NMC's Midwifery team had concerns about the root cause analysis; the midwifery team were separate from the fitness to practise team.

The initial complaint the NMC received related to the care provided to Baby A and his mother. It concerned midwives 1 to 6. In July 2009 further concerns were raised over the quality of the independent review by midwife 7, and of a potential cover up; the complaint detailed discrepancies between the statements given by the midwives in the local investigation report and the family's recollections of what had happened. The subsequent NMC investigation of the concerns around midwives 1 and 6 has been criticised as slow and formulaic, the same allegations were sent to all the midwives concerned, regardless of their roles in the care of mother and baby.

The NMC then paused their fitness to practise investigation as there was a coroner's inquest into the death of Baby A. Similarly, when a police investigation was opened shortly after the coroner's inquiry concluded the NMC again paused their investigation until January 2014 when the police investigation had been closed. A particularly concerning aspect of this was that in April 2012 Cumbria police sent the NMC information about 20 more cases where they considered there were concerns about midwives' fitness to practise that should be investigated, and the NMC did not act on this information. In November 2014 the investigating committee decided to refer the cases of five of the midwives involved in

Baby A's care to the Conduct and Competence Committee (CCC). For various reasons the CCC hearings did not start until March 2016, some 16 months after the referral decision. Hearings began in March 2016 and the final hearing was held in January 2017. This is clearly many years after the concerns were first raised with the NMC. The outcomes of these hearings are detailed in table 7. Cases against midwives 5, 8 and 10 were all considered, but did not result in fitness to practise hearings.

A raft of concerns were raised about how the hearings were conducted including: substantial delays; families given insufficient time to consider documents; lack of support during the hearings (families not being sufficiently prepared for and supported through the adversarial hearing process which included cross-examination); failure to include information supplied by complainants.

One particularly distasteful aspect of the way the NMC handled the events related to Baby A's death came to light when his father made a subject access request as he wanted to know more about the culture of the NMC. This revealed what the PSA termed 'low level, in one case puerile, disrespectful comments about him between members of staff at the NMC'.

Baby A was by no means the only patient who had received poor care at Furness General Hospital: his case has been outlined above as it provided the earliest opportunity for the NMC to take action about what was occurring in this hospital. However, the NMC were also notified about the care relating to other mothers and babies.

The 2018 PSA Lessons Learned report recognised that there were difficulties for the NMC in dealing with these cases nonetheless it was highly critical of the NMC

in our view, before 2014 the NMC did not take credible information which it received about the midwives at the FGH seriously or take action to satisfy itself that the midwives were fit to practise. Its handling of the cases before 2014 generally was frequently incompetent. Even after that:

- Cases took longer to be investigated than was necessary causing distress to families and registrants
- The full range of the conduct allegedly involved – clinical concerns, collusion and individual dishonesty – was not fully explored
- The families we spoke to were dissatisfied and our study of the files showed that all of the bereaved families were unhappy with aspects of the way in which they were treated or their cases handled by the NMC.

The NMC recognised that there had been significant failings in the way that it had dealt with the situation at Furness General Hospital. In particular changes were needed to the way that complainants were communicated with and the fitness to practise procedure.

Even prior to the Morecambe Bay scandal there had been concerns over the NMC's fitness to practise processes. It was recognised that overhaul was needed and in October 2016 a consultation on modernising the 2004 Fitness to Practise was launched.[70] As a result of this consultation the case examiner role significantly changed. From 31 March 2017 case examiners had the power to issue advice, warnings and undertakings.[71] This was followed

---

[70] www.nmc.org.uk/about-us/consultations/past-consultations/2016-consultations/modernising-fitness-to-practise---changes-to-the-fitness-to-practise-rules-2004/.

[71] The Nursing and Midwifery Order (Legal Assessors) (Amendment) and the Nursing and Midwifery Council (Fitness to Practise) (Amendment) Rules Order of Council 2017 SI 2017/703 available at www.legislation.gov.uk/uksi/2017/703/contents/made.

in 2018 by the NMC launching a consultation[72] on their new strategy[73] for refocussing their fitness to practise procedures. The strategy sets out their two overarching aims for fitness to practise. Firstly, a professional culture that values equality, diversity and inclusion, and prioritises openness and learning in the interests of patient safety. Secondly, nurses, midwives and nursing associates who are fit to practise safely and professionally.

Twelve principles for fitness to practise cases have been developed to deliver their aims:[74]

1.   A person-centred approach to fitness to practise.
2.   Fitness to practise is about managing the risk that a nurse, midwife or nursing associate poses to patients or members of the public in the future. It isn't about punishing people for past events.
3.   We can best protect patients and members of the public by making final fitness to practise decisions swiftly and publishing the reasons openly.
4.   Employers should act first to deal with concerns about a nurse, midwife or nursing associate's practice, unless the risk to patients or the public is so serious that we need to take immediate action.
5.   We always take regulatory action when there is a risk to patient safety that is not being effectively managed by an employer.
6.   We take account of the context in which the nurse, midwife or nursing associate was practising when deciding whether there is a risk to patient safety that requires us to take regulatory action.
7.   We may not need to take regulatory action for a clinical mistake, even where there has been serious harm to a patient or service-user, if there is no longer a risk to patient safety and the nurse, midwife or nursing associate has been open about what went wrong and can demonstrate that they have learned from it.
8.   Deliberately covering up when things go wrong seriously undermines patient safety and damages public trust in the professions. Restrictive regulatory action is likely to be required in such cases.
9.   In cases about clinical practice, taking action solely to maintain public confidence or uphold standards is only likely to be needed if the regulatory concern can't be addressed
10.   In cases that aren't about clinical practice, taking action to maintain public confidence or uphold standards is only likely to be needed if the concerns raise fundamental questions about the trustworthiness of a nurse, midwife or nursing associate as a professional.
11.   Some regulatory concerns, particularly if they raise fundamental concerns about the nurse, midwife or nursing associate's professionalism, can't be addressed and require restrictive regulatory action.
12.   Hearings best protect patients and members of the public by resolving central aspects of a case that we and the nurse, midwife or nursing associate don't agree on.

---

[72] www.nmc.org.uk/about-us/consultations/past-consultations/2018-consultations/ensuring-patient-safety-enabling-professionalism/.

[73] www.nmc.org.uk/globalassets/sitedocuments/consultations/2018/ftp/ensuringpublicsafety_v6.pdf.

[74] www.nmc.org.uk/ftp-library/understanding-fitness-to-practise/using-fitness-to-practise/.

iii. Current NMC Fitness to Practise Procedures

Enquiries and concerns are screened for eligibility, do they relate to professional on the NMC register, and if so could the case raise concerns about that individual's fitness to practise?[75] If a case meets these criteria the seriousness of the case is assessed[76] to see if an interim order is needed.

Investigations will take place into serious concerns about a registrant's fitness to practise which could place patients at risk, or negatively impact public confidence in the nursing and midwifery professions. The NMC also investigate concerns about whether the accuracy of entry register including any potential fraud. Investigations will vary according to the concerns raises, information will be gathered which could include witness statements, expert testimony, medical assessments, English language assessments.

At the end of the investigation a case examiner will consider the evidence and decide if there is a case to answer.

If case examiners decide there is **no case to answer**, they can:

- close the case,
- give the nurse, midwife or nursing associate advice, or
- issue the nurse, midwife or nursing associate with a warning.

If case examiners decide there is a **case to answer**, they can:

- recommend undertakings to be agreed with the nurse, midwife or nursing associate, or
- refer the case to the Fitness to Practise Committee.

Case examiners can make a recommendation that the case be referred to the Fitness to Practise Committee for an interim order. Alternatively, if a case examiner does not make this recommendation the investigating committee can make an interim order at any point until the Fitness to Practise Committee starts to consider the case.

If the decision is made by the case examiner to send the case to the Fitness to Practise Committee it will be reviewed by the NMC's legal team. What follows is a fairly straightforward legalistic process involving drafting charges, compiling a hearing bundle,[77] potentially gathering further evidence. The registrant is notified and information is sent to them. Case management follows with teleconferences, preliminary hearings and discussions around whether the case can be resolved either by consent using the consensual panel determination process or by voluntary removal (this is not available in all cases).

If resolution cannot be achieved a panel is convened and the case progresses to a hearing. The panel can refer the case back for further investigation if it feels the evidence base is insufficient. The available sanctions are

- taking no further action
- voluntary removal from the register in some circumstances[78]

---

[75] www.nmc.org.uk/ftp-library/understanding-fitness-to-practise/fitness-to-practise-allegations/.

[76] www.nmc.org.uk/ftp-library/understanding-fitness-to-practise/how-we-determine-seriousness/.

[77] Inclusion is determined on a 'fair and relevant' test set out in rule 31 of the Nursing and Midwifery Council (Fitness to Practise) Rules 2004.

[78] www.nmc.org.uk/ftp-library/ftpc-decision-making/voluntary-removal-at-hearings/.

- a caution order of between one and five years
- a conditions of practice order of up to three years
- a suspension order of up to 12 months
- a striking-off order.

iv. NMC Statistics

Table 8 Fitness to practise concerns raised with the NMC 2010–20

Year	2010/ 2011	2011/ 2012	2012/ 2013	2013/ 2014	2014/ 2015	2015/ 2016	2016/ 2017	2017/ 2018	2018/ 2019	2019/ 2020
Size of register	667,072	671,668	673,567	680,858	686,782	692,550	690,773	690,278	698,237	716,607
Enquiries from a patient or the public	915	835	1,029	1,029	1,518	1,370	1,537	1,470	1,566	1,861
Enquiries from other sources	3,296	3,572	3,077	3,658	3,665	4,045	3,939	4,039	3,807	3,843
Total enquiries	4,211	4,407	4,106	4,687	5,183	5,415	5,476	5,509	5,373	5,704

As Table 8 shows the majority of the concerns raised are not raised by patients or members of the public. The proportion of concerns raised by patients/member of the public has been steadily increasing; these were 33 per cent of the concerns in 2019/20, 29 per cent in 2018/19, up from 27 per cent 2017/18.

The percentage of cases closed after an initial assessment is high.[79] In 2019/2020 64 per cent of referrals were closed after the initial assessment, which is broadly in line with closure rates over the preceding three years (in 2018/2019 it was 63 per cent of referrals, in 2017/2018 it was 56 per cent).

The use of interim orders remains fairly low, in 2019/2020 561 interim orders were issued. This is relatively consistent, in 2018/2019 506 were issued and in 2017/2018 580 were issued. Interim orders tend be comprised of around 55 per cent interim conditions on practice and 45 per cent interim suspensions.

The outcomes of cases that reach a case examiner have remained consistent since the powers for case examiners to issue advice, warnings and undertakings came in in April 2017.

---

[79] NMC Annual Fitness to Practise Report 2019–20, available at www.nmc.org.uk/globalassets/sitedocuments/annual_reports_and_accounts/ftpannualreports/2019-2020-annual-fitness-to-practise-report.pdf.

Table 9 NMC case examiner decisions 2017–20

Case examiner decision	2017/2018	2018/2019	2019/2020
Refer for hearing	819 (37%)	520 (32%)	534 (38%)
Advice	24 (1%)	12 (<1%)	7 (<1%)
Warning	93 (4%)	102 (6%)	6 (<1%)
Undertaking	28 (1%)	41 (3%)	46 (3%)
No Further action	1,270 (57%)	963 (59%)	812 (58%)
Total	**2,234**	**1,638**	**1,405**

It is very clear that there is a substantial whittling down at each state of the fitness to practise process, with only a relatively small number of cases getting to a hearing, as would be expected. Of those that do reach a hearing the outcomes remain fairly consistent from year to year, see Table 10.

Table 10 NMC Fitness to Practise Panel decisions 2017–20

Panel decision	2017/2018	2018/2019	2019/2020
Strike off	257 (21%)	162 (25%)	127 (28%)
Suspension	372 (31%)	231 (35%)	142 (32%)
Conditions imposed	165 (14%)	99 (15%)	69 (15%)
Caution	129 (11%)	57 (8%)	42 (9%)
Fitness to practise impaired – no sanction	0 (0%)	0 (0%)	0 (0%)
Subtotal	**923 (77%)**	**549 (83%)**	**380 (84%)**
Facts not proved	5 (<1%)	17 (3%)	5 (1%)
Fitness to practise not impaired	279 (23%)	95 (14%)	67 (15%)
Total	**1,207 (100%)**	**661 (100%)**	**452 (100%)**

The median time it takes from receipt of a concern to conclusion of a final hearing was 90 weeks in 2020.[80] This had been increasing for the last three years. It is right that a process that can deprive a registrant of their livelihood is thorough and comprehensive, but a gap of almost two years reduces the potential for system-wide learning. The time taken to close a case has been raised by the PSA in their annual reviews of the NMC and in 2020 they failed to reach standard 15,[81] which has contributed to the scores shown in Chart 1 PSA fitness to practise performance review scores 2015–20.

G. The Healthcare Professionals Council (HCPC)

The HCPC (known as the Health Professions Council between 2002–12) is the most recent of these three professional regulators, having been set up in 2002.[82] It replaced the Health Professionals Council, a statutory council[83] which had been set up in 1960, prior to this there had been some voluntary committees for specific professions that acted as quasi-regulators, such as the Board of Registration of Medical Auxiliaries which had been set up in 1937. The Health Professionals Council was the first multi-professional regulator, it regulated chiropodists/podiatrists; clinical scientists; dietitians; medical laboratory scientific officers (MLSOs); paramedics; physiotherapists; radiographers; speech therapists and others. The conduct provisions were accusatorial with both the council's solicitor and the registrant.

The HCPC remains the only multi-professional regulator currently regulating 15 professions: arts therapists; biomedical scientists; chiropodists/podiatrists; clinical scientists; dietitians; hearing aid dispensers; occupational therapists; operating department practitioners; orthoptists; paramedics; physiotherapists; practitioner psychologists; prosthetists/orthotists; radiographers; and speech and language therapists.[84]

i. Current HCPC Fitness to Practise Procedures[85]

Enquiries received by HCPC are triaged to see if they are within HCPC's remit; do they relate to the fitness to practise of an HCPC registrant? Cases which are not related to an HCPC registrant or which do not relate to a potential fitness to practise issue are closed after triage. HCPC has four standards frameworks; the two which are relevant to fitness to practise investigations are standards of conduct, performance and ethics and standards of proficiency.

---

[80] PSA, *Performance Review 2019/20 Nursing and Midwifery Council* available at www.professionalstandards.org.uk/docs/default-source/publications/performance-review---nmc-2019-20.pdf?sfvrsn=cbc4920_0.

[81] Standard 15: The regulator's process for examining and investigating cases is fair, proportionate, deals with cases as quickly as is consistent with a fair resolution of the case and ensures that appropriate evidence is available to support decision-makers to reach a fair decision that protects the public at each stage of the process.

[82] These are contained in the Health Professions Order 2001 SI2002/254 available at www.legislation.gov.uk/uksi/2002/254/contents/made as amended.

[83] Professions Supplementary to Medicine Act 1960 c 66 (Reg 8 & 9 Eliz 2) available at www.legislation.gov.uk/ukpga/Eliz2/8-9/66/contents.

[84] HCPC regulated social workers in England between August 2012 and December 2019.

[85] The Consolidated Fitness to Practise Rules (1) Health and Care Professions Council (Practice Committees and Miscellaneous Amendments) Rules 2009; (2) Health and Care Professions Council (Investigating Committee) (Procedure) Rules 2003; (3) Health and Care Professions Council (Conduct and Competence Committee) (Procedure) Rules 2003; (4) Health and Care Professions Council (Health Committee) (Procedure) Rules 2003.

Cases that have been triaged are then sent to one of two pathways. Serious cases are referred straight to the Investigating Committee. HCPC can seek an interim order at any stage of any investigation, but interim orders are most likely to be sought in serious cases. Interim orders are sought if the allegations made raise concerns that there is a risk to public safety, the public interest or to the registrant themselves if that registrant is allowed to continue to practise. The majority of cases that are still open after triage progress to an initial investigation overseen by a case manager.[86] At the end of the screening investigation cases are assessed to see if they meet the thresholds criteria for a fitness to practise investigation – does the information HCPC have amount to an allegation that the registrant's fitness to practise might be impaired? The decision is an assessment of whether the matter could comprise a breach of HCPC's standards.[87] Concerns which meet the threshold are referred to the Investigating Committee, (run by the Health and Care Professionals Tribunal Service (HCPTS)), cases that do not meet this threshold are closed.

a. The HCPTS[88]

The HCPTS is an operationally separate arms-length part of the HCPC with responsibility for delivering the fitness to practise hearings.[89] It operates three committees, the Investigating Committee and the Health Committee and the Conduct and Competence Committee.

The Tribunal Advisory Council assists the smooth running of the HCPTS. It is a non-statutory committee of the HCPC. It consists of six members, three Tribunal Panel Chairs and three independent members. It is accountable to the HCPC. Its role is to advise the Council on the recruitment, training and assessment of Tribunal panellists, panel chairs and legal advisors, including issuing Practice Notes.

If a case is submitted to the Investigating Committee the registrant must be given at least 28 days' notice of the Investigating Committee Panel meeting. The Investigating Committee is a three-person panel that meets in private. It comprises a Chair, an individual from the same profession as the registrant whose case is being considered and a lay person. The purpose of the committee is not to determine the facts of the case but to decide whether there is a realistic prospect of proving the allegation at a final hearing. Potential outcomes from the Investigating Committee are:

– to adjourn the case while further information is obtained and/or the allegations are amended;

– undertake mediation itself or refer the case back to the screeners for mediation with a view to resolving the case without taking it to the Health Care Professionals Tribunal Service (HCPTS);

– that there is no case to answer and the case should be closed;

---

[86] Sections 22, 23 and 24 of the Health Professions Order 2001, as amended.
[87] A breach of the standards does not in itself establish that fitness to practise is impaired, but may be taken into account in any proceedings, see s 4(1) of the Health Professions Order 2001.
[88] www.hcpts-uk.org/.
[89] The operation and composition of the HCPTS are set out in part V of the Health Professions Order 2001.

– that there is a case to answer and the case should go to a final hearing at the Health Care Professionals Tribunal Service (HCPTS).

When making their decision the Investigating Committee can take into account any similar concerns raised about the registrant in the previous three years.

If they decide there is a realistic prospect of proving the allegation the Investigating Committee will refer the case to the to either the Conduct and Competence Committee or the Health Committee depending on the nature of the allegation.

If the Investigating Committee decides there is no case to answer they must make a declaration to that effect if the individual they investigated requests it, in all other cases they may make such a declaration with the consent of the investigated individual.

Cases referred by the Investigating Committee are considered by a three person tribunal. At least one of the tribunal must be a registrant panel member from the same profession as the registrant concerned and at least one must be a lay member. The tribunal chair leads the hearing. The HCPTS has a pool of 300 tribunal members. Tribunals are sometimes supported by legal assessors, who advise them on points of law and drafting of decisions, but do not take part in the decision-making.

HCPC's Presenting Officer will attend the pre-hearing case management and the hearing to present the HCPC's case.

After the referral by the Investigation Committee what follows is a straightforward legalistic case management process.[90] Case management depends on the estimated length and complexity of the hearing; it may be a direct listing or it may involve a listings teleconference(s) and/or pre-hearing meeting(s) where key deadlines for the disclosure of evidence will be set and any outstanding issues can be resolved.

Hearings comprise of three stages:-

- Facts stage – this is a determination by the HCPTS that the facts are proved. This can be achieved either by the registrant admitting to the facts or if the facts are contested then the HCPC set out their allegations in examination in chief, the registrant presents their evidence in response in cross-examination, there is a re-examination by HCPC followed by Tribunal panel questions.

- Grounds stage – the HCPC will allege the facts amount to misconduct/lack of competence/impaired health/a conviction. The HCPC Presenting Officer will refer to the Standard which is alleged to have been breached.

- Impairment stage – this stage focuses on whether the registrant's fitness to practise is impaired. This looks at insight shown, conduct since the event, remedial actions, recurrence risk and individual competence. There is also consideration of the need to protect service users, to declare and uphold proper standards of behaviour and to maintain public confidence in the professions. Both parties can make submissions.

---

[90] See www.hcpts-uk.org/globalassets/hcpts-site/publications/practice-notes/hcpts-practice-notes---consolidated.pdf.

- Determination – the Tribunal then decides in camera if each step has been proved (facts, grounds and impairment) after receiving legal advice from a legal assessor. This is usually done as a single process at this point in the hearing, but each step can be determined separately in complex cases. If they find fitness to practise is impaired the case progresses to the sanctions stage. If the panel finds fitness to practise is not impaired that is the end of the case. If the panel decides there is no case to answer they must make a declaration to that effect if the individual they investigated requests it, in all other cases they may make such a declaration with the consent of the individual concerned.

- Sanctions stage – this stage focuses on whether the HCPTS should impose a sanction on the registrant. Both parties can make submissions. The Tribunal panel will have regard to the HCPC Sanctions policy[91] which sets out indicative sanctions. The HCPTS may decide that no sanction is appropriate. If the MPTS decide to impose sanctions these can be a caution (this appears on the register, but does not restrict a registrant's ability to practise) conditions, suspension or erasure. Ordinarily any sanction cannot take place until 28 days after notice is deemed served on the registrant. In cases where the HCPC Presenting officer determines that sanctions should be imposed immediately they will make submissions for an interim order, which take effect immediately. The Presenting officer will provide submissions as to why they thing these sanctions should be applied immediately and the registrant responds. The HCPTS then makes a determination on this point in camera.

The outcomes from an MPTS are:

- taking no further action
- issuing a caution to the registrant (maximum of five years)
- voluntary removal from the register in some circumstances
- placing conditions on the registrant's practice (for a maximum of three years)
- suspending the registrant's registration (for a maximum of one year)
- erasing the registrant's name from the relevant register so they can no longer practise.

There is a right of appeal within 28 days of the MPTS decision or notification of the decision to the High Court in England and Wales, the Court of Session in Scotland or the High Court of Justice in Northern Ireland.

Where a Tribunal panel has imposed either conditions or a suspension the order must be reviewed by a panel before it expires.[92] This is done at a substantive review hearing, a more limited hearing where the panel can change the sanction for a different type of sanction, extend the existing sanction or decide the condition or suspension is no longer necessary.

---

[91] www.hcpts-uk.org/legislation/panellegislation/sanctions-policy/.
[92] Article 30 The Health Professions Order 2001.

ii. HCPC Statistics[93]

Table 11 Fitness to practise concerns raised with the HCPC 2012–19

Year	2012/13	2013/14	2014/15	2015/16	2016/17	2017/18	2018/19
Registrants on HCPC's registers	310,942	322,021	330,887	341,745	350,330	361,061	369,139
Enquiries from members of the public	–	–	–	910 (43%)	924 (41%)	983 (42%)	1,139 (47%)
Total enquiries	**1,653**	**2,069**	**2,170**	**2,127**	**2,259**	**2,302**	**2,424**

As Table 11 shows a large proportion of the concerns raised are raised by members of the public, they make up the largest group of complainants. In 2018/19 the next largest group raising concerns was employers who raised 24 per cent of concerns, with 18 per cent of concerns being self-referrals, 4 per cent being referred by another professional, 3 per cent anonymous/article 22(6),[94] 2 per cent other and 1 per cent each from the police and professional bodies. The proportion of concerns raised by patients/member of the public concerns has been fairly consistent for a number of years; these were 47 per cent the concerns in 2018/19, 42 per cent in 2017/18, and 41 per cent 2016/17.

The percentage of cases because they do not meet the threshold for investigation is high, but not necessarily consistent from year to year. In 2018/19 74 per cent of referrals were closed after the initial assessment, the rates have been quite variable over the preceding years (in 2017/18 it was 54 per cent of referrals, in 2016/17 it was 82 per cent), making it difficult to draw conclusions.

The use of interim orders tribunals remains fairly low, see Table 12. These can be used at any part of the HCPC investigation process or at the end of a tribunal decision.

Table 12 HCPC interim orders 2014–20

	2014/15	2015/16	2016/17	2017/18	2018/19	2019/20
Total Interim Orders	265	337	346	466	505	493

The investigation outcomes for cases that reach the investigation committee have varied slightly, see Table 13. The percentage of cases that are closed has remained fairly consistent between 2015 and 2019. The percentage of referrals to the MPTS has increased year on year, having more than doubled between 2019 and 2015. By contrast the proportion of cases where the outcome from the case examine stage is advice has dropped over the same time period.

---

[93] HCPC Annual Fitness to Practise Statistics, available at www.hcpc-uk.org/about-us/insights-and-data/ftp/.

[94] Article 22(6) of The Health Professions Order 2001 allows HCPC to investigate a matter which has not been raised in the normal way.

Table 13 HCPTS Investigating Committee Panel decisions 2015–19

Investigating Committee Panel decision	2015/16	2016/17	2017/18	2018/19
Refer to tribunal	496	443	375	347
	(63%)	(68%)	(70%)	(56%)
Further information needed	48	27	59	65
	(6%)	(4%)	(11%)	(10%)
No case to answer	243	183	100	20
	(31%)	(28%)	(19%)	(34%)
Total	**787**	**653**	**534**	**621**
	(100%)	**(100%)**	**(100%)**	**(100%)**

It is very clear that there is a substantial whittling down at each stage of the fitness to practise process, with only a relatively small number of cases getting to an HCPTS hearing, as would be expected, see Table 13. Of those that do reach a Conduct and Competence Committee Panel hearing the outcomes remain fairly consistent from year to year, see Table 14.

Table 14 HCPTS Conduct and Competence Committee Panel decisions 2015–19

Conduct & Competence Committee	2015/16	2016/17	2017/18	2018/19
Caution	33	39	53	36
	11%	9%	13%	11%
Conditions imposed	38	39	48	31
	13%	9%	12%	9%
No further action	5	8	13	7
	2%	2%	3%	2%
Not well founded/ discontinued	82	115	88	106
	27%	27%	21%	31%
Struck off	69	92	91	70
	23%	21%	22%	21%
Suspension	53	110	87	80
	18%	25%	21%	23%
Voluntary removal	20	26	34	11
	7%	6%	8%	3%
Well founded	0	3	0	0
	0%	1%	0%	0%
Total	**300**	**432**	**414**	**341**
	100%	**100%**	**100%**	**100%**

As just a handful of cases come before the Health Committee Panel it is difficult to draw any conclusions on trends in sanctions, see Table 15.

Table 15 HCPTS Health Committee Panel decisions 2015–19

Health Committee	2015/16	2016/17	2017/18	2018/19
Caution	0	0	0	0
	0%	0%	0%	0%
Conditions imposed	4	1	3	2
	22%	8%	18%	18%
No further action	0	0	0	0
	0%	0%	0%	0%
Not well founded/ discontinued	2	2	5	4
	11%	15%	29%	36%
Struck off	0	0	0	0
	0%	0%	0%	0%
Suspension	7	5	8	2
	39%	0%	47%	18%
Voluntary removal	5	5	1	3
	28%	38%	6%	27%
Well founded	0	0	0	0
	0%	0%	0%	0%
Total	**18**	**13**	**17**	**11**
	100%	**62%**	**100%**	**100%**

The time it takes from receipt of a concern to conclusion of a final hearing was 25 months in 2018/19. This has been consistent for the last three years. It is right that a process that can deprive a registrant of their livelihood is thorough and comprehensive, but a gap of over two years reduces the potential for system-wide learning. The time taken to close a case has been raised by PSA in their annual reviews of HCPC who have consistently failed to meet PSA's standard 15,[95] and has contributed to the scores shown in Chart 1 PSA fitness to practise performance review scores 2015–20.

III. Conclusions on Complaints to Regulators

These figures clearly show that there is a willingness to raise concerns to healthcare regulators, but that these concerns may not be considered appropriate by the regulator. As the professional regulators have long known, a large proportion of the concerns raised with

---

[95] Standard 15: The regulator's process for examining and investigating cases is fair, proportionate, deals with cases as quickly as is consistent with a fair resolution of the case and ensures that appropriate evidence is available to support decision-makers to reach a fair decision that protects the public at each stage of the process.

them are outside their remit. The GMC, for example, has commissioned reports into this and has extensive signposting on its website. This indicates there is a willingness to raise concerns by members of the public, but that the pathway for them to do so needs to be clearer.

The regulatory system is not straightforward, and the provision for dealing with complaints from members of the public is very variable. Each regulator has a slightly different process. What is consistent across all three of the regulators considered above is that the majority of concerns raised are not investigated. For concerns that are investigated, the process is slow and the final hearing is adversarial. For a member of the public intent on raising a concern, these systems could be perceived as deeply frustrating at best and entirely off-putting at worst. This does not prevent some people from raising concerns with professional regulators, though there is little research to indicate whether or not it inhibits other people from raising concerns.

The PSA have acknowledged that the current position is complex and fragmented. This chapter outlines the processes of three key regulators, but as the PSA point out

> In health and care professional regulation in the UK there are 13 regulators. Ten of these fall under our oversight. Seven have a UK-wide remit,5 three cover different parts of the UK.6 One social work regulator (for England) falls under our remit and the other three social care regulators, for Scotland, Wales and Northern Ireland do not.[96]

The Health and Care Act 2022 gives the Secretary of State substantial new powers in relation to professional regulators. The existing powers are the ability to create a regulator and to bring a profession into regulation. In addition, the proposed reforms amend section 60 of the Health Act 1999 to permit the Secretary of State to:

- abolish a health and care regulator
- remove a profession from regulation if regulation is not required for the protection of the public.

The PSA propose that a single regulator should be created, which they propose would remove boundaries and create a simpler more coherent proposition for all. While this sounds radical, the HCPC demonstrates that the multi-professional regulatory framework is viable in a UK context. The PSA advocate for a development of a 'common code' that would improve public understanding of what to expect from HCPs and when to report a concern to a regulator. The single regulator model would have the major advantage that when an incident involves members of a team from different professional disciplines these could be investigated together rather than by separate bodies. While this would clearly streamline the landscape and make it simpler for patients and the public to identify where and when to complain, it is likely to be heavily opposed by the existing regulators and it is uncertain whether there is the political appetite to take it forward. A more modest ambition would be to reduce the number of professional regulators. The powers given to the Secretary of State have the potential to entirely reshape the regulation of healthcare professionals and it will be interesting to see how they are used in the future.

---

[96] Professional Standards Authority, *Reshaping Regulation for Public Protection: Our View on the Implications of the Health and Care Bill for Professional Regulation for Health and Social Care* (October 2021) available at www.professionalstandards.org.uk/docs/default-source/publications/thoughtpaper/reshaping-regulation-for-public-protection.pdf?sfvrsn=94d74820_7.

PART III

Raising Standards

The systemic goals for the NHS are consistently to deliver safe and effective healthcare. No system can be risk-free. Mistakes will occur. The reality of human actions and systems is that a certain amount of unintended harm will always be caused. The overriding response to such harm should be to care for the individuals who have been harmed, and to ensure that relevant lessons are learned so that future risk is reduced and thus performance is improved and medical and social support is delivered to the best standard that society can achieve.

In relation to the improvement of performance, what is required are systems that swiftly collect all relevant information, expertly monitor and evaluate the information, feedback relevant learning, apply relevant changes to practice, behaviour and systems and continue to monitor changes to see if further changes are needed. The achievement of these goals requires attention both to operational systems and to the individual behaviour of all individuals working in or interacting with those systems. The need to affect the personal behaviour of individuals arises especially in relation to the first stage of sharing information (raising concerns) and the later stage of changing behaviour and practice (raising standards).

Parts I and II of this book have examined the NHS and the means for raising concerns about the NHS respectively. This Part identifies core objectives in relation to NHS concerns. It contextualises the role of raising concerns about the NHS in the wider ambit of raising concerns more generally and proposes policies which have the dual objective of improving the experiences of those who suffer harm and driving improvements in the NHS.

13

Raising Concerns and Raising Standards

I. The Rationale: Delivering Care and Improving Performance

Life involves risk. Providing healthcare certainly involves risk, and unintended harm occurs. Many studies have documented the realities of uncertainty in clinical practice.[1] Every doctor who has practised medicine has made mistakes. Most have at some time made major mistakes and precipitated the death of a patient. It is 'part of being a doctor', and it leaves one feeling uncomfortable.[2] The question, therefore, is how to support constant good practice, learning and improvement.

Some decades ago, the 'perfectibility' model assumed that training and punishment would eliminate all medical error.[3] The thinking aligned with the focus of tort liability law in concentrating on the actions of a particular individual: it was too complicated for liability law to award compensation based on failures in a system. It was only more recently that independent inquiries, outside the formal legal system, have been able to highlight systemic and cultural issues as causative of harm. That wider approach mirrors changes in general regulatory practice, which has moved to look at culture and systemic issues. Similarly, Leape noted that reliance on inspection as a mechanism of quality control was discredited long ago in industry.[4] An emphasis on the incompetent doctor shifts the emphasis away from the more fundamental questions posed by Vincent and Reason about systemic approaches to mishaps.[5]

---

[1] R Fox, 'Training for Uncertainty' in R Merton, G Reader and P Kendall (eds), *The Student Physician: Introductory Studies in the Sociology of Medical Education* (Harvard University Press, 1957); E Friedson, *Professional Dominance* (Atherton Press, 1970); C Bosk, *Forgive and Remember: Managing Medical Failure* (University of Chicago Press, 1979); RE Anderson, RB Hill and CR Key, 'The Sensitivity and Specificity of Clinical Diagnostics During Five Decades' (1989) 261(11) *Journal of the American Medical Association* 1610; WB Barendregt, HH de Boer and K Kubat, 'Autopsy Analysis in Surgical Patients: A Basis for Clinical Audit' (1992) 79(12) *British Journal of Surgery* 1297; M Rosenthal, *The Incompetent Doctor: Behind Closed Doors* (Open University Press, 1995).

[2] R Smith, 'Foreword' in MM Rosenthal, L Mulcahy and S Lloyd-Bostock (eds), *Medical Mishaps. Pieces of the Puzzle* (Open University Press, 1999) xviii.

[3] LL Leape, 'Error in Medicine' (1994) 272(23) *Journal of the American Medical Association* 851.

[4] ibid; citing DM Berwick, 'EM Codman and the Rhetoric of Battle: A Commentary' (1989) 320 *Milbank Quarterly* 262; WE Deming, *Quality, Productivity and Competitive Position* (MIT Press, 1982).

[5] L Mulcahy and MM Rosenthal, 'Beyond Blaming and Perfection: A Multi-dimensional Approach to Medical Mishaps' in MM Rosenthal, L Mulcahy and S Lloyd-Bostock (eds), *Medical Mishaps. Pieces of the Puzzle* (Open University Press, 1999) 8.

Medical negligence based on fault and the litigation mechanism are central to our current compensation system. The problems outlined in Part II indicate it is time to take a fresh objective systemic view of the issues and the evidence, and their implications for systems and culture. We have a crisis in the cost of clinical negligence, and a succession of major scandals resulting in costly inquiries. There are clear examples of the inadequacy of the complaints system, with a rising tide of dissatisfaction at the unresponsiveness of the system. Blame as a means of improvement has not delivered. Rather than automatically assuming that the answer can be found in tinkering with existing structures, our research indicates it is time to take a fresh look for more effective solutions which can be applied systemically.

Any organisation that delivers services and products to people should have two basic objectives. One is *to perform well* – to do its job well in delivering safe and effective services and products, constantly improving its performance – and the second is *to care* for those who are recipients of its work, whether patients/customers, staff or relevant third parties. There is no difference in these basic objectives between a private commercial organisation and a public organisation, and no difference based on the type of services or products involved.

Delivering these two objectives requires the operation of a system that is based on a constant cycle of setting and monitoring standards of performance and outcomes, identifying where things are doing right and wrong, identifying the root causes of where things have gone wrong, identifying the root causes of inadequate performance as well as where things could be done differently, including through innovation, applying the relevant knowledge and learning so as to improve performance and reduce risk, delivering extra care to those who have been harmed, and continuing to monitor things to see if further steps are necessary. This model can be represented simply, as in Figure 1, as a continuous circle of functions. It is based on quality systems that have been applied in industry for many years, and is now the core model in approaches to regulatory systems.[6] The core objective is not to identify breaches of rules, or non-compliances, although such information may be useful, but to constantly strive to improve performance. Any level of performance, whether less than average or outstanding, can always be improved, and this state of constant learning and improvement is the essential purpose of the system in monitoring the delivery of each individual parcel of care, service or product.

It will be seen that the core functions involve both prospective and retrospective elements. Looking backward is necessary to identify what has happened, so as to be able to apply the knowledge to future activities and to reduce risk. Delivering appropriate responses to those who have suffered harm also involves an honest response to past events, so as to provide care for those harmed now and in the future.

---

[6] Versions of this model have been quoted with approval by the Irish Law Reform Commission and the Australian Law Reform Commission: *Report on Regulatory Powers and Corporate Offences. Volume 1: Regulatory Powers* (Law Reform Commission, 2018) 51. *Integrity, Fairness and Efficiency – An Inquiry into Class Action Proceedings and Third-Party Litigation Funders. Final Report* (Australian Law Reform Commission, 2018) para 8.30.

Figure 1 Performance improvement and problem solving model

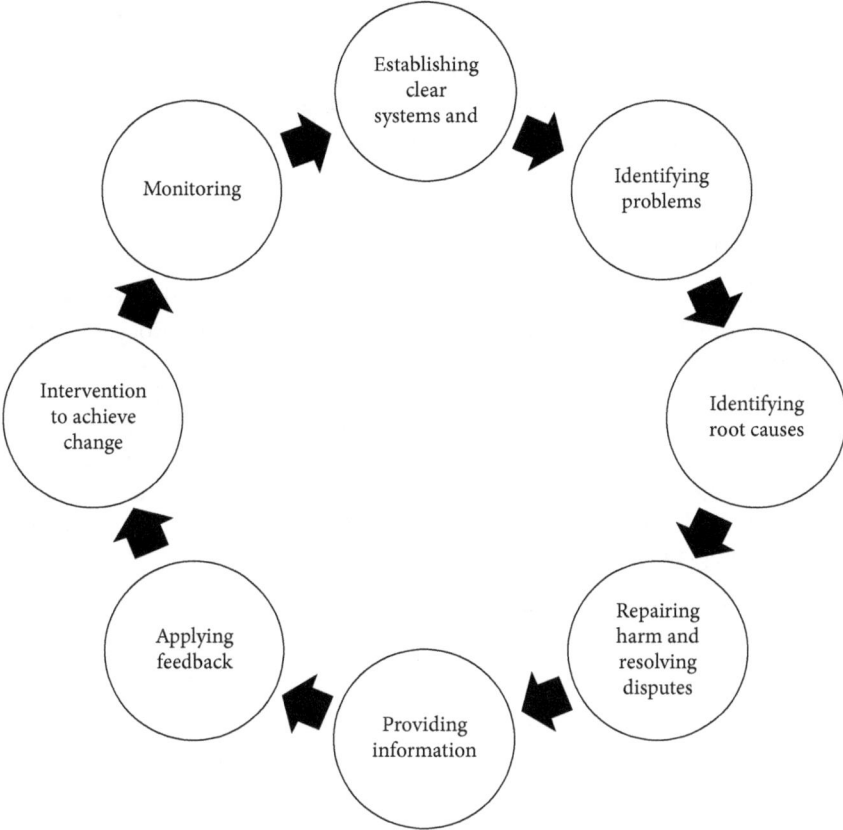

II. What Do People Want When They Raise Concerns?

In designing and evaluating a system, we should begin by defining and agreeing the core purposes, objectives and outcomes that the system is intended to deliver.[7] By definition, harming patients is not an intended or desired outcome of a healthcare system. The overriding goal is to make people better, and not worse. We start this analysis by reviewing highlights from the now considerable and consistent body of research that has accumulated especially since 1990[8] into what people want when they complain in general,[9] and specifically what patients and families want when they complain about healthcare services and the NHS.

---

[7] As prescribed in C Hodges, *Outcome-Based Cooperation in Communities, Organisations, Regulation and Dispute Resolution* (Hart, 2022).

[8] L Mulcahy and MM Rosenthal, 'Beyond Blaming and Perfection: A Multi-dimensional Approach to Medical Mishaps' in MM Rosenthal, L Mulcahy and S Lloyd-Bostock (eds), *Medical Mishaps. Pieces of the Puzzle* (Open University Press, 1999) 4.

[9] See review at C Hodges, *Delivering Dispute Resolution* (Hart, 2019) ch 3.

We know that a substantial number of patients suffer iatrogenic injuries,[10] but relatively few of them subsequently raise a concern, and even fewer complain to regulators, litigate or go to an ombudsman. The evidence from Part II of this book indicates that there seems to be more concerns raised than are investigated by the ombudsmen, the professional regulators and as part of the litigation process. This section will identify key themes that harmed individuals have said they want their complaint or claim to achieve.

A. NHS Complaints

Lloyd-Bostock and Mulcahy published a review in 1994 of 342 hospital complaints entering the NHS formal complaints procedure under the Hospital Complaints Procedure Act 1985.[11] From the patient's perspective, they suggested that a unified system for reporting incidents, complaints and claims as concerns should alleviate the stress involved in expressing their dissatisfaction, and should also mean that patients receive an explanation and apology at a relatively early stage, together with an action plan aimed at avoiding similar mistakes in future. Their findings inspired them to propose a theoretical framework which conceptualised complaints quite broadly as a social process of calling the hospital to account. The motivations of complaints were:

- – Specific remedy for this complainant/patient   15.3%
- – Remedy for others/future   20.5%
- – Investigation/explanation   22.7%
- – Vague   28.8%
- – No statement   28.7%

In relation to NHS complaints, the PHSO commented in 2015: 'Often people complain to us because they don't want someone else to go through what they or their loved one went through …'[12] The PHSO confirmed the message in late 2015: 'People bring their unresolved complaints to us because they want an explanation, an apology and for the service to improve for others.'[13] The same conclusion was stated by the Public Accounts Committee in December 2017: 'There is a growing body of evidence that when things go wrong many people simply want an apology, or want to know that the issue is being dealt with and it won't happen again.'[14]

It is striking that consumers rank complaints against their GPs as one of the most frequent issues: in the two years to mid-2016 complaints to the PHSO were most numerous

---

[10] T Brennan, L Leape, N Laird et al, 'Incidence of Adverse Events and Negligence in Hospitalised Patients: The Results from the Harvard Medical Practice Study I' (1991) 324 *New England Journal of Medicine* 370; L Leape, T Brennan, N Laird et al, 'Incidence of Adverse Events and Negligence in Hospitalised Patients: The Results from the Harvard Medical Practice Study II' (1991) 324 *New England Journal of Medicine* 377.

[11] S Lloyd-Bostock and L Mulcahy, 'The Social Psychology of Making and Responding to Hospital Complaints: An Account Model of Complaint Processes' (1994) 16 *Law and Policy* 123.

[12] J Mellor, *Report on Selected Summaries of Investigations by the Parliamentary and Health Service Ombudsman. October to November 2014* (Parliamentary and Health Service Ombudsman, 17 June 2015).

[13] *RESOLVE News from the Ombudsman Service* (PHSO, December 2015).

[14] House of Commons, Committee of Public Accounts, *Managing the Costs of Clinical Negligence in Hospital Trusts* Fifth Report of Session 2017–19, HC 397, 1 December 2017, para 5.

for GP services (37 per cent), local authorities (29 per cent), hospitals (28 per cent), HMRC (20 per cent), another government department (14 per cent): see Figure 2.[15]

Figure 2 Services people have had a poor experience with in the two years to mid-2016

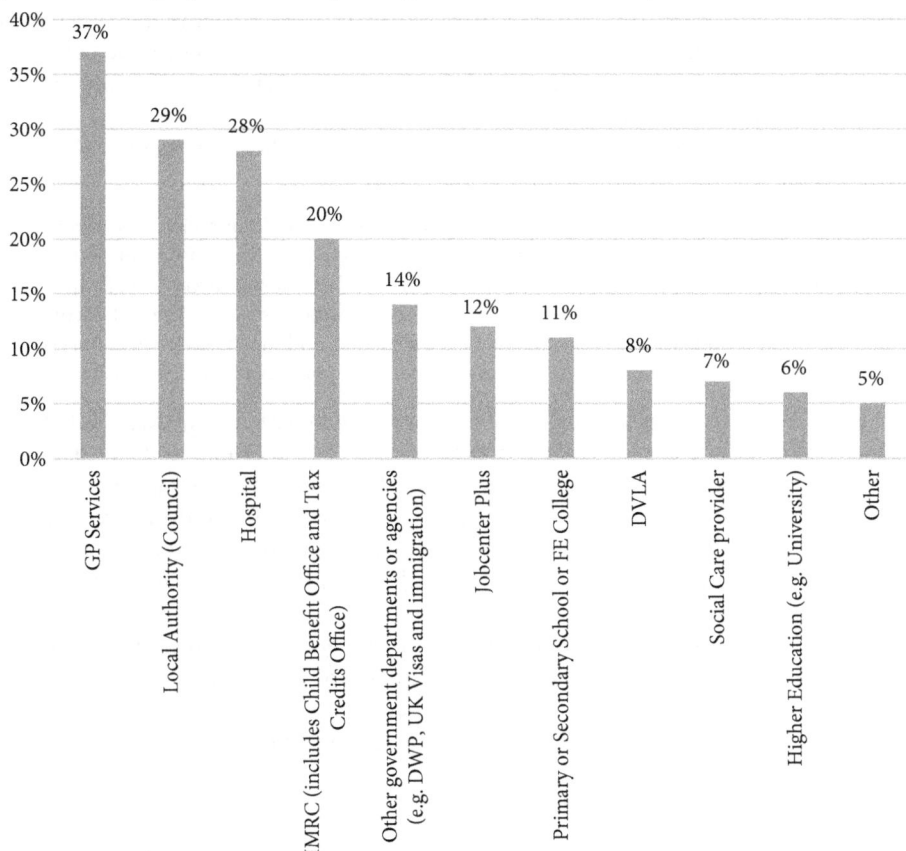

B. NHS Clinical Negligence Claims

A 1994 study surveyed 227 patients and relatives who were taking legal action through five firms of plaintiff medical negligence solicitors.[16] Over 70 per cent of respondents were seriously affected by incidents that gave rise to litigation with long-term effects on work, social life and family relationships. Intense emotions were aroused and continued to be felt for a long time. The decision to take legal action was determined not only by

---

[15] *Learning from Mistakes: How Complaints Can Drive Improvements to Public Services* (Citizens Advice, 2016) Figure 2.

[16] C Vincent, M Young and A Phillips, 'Why Do People Sue Doctors? A Study of Patients and Relatives Taking Legal Action' (1994) 343 *The Lancet* 1609.

the original injury, but also by insensitive handling and poor communication after the original incident. Where explanations were given, less than 15 per cent were considered satisfactory. Four main themes emerged from the analysis of reasons for litigation: concern with standards of care – both patients and relatives wanted to prevent similar incidents in the future; the need for an explanation – to know how the injury happened and why; compensation – for actual losses, pain and suffering or to provide care in the future for an injured person; and accountability – a belief that the staff or organisation should have to account for their actions.

The experience of the charity Action for Victims of Medical Accidents (AVMA) as at 1999 was that:

> … more than anything else, what concerned patients was the issue of information and accountability. They wanted to know what had happened and why it had happened; they wanted an assurance that a similar accident would not happen to other patients; and they wanted to know that whoever was responsible would be appropriate held to account. Many … were also clearly in need of compensation to restore some quality to a life which had been shattered, and that obviously was not an aspect that could be ignored, but it was rarely the thought that was uppermost in their minds.[17]

Studies around 2000 found 'a striking consensus'[18] over what patients say they want, namely compensation, an admission of fault, the prevention of future accidents and an explanation and apology.[19] Similarly, an American study of 2013 found that the 'principal gestures' that patients expect are: an apology, timely and honest communication and information flow; acknowledgement of the error and for responsibility to be taken; reassurance that the incident will not happen again and that the service seeks to improve as a result of the incident; and emotional support.[20]

A 2012 survey of 1,675 people into why they seek legal advice found that 'preventing something that had gone wrong from going wrong again' was a significant motivation.[21] The complete list of motivations for seeking legal advice, and percentages of respondents' motivations and objectives, noted in the survey are shown in Table 1.

Table 1 Motivation for seeking advice: Legal Services Board 2012 survey results

Motivation for seeking advice: I wanted to	What was your main objective for seeking advice to resolve problems?	What was your other objective for seeking advice to resolve problems (choose more than one)?
Obtain or preserve money or property	35.4%	10.9%
Put right something that had gone wrong	11.3%	18.0%

(continued)

[17] A Simanowitz, 'The Patient's Perspective' in MM Rosenthal, L Mulcahy and S Lloyd-Bostock (eds), *Medical Mishaps. Pieces of the Puzzle* (Open University Press, 1999) 228.

[18] L Fleck, 'NHS Redress Scheme for Severely Neurologically Impaired Babies' at the No-fault Compensation Scheme conference, Centre for Socio Legal Studies, University of Oxford, 16 March 2005.

[19] National Audit Office, Handling Clinical Negligence Claims in England: Report by the Comptroller and Auditor General, Session 2000–2001, HC 403, 3 May 2001; L Mulcahy, *Mediating Medical Negligence Claims: An Option for the Future* (The Stationery Office, 2000).

[20] R Iedema and D Piper, 'Do Patients Want and Expect Compensation Following Harm?' (2013) 116 *Precedent* 48.

[21] *Evaluation: How can we measure access to justice for individual consumers? A discussion paper* (Legal Services Board, 2012).

Table 1 *(Continued)*

Motivation for seeking advice: I wanted to	What was your main objective for seeking advice to resolve problems?	What was your other objective for seeking advice to resolve problems (choose more than one)?
Get compensation	10.6%	7.5%
Understand what had happened	9.6%	18.7%
Prove that I was right	7.8%	12.2%
Motivated by the sense of injustice	7.3%	15.5%
Prevent something that had gone wrong from going wrong again	7.0%	16.8%
Change the behaviour of a person	5.4%	7.6%
Clear my name	3.4%	6.4%
Obtain recognition of a mistake/receive an apology	2.1%	8.7%

The 2016 National Maternity Review was particularly clear about the adverse effects of litigation on creating a blame culture.[22]

The funding of clinical negligence claims has been examined in two surveys by the same lead author. The first in 2001 was survey of 8,206 people.[23] A 2013 survey[24] on funding clinical negligence had 19,746 participants and was administered by Ipsos MORI. This dual survey approach allowed for comparison between the 2001 and 2013 surveys. Key findings were as follows:

- In the 2001 survey 4.8 per cent of the sample believed that over the last three years they had suffered some illness, injury or impairment that in their opinion was caused by their medical treatment or care. This annual rate of 1.6 per cent is broadly consistent with Vincent et al's (2001) estimate that 10 per cent of hospital episodes involve some form of adverse event, and it provides an upper bound for the potential number of claims. Approximately 55 per cent of those reporting some event claimed that it was insignificant, emotional only or minor and temporary, 15 per cent reported a temporary major disability and almost 30 per cent claimed that the event had had a permanent impact on their health. A similar pattern of response was found with respect to impact on employment: of the 70 per cent of respondents who were in work at the time of the event, approximately 48 per cent stated that the impact was not relevant, non-existent or minor, 16 per cent reported having to take at least one month off work as a result of the

---

[22] *Better Births: Improving Outcomes of Maternity Services in England: A Five Year Forward View for Maternity Care* (National Maternity Review, 2016).

[23] P Fenn, A Gray and N Rickman, 'The Economics of Clinical Negligence Reform in England' (2004) 114 *The Economic Journal* 272.

[24] P Fenn, A Gray, N Rickman and D Vencappa, 'Funding Clinical Negligence Cases Access to Justice at Reasonable Cost? (Nuffield Foundation, 2016), available at www.nuffieldfoundation.org/sites/default/files/files/Funding_clinical_negligence_cases_Fenn_v_FINAL.pdf.

event and 35 per cent stated that they had had to take at least one year off work, retire or move to a less demanding job.

- The proportion of people who have experienced an adverse event and subsequently pursued a legal claim for damages was stable (10.5 per cent in 2001, 10.8 per cent in 2013).

- In 2001 respondents who considered that they had experienced an adverse event were then asked what remedy they considered to be most appropriate. The remedy most commonly considered appropriate was an apology or explanation (34 per cent), followed by an inquiry into the causes (23 per cent) or support in coping with the consequences (16 per cent). 11 per cent of respondents indicated that financial compensation would have been the most appropriate response.

- In line with this finding, only 11.4 per cent of respondents in 2001 and 10.7 per cent in 2013 stated that they had in fact pursued a legal claim for financial compensation. Those with more severe claims were more likely to have considered financial compensation. This is a remarkable figure as it suggests that just under 90 per cent of claimants are looking to clinical negligence to deliver a remedy it is simply not intended or equipped to deliver.

- The main reasons given for not pursuing a claim were that the respondent did not want financial compensation (36.7 per cent in 2001, 44 per cent in 2013) or that it had not occurred to them (19.5 per cent in 2001, 14.9 per cent in 2013). Some 6.8 per cent in 2001 and 7.8 per cent in 2013 were worried about time-consuming complexity and 2.3 per cent in 2001 and 1.6 per cent in 2013 were worried about cost. This has been interpreted as suggesting that the proportion of potential claimants seeking financial compensation could increase by 80 per cent–88 per cent ((2.3+6.8)/11.4 in 2001 (7.8+1.6)/10.7 in 2013) if the costliness and complexity of the process was significantly reduced. However, that assumption requires that the base level of advertising and other mechanisms to attract potential claimants into the compensation system remain the same.

- In 2001 the distribution of financial claims by income distribution was clearly bimodal, with higher proportions seeking financial compensation at lower and higher incomes. This evidence is consistent with the interpretation that, whereas patients in lower income bands are able to pursue compensation through legal aid, and those in upper income bands have the means to access costly legal services, middle income households are less able to obtain access. It also suggests a plausible limit to the propensity to make a legal claim in England: in the absence of significant cost pressures, some 18–20 per cent of those with injuries are prepared to pursue financial compensation.

- In the 2016 survey the distribution of financial claims by income distribution had altered substantially, with the highest proportion of those seeking compensation in the middle income quintile, and the poorest and second poorest quintiles having the lowest rates of claiming. The CFA model and removal of legal aid had clearly significantly impacted on claiming behaviours, the authors propose

A reasonable inference from these findings is that the legal aid 'means' test was working as intended during the earlier period – it was providing support to those sections of society who were unlikely to have recourse to other means in order to bring a claim of negligence. The corollary of this, however, is that the level of claiming amongst the middle income groups was relatively low, and the subsequent growth of CFA funding over the following decade may have gone some way to filling that gap.

A 2018 Study by the Behavioural Insights Team[25] was carried out on the motivations behind clinical negligence claiming behaviour of those who had already made a claim.

- A survey was sent to 10,000 past claimants, of whom half had received damages (awarded damages were for £100,000 or less). 516 people fully responded to the survey, another 212 submitted partial responses. Of those who responded 65 per cent had had their claim settled with financial compensation.

- There is not a clear trajectory from complaint to claim: in general 52 per cent of claims are made without a complaint attached, 10 per cent of claims have no complaint information recorded and 7 per cent are unclear. Among survey respondents 53 per cent had made a complaint, a further 28 per cent had made a complaint with some support and 19 per cent had not complained. Among the people who did not complain or complained with support 72 per cent were unaware of how to make an official complaint. This indicates that one third (33.8 per cent) of those who have successfully identified a path to litigation were unaware of how to raise an NHS complaint.

- Survey participants were asked to tick any of the reasons that might apply for making a claim. The results were: to prevent similar incidents happening again to others (87 per cent), to get an apology (80 per cent), to get a detailed investigation and explanation of the incident (79 per cent), to hold the clinician to account (77 per cent), frustration with the handling of the incident (76 per cent), to get financial compensation (41 per cent), financial support in coping with the future (35 per cent), and making a claim seemed a straightforward option (25 per cent). This is interesting as the motivations which matter to most people, eg future harm prevention and an apology, simply are not factors that litigation can deliver. Financial support, which litigation can deliver, comes much lower on the list. This supports the notion that people are using litigation to obtain outcomes that it is not intended or able to provide.

C. Healthcare Investigations

A 2011 study involved 100 semi-structured, in-depth interviews with 39 patients and 80 family members who were involved in high severity healthcare incidents (leading to death, permanent disability or long-term harm) and incident disclosure.[26] Most patients and family members felt that the health service incident disclosure rarely met their needs and expectations. They expected better preparation for incident disclosure, more shared dialogue about what went wrong, more follow-up support, input into when the time was ripe for closure and more information about subsequent improvement in process. The researchers concluded that there was a need for principles of effective incident disclosure: if clinicians and services are to meet patients' and relatives' expectations, all concerned should be properly prepared for the incident disclosure meeting(s) on the following basis:

- They investigate and agree on what went wrong and inform those harmed of the need for a discussion about the unexpected outcome.

---

[25] Behavioural Insights Team, *Behavioural Insights into Patient Motivation to Make a Claim for Clinical Negligence: Final Report by the Behavioural Insights Team* (August 2018).

[26] R Iedema, S Allen, K Britten et al, 'Patients' and Family Members' Views on How Clinicians Enact and How They Should Enact Open Disclosure: The "100 Patient Stories" Qualitative Study' (2011) 343 *British Medical Journal*, www.bmj.com/content/343/bmj.d4423.

- Clinicians point out that the disclosure discussion(s) will benefit from a patient support person being present, and from those harmed presenting their own account, views, and questions about what went wrong and what needs to happen.

- The disclosure discussion is performed as a two way, exploratory dialogue that produces an explanation that satisfies all stakeholders, bolstered by a sincere apology, a care plan redressing the patient's harm, a strategy for preventing the incident from recurring, and a clear outline of whether, why, and how other agencies (such as a neighbouring health service or hospital, the police, or the coroner) are involved.

- Closure becomes feasible when the patient and family members feel they have asked everything they wanted to ask, have received adequate answers to their questions, and are satisfied that their concerns have been taken seriously.

- To reassure them that incident disclosure links to practice improvement, they are informed about how the service has addressed the incident and what difference this has made or is making to care outcomes.

D. International Research

Considerable academic research has occurred in the United States on whether tort liability, and some examples of switches to 'no fault' schemes, affect safety practice and outcomes. A recent meta study continued the general trend by finding that that increased tort liability, at least in its current form, was not associated with improved quality of care.[27] A review by a leading legal American academic concluded that medical malpractice liability remains an inefficient way to transfer funds to injured patients.[28] Fear of litigation, damage to reputation and embarrassment have been found to be the main barriers to the practice of open disclosure.[29]

E. Conclusions on What People Want

The findings are consistent and clear. People expect healthcare systems to demonstrate qualities of openness, caring and improvement. They expect individual apologies and care. They show remarkable stoicism in relation to personal adversity, which they are prepared to cope with provided that lessons are learned and performance improves, so that the same thing does not happen to others. Hence, they expect that the individual professionals and the system within which they operate will demonstrate improvement in performance.

---

[27] Michelle M Mello, Michael D Frakes, Erik Blumenkranz and David M Studdert, 'Malpractice Liability and Health Care Quality: A Review' (2020) 323(4) *Journal of the American Medical Association* 352–66.

[28] W Kip Viscusi, 'Medical Malpractice Reform: What Works and What Doesn't' (2019) 96(4) *Denver Law Review* 775.

[29] TH Gallagher, AD Waterman, AG Ebers et al, 'Patients' and Physicians' Attitudes Regarding the Disclosure of Medical Errors' (2003) 289 *JAMA* 1001; D Studdert, D Piper and R Iedema, 'Legal Aspects of Open Disclosure II: Attitudes of Health Professionals – Findings from a National Survey' (2010) 193 *Med J Australia* 351.

F. Some Challenges in Delivering What People Want

Much of this book focuses on the mechanics of the complaint and disputes pathway(s), but it is salutary here to note some of the major barriers and impediments that people and the system face in delivering the objectives of learning and improvement.

A system that fails to demonstrate that it is capable of changing practice, improving performance and reducing risk, and that it actually achieves these outcomes in practice, will fail to attract the trust and confidence of its stakeholders. Such failures will also depress the motivation of people to assist by raising instances of problems. As a Complaints Survey carried out for Citizens Advice in 2015 said, over half (52 per cent) of respondents did not complain because they 'didn't think it would change anything'.[30]

There has been mounting recognition since Dame Hazel Genn's first *Paths to Justice* study that where problems are unresolved they can cascade, multiply and cluster,[31] making people's lives more stressful and making the problems more difficult for external services to unpick and resolve.

A legal system can essentially only respond through providing money, as a proxy for other elements, but it is fundamentally not capable of delivering improvements in performance and culture, especially by a complex system over time. While there are clear cases where compensation is necessary to ensure that an injured individual can obtain the physical care that they may need, it is striking that people rarely say that they want *money* as such. The theoretical analysis of the legal system has to rely on a model of restorative justice in paying adequate financial *compensation*, but the legal system cannot itself provide the other factors that are important to harmed individuals, such as an apology, full explanations or any kind of swift caring response.

In theory, ensuring that monitoring, learning and improvement occurs is the responsibility of institutions' and professional management and of independent regulation. But achieving these functions will be difficult where responsibilities are spread across multiple people, institutions and systems. It will be a considerable challenge to the success of those parts of the system that are responsible for addressing behaviour, culture and performance if other parts of the system operate so as to create significant barriers and impediments. This is precisely the case where the civil legal system is based on finding fault in an adversarial environment. That simple fact will form a major barrier to people sharing relevant information, both within the professional system, and between patients and professionals, as discussed below. The legal system will, in fact, drive all the wrong cultures and behaviours, seriously impeding learning, transparency and improved performance. As Dr Pelle Gustafson, the Medical Director of the Swedish Patient Compensation Scheme, has said, mistakes happen, and looking for scapegoats through a legal system for medical injuries based on fault is 'a very efficient way of killing more patients'.[32]

---

[30] *Learning from Mistakes: How Complaints Can Drive Improvements to Public Services* (Citizens Advice, 2016) 15. See also P Vaze, J Hinde and G Higginson, *Dealing with Dissatisfaction. Complaint Handling in Energy, Water, Telecoms, Royal Mail and Financial and Legal Services* (Consumer Focus, 2012); *Consumer Action Monitor* (Ombudsman Services, 2018).

[31] H Genn, *Paths to Justice: What People Do and Think About Going to Law* (Hart, 1999).

[32] S Macleod and C Hodges, *Redress Schemes for Personal Injuries* (Hart, 2017) 646.

III. The Core Objectives

We have identified five core objectives which marry the needs of harmed individuals and the needs of the NHS to drive improvements in performance, these are:

A.   caring for those how have been harmed (the caring objective);
B.   reporting concerns (the reporting objective);
C.   establishing what happened and how this differed from what should have happened (the investigation objective)
D.   demonstrating systemic and actual learning (the improvement objective); and
E.   financial efficiency (the financial objective).

These will be outlined in turn below.

A. Caring for Those Who Have Been Harmed (the Caring Objective)

The NHS's raison d'etre is to provide healthcare – providing care to those who have been harmed should be the most natural response of the NHS, too often it is not. The objective is to help individuals to recover, and not inadvertently to make them worse, physically or psychologically.

There are two main rationales for providing a caring response to harmed individuals. The first rationale is to maintain the social cohesion and solidarity of society by demonstrating support for those members of society who suffer harm through no fault of their own. The second rationale is to return those harmed to a state in which they can contribute as fully to society as they are able to. Both rationales, therefore, support the delivery of medical and social services in caring for and rehabilitating those who are harmed. In other words, the requirement is to provide for each individual a package of care and support aimed at recovery and, where required, assistance with coping with ongoing disability.

The care required for those who have been harmed is not just physical healthcare, but should encompass recovery in a broader sense and should address the emotional dimensions of the harm caused (including the desire for understanding of events and for a meaningful apology) and the need for rehabilitation. There is a fitting Dutch phrase that an injured person is 'overdrawn on his emotional bank account' which recognises that the rehabilitation needs are not restricted solely to the physical.

There is an emerging recognition that perceptions of injustice or unfairness in justice-related appraisals that take place after injury can inhibit recovery and result in worse outcomes.[33] This highlights the importance of ensuring that any process that appraises or judges the circumstances of the injury is perceived as fair and just.

---

[33] For a summary see A Akkermans, 'Achieving Justice in Personal Injury Compensation: The Need to Address the Emotional Dimension of Suffering a Wrong' in P Vines and A Akkermans, *Unexpected Consequences of Compensation Law* (Hart, 2020).

B. Reporting Concerns (the Reporting Objective)

It is impossible to learn from an incident you know nothing about. Increasing reporting of experiences is a stated goal for the NHS. For example, the objective of the common approach to handling complaints in hospitals and social care introduced in 2009 was to 'encourage a culture that seeks and then uses people's experiences to make services more effective, personal and safe'.[34] The problem here is to reduce the barriers to reporting and sharing information, as discussed below.

C. Establishing What Happened and Any Deviation from Good Practice (the Investigation Objective)

The literature is clear: individuals who have been harmed want to know what happened. Knowing what has happened to one and why is part of the process of coming to terms with adverse experiences, and healing. It also often transforms into wanting to be reassured that the same harm will not happen to others. There is an imbalance of knowledge and information which can make this very difficult. Although medical records are the patient's records, they are held by the healthcare provider, and are not always easy to access, as was seen in the Morecambe Bay scandal. Medical records require specialist knowledge to decipher the terminology and to interpret. This can make establishing what happened difficult for a harmed individual and often necessitates obtaining the views of an expert. If there is any disagreement on the actions taken (or not taken) this task is more complex. As events do not happen in isolation establishing what happened has to be appropriately contextualised; put simply it would be unreasonable to expect the same specialist diagnostic testing from a GP as would be expected from a specialist consultant with a particular interest in that condition and access to all the required types of tests.

Establishing the facts of what happened is necessary for holding service providers accountable to patients, but it is not sufficient. It is also necessary to establish whether the outcome that is a cause for concern resulted from a departure from good practice. At one end of the spectrum are acts which are so flagrantly wrong that no specialist or technical knowledge is needed to know this, for example the case of the surgeon Simon Bramhall who was convicted of assault for branding his initials into the livers of two transplant patients. The majority of concerns feature deviations which are more subtle. Additionally, there may be more than one view on what constitutes good practice, adding to the challenge.

There has been a clear emphasis on encouraging healthcare organisations to provide information, for example the requirements of the statutory duty of candour, the guidance in the NHS Constitution, and so on. Despite these efforts, it is clear that the requirements to provide patients with relevant information have not always been observed, leaving people looking for other ways to obtain this information, as outlined in Part II.

---

[34] *Listening, Responding, Improving: A Guide to Better Customer Care* (Department of Health, 2009) at http:// webarchive.nationalarchives.gov.uk/+/www.dh.gov.uk/en/publicationsandstatistics/publications/publicationspolicyandguidance/dh_095408. See also *A Promise to Learn – A Commitment to Act. Improving the Safety of Patients in England* (National Advisory Group on the Safety of Patients in England, 2013).

D. Demonstrating Systemic and Actual Learning (the Learning Objective)

It has been found above that people who suffer harm wish to see the healthcare system learn lessons from their predicament and ensure that the same fate is not suffered by others. If they are not convinced that the healthcare system is responsive to their concerns and that lessons have been learned and applied, they may seek alternative means to achieve this objective. For example, if individuals feel that learning does not seem to have happened, then a desire to hold the healthcare system 'accountable' (in the traditional sense) may be sought through the legal system despite the fact that the legal system does not perform behavioural or regulatory functions in delivering improvement in performance and the only remedy as such is the payment of damages.

The ability of the system to improve must be seen at the theoretical and actual levels, if the institutions, people and system are to be trusted. Thus, the system must demonstrably be capable of delivering learning and improvement. Developing policies and guidance is not sufficient, as the IMMDS Review report stated: 'Across all three of the interventions we have seen the impact of a failure to implement available information and guidance.' This was by no means unique, Mid-Staffs had a whistleblowing policy, but the day-to-day reality did not match what was written down in the policy.[35]

It is critical that the system must be shown to deliver actual learning and improvement, including in individual cases. This learning and improvement can take many forms. It could be something as simple as a practical change in one place, for example improving the signing in a hospital so patients can locate the PALS team. It could also be a sweeping system-wide reform, such as the statutory duty of candour. Where there is evidence that an individual practitioner's actions are such that they are not fit to practice, this could be removing them from the register.

E. Financial Efficiency (the Financial Objective)

It almost goes without saying, but as the NHS is taxpayer-funded the standard requirements that apply to all public spending must be adhered to.[36] Maximising financial efficiency is a clear priority at all levels of the NHS, the same provisions apply to other public agencies such as the PHSO and NHS Resolution, etc. While claimant lawyers are not taxpayer-funded in cases where the claimant succeeds their fees come from the public purse via NHS Resolution, who have long focused on reducing claimant costs as part of their core remit.

Of the other entities considered in Part II only the professional regulators are not subject to the same externally imposed financial efficiency framework as they are funded by member fees.

---

[35] Paragraph 2.381 of the *Report of the Mid Staffordshire NHS Foundation Trust Public Inquiry. February 2013 Chaired by Robert Francis QC*, HC947. available at www.gov.uk/government/publications/report-of-the-mid-staffordshire-nhs-foundation-trust-public-inquiry.

[36] www.gov.uk/government/publications/managing-public-money.

IV. The Just Culture Model

It is helpful to review systems other than healthcare to see how they do things. High-risk safety systems such as aviation and nuclear safety in fact provide deep learning on how to achieve constant improvement in performance. The aviation safety model, which has been widely cited as a model applicable to the NHS, is particularly relevant. It is also inspiring new approaches to all regulatory systems, including those aimed at economic, consumer protection or social goals, and not just at safety goals.[37]

We fully acknowledge that aviation is very different from healthcare. The essence of the aviation model – which is appropriately named Performance-Based Regulation (PBR) – involves the constant operation of the cycle set out in Figure 1 (albeit it is not usually necessary to invoke a function dealing with response to injury or death) so that all relevant information about deviations from norms and standards, and abnormal behaviour and outcomes, are captured immediately, are reviewed so that appropriate action can be taken to improve performance. PBR is a process-based approach that focuses on monitoring performance (quality assurance activities) to ensure that the system is capable of reliably producing an acceptable level of output.[38] PBR includes the documented, repeatable processes of a quality management system. It comprises four components: *safety policy, safety risk management, safety assurance* and *safety promotion*. It also involves the classic tasks of risk management: hazard identification, analysis of data and risk and risk reduction activity. There is significant reliance on checklists.[39] The primary objective of a performance-based system is to identify risks *before* they cause significant harm. As the Civil Aviation Authority has said, 'reacting after an incident or near miss is not the best way to prevent it happening again' and hence a system was needed to produce much more information and do so quickly, so that the real causes of risks can be identified and changes implemented to avoid them.[40] Further, information is needed from multiple sources, not least because different actors have differing viewpoints on what occurred and why, and it is necessary to take an holistic and objective overview in order to be able to address risk effectively.

The International Civil Aviation Organization (ICAO) has set out five principles of human performance that are fundamental in the approach:[41]

Principle 1: People's performance is shaped by their capabilities and limitations;

Principle 2: People interpret situations differently and perform in ways that make sense to them;

---

[37] See C Hodges, *Outcome-Based Cooperation In Communities, Business, Regulation and Dispute Resolution* (Hart, 2022); C Hodges and R Steinholtz, *Ethical Business Practice and Regulation* (Hart, 2017).

[38] AJ Stolzer, CD Halford and JJ Goglia, 'Introduction' in AJ Stolzer, CD Halford and JJ Goglia (eds), *Implementing Safety Management Systems in Aviation* (Ashgate, 2011) xlviii.

[39] A Gawande, *The Checklist Manifesto. How to Get Things Right* (Metropolitan Books of Henry Holt and Company LLC, 2009).

[40] *The Transformation to Performance-based Regulation* (Civil Aviation Authority, 2014) 1. D McCune, C Lewis and D Arendt, 'Safety Culture in Your Safety Management System' in AJ Stolzer, CD Halford and JJ Goglia (eds), *Implementing Safety Management Systems in Aviation* (Ashgate, 2011) 138; S Dekker, *Just Culture. Balancing Safety and Accountability* (Ashgate Publishing, 2007) ix; *Building a Culture of Candour: A Review of the Threshold for the Duty of Candour and of the Incentives for Care Organisations to be Candid* (Royal College of Surgeons of London, 2014).

[41] *Manual on Human Performance (HP) for Regulators* (International Civil Aviation Organization, 2021), Doc 10151, para 1.4.

Principle 3: People adapt to meet the demands of a complex and dynamic work environment;

Principle 4: People assess risks and make trade-offs; and

Principle 5: People's performance is influenced by working with other people, technology, and the environment.

ICAO goes on to specify that a national safety regulatory system should cover the following activities:[42]

- collecting and analysing data;
- developing regulatory material;
- evaluating, accepting and approving (eg, systems and equipment, procedures, personnel);
- providing ongoing surveillance; and
- promoting safety.

The critical ingredient in PBR is a *culture* that operates in every organisation involved in aviation, and applies to all staff, however insignificant their roles might be.[43] There are two elements to this culture: an *open culture* and a *just culture*. In an *open culture*, all information relevant to safety and performance is shared openly and immediately. There are no 'ifs or buts'. However, it is recognised that humans simply will not share information if they fear potential adverse consequences, whether personal criticism, official investigations, criminal action, employment disciplinary action, social censure, embarrassment or simply uncertainty over what will happen.[44] This was confirmed in a series of studies.[45] What is needed is a culture of psychological safety.[46]

Accordingly, a *just culture* must operate, so that there are always just consequences taken in response to relevant behaviour and information. The consequences are usually, however, not those of sanctions imposed by a traditional legal system, which are manifestations from an earlier era of attempts at controlling behaviour, and are now shown to impede learning. The essential point is to reduce future risk, so the primary consequences will be to adopt all relevant steps and changes to achieve that outcome. It is recognised that anyone may make a mistake, or act in a way that produced unintentional harm. The question is not usually 'Why did that person behave like that' (triggering a response 'He ought to be blamed and

---

[42] ibid, para 2.

[43] It is misleading to think that the culture only applies to pilots, who have 'skin in the game' as they may lose their lives. The same culture applies to air traffic controllers, the Civil Aviation Authority, design and engineering organisations, those who supply fuel and maintenance services, and so on. Relevant actions and providing relevant information involves *everyone* in the industry.

[44] S Dekker, *Just Culture. Restoring Trust and Accountability in Your Organization* 3rd edn (Ashgate Publishing, 2017); *Report on Legal and Cultural Issues in Relation to ATM Safety Occurrence Reporting in Europe: Outcome of a Survey Conducted by the Performance Review Unit in 2005–2006* (Eurocontrol Performance Review Commission, 2006).

[45] See especially the following: E Tarnow, 'Self Destructive Obedience in the Airplane Cockpit and the Concept of Obedience Optimization' in T Blass (ed), *Obedience to Authority: Current Perspectives on the Milgram Paradigm* (Erlbaum Associates, 2000); S Griffith, *American Airlines ASAP*. Paper presented at the Global Analysis and Information network (GAIN) Workshop (Cambridge, MA, 1996); M Tamuz, 'The Impact of Computer Surveillance on Air Safety Reporting' (1987) *Columbia Journal of World Business* 69; US FAA, Office of Aviation Safety, *Near Midair Collisions in the U.S.* (unpublished statistics, 1987); M Tamuz, 'Learning Disabilities for Regulators. The Perils of Organizational Learning in the Air Transportation Industry' (2001) 33(3) *Administration & Society* 276.

[46] AC Edmondson, *The Fearless Organization* (John Wiley & Sons, Inc., 2019).

sanctioned') but 'Why would any human have behaved like that' triggering the response 'How do we prevent that type of behaviour or consequence from occurring in future?' In a just culture, therefore, front line operators or others are not punished for actions, omissions or decisions taken by them that are commensurate with their experience and training, but where gross negligence, wilful violations and destructive acts are not tolerated. The culture draws a line between acceptable and unacceptable behaviour: it is not 'no blame'. 'A wilful violation is not acceptable. An honest mistake is.'[47] Standards of behaviour require professional competence, openness, sharing and taking responsibility for one's mistakes by correcting them and improving.[48] There is a long-stop legal protection, but one which is not punitive.[49]

A just culture must operate in *every* context across *all* organisations involved in a combined endeavour: public system regulation, professional regulation, employment discipline, legal liability for compensating harm and social and professional relationships. If there is a conflict in the approach between any of these groups, then the sharing and learning process will not work.

The model of an integrated operating, management and regulatory system that is based on open and just culture is an evolution in how the behaviour of others is controlled. It is based on extensive evidence from research into human psychology and behaviour, and into the relevance of ethical culture in organisations. It transcends earlier understandings that behaviour could be controlled by use of external authority and force, whether staff disciplinary measures, regulatory enforcement measures or civil sanctions. It leaves behind the theory that deterrence controls people's future actions in obeying laws.[50] It rests on enlisting actors' intrinsic motivation through supporting their competence, autonomy and relatedness,[51] coupled with emphasis on ethical behaviour and culture.[52] For some people, the ideas are counter-intuitive, yet they are based on extensive scientific evidence on how people behave and how behaviour can best be affected.

V. Open and Just Culture in the NHS

NHS leaders have realised that much was to be learned from the civil aviation industry's adoption of root cause analysis, human factors research and cognitive psychology. However, these scientific lessons have taken time to be understood and even longer to be applied. In

[47] S Dekker, *Just Culture* (Ashgate Publishing, 2007) 15.

[48] D McCune, C Lewis and D Arendt, 'Safety Culture in Your Safety Management System' in AJ Stolzer, CD Halford and JJ Goglia (eds), *Implementing Safety Management Systems in Aviation* (Ashgate, 2011) 195.

[49] Commission Regulation (EU) No 691/2010 of 29 July 2010 laying down a performance scheme for air navigation services and network functions and amending Regulation (EC) No 2096/2005 laying down common requirements for the provision of air navigation services, art 2(k).

[50] C Hodges, *Law and Corporate Behaviour* (Hart, 2015); Y Feldman, *The Law of Good People. Challenging States' Ability to Regulate Human Behavior* (Cambridge University Press, 2018); B van Rooij and A Fine, *The Behavioural Code. The Hidden Ways the Law Makes Us Better .... Or Worse* (Beacon Press, 2021).

[51] RM Ryan and EL Deci, *Self-Determination Theory. Basic Psychological Needs in Motivation, Development, and Wellness* (Guilford Press, 2017).

[52] A Tenbrunsel and K Smith-Crowe, 'Ethical Decision Making: Where We've Been and Where We're Going' (2008) 2(1) *Academy of Management Annals* 545–607.

the past decade, there have been growing references to the idea of adopting open and just culture in the NHS, emulating the aviation model. As noted in Part II, achieving an open and just culture was said by Secretary of State Jeremy Hunt to be an objective of the NHS. But it has only happened in limited pockets. As discussed below, the fact that embedded systemic impediments exist has not been recognised or tackled. Recently, the language has dropped the 'open and just culture' tag and adopted a 'just and learning' label. This partly reflects the continued unwillingness to de-emphasise the responsibility of individuals.

A *Just Culture Guide* was developed following Professor Sir Norman William's 2018 Report on gross negligence manslaughter in healthcare triggered by the Bawa-Garba Case.[53] The Report stated that it aimed

> to support a just and learning culture in healthcare, where professionals are able to raise concerns and reflect openly on their mistakes but where those who are responsible for providing unacceptable standards of care are held to account [which will] lead to improved patient safety.

The Report defined just culture as recognising systemic factors rather than just individual accountability: 'A just culture considers wider systemic issues where things go wrong, enabling professionals and those operating the system to learn without fear of retribution.'[54] It said:[55]

> … generally in a just culture inadvertent human error, freely admitted, is not normally subject to sanction to encourage reporting of safety issues. In a just culture investigators principally attempt to understand why failings occurred and how the system led to sub-optimal behaviours. However a just culture also holds people appropriately to account where there is evidence of gross negligence or deliberate acts.

In promulgating its NHS Complaint Standards in 2021, setting out how organisations providing NHS services should approach complaint handling, the PHSO published the following comments that adopted the language of a 'just and learning culture':[56]

> Promoting a just and learning culture

> An effective complaint handling system promotes a culture that is open and accountable when things do not go as they should. It creates an environment where staff feel supported and empowered to learn when things do not go as expected, rather than feeling blamed.

> It uses learning to improve its services and makes sure every member of staff knows their role in promoting a just and learning culture. It puts in place clear ways to demonstrate how the organisation uses learning to improve.

> • Senior staff make sure every member of staff knows how they can create and deliver a just and learning culture in their role. Staff can demonstrate how they meet these objectives through practical examples.

---

[53] *Gross Negligence Manslaughter in Healthcare. The Report of a Rapid Policy Review* (2018), at https://assets.publishing.service.gov.uk/government/uploads/system/uploads/attachment_data/file/717946/Williams_Report.pdf.

[54] ibid, paras 9.14 and 3.4.

[55] ibid, Glossary at p 59.

[56] *NHS Complaint Standards. Summary of Expectations* (PHSO, 2021), available at www.ombudsman.org.uk/organisations-we-investigate/nhs-complaint-standards/complaint-standards-nhs/promoting-just-and-learning-culture.

- Every organisation has appropriate governance structures in place to ensure that senior staff review information arising from complaints regularly, and are held accountable for making sure that the learning is acted on to improve services.
- Organisations make sure staff are trained to identify complaints in a way that meets the expectations set out in the Complaint Standards.
- Organisations have clear processes in place to show how they capture learning from complaints, and use it to improve services. In their annual report, organisations provide details of what learning they have identified in complaints and how they have used it to improve their services. This information is easy to compare with that of other organisations.
- Organisations put measures in place to capture feedback from those who make complaints (as well as the staff involved) on their experience. They use this to demonstrate how the organisation has performed towards meeting the Complaint Standards and what users expect to see, as set out in My Expectations.
- Staff are trained to identify those complaints where mistakes have been made that may have resulted in significant impact. Staff ensure these mistakes are reviewed through the organisation's Duty of Candour processes. Organisations routinely share learning from complaints with other organisations (both locally and nationally) to build on insight and best practice.

The PHSO commented in the NHS Complaints Standards document on the importance of a just and learning culture, and also on the difficulties in achieving this:

It is important that:

- organisations promote a just and learning culture, in which complaints are welcomed and handled well
- staff have the skills and experience they need to be confident in handling complaints
- people using NHS services know how to give feedback or make a complaint, can get support when they need it, and are confident their concerns are taken seriously and addressed
- people making complaints about NHS services get a consistent, positive experience each time
- staff being complained about are supported and involved throughout the process.

It can often be difficult for staff to achieve these aims because:

- many organisations do not actively promote a just and learning culture, failing to ensure complaints are welcomed and used as a valuable source of learning
- there is no single set of guidelines for managing complaints about NHS services
- staff cannot always get the right training and support to handle and resolve complaints
- managers and leaders approach learning from complaints in different ways
- people making complaints do not get a consistent, positive experience, and do not always feel that their concerns are taken seriously and addressed.

This can lead to a culture in which complaints are feared or ignored, rather than embraced. As a result, staff can feel unsupported in this important and complex area of work.

The continued debate over several years about the relevance of systemic and individual accountability, and the correct balance between those factors, in practice exposed healthcare staff to face a barrage of different systems with differing, and sometime conflicting, emphasis on individual and systemic accountability. This added an additional layer of complexity to an already crowded accountability landscape; Goodwin[57] describes it thus 'Although

---

[57] D Goodwin, 'Cultures of Caring: Healthcare "Scandals", Inquiries, and the Remaking of Accountabilities' (2018) 48(1) *Social Studies of Science* 101–24. doi: 10.1177/0306312717751051. Epub 2018 Jan 9. PMID: 29316861.

individualized forms of accountability are conventional, when individuals are held accountable for collective norms and practices, the outcome, rightly or wrongly, is resentment.' A major issue is that experts recognise the need for an open and just culture, and for the need to examine systemic and human factors, but politicians, the media and unsatisfied patients and their relatives react to problems by simply asking 'Who's to blame?' That approach has to be unlearned, by showing that it impedes improvement rather than assists it.

VI. Outcome Based Cooperation

There is a clear desire, and accompanying rhetoric, to develop an Open, Just and Learning Culture in the NHS. While there is typically, in such cultures, very little 'blame' or individual adverse sanctioning in practice, there is always accountability. This is accountability both for actions and for contributing to improvement, but it is very rarely punitive. A potential model which would allow the NHS to become the Open, Just and Learning Culture it wants to be is Outcome Based Cooperation. This model has been developed from the open and just culture model, coupled with extensive research into effective management and regulatory models. It provides a new general model of how human behaviour in organisations and regulatory systems can support the maximisation of trust and achievement of desired outcomes. The Outcome Based Cooperation (OBC) model has been applied in communities, commerce, regulation and dispute resolution.[58] One advantage of this approach is to support the same ethical behaviour in all contexts, by adopting an integrated approach in each of them.

The basic OBC model involves agreeing purposes, objectives and outcomes between all stakeholders, and supporting ethical cooperation through each actor producing relevant evidence that it is trustworthy. The evidence produced will indicate the strength of trust that an actor deserves, and the extent to which it achieves its agreed outcomes and increases in its performance in achieving them. Achieving undesired outcomes, and unacceptable responses to inadequate performance and to harm caused, will be negative evidence. The converse will be positive evidence. The system is based on involvement of all stakeholders in respectful engagement through transparent open processes. The evidence and outcomes will differentiate between those who deserve trust and those who do not, such as those who intend to cause harm or are indifferent to that outcome. Protection of society from harm justifies taking firm action against people or organisations in the latter category.

The OBC model is particularly effective where it is adopted holistically by all organisations in a sector. This drives consistent ethical behaviour and production of consistent evidence of trustworthiness.

VII. Barriers to an Open and Just Culture

We have identified three key areas where reforms are necessary to allow the development of an open and just culture in the NHS.

---

[58] C Hodges, *Outcome-Based Cooperation in Communities, Business, Regulation and Dispute Resolution* (Hart, 2022).

- Improving operational culture
- Reducing barriers to reporting concerns
- Removing the blame culture

A. Improving Operational Culture

Poor operational culture is referred to time and again in the succession of Inquiry Reports noted in Part II. There has been frequent recognition of the point well-established by academic research into organisations that openness in the NHS is constrained by fear. One of many official references, for example, said:[59]

> To expect a doctor to admit that he or she has made a mistake is dependent on the NHS operating a culture in which it is accepted that the very best of doctors will on occasions make mistakes. It also requires other doctors and managers to provide support, to talk about the matter openly and to help doctors avoid any repetition. Without such a culture, doctors may try to hide mistakes and act defensively, even attempting to blame others, rather than look into why the error occurred in the first place and learn how to prevent it happening again.

A considerable number of the processes outlined in Part II of this book, notably professional regulation and litigation, focus heavily on the role of the individual in adverse events. This strongly contrasts with the emphasis that is, and always has been, placed on *systems* by the patient safety movement and by effective safety management systems such as in aviation. It is worth briefly returning to *To Err is Human*[60] published in 1999. It marked a watershed in the birth of the modern patient safety movement. It described the very large number of hospital deaths in US hospitals that were due to medical errors – possibly up to 98,000 per year. It outlined that understanding errors was key to improving patient safety. This includes recognising the value of feedback and information on mistakes or near misses. *To Err is Human* promulgated that responsibility for improvement did not rest on any single group or individual, but belonged to a multitude of stakeholders. That included those 'inside' the healthcare system, including health care organisations, healthcare professionals, policy makers, regulators and crucially, patients and their families. It also recognised the potential impact of aspects 'outside' the healthcare system such as legal liability.

One of the most important questions facing the patient safety movement in its early days was how to distribute responsibility between individual professionals and the organisational systems they operated within. Initially the dominant view was that error was not the result of individual failing, but could be attributed to poorly designed systems. Accordingly, it was argued that it was more appropriate to modify systems to prevent or mitigate error, rather than to blame individuals for safety incidents.[61] This is reflected in the focus on

---

[59] Ledward inquiry, REPORT.FIN.doc (nationalarchives.gov.uk) para 16.
[60] *To Err is Human* (Institute of Medicine, 1999).
[61] LL Leape, AI Kabcenell, TK Gandhi, P Carver et al, 'Reducing Adverse Drug Events: Lessons from a Breakthrough Series Collaborative' 2000 (26(6) *Joint Commission Journal on Quality and Patient Safety* 321–31.

'clinical governance', first introduced in the NHS in the late 1990s,[62] and defined in the 2007 *Safeguarding Patients* Report[63] as follows:

> At the most general level, clinical governance asserts that healthcare organisations have a corporate responsibility, over and above the responsibility of individual health professionals working in the organisation, to provide safe and high quality care and to strive for continuous quality improvement. Clinical governance seeks to embed the culture and systems needed to promote quality improvement and patient safety into the everyday routines of every clinical team.

Leading practitioners emphasised in 2014 the lesson practised in aviation safety, that a focus on compliance with rules fails in practice:[64]

> A compliance-focused approach will fail. If organisations do not start from the simple recognition that candour is the right thing to do, systems and processes can only serve to structure a regulatory conversation about compliance. The commitment to candour has to be about values and it has to be rooted in genuine engagement of staff, building on their own professional duties and their personal commitment to their patients.[65]

A pure 'no blame approach' with its attribution of all responsibility for safety to systems is not the answer, as accountability and learning are required,[66] and is not the essence of open and just culture in aviation safety. The aviation model balances the accountabilities of both individuals and systems,[67] as noted above.

The systemic impediments that prevent development of an open and just culture start with lack of respect in some professional, managerial, institutional and regulatory relationships and systems, and end with the culture of blame and adversarialism in responding to complaints and injuries. It will simply not be possible to sustain an open learning culture for as long as any of these elements remain allowed to continue. As a consequence, the NHS and its patients are condemned to continue to suffer from repetitive cycles of poor relations, limited institutional learning, major disasters, major investigations that find the continuation of bad practice and cultures, political and media criticism and lack of public trust.

B. Reducing Barriers to Reporting Concerns

The desired culture must seek the views of two separate cohorts:

- the experiences of those the NHS treats and their friends and families, and
- the experiences of those who work within the system.

---

[62] This was first outlined in *The New NHS: Modern, Dependable* (Department of Health, December 1997), but was more fully described in *A First Class Service: Quality in the New NHS* (Department of Health, July 1998)

[63] Paragraph 2.6 of *Safeguarding Patients The Government's Response to the Recommendations of the Shipman Inquiry's Fifth Report and to the Recommendations of the Ayling, Neale and Kerr/Haslam Inquiries* HMSO London, February 2007, available at https://assets.publishing.service.gov.uk/government/uploads/system/uploads/attachment_data/file/228872/7015.pdf.

[64] *Building a Culture of Candour: A Review of the Threshold for the Duty of Candour and of the Incentives for Care Organisations to be Candid* (Royal College of Surgeons of London, 2014) para 1.32.

[65] Reference from original text: For the impact of a lack of an enabling environment for candour/open disclosure, see Mazor et al (2004) 'Communicating with patients about medical errors', *Archives of Internal Medicine* 164, 1690; Vincent (2003) 'Understanding and responding to adverse events' *New England Journal of Medicine* 348 (11) 1051.

[66] RM Wachter and PJ Pronovost, 'Balancing "No Blame" With Accountability in Patient Safety' (2009) 361(14) *New England Journal of Medicine* 1401–06.

[67] RM Wachter, 'Personal Accountability in Healthcare: Searching for the Right Balance (2013) 22(2) *BMJ Quality & Safety* 176–80.

There is some crossover, but the potential barriers to, and inhibitors of, reporting for these two groups are distinct. The barriers to staff sharing information, which largely revolve around fear of adverse criticism of individuals, colleagues, units or the system, will be addressed below.

There is a clear disparity between the patient and the healthcare provider in access to information and in understanding its relevance. This can impact on willingness and ability to raise a concern. In the Mid-Staffs inquiry it was noted that people did not want to raise concerns for fear of negatively impacting the care being provided. There is also an imbalance of information and power, which can make it difficult for even the most eloquent of patients to raise concerns. The IMMDS review took evidence from the Mesh campaigner Yvette Greenway and her partner Michael Mansfield QC. He told the IMMDS Review about an incident where a consultant dismissed Yvette's symptoms and concerns:

> I'm used to asking questions all the time. But actually I suddenly experienced what a lot of people tell me which is, you're in the presence of an expert … You have to reflect, and so you're mildly humble about it all and think well maybe he knows more than we do? Maybe there's something we're missing here. The full impact of the way he's treated you doesn't really impact itself at the time until moments later. Then you think, we've just been through what everybody talks about.

Once patients have decided to raise a concern, reviews of the NHS complaints system have consistently found that patients and families are unclear how to raise complaints, or are confused by the availability of multiple avenues,[68] or feel that the process was too complex.[69] Part II of this book sets out the various mechanisms for raising concerns, and it is notable that some of the mechanisms – such as the regulators, the ombudsman and litigation – filter out a significant proportion of those seeking to raise a concern as not within their remit. This reinforces the observation that there is a lack of clarity around how and where to raise concerns. It also reinforces patients' impression that the NHS does not want to listen or improve.

Part of the difficulty is the inter-relation between the different bodies who deal with concerns.[70] For example, the complaints and NHS Ombudsman systems are effectively two-tier structures, directing complaints first to the local level and only after that to the Ombudsman, but the proportion of complaints that the Ombudsmen rejects as not properly made out indicates that there are fault lines in this process.

All complaints should be facilitated and listened to. Thought should be given to adopting the Welsh approach of removing the formal requirements for complaints to be written and of putting a positive duty on all staff to support those raising a concern.

C. Removing Blame Culture

The main problem is that blame and lack of psychological safety continue to exist systemically across the NHS – in professional and hierarchical relationships, in management

---

[68] *NHS Complaints Reform: Making Things Right* (Department of Health, 2003); A Clwyd and T Hart, *A Review of the NHS Hospitals Complaints System. Putting Patients Back in the Picture* (Department of Health, 2013); K Evans, *"Using the Gift of Complaints": A Review of Concerns (Complaints) Handling in NHS Wales* (Welsh Government, 2014).

[69] *Making Experiences Count: A New Approach to Responding to Complaints* (Department of Health, 2007).

[70] *Listening, Responding, Improving: A Guide to Better Customer Care* (DH, 26 February 2009).

relationships, in regulatory systems, in inquiries and in delivering redress after harm. Those conditions together form almost insurmountable barriers to sustaining an open and just culture in which information is shared freely and swiftly, learning can occur and relevant changes and consequences are implemented that are viewed as justified so as to improve performance and reduce risk.

The lesson from the aviation experience is that strenuous efforts have to be applied in *every* context to remove the primacy of blame, and to take actions that will support the operation of open and just culture across the entire system. For example, prior to 2005 New Zealand had a non-adversarial administrative compensation scheme, which used a blame-based threshold of 'medical malpractice' and which required ACC[71] to report individual practitioners to the Health and Disability Commissioner. In 2005 the compensation threshold was changed to a non-fault based 'treatment injury' and the reporting requirements to the commissioner were changed: ACC now have an 'obligation to report the risk of harm, without being in any way focused on the individual practitioner who might or might not be responsible'.[72]

As a result of these changes claim numbers went up by 42 per cent, the proportion that were paid went from 38 per cent to 64 per cent, and the average decision time for a claim fell from over five months to 13 days. These changes have been attributed to a willingness on the part of healthcare professionals to report patient injuries.[73] The findings indicate that all elements of blame need to be removed; replacing adversarial litigation is part of the solution, but not all of it.

The changes outlined above may seem counter-intuitive to some people, not least the media, politicians and those who have suffered harm and their relatives. But the cycle of mistakes and poor performance that is recorded earlier in this book will simply not be disrupted and removed unless changes in behaviour, culture and systems are implemented. Unacceptable levels of harm will continue. This leads inescapably to the conclusion that punitive professional regulatory sanctions (see 'Improving Operational Culture, above Section VII.A) and adversarial redress and compensation systems based on proof of negligence (blame) are a clear impediment to sustaining an open and just culture in the NHS.

i. Improving Dispute Resolution

Removing adversarial processes and removing blame from compensation require two elements. Inquisitorial processes can replace adversarial processes. The most well-known examples of non-adversarial compensation mechanisms after treatment injuries can be found in the Scandinavian countries and in New Zealand. These systems have also removed blame by using a non-fault based threshold for compensation eligibility. They have also entirely decoupled compensation, which is based on the circumstances the harmed

---

[71] The Accident Compensation Corporation (ACC) provides no-fault compensation coverage, see www.acc.co.nz.

[72] See Evidence given by Michael Mercer Principal Solicitor at ACC at page 39 of the Health and Social Care Select Committee, *NHS Litigation Reform* Thirteenth Report of Session 2021–22, HC 750, 28 April 2022, available at https://committees.parliament.uk/publications/22039/documents/163739/default/.

[73] J Manning, 'Access to Justice for New Zealand Health Consumers' (2010) 18(1) *Journal of Law and Medicine* 178–94 at fn 65.

individual is in, from any form of regulatory action or assessment of fault on the part of the individual healthcare provider.

ii. Fundamental Reforms in Dispute Resolution Systems: Techniques, Processes, Pathways, Functions, Institutions, Landscapes

Debate over reform of NHS redress takes place against a backdrop of major change in both technology and policy on dispute resolution generally. A complex picture emerges from changes in multiple factors, which are themselves changing the approaches to dispute resolution in different ways and at different paces in different contexts.

Significant changes on systems, pathways and behaviour/cultures are being undertaken elsewhere in the dispute resolution landscape, so contemplating radical change in the NHS and injury contexts are by no means unique. Hodges reviewed the overall picture in England and Wales in 2019, looking at changes in disputes relating to consumers, employment, families, small businesses, intellectual property, property and claims against the state, as well as injuries arising in road traffic, workplace and clinical contexts of various kinds.[74] He concluded that the court and justice system in England and Wales was broken and not fit for purpose, a conclusion echoed by Lord Thomas of Cwmgiedd in his Foreword to the book, and in a related review that Lord Thomas chaired on Justice in Wales.[75] Hodges reviewed each 'vertical' system for the different types of claim and made detailed recommendations under three broad headings:

1. Improving the provision of information, advice, assistance, and support.
2. Improving the dispute resolution pathway.
3. Delivering change to reduce future risk.

The major changes have related to processes, alternative pathways, new techniques and how they are integrated into existing processes, and the emergence of new institutions as dispute resolution intermediaries.

A fundamental review by the Legal Services Board concluded that access to justice is fundamentally about *outcomes and relationships* more than legal processes, noting[76]

> justice is more than the resolution of disputes: it includes just relationships underpinned by law. ... Justice is underpinned by legal knowledge, legislative frameworks, dispute resolution and the infrastructure of the legal services market and the court system as well as by the outcomes that consumers secure. Access to justice is the securing of these just outcomes rather than the process of dispute resolution.

All dispute resolution formats have been reforming themselves to adopt digital technology, including platforms, online procedures and in some instances artificially intelligent assistance. Some have moved more quickly than others. The consumer Ombudsmen and the creation of commercial online dispute resolution (ODR) platforms and schemes[77] led the

---

[74] C Hodges, *Delivering Dispute Resolution: A Holistic Review of Models in England & Wales* (Hart, 2019).
[75] *Justice in Wales for the People of Wales* (The Commission for Justice in Wales, 2019).
[76] *Evaluation: How Can We Measure Access to Justice?* (Legal Services Board, 2012) para 3.6.
[77] AJ Schmitz and C Rule, *The New Handshake. Online Dispute Resolution and the Future of Consumer Protection* (American Bar Association, 2017) ch 3; C Rule, 'Online Dispute Resolution and the Future of Justice' (2020) 16

way. The Online Court model,[78] now spreading through courts and tribunals in England and Wales, was based on these initial models.[79] The 2020–21 COVID pandemic strongly reinforced the switch to use of online processes.

The combined effect of these evolutions in technology and techniques has profoundly changed the dispute resolution architecture and processes. The fact is that systems for resolution of some types of disputes in this country, especially personal injuries involving the NHS, are now lagging behind in terms of innovation. Senior judiciary have recently signalled major reforms in the court system generally,[80] tribunals and family law.[81] The Master of the Rolls, head of civil justice, has outlined not only further reforms but also a system that would integrate each of the (best of the) different pathways into an holistic system.[82] He expects very considerable further change.[83]

Given this background, there is a strong case that pursuing medical injuries through adversarial processes and traditional court procedures is out of date, and does not deliver the outcomes that are needed in terms of efficiency or assistance in improving performance and behaviour.

In the healthcare context, of course, the 'alternative process or institution' to the courts is an administrative redress scheme, which would mirror the switch to Ombudsmen that has occurred some decades ago in the consumer disputes context. Two significant forces that have held that switch back are objections by lawyers, who would of course lose work, and concerns by officials that the removal of 'blame' as a gateway to complaints by NHS patients would produce a flood of claims and overwhelming cost. This was considered by the Health and Social Care Select Committee in their Inquiry into Clinical Negligence, Table 2 is taken from the evidence submitted by the Department of Health and Social Care to the inquiry.[84] It is difficult to compare across different systems, but what is clear is that England's spend is far higher than any of the comparator nations. No other international scheme was as expensive, despite receiving a higher number of claims.

Annual Review of Law and Social Science 277; MA Wahab, D Rainey and E Katsh (eds), *Online Dispute Resolution: Theory and Practice* (Eleven International Publishing, 2021).

[78] Lord Justice Briggs, *Civil Courts Structure Review: Final Report* (Judiciary of England and Wales, 2016); *Early Progress in Transforming Courts and Tribunals* (National Audit Office, 2018); *HMCTS Response to Public Accounts Committee Report on Court Reform Programme*, 20 July 2018, at www.gov.uk/government/news/hmcts-response-to-public-accounts-committee-report-on-court-reform-programme.

[79] R. Susskind, *Online Courts and the Future of Justice* (Oxford University Press, 2019).

[80] Sir Geoffrey Voss C, 'The Law Society's Inaugural Lecture on the Future of Law', 8 May 2018.

[81] *Supporting Families in Conflict: There Is a Better Way. An Address by Sir Andrew McFarlane to the Jersey International Family Law Conference 2021*, 9 October 2021.

[82] Rt Hon Sir Geoffrey Vos, 'The Relationship between Formal and Informal Justice', speech at Hull University, 26 March 2021. Rt Hon Sir Geoffrey Vos, 'London International Disputes Week 2021: Keynote Speech' London, 10 May 2021. Rt Hon Sir Geoffrey Vos MR, 'Recovery or Radical Transformation: The Effect of Covid-19 on Justice', Speech at London School of Economics, 17 June 2021.

[83] Rt Hon Sir Geoffrey Vos MR, 'The Future for Dispute Resolution: Horizon Scanning' Speech at the Society of Computers and Law, 17 March 2022.

[84] Page 145 of Health and Social Care Select Committee, *NHS Litigation Reform* Thirteenth Report of Session 2021–22, HC 750, 28 April 2022, available at https://committees.parliament.uk/publications/22039/documents/163739/default/.

Table 2 International comparison of claim rates and spends following clinical harm

	Country	Population (millions)	Claims/ 100,000	Cost per capita (£)	% GDP	% Health Spend
Tort litigation	England	56	19	42.1	0.1%	2%
	Wales	3.1	14	29.2	0.1%	1%
	Scotland	5.4	9	6.9	0.02%	0.3%
	Canada	37	2	4.1	0.01%	0.1%
	Australia	25	26	6.8	0.02%	0.2%
Avoidable harm scheme	Sweden	10	167	5.0	0.01%	0.8%
	Denmark	6	183	–	–	–
No-Fault scheme	New Zealand	4.9	332	18.7	0.1%	1%

Figures use 2018/19 data except for Wales which uses 2017 data

Given the spend from clinical negligence comes from the public purse there are valid concerns around making sure it is as financially efficient as possible. There are mechanisms which can be used to control costs. First, if you shift from an adversarial court process into an administrative inquisitorial process this effectively removes lawyers, who account for just over a quarter of the clinical negligence spend. There should be parity between the value of an award made by an administrative scheme and what the courts would have awarded; the sum taken home by the claimant under each system should be the same. The quantum awarded by an administrative scheme is likely to be lower than the quantum a court would award as litigation allows for success fees to be deducted from court award. Given the high value of legal fees these savings are potentially substantial. The costs of establishing and administering the scheme are often raised as an objection to setting up a scheme. However, the cost of courts is not generally included in assessments of the cost of clinical negligence; any saving in court time should be offset against scheme set up and administration costs.

The Select Committee Inquiry into NHS Litigation[85] recommended

> Compensation should be based on the additional costs necessary to top up care available through the NHS and social care system, rather than the current assumption that all care will be provided privately. Whilst we recognise that additional care costs are difficult to calculate, we recommend that they should be modelled using practice established in international patient injury compensation schemes. We further recommend that Section 2(4) of the Law Reform (Personal Injuries) Act 1948 should be repealed for clinical negligence cases brought against NHS organisations in England.

Repealing section 2(4) is a solution that has proved contentious. A less charged alternative might be to ramp up the rate at which payments can be recovered by the Compensation Recovery Unit, so that they reflect the cost of care provided rather than their current capped

---

[85] Health and Social Care Select Committee, *NHS Litigation Reform* Thirteenth Report of Session 2021–22, HC 750, 28 April 2022 available at https://committees.parliament.uk/publications/22039/documents/163739/default/.

levels. This would not be as effective as repealing section 2(4) of the 1948 Act, but it might be a more achievable goal.

For the complete removal of blame litigation should be removed and replaced by a scheme which is the exclusive remedy for those seeking compensation. This would represent a significant shift in position and would be subject to considerable opposition, not least from the legal community. A more politically palatable option, as recommended by the Health and Social Care Select Committee is to retain the right to litigate (resolving any potential Article 6 Human Rights questions) but to have a compulsory ADR as a first stage. This ADR would work in an inquisitorial manner using a non-blame based system-focused test. Any claimant who was not satisfied with the decision of the ADR scheme could subsequently litigate. The Select Committee recommended

> Once an administrative scheme is established for all clinical negligence claims the future of Qualified One-Way Costs Shifting (QOCs) in clinical negligence cases against the NHS should be considered. The Government has said the purpose of QOCs is to minimise the financial risk to claimants, but, as the administrative system will provide risk free access to compensation which is no less generous than that awarded by the courts, QOCs will become redundant. We believe that any claimant who pursues litigation having been offered compensation by the independent administrative body should have to pay the defendant's costs if they subsequently lose their case. Part 36 offers will remain vital. We recommend that NHS Resolution should consider using the quantum of compensation made by the independent administrative body as a part 36 offer.

The format of payments and whether a lump sum or periodic payment is offered will impact on the spend, particularly where the Personal Injury Discount Rate (PIDR) adds considerable amounts to the quantum offered. Periodic payments provide greater opportunities for adjusting payments to meet developing or changing needs and therefore ensuring the care that injured individuals need.

Most importantly in order to be credible any alternative scheme has to be sufficiently independent that it would be recognised by the Courts as such.

The factors above cover the top line requirements for any alternative to litigation. On a more granular level any administrative scheme has to be accessible and responsive, as the 2017 Legal Problem and Resolution Survey (LPRS) based on 2014/15 data stated:[86]

> the types of legal problem people commonly encounter present a complex and variable set of circumstances and issues and they cannot be easily categorised based on a single dimension, such as the type of legal dispute. The provision of help, advice and services to support people with such problems therefore needs to be sufficiently broad and flexible to meet a diverse range of needs.

Some important generic lessons from a great deal of reform in dispute resolution, nationally and internationally, are the need for simplicity in identification of pathways and operation of processes, trust in intermediaries and the system,[87] an integrated landscape, the ability to collect as much data and possible and then feed it back to identify risks and support action to reduce risk and to improve performance and a focus on delivering purposes and desired

---

[86] R Franklyn, T Budd, R Verrill and M Willoughby, *Findings from the Legal Problem and Resolution Survey, 2014–15* (Ministry of Justice, 2017). See earlier *Evaluation: How Can We Measure Access to Justice for Individual Consumers? A Discussion Paper* (Legal Services Board, 2012).

[87] TR Tyler, *Why People Obey the Law* (Yale University Press, 2006); TR Tyler, 'Psychology and the Law' in RE Goodin (ed), *The Oxford Handbook of Law & Politics* (Oxford University Press, 2011).

outcomes. Most commercial markets have instituted huge changes along these lines: the NHS is a long way behind being able to operate in this fashion as a system that responds, learns and improves.

To summarise, there are two basic needs if things are to improve:

1. To shift from blame and an adversarial system to an administrative investigative system and objective criteria.
2. To shift to a culture in which information is shared openly, and this is then used in learning, feedback and changing behaviour, culture and performance.

iii. Early Facilitated Dispute Resolution

The above paragraphs set out what how an alternative dispute resolution scheme should be structured and what it should do. The next issue is how it should carry out its functions. Historical thinking has tended to conceive of different techniques and pathways as necessarily separate and distinct. However, delivering ease and speed of access to solutions for people requires greater integration. A major example of this is to integrate the functions of (a) providing people with information that might help them review and assess their problems, (b) assisting parties to a dispute to communicate their problems and to negotiate towards a solution, (c) provide for investigation of facts, whilst (d) avoiding unnecessary repetition of any of the above aspects. In other words, a system could deliver in an integrated fashion the functions of facilitation, mediation, claiming, investigation and resolution. Each of these functions does not need to be a separate stage in a lengthy linear process: the functions can be achieved as part of an integrated approach. There is no need for a pre-action protocol or mediation hurdle: the stages are automatically embedded in the process, and used to the extent that they are useful or swiftly passed over so as to get to the next stage in the pathway.

This integrated system has been implemented with great success by some of the consumer Ombudsmen, as part of their review and modernisation of their procedures on the basis of adopting more digital facilities and web platforms. The same basic model was, of course, copied in the Briggs model of the Online Court.[88] The approach is called Early Facilitated Communication. Function (a) above, providing information, can be done by providing information in various forms – on websites, in discrete packages, perhaps triggered by artificial intelligence-led analysis of the nature of a problem, or by oral independent advice/ assistance to one or both sides (replacing lawyers). Objective and even-handed information will be provided for both sides. Facts can be inputted online or by a case handler talking to one or both sides. The case handler, or in some cases an AI function, can initiate and support direct or facilitated communication between the parties, with the objective of them reaching a fair settlement.

The underlying approach is simply to encourage people to talk to each other, exchange views, facts and feelings and, if possible, resolve their differences as swiftly as possible. The

---

[88] Lord Justice Briggs, *Civil Courts Structure Review: Final Report* (Judiciary of England and Wales, 2016); *Early Progress in Transforming Courts and Tribunals* (National Audit Office, 2018); *HMCTS Response to Public Accounts Committee Report on Court Reform Programme*, 20 July 2018, at www.gov.uk/government/news/ hmcts-response-to-public-accounts-committee-report-on-court-reform-programme.

developing experience is that a case officer can provide relevant information and assistance to both parties without becoming partisan. The 'facilitated communication' function morphs imperceptibly into 'mediation', where the case officer facilitates further communication between the parties with a view to assisting them to reach a settlement if they so wish, 'in the shadow of a trusted independent'. The case officer also acts as a guard of fairness in treatment and outcomes, especially where there is an imbalance of power and resource between the parties, guarding against inappropriate pressure or abuse. As is often the case with mediation, fresh issues and wider means of resolving a problem can be raised and used effectively. If resolution is not achieved by the parties in this facilitated process, the case handler will have ensured that all the facts are assembled, so that the case can be passed for resolution by an independent ombudsman.

VIII. Conclusions on the Social Policy Objectives

As outlined above harmed individuals want: a meaningful apology; an explanation of what happened to them; accountability for what has happened; prevention of future harm; and, in some cases, compensation.

The five core social policy objectives identified above are:

- caring for those who have been harmed (the caring objective);
- reporting concerns (the reporting objective);
- establishing what happened and how this differed from what should have happened (the investigation objective);
- demonstrating systemic and actual learning (the improvement objective); and
- financial efficiency (the financial objective).

These requirements suggest that essential features of the system are as follows. First, a financially efficient system that is designed to minimise the barriers to reporting concerns, deliver learning, feedback, application of change has to be demonstrably in place. Second, since systems alone are insufficient, the local social, operational, employment and regulatory cultures have to be demonstrably conducive to supporting reporting of concerns and learning from them. Such cultures should facilitate the sharing of information and should avoid sanctions such as inappropriate embarrassment, ostracism for speaking up. Third, patients who suffer harm from the healthcare system should be provided with proof that the system and culture can be trusted, and that the information on what has happened to them has not only been fed into the system but has also contributed to improvements.

14

Conclusion

In Don Berwick's words

> In the end, culture will trump rules, standards and control strategies every single time, and achieving a vastly safer NHS will depend far more on major cultural change than on a new regulatory regime.[1]

To work effectively, an open, just and learning culture would have to be present throughout the NHS and there would have to be strong reciprocal links to regulators, administrators, managers, patients and the community. To achieve this culture any barriers to it, such as the use of blame, must be removed, along with any processes which inhibit the development of such a culture. All processes, whether they are for patient complaints, obtaining compensation following injury, for staff to raise concerns, requests for regulatory oversight, etc, should be easy to identify and use, fair, administrative and underpinned by clear and transparent rules. It is clear from Part II that this is not the case with the current systems.

There is no rationale for having multiple processes which are duplicative, or confusing to users. Nor is there any excuse for potentially valuable patient safety information being able to fall through gaps as currently happens with the vast majority of the issues raised with clinical negligence claimant lawyers. As Parts I and II of this book indicate, a single patient safety incident might be subject to multiple different investigations, with multiple purposes, for example no-blame HSIB maternity investigations with an Early Notification Scheme investigation for liability. There are also some clear examples of inconsistencies in what type of investigations are applied, for example in Shrewsbury and Telford Serious incident investigations were not initiated on occasions when another Trust would have carried out a Serious Incident investigation. The landscape at the moment is complex and siloed. In our view the time has come 'to recognise with clarity and courage the need for wide systemic change'.[2]

The current complex arrangements should be replaced with a new, more ethical, supportive ecosystem. The core objectives identified should become a values-based charter for all entities that deal with patient harm. They should be the core around which any reforms are based. The success of these objectives will depend on the processes utilised to deliver them.

There is a clear need first to integrate the information gathered from different data collection sources relating to patient harm to enable a fuller picture to be obtained. Second any feedback from different agencies should be aggregated so that individuals on the ground

---

[1] National Advisory Group on the Safety of Patients in England, *A Promise to Learn – A Commitment to Act Improving the Safety of Patients in England* (August 2013) available at www.gov.uk/government/publications/berwick-review-into-patient-safety.

[2] ibid.

are not bombarded by multiple varied messages. This will enable greater responsiveness on the ground.

An alternative to the current raft of investigations is the Welsh approach. The Welsh mantra 'investigate once, investigate well' and the 'Once for Wales Concerns Management' system which incorporate concerns, complaints and claims provides a model of this type of integrated approach. We would advocate that this unified approach be extended beyond concerns and developed into a fuller investigatory function.

Behaviour within any organisation can become subject to the prevailing culture of that organisation, and, as examples such as Mid-Staffs and Morecambe Bay illustrate, local culture can drift a very long way from value norms, and on occasion can become entirely unacceptable. External oversight and investigation is one potential solution to this. However, the examples in Part II, for example the NMC and Morecambe Bay, show there can be a disconnect, or worse, antagonism, between the external agency and the organisation being investigated. A more supportive approach is for the investigative agency to have a member of staff embedded within the NHS organisation. This allows a more integrated approach; the investigator is aware of the local personnel and specific issues within that setting, this local knowledge enables them to intervene early and to direct their concerns to the most appropriate individual. In addition, the external investigator adds specific expertise to the local investigatory team, which, over time, should raise the standards of local investigations. Crucially, local ownership of the investigation process and any resulting learnings is maintained. It is important that the external investigator be employed by an independent external body and is not employed by the organisation they investigate. The investigative body must ensure that investigators are rotated periodically around different organisations, so they are able to detect poor local cultures or drifts from acceptable bounds. This model provides a supportive way to facilitate higher quality local investigations into matters which are currently investigated locally, as we explained when we proposed this model for maternity investigations.[3] It is not a replacement for the HSIB national investigations, which focus on selected matters of the highest risk, and should be maintained. The output of an independent investigation could provide the information that many patients and their families are looking for. Time and time again people reiterate that they want an explanation and to understand what took place. This report could provide this information for them, as well as proving a more straightforward process for individuals seeking to raise concerns.

A more accessible straightforward process is badly needed. At the moment we have multiple external agencies carrying out investigations, often working in their own silos. There is a drive towards multidisciplinary team working; the mantra of 'train together, work together' as set out in the interim Ockenden report reflects the reality of team working within the NHS. Multiple professional regulators each investigating an incident separately is anachronistic and harks back to failed past practices and structures. The PSA have proposed a single professional regulator with a common code across all professions. Were this approach to be taken, it would radially simplify the professional regulatory investigations. However, a unified regulator seems unlikely to be created. In any event, a practical, more streamlined

---

[3] SA Macleod, A Sampson and C Hodges, 'The Rapid Resolution and Redress Scheme for Birth Injuries: An Alternative Scheme Design. Foundation for Law Justice and Society Policy Paper' (13 September 2017) available at www.fljs.org/rapid-resolution-and-redress-scheme-birth-injuries-alternative-scheme-design.

approach to investigations is needed, and that requires clarity on the scope and purpose of the investigations that are currently carried out. Rather than having multiple agencies trying to ascertain what happens, it would be more efficient to have an independent external investigator, with strong links to the professional regulators, establishing what happened and feeding this back. Ideally there would be consensus and all the facts would be agreed, but in very many cases there will be some discrepancies and it is therefore critical that any investigator is credible and genuinely independent. The investigator's report should encompass all the evidence of what happened, rather than focussing on the actions or inactions of an individual. As well as holding individuals to account there is a need for the system to shift emphasis and to hold organisations to account as well. The statutory duty of candour is an example of a shift from individual candour to institutional candour, but this trend needs to become more widespread. However, imposing such a duty sends a message to staff that they are not trusted to do the right thing and report. Having such a duty as a legal requirement should not be necessary in the right culture. We have had individuals prosecuted for manslaughter, but to date there has not been a conviction against an organisation for corporate manslaughter.[4] To protect the public there will always be a need to hold individual practitioners to account when that is appropriate; when this is the case the factual information in the report should form the backbone of any future fitness to practise investigation.

In order for staff to feel comfortable reporting, they must feel that the response to them raising concerns, both within the organisation and externally, will be reasonable and fair. A particular barrier to this approach is the persistence of clinical negligence litigation with its focus on blame. We support the Health and Social Care Select Committee's suggestion that before being permitted to commence litigation anyone wishing to obtain compensation must have their case assessed by an independent administrative scheme against a system-based test for compensation. The move away from blame is key, as was illustrated in 2005 in New Zealand when ACC shifted from a blame-based test to a system-based test. However, other aspects of the legal landscape also have to be considered. Clinical negligence litigation is a commercial enterprise and the opportunities offered by an administrative scheme, particularly for claims management companies (CMCs), need to be carefully considered. CMCs did very well from the PPI scandal despite the financial ombudsman scheme offering a free administrative scheme that did not need legal representation to access.

The independent investigatory service we advocate is akin to an ombudsman, but should be integrated into the organisation it oversees. This model combines independent oversight with local knowledge and allows for greater support. The reports from this investigatory agency can be used by others to deliver the caring objective. If the ombudsman finds that an incident met the system-based test for compensation then, as the Select Committee recommended, a recommendation should be made to NHS Resolution to provide the financial redress on a par with that which the courts would award.

In some ways this is a significant departure from the current arrangements, but it is clear from Part II that significant reform is needed. Our proposals allow the delivery of the core objectives. There is the need for a new entity to deliver these investigations; although they

---

[4] See Dr Jenny Vaughan's blog, 'The Long Road to Justice for Hadiza Bawa-Garba' *BMJ* (14 August 2018) available at https://blogs.bmj.com/bmj/2018/08/14/jenny-vaughan-the-long-road-to-justice-for-hadiza-bawa-garba/.

are an ombudsman it would be a mistake to ask PHSO to take on these functions. PHSO cannot offer the same level of efficiency that the other UK ombudsmen can because of its statutory constraints; to burden it further with additional cases and a new way of working is not a wise path. It would be better to allow PHSO to relinquish its health cases to this new entity and the remainder of the public service function to merge with the LGO as has long been planned. Each of the elements that we recommend can be found already to operate well in other sectors and contexts, and to accord with the direction of travel of reforms on regulation and dispute resolution.

Demonstrating learning is key. Too often recommendations are made, and then there is little or no follow up to see whether they have actually been implemented and if so what difference this has made. Having a local presence allows for greater follow up, and, importantly, provides a channel for this information to be fed back to those who raised these concerns in the first place.

These changes in culture and process outlined above are necessary to realise the ambition of a just NHS where raising concerns actually leads to raising standards.

INDEX

Abertawe Bro Morgannwg University Health Board Review, 170, 189–91
PSOW healthcare complaints, **109**
accountability:
complaint handing, 63–64, 68
Healthcare Safety Investigation Branch, 207
Integrated Care Systems, 16–17
just culture model, 274–76, 286
professional regulations, 200–1, 203
public inquiries, 200–1, 203
Public Ombudsman Service, proposals for, 103
Action Plan for Antimicrobial Resistance, 19, 47
Acute Data Alignment Programme (ADAPt):
patient safety, 41
Adoption and Spread Safety Improvement Programme (A&S-SIP), 48–49
after-the-event insurance, 149
post-LASPO, 161–62
pre-LASPO, 125–26, 149, 160–61
qualified one-way cost shifting, 126
see also conditional fee arrangements
air pollution, 19
allied health professionals:
recruitment, 21
alcohol, *see* **drug and alcohol services**
alternative dispute resolution, 92, 126, 280–85
early facilitated dispute resolution, 285–86
Jackson reforms, 162
Northern Ireland, 149–50
Woolf reforms, 157–58
ambulance staff, 8
access to patient records, 25
NHS Resolution claims, **130**
Patient Safety Collaboratives, 42
antimicrobial resistance, 19, 47
apologising for mistakes, 50–51
autism:
health inequalities, 17–18
Learning Disabilities Mortality Review Programme, 45–47
services, 19
Winterbourne View Hospital, 183–84
autonomy, *see* **professional autonomy**
Ayling (Clifford) Independent Inquiry, 70, **170**, 174–75, 201
response to, 180–81

Being Open **policy**, 50–51
Berwick Report 2013, 287
involvement of patients and carers, 39–40, 42, 72–73
Bolam **test**, 64, 95–96, 116–17
informed consent, 118–19
reasonable care and skill test compared, 117–18
scope in clinical negligence cases, 119
Bristol Royal Infirmary Public Inquiry, 170, 171–73
criticisms of GMC, 230

cancer care:
children and young people, 19
complaints, 61
COVID-19, impact of, 27
health inequalities, 18, 30
Long Term Plan, 19–20, 30
outcomes, 11
Paterson Inquiry, 193–95
Penny case, 117–18
cardio-vascular disease:
clinical negligence claims, **137**, *144*, **152**, *153*
Long Term Plan, 19–20
outcomes, 11
Care and Treatment Reviews (CTRs), 46
Care, Education and Treatment Reviews (CETRs), 46
Care Quality Commission (CQC), 11
maternity care, 11–12, 198
Morecambe Bay scandal, 186–87
Mental Health Improvement Programme, 44
regulatory responsibilities, 220–21
statutory duty of candour, 52–53
unregistered providers of care, 221–22
Centre for Effective Dispute Resolution (CEDR), 131, 158
Civil Justice Council:
Fixed Recoverable Costs in Lower Value Clinical Negligence Claims, 124, 126–27, 166–67
Civil Procedure Rules (CPR), 157–58
clinical negligence and litigation, 37–39, 116, 155–57
claims and costs
England, **128**
home nations compared, **154**
Northern Ireland, **150**, **151**
Scotland, **136**

claims in England, 122–23, 131
  Civil Justice Council Report into Fixed
      Recoverable Costs, 124
  costs, 122–23
  current process, *127*
  Health and Social Care Select Committee
      Inquiry, 124
  Marsh Report 2011, 123
  National Audit Office reports, 123–24
  NHS Resolution, 125–31
  see also NHS Resolution
claims in Northern Ireland, 148, 153
  filtering claims, 148–49
  funding claims, 148–49
  lack of centralised defence body, 149–50
  procedures, 149–53
  see also Northern Ireland Public Services
      Ombudsman, 110–11
claims in Scotland, 131–32, 137–38
  Central Legal Office, 133
  Clinical Negligence and Other Risks Indemnity
      Scheme, 132–37
  see also Clinical Negligence and Other Risks
      Indemnity Scheme
claims in Wales, 138, 147–48
  Learning From Events process, 145–47
  NHS Redress Scheme, 138–39, 140–42, 147
  Welsh Risk Pool claims, 139–40, 142–45, 145–47
  see also Welsh Risk Pool
Clinical Negligence Scheme for Trusts, 37, 122
comparison of home nations, 153–55
costs, 157, 159–67
  financial efficiency, 165
  fixed recoverable costs, 166–67
Getting it Right First Time, 37–39
institutional non-delegable duties of care, 119–21
international comparison, **283**
liability assessment, 116–17, 119, 121
  consent cases, 118–19
  diagnosis cases, 117–18
  reasonable care and skill cases, 117–18
litigation reform
  Health and Social Care Select Committee
      Inquiry, 124
  Woolf Review of Civil Procedure, 157–59
**Clinical Negligence and Other Risks Indemnity
    Scheme (CNORIS),** 132–33, 137–38
  claims and costs, **136**
  claims by specialty, **137**, *137*
  claims-handling, 135–37
  filtering of claims, 133–35
  funding of claims, 133–35
Clinical Negligence Mediation Scheme, 158
**Clinical Negligence Scheme for Trusts
      (CNST),** 37, 120, 122

Clostridium difficile, 47, 49
**Clwyd and Hart review of NHS complaints system
      2013,** 61, 73–75
co-payment charges, 7
Community Health Councils (CHCs), 61–62, 66
  Wales, 86, 142
  see also Patient Advice and Liaison Service
community healthcare:
  services, 15–17, 29
  staff, 8
compensation, 258, 273, 289–90
  blame threshold, 280–81, 284
  clinical negligence claims, 123, 124, 125–26,
      134–35, 154, 156–57
    minor injuries, 164
    upper limit, 164
    Wales, 141–42, 144, 147, 153
  cost to NHS, 123
  motivation for complaints, 262–65, **263**, 267
  ombudsmen, 114, 115
  right to, 67, 167
complaints and complaint-handling, 93–96
  clinical claims, 60, **69**
  complaints processes
    England, 63–69
    Scotland, 90–93
    Wales, 84–86
  England
    NHS complaints, 59–79,
    public service complaints, 58–59
  healthcare staff, impact on, 62–63
  inadequacies of, 258
  Independent Complaints Advisory Service, 62
  motivations for complaints, 61, 259–60, 266
    healthcare investigations, 265–66
    NHS clinical negligence claims, 261–65
    NHS complaints, 260–61
  non-clinical claims, 60, **69**
  Northern Ireland Public Services Ombudsman,
      110–11
    activity, 111–12
    complaints by organisation, **113**
    healthcare complaints, **111**, 113
    performance, **112**
  Parliamentary and Health Service Ombudsman
    complaints received, **100–1**
    inquiries and investigations, **101**
    recommendations, **99**
    review of complaints, 75–78
  Patient Advice and Liaison Service, 62
  Public Services Ombudsman for Wales, 107,
      114–15
    activity, 107–9
    healthcare complaints, **109–10**, 109–10
    targets and performance, **108**

patients, impact on, 61–62
recipients of healthcare complaints, **60**
reviews and reports, *see* inquiries and reviews
Scotland
  NHS complaints, 90–93
  outcomes, **93**
  public service complaints, 88–89
Scottish Public Services Ombudsman,
    104, 114–15
  activity, 104–6
  complaints received, **105**
  recommendations, **106**
  support and advocacy services, 61–62
Wales
  Evans' Review 2014, 86–88
  NHS complaints, **83–84**, 84–88
  NHS complaints, 83–88
  Once for Wales Concerns Management System
    project, 88, 95, 288
  public service complaints, 80–83
  social services complaints procedures, **81–82**
see also regulators
complexity of the NHS, 7–8
conditional fee agreements, 125–26, 157, 160–61,
    161–63, 166, 264
  Northern Ireland, 149
consent cases:
  clinical negligence, 118–19
    Wales, 147
  Paterson Inquiry, 193–95
coronavirus, *see* **COVID-19**
costs:
  clinical negligence claims in England, 122–23
    after-the-event insurance, 160–61
    Civil Justice Council Report into Fixed
      Recoverable Costs, 124
    conditional fee agreements, 160–61, 161–63
    funding cuts, 164–65
    funding, 159–60
    insurance, 159
    Jackson Review of Litigation Costs, 161–63
    legal aid, 160
    Woolf reforms, 160–61
COVID-19:
  impact of, 12–13, 21–22, 27, 31
    Care and Treatment Reviews, 46
    Care, Education and Treatment Reviews, 46
    complaint handling, 96, 100
    health-based Covid response, 9
    Healthcare Safety Investigation Branch
      investigations, 215
    Long Term Plan, 31
    Managing Deterioration Safety Improvement
      Programme, 48
    maternity investigations, 212

medical examiner system, 35–36
NHS App, 24
NHS Early Notification Scheme, 130
public perception of NHS, 9, 10
remote/online hearings, 281–82
telephone consultations, 22–23, 25

degree of harm:
  reported incidents, **34**
delays, 10
  complaints, 60, 87
  COVID, 27
dentistry:
  complaints, **60, 152**
  co-payment charges, 7
  General Dental Council, 219, **224**
  National Clinical Assessment Service, 57
Development of the Patient Safety Incident
    Management System, *see* **Learn from**
    Patient Safety Events
diabetes prevention, 18, 19–20, 24
digitally-enabled care:
  Long Term Plan, 23–24
    clinical care, supporting, 25
    clinical efficiency and safety, 26
    healthcare professionals, supporting, 25
    patient empowerment, 24
    population health, 25–26
  milestones, 26
  New Service Model, 14
  see also technology
disclosure:
  case management, 234, 248
  blame culture, impact of, 121, 168, 201
  clinical negligence procedures, 157
    Northern Ireland, 149
  healthcare investigations, 265–66
  safe-space protections, 209, 214, 217–18
  see also transparency
doctors, *see* **medical professionals**
drug and alcohol services, 17, 18
duty of candour, 51
  contractual duty of candour, 51
  statutory duty of candour, 52
    enforcement, 52–53
    prosecutions, 52–53

education and training:
  patient safety, 40
elderly persons, *see* **older persons**
end-of-life care, 48, 60
establishment of the NHS, 7
Evans' Review 2014 (Wales), 86–88
  response, 88
evolution of the NHS, 10–11

fitness to practice procedures, 223
  General Medical Council, 233
    Medical Practitioners Tribunal Service, 233–35
    statistics, 235–37
  Healthcare Professionals Council, 246–47
    Health and Care Professionals Tribunal Service,
      247–49
    statistics, 250–52
  investigations, 223
  Medical Practitioners Tribunal Service, 233–35
    Ayling case, 175
    Bawa-Garba case, 232
    Paterson case, 194
  Nursing and Midwifery Council, 237–38
    Council for Healthcare Regulatory Excellence
      reviews, 238–39
    current fitness to practice procedures, 243–44
    PSA performance review scores, *229*
    PSA standards, **228**
  standard of proof, 223
Five Year Forward View, 14, 30
  vanguards, 15
Fixed Recoverable Costs in Lower Value Clinical
    Negligence Claims, 124, 126–27, 166–67
funding arrangements:
  COVID-19, impact of, 27
  five-year funding plan, 27
  Long Term Plan commitments, 27–30
  negligence claims, 153–54, 159–61
    England, 125–26
    funding cuts, 164–65
    Northern Ireland, 148–49
    Scotland, 133–35
    Wales, 139
  see also conditional fee arrangements; legal aid

General Dental Council (GDC), 219, **224**
  PSA performance review scores, *229*
General Medical Council (GMC), 219, 229–30
  Bawa-Garba sanctions, 230–33
  fitness to practice procedures, 233
    case examiner decisions, **236**
    concerns raised, **235**
    Medical Practitioners Tribunal Service, 233–35
    outcomes, **236**
    PSA performance review scores, *229*
    statistics, 235–37
    see also Medical Practitioners
      Tribunal Service
General Optical Council (GOC), 219, 221, **225**
  fitness to practice performance
    review scores, *229*
General Pharmaceutical Council (GPhC),
    219–20, **226**
  fitness to practice performance review scores, *229*

general practice staff, 8
Getting it Right First Time (GIRFT), 30, 37–39
  surgical site infection programme, 47
Gosport War Memorial Hospital Independent
    Inquiry, 170, 191–93

Health and Care Professionals Tribunal Service
    (HCPTS), 247–49
  Conduct and Competence Committee Panel
    decisions, **251**
  Health Committee Panel decisions, **252**
  Investigating Committee Panel
    decisions, **251**
health and social care levy, 9, 12, 27
health inequalities, 17–18, 30
Health Select Committee recommendations 2011,
    71, 93–94
Health Services Safety Investigations Body
    (HSSIB), 37, 209
healthcare associated infections:
  patient safety, 47
Healthcare Commission, 11
  see also Care Quality Commission
Healthcare Professionals Council (HCPC), 219,
    227, 246
  current fitness to practice procedures, 246–47
    concerns raised, **250**
    Health and Care Professionals Tribunal Service,
      247–49
    interim orders, **250**
    PSA performance review scores, *229*
    statistics, 250–52
  see also Health and Care Professionals Tribunal
    Service
Healthcare Safety Investigation Branch (HSIB), 37,
    216–18
  establishment, 209
  Expert Advisory Group, 207–9
  maternity investigations, 210–11, **211–12**,
    213, **213**
    statistics, 212–13
  national investigations, 210–11, **210–11**,
    216, **216**
    full investigations, 215
    initial assessment, 214
    preliminary investigations, 215
    referrals, 214
    reports, 215
    statistics, 215–16
  objectives, 208
  origins, 207
  statutory framework, 209
Human Fertilisation and Embryology Authority
    (HFEA), 220
Human Tissue Authority (HTA), 221

improving performance, 257–58, *259*, 286
 barriers, 267
 motivations for complaints, 259–60, **262–63**, 266
  healthcare investigations, 265–66
  NHS clinical negligence claims, 261–65
  NHS complaints, 260–61
 objectives, 268
  caring objective, 268
  financial objective, 270
  investigation objective, 269
  learning objective, 270
  reporting objective, 269
 open and just culture model in the NHS, 273–76
  improving operational culture, 277–78
  non-adversarial dispute resolution, 280–81
  outcome-based cooperation, 276
  removing blame culture, 279–86
  reporting concerns, 278–79
 performance-based model, 271–72
  just culture model, 272–73
  open culture model, 272
incident reports and reporting systems, 33–34, 211–12
 failures of, 71, 182
 recommendations, 71
incorrect diagnoses and failure to diagnose:
 clinical negligence
  reasonable care and skill test, 117–18
 complaints, 87, 117–18
 COVID, impact of, 27
 Maternity and Neonatal Safety Improvement Programme, 43–44
 Paterson Inquiry, 193–95
Independent Complaints Advisory Service (ICAS), 62
independent healthcare providers, 8
 patient safety, 41
Independent Medicines and Medical Devices Safety (IMMDS) Review 2020, 38, 78–79, 94, **170,** 195–96, 199–200, 201–3, 270, 279
inquiries and reviews, 170, 199–206
 Abertawe Bro Morgannwg University Health Board Review, **109, 170,** 189–91
 Ayling (Clifford) Independent Inquiry, 70, **170,** 174–75, 180–81, 201
 Berwick Review 2013, 39–40, 42, 72–73, 287
 Bristol Royal Infirmary Public Inquiry, **170,** 171–73, 230
 Clwyd and Hart Report 2013, 61, 73–75
 Evans' Review 2014 (Wales), 86–88
 Gosport War Memorial Hospital Independent Inquiry, **170,** 191–93
 Health Select Committee recommendations, 71, 93–94

 Independent Medicines and Medical Devices Safety Review, 38, 78–79, 94, **170,** 195–96, 199–200, 201–3, 270, 279
 Keogh Hospitals Review, **170,** 184–85
 Kerr-Haslam (William/Michael) Independent Inquiry, 70, **170,** 178–81, 201
 Ledward (Rodney) Independent Inquiry, 170–71
 Mid-Staffs Independent Inquiry 2010, 71, **170,** 181–83, 201
 Mid-Staffs Public Inquiry 2013, 42, 71–75, **170,** 185–86, 201, 216
 Morecambe Bay scandal, **170,** 186–89, 202, 203, 239–43, 269, 288
 Neale (Richard) Independent Inquiry, 70, **170,** 176–77, 180–81, 201
 Ockenden Review of Maternity Services (Shrewsbury and Telford Hospital NHS Trust), 11–12, 79–80, **170,** 196–9, 201, 205, 288–89
 Once for Wales Concerns Management System project, 88, 95, 288
 Parliamentary and Health Service Ombudsman review of complaints, 75–78
 Paterson (Ian) Independent Inquiry, **170,** 193–95
 Shipman (Harold) Independent Inquiry, 62, **170,** 69–70, 173–74, 201, 203–5, 222, 223, 230, 278
 Shipman (Harold) Public Inquiry, **170,** 69–70, 174, 180, 201, 203–5, 222, 223, 230, 278
 Southern Health Review (Stage I) 2021, 78
 Winterbourne View Hospital Review, **170,** 183–84
Integrated Care Systems (ICSs), 15
 accountability, 16–17
 designing ICSs, 15–16
 geographic coverage, 16
 population health management, 25, 26
 public sector partnerships, 15
 statutory basis, 16–17
 transparency, 16–17
international recruitment:
 Long Term Plan, 21

Jackson Review of Litigation Costs, 161–63, 166–67

Keogh Hospitals Review, 170, 184–85
Kerr-Haslam (William/Michael) Independent Inquiry, 70, **170,** 178–81, 201

leadership and talent management, 23
Learn from Patient Safety Events (LFPSE), 33–34, 214
Learning Disabilities Mortality Review (LeDeR) Programme, 45–47

learning disability services:
   complaints, **100**
   health inequalities, 17–18
   inquiries
      Winterbourne View hospital, **170**, 183–84
   Long Term Plan, 19
   patient safety, 45–47
Learning From Events process (Wales), 145–47
   NHS Redress Scheme, 147
   Welsh Risk Pool claims, **140**, 145–47
Ledward (Rodney) Independent Inquiry, 170,
      170–71
legal aid, 125, 153–54, 157, 160, 164, 264
   Northern Ireland, 148–49
   Scotland, 133–34
Legal Aid, Sentencing and Punishment of
      Offenders (LASPO) Act 2012:
   negligence claims
      conditional fee arrangements, 125–26, 161–62
      damages based agreements, 162
      general damages, 162
      Jackson reforms, 161–63
      judicial cost management, 162
      personal injury claims, 161
      private litigation funders, 162
      qualified one-way costs shifting, 162
      recovery of costs, 126, 161–62
      referral fees, 162
      rising claims, 125–26, 127–28, 166
litigation, *see* **clinical negligence and litigation**
local authorities, 8
   complaints about public health organisations, **60**
   drug and alcohol services, 18
   Independent Advocacy Services, 62
   integrated care systems, 15, 16
   social care, 8–9
Local Health and Care Record (LHCR), 25, 26
Long Term Plan, 12, 14
   addiction programmes, 18
   air pollution, 19
   antimicrobial resistance, 19
   childhood obesity prevention, 18
   children and young people, services for, 19
   commitments, 27–30
   COVID-19, impact of, 27, 31
   diabetes prevention, 18
   funding arrangements, 27–30
   health inequalities, 17–18
   Integrated Care Systems, *see* Integrated Care
      Systems
   integration of health and social care, 8–9
   major health conditions, 19
   New Service Model, 8, *8*, 14–17
   obesity programmes, 18
   smoking cessation programmes, 18

   staffing, 20, 31
      allied health professionals, 21
      interim plan, 20
      international recruitment, 21
      leadership and talent management, 23
      medical workforce, 21
      midwives, 20
      nurses, 20
      staff retention, 21–22
      technology, 22–23
      volunteers, 23

Managing Deterioration Safety Improvement
      Programme (ManDetSIP), 42, 48
Maternity and Neonatal Safety Improvement
      Programme, 19, 43–44
maternity services:
   Morecambe Bay scandal, **170**, 186–89, 202, 203,
      239–43, 269, 288
   Ockenden Review, 11–12, 79–80, **170**, 196–9, 201,
      205, 288–89
   patient empowerment, 24
   patient safety improvements, 43–44, 146
   technology, 24, 146
   Long Term Plan, 19, 24
   Maternity and Neonatal Safety Improvement
      Programme, 19, 43–44
mediation, 51, 68, 92, 157, 285–86
   Health and Care Professionals Tribunal
      Service, 247
   NHS Resolution's Mediation Panel, 130–31
   Woolf reforms, 157–59
   see also alternative dispute resolution
Medical Examiner System, 35–36, 49
   Learning Disabilities Mortality Review
      Programme, 46
Medical Practitioners Tribunal
      Service (MPTS), 223
   fitness to practice hearings, 233–35
      Ayling case, 175
      Bawa-Garba case, 232
      panel decisions, **237**
      Paterson case, 194
medical professionals, recruitment of:
   international recruitment, 21
   Long Term Plan, 21
Medicines Safety Improvement Programme, 44
Mental Health Safety Improvement
      Programme, 44–45
mental health services, 8
   adults, 19–20
   children and young people, 19
   patient safety improvements, 44–45
methicillin-resistance *Staphylococcus aureus*
      (MRSA), 47, 49

Mid-Staffordshire NHS Foundation Trust,
11, 114, 279
independent inquiry (2010), 71, **170**, 181–83, 201
public inquiry (2013), 42, 71–72, **170**, 185–86, 201
Berwick Report, 72–73
Clwyd and Hart's Report, 73–75
Healthcare Safety Investigation Branch, 216
midwives:
recruitment of
Long Term Plan, 20
see also Nursing and Midwifery Council
mistakes, responding to, 53
apologies, 51
Being Open policy, 50–51
duty of candour, 51, 52–53
Morecambe Bay scandal, 170, 186–89, 202, 203,
269, 288
fitness to practice procedures, 239–43
MRSA, *see* **methicillin-resistance** *Staphylococcus*
aureus, 47, 49

National Audit Office (NAO):
Citizen Redress: What Citizens Can Do if Things
Go Wrong with Public Services (2005), 58
Clinical Negligence in the NHS in Wales (2001), 138
Feeding Back? Learning from Complaints Handling
in Health and Social Care (2008), 66, 93
Handling Clinical Negligence Claims in England
(2001), 123, 157
inquiries, 200
Investigation into Government-funded Inquiries
(2019), 204–5
Managing the Costs of Clinical Negligence in Trust
(2017), 123–24, 165–66, 205–6
Public Service Markets: Putting Things Right When
They Go Wrong (2015), 58–59
National Clinical Assessment Service (NCAS), 57
National Institute for Health Research (NIHR):
Patient Safety Translational Research Centres, 47
National Patient Safety Agency (NPSA), 32, 33
abolition, 57
Being Open policy, 50–51
National Patient Safety Alerts system, 33, 36, 49
National Patient Safety Committee, 36, 37
National Patient Safety Improvement
Programme, 42
COVID-19, 48
Neale (Richard) Independent Inquiry, 70, **170,**
176–77, 180–81, 201
neonatal services:
early notification scheme, 130
Long Term Plan, 19
Maternity and Neonatal Safety Improvement
Programme, 19, 43–44
Morecambe Bay scandal, 186

Ockenden Review, 196–99
patient safety improvements, 42, 43–44
New Service Model, 8, *8*
objectives, 14
proposed changes, 14–15
NHS Redress Scheme, 282
Wales, 138–39, 140–42
Learning From Events process, 147
NHS Resolution, 11
clinical negligence claims, 122
claims and costs, **128**
claims by specialty, **129–30**
claims by value tranche, *129*
claims-handling, 126–27
Clinical Negligence Scheme for
Trusts, 120–21, 125
early notification scheme, 130
estimated value tranche, *129*
filtering process, 125–26
funding claims, 125–26
litigants in person, 125
mediation, 130–31
settlement profile, *128*
Maternity Incentives Scheme, 11–12
Mediation Panel, 130–31
no win no fee arrangements, *see* **conditional fee**
agreements
non-delegable duty of care, 119–21
Northern Ireland:
clinical negligence claims, 148, 153
claims and costs, **150, 151**
claims by specialty, **152**
filtering claims, 148–49
funding claims, 148–49
lack of centralised defence body, 149–50
procedures, 149–53
Northern Ireland Public Services Ombudsman,
110–13
see also Northern Ireland Public Services
Ombudsman
Northern Ireland Public Services Ombudsman
(NIPSO), 110–11
activity, 111–12
clinical negligence payments, *153*
complaints by organisation, **113**
healthcare complaints, **111,** *113,* 113
performance, **112**
nurses:
Nursing and Midwifery Council, 237–39
Council for Healthcare Regulatory Excellence
reviews, 237–39
current fitness to practice procedures, 243–44
fitness to practice procedures, reviews of,
238–39
Morecambe Bay scandal, 239–43

PSA performance review scores, *229*
   statistics, 244–46
recruitment
   Long Term Plan, 20
Nursing and Midwifery Council (NMC), 237–38
   Council for Healthcare Regulatory Excellence
     reviews
     2008 review of fitness to practice procedures, 238
     2011 review of fitness to practice procedures,
      238–39
     2012 review of fitness to practice procedures, 239
   current fitness to practice procedures, 243–44
   fitness to practice procedures
     case examiner decisions, **245**
     concerns raids, **244**
     outcomes, **240**
     panel decisions, **245**
     reviews of, 238–39
   Morecambe Bay scandal, 239–43
   PSA performance review scores, *229*
   statistics, 244–46

obesity prevention, 18
**Ockenden Review of Maternity Services
   (Shrewsbury and Telford Hospital NHS
   Trust),** 11–12, 79–80, **170,** 196–9, 201, 205,
   288–89
older persons, 45
   patient safety, 45
   urinary tract infections, 47
ombudsmen:
   Northern Ireland Public Services Ombudsman,
     110–13
   see also Northern Ireland Public Services
     Ombudsman
   Parliamentary and Health Service Ombudsman,
     75–78, 97–103, 114
   see also Parliamentary and Health Service
     Ombudsman
   Public Service Ombudsman, unified
     proposals for, 102–3
   Public Services Ombudsman for Wales, 107–10,
     114–15
   see also Public Services Ombudsman for Wales
   Scottish Public Services Ombudsman, 104–6, 114–15
   see also Scottish Public Services Ombudsman
*Once for Wales Concerns Management System
   project,* 88, 95, 288
online dispute resolution (ODR), 281–82
out-of-hospital care, 14, 15–16
outcomes, 11–12
   complaints
     General Medical Council, **236**
     Nursing and Midwifery Council, **240**
     Scotland, **93**

Long Term Plan, 19
outcome-based cooperation
   open and just culture model, 276

**Parliamentary and Health Service Ombudsman
   (PHSO),** 97–98, 114
   activity, 98–99
   complaints
     complaints received, **100–1**
     inquiries and investigations, **101**
     recommendations, **99**
     review of complaints, 75–78
   operating costs, 98
   procedure for healthcare complaints, **76–77,** 99–101
     recommendations, **99**
   proposals for a unified public services
     ombudsman, 102–3
     principles proposed, **103**
   review of complaints investigations, 75–78
Paterson (Ian) Independent Inquiry, 170, 193–95
Patient Advice and Liaison Service (PALS), 62, 66, 71
   Kerr-Haslam Inquiry, 70
**Patient Safety Incident Response Framework
   (PSIRF),** 34–35
patient safety specialists, 40
Patient Safety Strategy, 12, 32–33, 49
   improvement aim
     Adoption and Spread Safety Improvement
      Programme, 48–49
     antimicrobial resistance, 47
     continuous improvement, 43
     healthcare associated infections, 47
     Managing Deterioration Safety Improvement
      Programme, 48
     Maternity and Neonatal Safety Improvement
      Programme, 43–44
     Medicines Safety Improvement Programme, 44
     Mental Health Safety Improvement Programme,
      44–45
     National Patient Safety Improvement
      Programme, 42
     patient safety workstreams, 42–43
     research and innovation, 47–48
     safety and learning disabilities, 45–47
     safety of older people, 45
   insight and information sources
     clinical negligence and litigation, 37–39
     Health Services Safety Investigations Body, 37
     Healthcare Safety Investigation Branch, 37
     Learn from Patient Safety Events, 33–34
     medical examiners, 35–36
     national clinical reviews and responses, 36
     National Patient Safety Alerts system, 36
     National Patient Safety Committee, 37
     Patient Safety Incident Response Framework, 34–35

involvement aim
  education and training, 40
  Patient Safety Partners, 39–40
  patient safety specialists, 40
  private providers, 41
  Safety I approach, 41
  Safety II approach, 41
**Patient Safety Translational Research Centres
  (PSTRCs),** 47
personalised care:
  New Service Model, 14
  older people, 45
  personalised care and support planning, 48
  technology, 24
**personalised care and support planning
  (PCSP),** 48
population health management systems, 25–26
Practitioner Performance Advice Service, 57
pre-action protocols:
  clinical negligence, 155–56
  NHS Resolution's mediation service, 130–31
  Personal Injury Pre-Action Protocol, 135–36
  Pre-Action Protocol for the Resolution of Clinical
    Disputes, 126, 158
prescription medicines:
  co-payment charges, 7
prevention programmes:
  addiction programmes, 18
  antimicrobial resistance, 19
  childhood obesity prevention, 18
  diabetes prevention, 18
  smoking cessation programmes, 18
**Private Healthcare Information Network
  (PHIN),** 41
private healthcare, 7
  complaints mechanisms, 66, 79, 93
  insurance policies, 7
private providers, *see* **independent healthcare
  providers**
professional autonomy, 63, 273
professional regulators, 219, **224–27**
  Care Quality Commission, 220–21
  complaints to, 222–23, 252–53
    adjudication, 223
    fitness to practise hearings, 223–24
    General Medical Council, 219, 229–37
    Healthcare Professionals Council, 219, 246–52
    Nursing and Midwifery Council, 219, 237–46
  fitness to practise hearings
    investigations, 223
    procedures, 223
    PSA performance review scores, *229*
    PSA standards, **228**
    standard of proof, 223
  General Dental Council, 219, **224**

General Medical Council, 219, **224**, 229–30
  fitness to practice procedures, 233–37
  Jack Adcock case, 230–33
  see also General Medical Council
General Optical Council, 219, 221, **225**
General Pharmaceutical Council, 219–20, **226**
Healthcare Professionals Council, 219, **227**, 246
  current fitness to practice procedures, 246–49
  statistics, 250–52
  see also Healthcare Professionals Council
Human Fertilisation and Embryology Authority, 220
Human Tissue Authority, 221
Nursing and Midwifery Council, 219, **224**, 237–38
  current fitness to practice procedures, 243–44
  fitness to practice procedures, reviews of,
    238–39
  Morecambe Bay scandal, 239–43
  statistics, 244–46
  see also Nursing and Midwifery Council
oversight
  Professional Standards Authority, 228–29
Professional Standards Authority (PSA), 228–29, 253
  Bawa-Garba case, 232
  fitness to practice standards, **228**
A Promise to Learn: A Commitment to Act, *see*
  Berwick Report 2013
public health, 8
  commissioning services, 17
  complaints, **60**
    Northern Ireland, **113**
Public Health England, 8, 36
public inquiries, *see* **inquiries and reviews**
public perception of NHS, 9–10
public sector partnerships:
  drug and alcohol services, 18
  Integrated Care Systems, 15–16
public service complaints:
  England, 58–59
  Scotland, 88–89
  Wales, 80–83
Public Services Ombudsman for Wales (PSOW),
    107, 114–15
  activity, 107–9
  healthcare complaints, **109–10**, 109–10
  targets and performance, **108**

raising concerns, 55
  staff raising concerns
    mechanisms for, 57
    resolving concerns, 57
  see also complaints and complaint-handling
reasonable care and skill test, 117–18, 121
recruitment:
  allied health professionals, 21
  international recruitment, 21

Long Term Plan, 20–21, 31
medical professionals, 21
midwives, 20
nurses, 20
Workforce Implementation Plan, 20, 31
regulators, 224–27
activity regulators, 219
complaints to, 221
Care Quality Commission, 220–21
entity regulators, 219
complaints to, 221–22
General Dental Council, 219
General Optical Council, 219, 221
General Pharmaceutical Council, 219–20
General Medical Council, 219
see also General Medical Council
Healthcare Professionals Council, 219
see also Healthcare Professionals Council
Human Fertilisation and Embryology
Authority, 220
Human Tissue Authority, 221
Nursing and Midwifery Council, 219
see also Nursing and Midwifery Council
professional regulators, 219
complaints to, 222–52
see also professional regulators
reporting requirements:
early notification scheme, 130
Healthcare Safety Investigation Branch,
37, 130, **211**
improving performance, 268, 269, 278–79, 286, 289
independent healthcare providers, 41
medical examiners, 36
patient safety incidents, 33–34, 49
recommendations, 71, 182
risk of harm, 280
Wales, 88
research and innovation:
patient safety, 47–48
Resolution, *see* NHS Resolution
respiratory disease, 18, 19–20
reviews and reports, *see* inquiries and reviews;
reporting requirements

Scotland:
clinical negligence claims, 131–32, 137–38
Central Legal Office, 133
Clinical Negligence and Other Risks Indemnity
Scheme, 132–37
see also Clinical Negligence and Other Risks
Indemnity Scheme
complaints processes
NHS complaints, 90–93
outcomes, **93**
public service complaints, 88–89

personal injury claims, *132*
Scottish Public Services Ombudsman (SPSO),
104–6, 114–15
see also Scottish Public Services Ombudsman
Scottish Public Services Ombudsman (SPSO), 104,
114–15
activity, 104–6
complaints received, **105**
recommendations, **106**
Serious Incident Framework (SIF), *see*
Patient Safety Incident Response
Framework
Shipman Inquiry, 62, 201, 203–5, 222
Clwyd and Hart Report, 73–74
Good Doctors, Safer Patients Report, 223
Independent Inquiry, **170**, 69–70, 173–74
Public Inquiry, **170**, 69–70, 174, 230
Safeguarding Patients Report, 180, 278
smoking cessation programmes, 18
social policy objectives:
improvements in performance, 268–70
Southern Health Review (Stage I) 2021, 78
staffing, 20
interim plan, 20
allied health professionals, 21
international recruitment, 21
leadership and talent management, 23
medical workforce, 21
midwives, 20
nurses, 20
staff retention, 21–22
technology, 22–23
volunteers, 23
Long Term Plan, 20–21
staff retention, 21–22
stroke prevention, 19–20
support staff, 8
Sustainability and Transformation Partnerships
(STPs), 15–16
System Transformation Group, 15

technology:
digitally-enabled care
clinical care, supporting, 25
clinical efficiency and safety, 26
healthcare professionals, supporting, 25
Long Term Plan, 23–26
patient empowerment, 24
population health, 25–26
dispute resolution, 281–82
efficiency, 22–23, 25, 26
e-job planning, 22–23
telephone triage and consultations, 22–23, 25
telephone consultations, 22–23, 25
tort liability, impact of, 95–96, 257, 266

transparency:
  Being Open policy, 50–51
  Berwick Report, 73
  duty of candour, 51
    contractual duty of candour, 51
    enforcement, 52–53
    prosecutions, 52–53
    statutory duty of candour, 52
  fees
    Scotland, 135
  funding arrangements, 103
  Independent Medicines and Medical Devices
    Safety Review, 203
  Integrated Care Systems, 16–17
  Mid-Staffordshire inquiries, 182, 185
  Ockenden Reports, 79, 197
  open and just culture model in the NHS, 273–76
    improving operational culture, 277–78
    non-adversarial dispute resolution, 280–81
    outcome-based cooperation, 276
    removing blame culture, 279–86
    reporting concerns, 278–79
  outcome-based cooperation, 276

vaccine passports, 24
vanguards programme for new models of care:
  enhanced health in care homes, 15
  integrated primary and acute care systems, 15
  multispecialty community providers, 15
  urgent and emergency care, 15
volunteers, 9, 23, 218

Wales:
  clinical negligence claims, 138, 147–48
    Learning From Events process, 145–47
    NHS Redress Scheme, 138–39, 140–42, 147
    Welsh Risk Pool claims, 139–40, 142–45, 145–47
  complaints processes
    Evans' Review 2014, 86–88
    NHS complaints, **83–84**, 84–88
    Once for Wales Concerns Management System
      project, 88, 95, 288
    public service complaints, 80–83
    social services complaints procedures, **81–82**
  learning from claims, *146*
  Public Services Ombudsman for Wales,
    107–10, 114–15
  see also Public Services Ombudsman
    for Wales
Welsh Risk Pool claims, 139–40, **140**, 142–45, *143*
  Learning From Events process, 145–47
  provisions for claims, **144, 145**
  value of claims, **143**, *144*
whistleblowing, 41, 57, 171
  Bristol Royal Infirmary Inquiry, 171–73
  Healthcare Safety Investigation Branch, 214
  Ledward Inquiry, 170–71
  Mid Staffordshire Hospital Trust Independent
    Inquiry, 181–83
  Scotland, 104
  Winterbourne View Hospital Review, 183
Winterbourne View Hospital Review, **170**, 183–84
Woolf Review of Civil Procedure, 157–59, 160

Lightning Source UK Ltd.
Milton Keynes UK
UKHW051230040123
414802UK00006B/264